LEARNING TO WRITE

LEARNING TO WRITE

By

REED SMITH

CANADIAN EDITION
COMPLETELY REVISED AND RESET

Authorized in the Provinces of Manitoba, Ontario, and Saskatchewan

TORONTO: THE MACMILLAN COMPANY OF CANADA LIMITED, AT ST. MARTIN'S HOUSE

Printed in Canada

THINKING AND WRITING

A composition is an oral or written proof of clear thinking.
—RACHEL SALISBURY

Three-fourths of writing well consists in giving definite, well-chosen details and plenty of them. The other fourth doesn't matter.

Learning to write is a serious business, but it need not be a solemn one.

Acknowledgments

The obligations of the author of this book are of two kinds: first to various authors, agents, and publishers for permission to reprint copyrighted material, and second to friends and fellow-teachers who assisted with the manuscript.

Detailed acknowledgments of copyright permissions are made throughout the text, but it is fitting that general acknowledgments also be made here as follows:

Atlantic Monthly Press
Jonathan Cape Ltd. and the Trustees of the Mary Webb Estate
Chicago Tribune
Clarendon Press
Clarke, Irwin & Co. Ltd., Canadian representative of Messrs. G. Bell and Sons Ltd.
Collier's Weekly
Reginald C. Dingle and Allen Upward's sister
Dodd, Mead and Company, Inc.
Doubleday, Doran and Company
E. P. Dutton and Company
Famous Features Syndicate
Garden City Publishing Company
Ginn and Company
Harcourt, Brace and Company, for selections from Sinclair Lewis, John Dos Passos, William Beebe, and William Albert Robinson
The Trustees of the Hardy Estate and Macmillan & Co. Ltd., for a selection from Thomas Hardy
Harper and Brothers, for selections from Trevelyan, Mark Twain, Philip Wylie, and *Harper's Magazine*
D. C. Heath and Company
William Heinemann Ltd.
Houghton, Mifflin Company, for selections from Husband, Holmes, Emerson, Aldrich, Wren, and Anna Hempstead Branch
Little, Brown and Company
Longmans, Green and Company
The Magnet, Jarvis Collegiate Institute
The New Yorker

The New York Times
Publishers Syndicate
Reader's Digest
Charles Scribner's Sons, for selections from Harris, Stevenson, F. Hopkinson Smith, and Thomas Wolfe
Eliza London Shepard, for a selection from Jack London
The Macmillan Company for selections from J. M. Kierzek's *Practice of Composition*
The Twig—University of Toronto Schools
Writer's Digest

Individual acknowledgment also goes to Charles Dana Gibson for his pictures, "The Ninth Inning" and "You Are Going on a Long Journey", and to Mrs. George Bambridge and A. P. Watt & Son for "The Miracle of Purun Bhagat" from *Second Jungle Book* by Rudyard Kipling.

Special thanks are due also to the editor and publishers of the *English Journal* for the many devices and suggestions taken from that excellent publication, and to the teachers who generously supplied the many student themes from which the present selection was made.

The editors of The Macmillan Company of Canada Limited are deeply indebted to Reed Smith, author of the original book, *Learning to Write*, for permission to rearrange the material in this book to meet the special demands of the Canadian market.

Preface

Writing is a highly personal matter. The ideal composition class would consist of an instructor on one side of the table and a student on the other. Nothing can take the place of personal coaching and personal consultation. Since, however, there are so many students and, comparatively, so few teachers, composition classes and textbooks become a necessity.

This book is the outgrowth of twenty-five years' experience in teaching composition. Its method throughout is three-fold: first, the definite statement and clear explanation of the general principles and techniques underlying all effective writing; second, the illustration of these principles and techniques from the work of both students and successful authors; third, the discussion and application of these principles and techniques by means of an abundant variety of exercises, questions, Round-Table discussion hints, and assignments.

Since this book covers the work of two years, both the subject matter and the treatment increase progressively in difficulty and maturity of appeal in order to keep pace with the development of the student during two of the most precipitate years of his life.

The numerous Round-Table discussions have been prepared with special care. Taken together they constitute a complete practical work book covering the entire field of grammar, analysis, and composition. Their purpose is, first, to appeal to the student's reason and make him really think about himself and his environment as well as about the processes of learning to write; and, second, to stimulate interesting class discussion. More questions are suggested than could always be used with profit. The training and ability of composition classes vary not only in different schools, but also in the same school.

Knowing the class as the teacher will do, he can select wisely and suggestively among the various questions. So important does the author deem them that he would advise any teacher, rather than study the text and slight the exercises, to emphasize the exercises and the Round Tables and to slight the text.

The arrangement of the book into parts will enable each teacher to adapt it to the needs of his particular class, either as those needs are already familiar to him from past personal experience with the students or as they may become known to him through the use of diagnostic and achievement English tests at the beginning of the term.

A poorly prepared class may need careful and detailed drill in Part I, Fundamentals; a better prepared group may need only a rapid review and check-up of this material, with primary emphasis on analysis rather than on grammar; a particularly bright and advanced group might conceivably be ready to begin at Part II, with writing the independent paragraph.

To all subjects pertaining to composition, but especially to the three important ones of punctuation, sentence usage, and the study of words, the approach is entirely fresh and modern. Both language and literature are alive and growing, and the usage of today is in many particulars not that of yesterday. Through the use of such sources as the new Merriam-Webster International Dictionary, *Current English Usage*, and *An Experience Curriculum in English*, two recent monographs of the National Council of English Teachers, the files of the *English Journal*, and other publications listed throughout the text, the results of the latest and best research scholarship have been utilized.

The author has tried to keep three guiding ideas constantly before him: (1) teaching students to write is largely a matter of teaching them to think; (2) the secret of all good writing is the secret of going into details; and (3) humour should have a part both in writing and in the teaching thereof.

REED SMITH

Contents

PART THREE

VOCABULARY BUILDING

PART FOUR

SPECIAL FORMS OF WRITING

PART ONE

FUNDAMENTALS

CHAPTER I

The Road Ahead: Learning to Write

I am convinced more and more every day, that fine writing is, next to fine doing, the top thing in the world.

—JOHN KEATS

1. Writing Can Be Learned

To write and to speak well *are* within your grasp. No matter how weakly and wrongly you write now, you can learn to write strongly and effectively if you only try hard enough and try often enough. The price is the same to all: Never give up; keep on trying. It takes determination to pay the price, and you can pay it only if you have enough.

Do not think that writing comes easier for your companions than for you. It doesn't—except for a gifted and fortunate few. All beginning writers face the same long, slow process of learning. Great writers, like poets, are born and not made. But *good* writers can be made, or rather can make themselves.

2. It Is Not Easy

Although any determined student can learn to write, the task is neither easy nor brief. It takes years of practice—eight or ten years in all. Even then we fall far short of real skill and effectiveness.

There are two good reasons why writing is very hard. The first is that before we can write we must think. And to think has been called the hardest thing in the world. The material we work with when we write is our own experience and observation coined into sentences by our minds. Before we can write, we must see and feel and think. If we do not see and feel and think, to ask us to write is like asking a carpenter to build a house without any lumber, or an artist to paint a picture without any paint. When we try to write, we often work the pump handle very hard, but no water comes, for the well is empty. Learning to write, as has been truly said, is learning to grow up. If you want to realize why writing is very hard, take a walk through the woods with a friendly forester or hunter, and then see, as it were, how much you don't see; or look at a famous picture with an artist or an art critic and realize how amazingly much you miss that he observes. It is an eye-opening experience. Seeing, feeling, thinking, these three are the great fountain-heads of the writer's art, and not the least of these is thinking.

The other reason why writing is hard is the fact that words are astonishingly numerous, tricky, and stubborn.

No one that ever lived has been able to write well without rigorous self-training. Even Shakespeare, supremely gifted as he was, showed marked and continuous improvement during the first eight years of his life as a writer. He learned by writing. Nearly all of the famous writers whom we look up to as master craftsmen have left us records of the difficulties and discouragements they overcame in learning their art. Turn to the chapter on Revising and Rewriting and read what such men as Robert Louis Stevenson, Benjamin Franklin, Huxley, Newman, and Macaulay have to say on this subject. The story of their efforts and methods is one of almost incredible perseverance and the will to succeed. While training themselves, they wrote more in a week than most of us write in a year, and wrote more in a year than most of us will write in a lifetime. Think of recasting the same sentence twelve or fifteen times, and of spending a week perfecting a paragraph.

"But," you say, "these were professional writers, who received pay for their work. I can never hope to write like them."

Probably not, for it is possible that you are not as gifted by nature as they were. But one fact is not only probable but certain: even they could never have reached the heights unless they had given themselves whole-heartedly and devotedly to the task of learning how. In the end some go higher than others, but in the beginning all stand equal at the bottom of the slope, and the road winds uphill most of the way.

There is only one way to learn: practise, practise, practise. Since the beginning of time all persons concerned—amateur writers and professional writers, teachers and pupils alike—have sought for some other way, but there isn't one. Writing themes may not be your favourite indoor sport, but ask your teacher if writing compositions isn't pleasanter than correcting them.

Learning to write, therefore, resolves itself frankly and entirely into a matter of how hard you are willing to try. During the composition course you will be called upon to write compositions oftener than you feel like doing. Frequently, too, the subjects will seem hard and uninteresting—this in spite of the fact that sometimes the teacher spends as much time and thought on choosing a subject as you do on writing the theme.

But whether you feel like writing themes or not, or whether the subject is inviting or not, your improvement will depend almost entirely upon what *you*, not what the teacher, may do. Like tennis, boxing, fencing, and golf, writing is learned by doing, not by hearing or reading. All the instructor can do is to guide, to direct, and to point out errors. Properly speaking, he is a coach, not a teacher. The progress each student makes depends first upon how *hard* he tries, and secondly upon how *often* he tries. An experienced teacher of composition once told his class: "You can learn to write, all of you, if you really want to. But I can't teach you. I can only help you to teach yourselves."

3. It Is Richly Worth While

The process of learning to write is so long and hard that were the ability not so all-important, were it not so imperative under modern conditions, it would not be worth the trouble it takes.

But consider this reflection carefully and thoughtfully: Nothing that you learn in school, from athletics, dramatics shop work, domestic science, or stenography, on through the entire range of theoretical subjects, *nothing* will be half so valuable or constantly in demand after you graduate as writing and speaking. Well does Walter Lippmann call English "the main instrument of civilized living." And well does he add, "To give that instrument edge and point is a sacred task."

Never in the history of this country has the written and spoken word been as all-powerful and as all-prevalent as today. If you rise above the bottom in any trade or profession, or if you attain to even the slightest influence in church, community, business, politics, club life, or society in general, you will undoubtedly be called on frequently to express yourself in public. As life is constituted today, this is inevitable. The only way to avoid it is to sink so low in the business and social scale that nothing that you can do or say will make any difference to anybody else. The higher you rise, the oftener you will have to write and speak. And, conversely, the better you write and speak, the higher you will rise. Success in life and efficiency in expression are intimately interwoven.

Justly or unjustly, human nature being what it is, a movement usually stands or falls with its leader. A good cause is often lost because at the critical time a weak speech was made when a strong one was needed, or a vague, rambling report was offered when a clear, vigorous one would have saved the day. In fact, in almost every group—whether men's or women's club, committee or mass meeting, faculty or student gathering, political, religious, or social assembly—there is usually a moment when a convincing speech or a striking article will turn the tide of opinion definitely one way or the other. Happy is the man or woman who can respond successfully to the challenge of that moment! His "is the Earth, and everything that's in it", as Kipling says in another connection.

To grow into manhood and womanhood and still speak in public stammeringly and painfully, and still write crudely and awkwardly, is to go into battle lacking the most powerful weapon you will ever have the chance to obtain. And if you don't get it while you can, all your life you will have to compete daily with men and women who, although no more intelligent or better trained in other ways than you, because they possess this ability will forge ahead of you at every turn in both your business and your social careers. Don't put yourself under the sad necessity of facing life with a stout heart, a trained mind, and an eager sympathy, but with a trembling tongue and a lame pen. You could as well afford to enter a steeplechase mounted on a rocking-horse, or to compete in an automobile race driving an oxcart.

Only your worst enemy could wish for you such a future, but fortunately for you the remedy lies entirely in your own hands.

You can succeed if you will.

THE ROUND TABLE

1. If you had the power, what would you rather do or be than anything else?

2. After reading this chapter, (*a*) Do you agree that learning to write is within your grasp? (*b*) Do you think it is easier, or harder, than is stated? (*c*) Do you believe that the ability to write and speak well is the most valuable thing the school can help you to attain, or do you think its importance is overestimated? Be frank in expressing your views. Give facts in addition to opinions.

3. What profession are you planning to follow, and in it what need will you have for the ability to write well and to speak well?

4. If there is any point or paragraph in this chapter with which you emphatically (*a*) agree or (*b*) disagree, bring it up for discussion in class.

5. Do you know of any occasion in school or in life when a good

speaker or article helped carry a point or a poor speech or article helped defeat it? Ask your father and mother if they know of any.

6. Have you heard or read any incident of a writer's taking unusual time and care in perfecting his work?

7. Do you know of any instances, historic or personal, going to prove the truth of the old saying, "The pen is mightier than the sword"?

8. In your own writing, (*a*) How much time do you spend, on the average, on a page? (*b*) How long, on the average, does it take you to write a theme?

9. What is the moral of the following comment which a high-school graduate entering college made upon her high-school English teacher? "I find it hard to forgive my high-school teacher for the good grades she gave me. When I entered college I had to teach myself spelling, punctuation, organization of material, or fail, all because I believed from my high-school marks *that my work was satisfactory.*"

"But your teacher surely blue-penciled your errors," I said, knowing the abnormal conscience of teachers in these matters.

"Oh, yes, I suppose she did; I never noticed, for as long as she gave me a recommending grade I thought errors like those didn't matter. It took threatened failure to show me that they did."[1]

[1]Florence Humphries, "Some Principles Underlying Grading", *English Journal,* Vol. 12, 1923, p. 33.

CHAPTER II

The Parts of Speech

In general, grammar may be described as a great observational science, dealing with the facts and laws of language, just as botany deals with plant life and geography deals with the earth's surface. The facts and laws of language are manifold and complicated. Anything that aids us to understand them properly is worth while, for, as has been said, to write and speak one's language well are both the hardest and the finest tasks that face us in school and in life. Grammar and analysis—parsing words and analysing sentences—are helpful preparatory steps toward success. They lay the foundation, as it were, for a more rapid and intelligent progress in the art of writing.

There are hundreds of thousands of words in the English language. In spite of their tremendous numbers, however, all words can be put into eight classes or groups, according to the way they are used in sentences. These eight family groups are called "parts of speech" and are termed, respectively, (1) Nouns, (2) Pronouns, (3) Adjectives, (4) Verbs, (5) Adverbs, (6) Prepositions, (7) Conjunctions, (8) Interjections.

These are all of the parts of speech. No matter how often we speak, no matter how often we write, no matter how often we read, each and every word we come in contact with from the cradle to the grave is either a noun, a pronoun, an adjective, a verb, an adverb, a preposition, a conjunction, or an interjection.

The eight parts of speech may be grouped as follows:

1. The **Verb** (usually the action word), always the key word in the sentence

2. The Two Modifiers or Qualifiers
   Adjectives, modifying nouns and pronouns
   Adverbs, modifying verbs, adjectives, or other adverbs
3. The Two Name Words, or Substantives
   Nouns
   Pronouns, substitutes or place-takers for nouns
4. The Two Link Words or Connectives
   Conjunctions
   Prepositions, which govern objects as well as connect
5. **Interjections,** exclamations expressing feeling, which have no grammatical connection with the other words in the sentence

A word does not really become a part of speech till it is used in a sentence and enters into relationship with other words in the sentence. In short, it is not what a word looks like, but what it does that settles what part of speech it is. To express it more formally, it is function, not form, that determines.

We cannot tell what part of speech a word is unless we can see how it is behaving in company with other words in a sentence. We should not ask, for example, "What part of speech is the word *fast* or *steel*?" *Fast* might be any of four parts of speech, according to the work it does:

1. When the siege was lifted, the soldiers broke their long *fast.* (A noun because it names)
2. Many people *fast* during Lent. (A verb, because it asserts action)
3. Only a very *fast* runner can do the hundred-yard dash in ten seconds. (An adjective, because it modifies a noun)
4. Greyhounds can run very *fast.* (An adverb, because it modifies a verb)

Similarly, *steel* is three different parts of speech in the three following sentences:

1. *Steel* is used all over the world.
2. Trains run on *steel* rails.
3. Hard-hearted men *steel* themselves against the requests of the needy.

Consider the exchange made by *pipe* and *clay* in the two sentences:

1. He has a valuable deposit of *pipe clay* on his land.
2. He is smoking a *clay pipe.*

In fact, words in a sentence are very much like members of a baseball or a football squad. When a baseball team comes out on the field, it is impossible at first to tell what position the members will play. The catcher and the first baseman can possibly be identified by the kinds of mitt they are carrying, but no one can at sight single out the shortstop from the third baseman or the left fielder from the right fielder. It is only when the team goes out on the field that we can distinguish the different players. In fact it is only because he pitches, for example, that a player becomes a pitcher, and so on for the other positions on the team. Sometimes, too, when a substitution is made, the players on the same team shift positions. Let the pitcher lose control, for instance, and if he is a good batter he may be transferred to centre field, the third baseman may be put in to pitch, and the centre fielder be placed on third. Thus, in a moment, three members of the team change places and by virtue of the change, while remaining the same persons, play different positions. Again, it is function, not form, that determines.

So, in the sentence, it is what each word does, the part it plays, that makes it what it is. Recognizing the parts of speech is thus a mild kind of detective game, in which we first have to find out what any given word is up to, and thereby assign it to its proper class or group.

Ability to recognize the parts of speech is fundamental in grammar. Enough practice, both oral and written, should be given to bring the class up to the desired average in accuracy and speed.

Exercises in the Parts of Speech

I

What parts of speech are the two *firsts* and the four *thats* in these sentences:

1. Put *first* things *first.*
2. He said *that that that that* you used was unnecessary.

II

Tell what part of speech the italicized words are:

1. (a) Cheap things don't *last* long.
   (b) Her shoes are made on a narrow *last*.
   (c) *Last* came the Pilot of the Galilean Lake.
   (d) The *last* time I saw him was the day before yesterday.
2. (a) And Jill came tumbling *after*.
   (b) We left immediately *after* dinner.
   (c) *After* we got home, we rang you up.
3. (a) We broke *camp* soon after daybreak.
   (b) Please hand me the green *camp* stool.
   (c) We shall probably *camp* near the bend of the river.
4. (a) Put the money back in the *till*.
   (b) Can you stay *till* bedtime?
   (c) Please don't go *till* I get back.
   (d) If you *till* the ground carefully, you will raise a good crop.
5. (a) He said *that* you told him about me.
   (b) *That* is not true.
   (c) *That* time she guessed wrong.
   (d) The last book *that* you lent me is certainly interesting.
6. (a) He looks *like* his father.
   (b) Do you *like* olives?
   (c) There is an old proverb, *Like* master, *like* man.
   (d) I shall not look upon his *like* again.

III

Write sentences using the italicized words as directed:

1. *Since* as a conjunction, a preposition, and an adverb.
2. *Light* as a noun, an adjective, and a verb.
3. *Second* as a noun, an adjective, a verb, and an adverb.
4. *Iron* as a noun, an adjective, and a verb.
5. *Still* as a noun, a verb, an adjective, and an adverb.
6. *Clear* as a verb, an adjective, and an adverb.

IV

Using the sentences on page 51 and pages 66-69, continue practice on the parts of speech as long as needed.

For written parsing either of the following forms is convenient:

1. The chief pleasure in using a taxi is the carefree feeling you have when the fenders crumple.
2. A detour is the roughest distance between two points.

First Form

1. The = definite article
chief = adjective
pleasure = noun
in = preposition
using = verb
a = indefinite article
taxi = noun
is = verb
the = definite article
carefree = adjective
feeling = noun
you = pronoun
have = verb
when = conjunction
the = definite article
fenders = noun
crumple = verb

2. A = indefinite article
detour = noun
is = verb
the = definite article
roughest = adjective
distance = noun
between = preposition
two = adjective
points = noun

Second Form

	Noun	*Pronoun*	*Adjective*	*Verb*	*Adverb*	*Preposition*	*Conjunction*	*Interjection*
1.	pleasure	you	the	using		in	when	
	taxi		chief	is				
	feeling		a	have				
	fenders		the	crumple				
			carefree					
			the					
2.	detour		A	is		between		
	distance		the					
	points		roughest					
			two					

CHAPTER III

Parsing and Review of Grammar

When operating together to form a sentence, the parts of speech have various contacts with or relations to the other parts of speech. They stretch forth, as it were, one or more hands to some other part of speech which stretches out an answering hand in return.

Sometimes these relationships between words are shown by changes in the form of the word itself. We can recognize them with the eye. For example, there is the difference in number between *dollar* and *dollars,* one *tooth* and a set of *teeth,* one *ox* and a yoke of *oxen*; there is the difference in case between *boy* (nominative or objective) and *boy's* (possessive singular) and *boys'* (possessive plural), or between *I* and *me*; or in tense between *come* and *came,* or between *go* and *have gone.* Such changes take place in nouns, pronouns, verbs, adjectives, and adverbs, and help to make clear exactly what the word is doing in the sentence.

Just as often, however, the looks of a word give no clue to its relationships. Then we have both to consider the sentence as a whole and also to examine each part in order to tell what any given word is doing in that particular place at that particular moment. For example, *The dog bit the boy* means one thing, and *The boy bit the dog* means something entirely different, although the forms of the words have not changed in the slightest. In the following sentences the word *man* is used in six different constructions without the slightest corresponding change in form.

The *man* came. (Subject of a verb)
The lion killed the *man.* (Object of a verb)
She gave the *man* a dollar. (Indirect object of a verb)

The tree fell on the *man*. (Object of a preposition)
Mr. X, the *man* in question, has gone away. (In apposition with a noun in the nominative case)
She failed to find Mr. X, the *man* she was looking for. (In apposition with the noun in the objective case)

To parse a sentence is to tell first what part of speech every word in it is, and then by means of either form or function to discover exactly what each word is doing in the sentence. Sometimes this is easy. Again it may be hard, calling for no little logical ingenuity and skill.

The chief functions of the various parts of speech and their most important sentence contacts are indicated in the following charts, together with a review of grammar and examples of detailed written parsing.

The study of grammar and practice in parsing can be carried out with as much thoroughness and detail as each teacher desires. The sentences on page 51 and pages 66-69 contain abundant material for both parsing and analysis.

1. The Noun

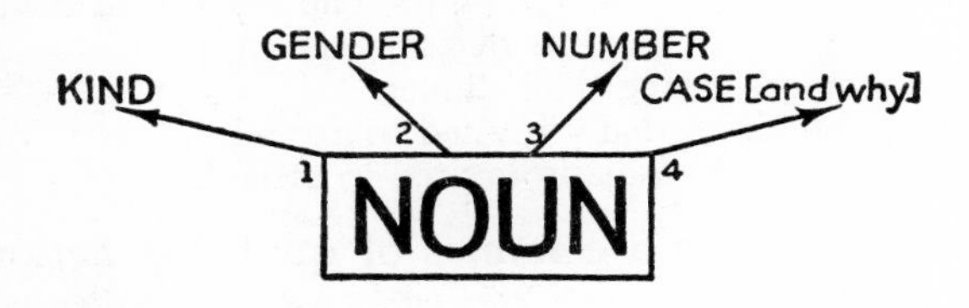

(1) KINDS OF NOUNS

There are two chief kinds or classes of nouns:

1. Proper nouns, or the particular names of individual persons, places, and things, such as *Canada, London, Napoleon, Mary, John, Amazon, Ontario.*

In writing, the proper noun (and any adjective formed from it such as Napoleonic or Canadian) begins always with a capital letter.

2. Common nouns, or the names of classes or groups of objects, such as *country, city, man, girl, boy, river, dog, cat, flowers.*

In addition to common nouns, many grammars recognize also (3) collective nouns, (4) abstract nouns and (5) verbal nouns.

3. Collective nouns are the names of collections or special groups of persons, animals, and objects, such as *army, flock, mob, jury, herd, troop, band, company, family, covey, brood, audience, choir, drove, squadron, swarm, team, fleet, regiment, committee.*

The important thing about collective nouns is the fact that they may take either the singular or the plural verb according as they are thought of as a unit (the collection or group taken as a whole) or thought of as individuals making up the group or collection. For the same reason, collective nouns can be referred to by either a singular pronoun or a plural pronoun. Consider the following sentences, all of which are correct:

1. The mob was dispersed.
2. The public are often deceived by appearances.
3. The board are of the opinion (*or* The board is of the opinion).
4. The jury has reached its decision.
5. The jury are eating their dinner.
6. The public is cordially invited to attend.
7. The public are cordially invited to attend.

4. Abstract nouns are names of qualities, actions, and conditions. Examples are *swiftness, grace, courage, pride, rejoicing, height, dancing, faith, friendship, beauty, fragrance, redness, blackness.* Such nouns are called abstract because they do not exist in the actual, concrete world of experience where we can see, hear, smell, taste, and touch, as do such objects as *stars, bells, lavender, onions,* and *satin.* Abstract nouns are only imagined or thought of. They exist in men's minds, not in nature.

5. Verbal nouns are words derived from verbs but used as nouns. (See page 36)

(2) GENDER

There are three genders, corresponding exactly to the facts of sex in life and in nature.

1. Names of males are **masculine,** such as *man, father, son, uncle, brother, prince, king, Joseph, Francis, cock, gander, drake, bull, stallion.*

2. Names of females are **feminine,** such as *girl, woman, actress, waitress, aunt, sister, princess, queen, Josephine, Frances, hen, goose, duck, cow, mare.*

3. Names applying to neither males nor females—in other words, things without life—are **neuter,** such as *tree, house, car, street, window, courage, moon.*

4. Names applying to either males or females are sometimes considered to be of **common** gender, such as *animal, teacher, agent.*

(3) NUMBER

There are two numbers, the singular applying to one, and the plural applying to more than one.

This distinction offers little difficulty either theoretically in parsing, or practically in writing and speaking, except in two instances: (1) nouns with foreign plurals, and (2) nouns ending in *-ics.*

1. Nouns with Foreign Plurals

Singular	*Plural*	*Singular*	*Plural*
alumna	alumnae	crisis	crises
alumnus	alumni	datum	data
analysis	analyses	formula	formulas (or formulae)
axis	axes		
bandit	bandits (or banditti)	oasis	oases
		phenomenon	phenomena
beau	beaux (or beaus)	radius	radii (or radiuses)
cherub	cherubs (or cherubim)	stratum	strata
		thesis	theses

2. Nouns Ending in *-ics*

There is a small but important group of words ending in *-ics* which are puzzling in practical use because they sometimes take a singular and sometimes a plural verb. Examples are

acoustics	gymnastics	politics
athletics	mathematics	statistics
economics	phonetics	tactics
ethics	physics	

When such words denote a scientific subject or study, or a book about it, they are construed as singular.

Mathematics (or economics, or ethics, or phonetics, or physics) *is* an important branch of learning.

When such words denote matters of practice or procedure, they may be construed as plurals.

1. Gymnastics are of many kinds and varieties.
2. The tactics employed by Stonewall Jackson in his valley campaign are highly regarded in Europe.

Like collective nouns, which these words resemble, they may be used in either the singular or the plural sense according to the idea to be conveyed:

1. Acoustics is a branch of physics.
2. The acoustics of this building are bad.
3. Athletics has come to be an important feature of modern education.
4. Athletics [in the sense of athletic sports and exercises] often take up too much of a student's time.
5. Politics makes strange bedfellows.
6. Politics of that kind [in the sense of political tricks and intrigues] are on a low level.

(4) CASE

There are three cases in English grammar, nominative, possessive, and objective.

1. Nominative Case

The nominative case is used:

(1) chiefly as the subject of a verb.

(2) in apposition with a noun or pronoun in the nominative case.

James Hilton, the *novelist*, wrote the article.

(3) as complement—(predicate nominative) after a linking verb. (See page 30)

The captain was the *hero* of the hour.

(4) as nominative of address.

Arthur, come here.

(5) as nominative absolute.

The *bell* having rung, we came in.

2. Possessive Case

As its name indicates, the possessive case indicates possession or ownership. In regularly inflected nouns, the possessive singular case can be recognized by the *apostrophe s* ('s) and the possessive plural by the *s apostrophe* (s').

3. Objective Case

In nouns there is no difference in form between the nominative and the objective case.

The objective case is used:

(1) as the direct object of a transitive verb.

The batter struck the *ball.*

(2) as the object of a preposition.

We stopped at the *station.*

(3) as the indirect object of a verb. Instead of being called the objective case, this use is often known as the case of the indirect object or the dative case.

Ask *him* the answer.

(4) in apposition with another noun or pronoun in the objective case.

We gave them to Smith, the *grocer*.

(5) to indicate measure and direction, such as duration of time and extent of space. This use is called the adverbial objective, for the nouns are used as adverbs to modify verbs, adjectives, or adverbs.

We walked *miles*.

(5) PARSING NOUNS

To parse nouns in detail means to tell their (1) Kind, (2) Gender, (3) Number, (4) Case and Why.

1. The four tests of a noun.

There are four chief constructions, or uses in the sentence, that only a noun is capable of (only a noun and, of course, a pronoun, which both in purpose and in effect is a substitute noun). The four uses are these:

(a) The subject of a verb.
(b) The object of a verb.
(c) The object of a preposition.
(d) Being modified by an adjective.

If a word is used in any of these four ways, it automatically and invariably is a noun. These four tests also determine whether or not a phrase or a clause is a noun phrase or a noun clause. The four tests are thus of great practical importance in parsing and analysing.

2. Noun Phrases.

Over the fence is out. (Subject of a verb)
It's no use *to cry over spilt milk.* (Logical subject of a verb)
Cats hate *getting their feet wet.* (Object of a verb)
Nearly everyone dislikes *being corrected.* (Object of a verb)
You can depend upon *his keeping his word.* (Object of a preposition)
I never heard of *a girl's kissing her own elbow.* (Object of a preposition)
They were afraid of *being late.* (Object of a preposition)

3. Noun Clauses.

How the cat got into the room is still a mystery. (Subject of a verb)
Whether you go or stay will make little difference in the long run. (Subject of a verb)
I fear *that you are mistaken.* (Object of a verb)
He denied positively *that he had said it.* (Object of a verb)
Don't count too heavily on *what he promised you last month.* (Object of a preposition)
I judge by *what I see and hear.* (Object of a preposition)
What you do makes so much noise I can't hear *what you say.* (First clause, subject of a verb; second clause, object of a verb)

Written Parsing of Nouns

1. I have no expectation of making a hit every time I come to bat.
—FRANKLIN D. ROOSEVELT

2. Courage is grace under pressure.

	Noun	*Kind*	*Gender*	*No.*	*Case*	*Construction*
1.	*expectation*	common (abstract)	neuter	sing.	obj.	object of *have*
	hit	common	neuter	sing.	obj.	object of *making*
	time	common	neuter	sing.	obj.	adverbial objective modifying *making*
	bat	common	neuter	sing.	obj.	object of preposition *to*
2.	*courage*	common (abstract)	neuter	sing.	nom.	subject of *is*
	grace	common (abstract)	neuter	sing.	nom.	predicate nominative after intransitive verb *is*
	pressure	common (abstract)	neuter	sing.	obj.	object of preposition *under*

Exercises

Parse the nouns in any group of five successive sentences on pages 51 or 66-69 (*a*) orally in class; or (*b*) written in class; or (*c*) as home work to be handed in in class.

In class the pupils may exchange papers and correct them as the teacher calls out the correct answers.

Such practice should be continued in the case of the class as a whole until a high average of both accuracy and speed is attained. If any one of you falls much below the average, additional exercises and practice work, with advisory coaching by a well-informed pupil, should be assigned.

2. The Pronoun

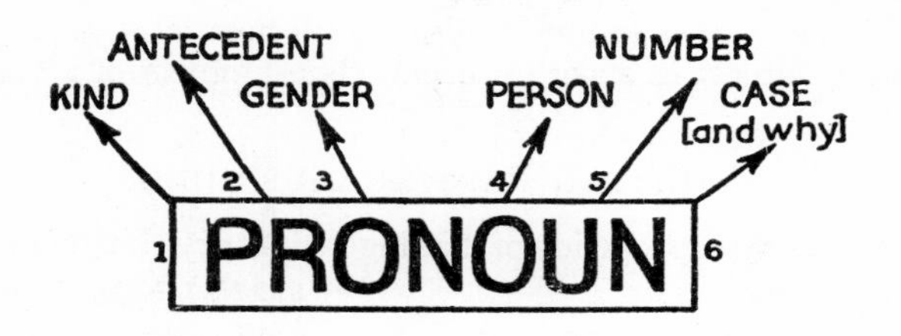

The word **pronoun** means a **for-noun.** Pronouns are substitutes, or place-takers, for nouns, and came into use to avoid the awkward and tiresome repetition of nouns.

Being substitutes for nouns, pronouns have the same sentence uses and obey the same sentence laws as nouns do. They have, for example, the same gender, number, and case functions, and likewise answer to the four chief tests of a noun, in that they are used as (1) the subject of a verb, (2) the object of a verb, (3) the object of a preposition, and (4) are modified by adjectives.

Pronouns, except indefinite pronouns, refer to a noun or another pronoun, which is called their antecedent, since it usually comes before or antecedes the pronoun that refers to it.

One special class of pronouns, moreover, the personal pronouns, distinguish between the person speaking, the person spoken to, and the person spoken of. In addition, therefore, to telling the kind, gender, number, case and why of pronouns, at need we should tell also their antecedent and person.

(1) KINDS OF PRONOUNS

1. Personal pronouns show by their form whether they refer to the person speaking, the person spoken to, or the person or thing spoken of:

First person (person speaking)	*I*	*we*
Second person (person spoken to)	*you* (*thou*)	*you* (*ye*)
Third person (person or thing spoken of)	*he*, *she*, *it*	*they*

2. Interrogative pronouns are used to ask questions:

who? which? what?

3. Demonstrative pronouns point out (*demonstrate*) or direct emphatic and definite attention to:

this these that those

When these words are used with nouns rather than in place of nouns, they become demonstrative adjectives.

4. Relative pronouns (*a*) refer or relate to an antecedent in the same sentence and (*b*) connect adjective clauses, of which they are a part, with their antecedents. Relative pronouns thus have the combined powers of pronouns (to refer to antecedents) and of conjunctions (to join clauses).

who which what (= *that which*) *that*

5. Indefinite pronouns. Besides the personal, relative, interrogative, and demonstrative pronouns, there is a large group of indefinite pronouns, between forty and fifty in number. As their name indicates, they do not refer to any particular individual or definite antecedent. Most of them can be used as adjectives also, to modify a noun. They are about half-way between real pronouns on the one hand, and nouns and adjectives on the other.

Among the most important are *all*, *any*, *anybody*, *anything*, *both*, *each*, *each other*, *either*, *neither*, *everything*, *few*, *many*, *nothing*, *one*, *one another*, *anyone*, *everyone*, *no one*, *none*, *someone*, *other*, *several*, *some*, *somebody*, *something*, *such*.

(2) ANTECEDENT

An antecedent is the noun or noun equivalent to which a personal or relative pronoun refers. *Antecedent* means "going before, preceding". The term comes from the fact that the antecedent usually comes before or precedes the pronoun that refers to it.

(3) GENDER

Pronouns have the same gender uses as nouns do. When pronouns refer to definite antecedents, they of course take their gender from their antecedents. *They*, for example, is masculine if it refers to a word like *men* or *boys*; feminine if it refers to *women* or *girls*; neuter if it refers to *trees* or *stones*; and common if it refers to *people* or *children*.

The third personal pronoun is unusual in showing three gender forms in the singular, *he, she, it*. It is the only word in English that does this.

(4) PERSON

As has been said, personal pronouns are the only pronouns which have the power to indicate person by means of their forms.

Other pronouns derive their person, as they also do their gender, from their antecedents. All nouns are in the third person except those in apposition with pronouns in the first or second person and those indicating someone directly spoken to, as "John, come here."

(5) NUMBER

Like their gender and person, pronouns derive their number from their antecedents. If the antecedent is singular, the pronoun is singular; if the antecedent is plural, the pronoun is plural.

1. He *who* comes is a friend. (Singular)
2. They *who* come are friends. (Plural)
3. All *that* believe this hold up their hands. (Plural)
4. Everything *that* lives must die. (Singular)

Only the personal and demonstrative pronouns and a few of the indefinite pronouns have different forms for singular and plural.

Personal

Singular	*Plural*
I	we
thou	you (ye)
he, she, it	they

Demonstrative

Singular	*Plural*
this	these
that	those

Indefinite

Singular	*Plural*
one	ones
other	others
somebody	somebodies

(6) CASE

Of all the words in the English language only the personal, relative, and interrogative pronouns have different case forms for the nominative and objective cases:

Personal

Nominative	*Objective*
I, we	me, us
he, they	him, them
she	her

Interrogative

Nominative	*Objective*
who?	whom?

Relative

Nominative	*Objective*
who	whom

This unusual richness in objective case forms makes it easier to parse pronouns in grammar but harder to use them correctly in speaking and in writing.

The case of a pronoun is determined by its use in its own clause or sentence, not by that of its antecedent. Pronouns derive their gender, person, and number from their antecedents, but their cases are, as it were, their own private affair, with which their antecedents have nothing to do. For example, in the three following sentences the relative pronoun *that* is in three different constructions, while the construction of its antecedent, *man*, remains unchanged:

1. He is the man *that* came yesterday. (Subject of a verb)
2. He is the man *that* I saw yesterday. (Object of a verb)
3. He is the man *that* I spoke to yesterday. (Object of a preposition)

Consider, too, the cases of the pronouns in these paired sentences:

1. (*a*) I don't know *what* you are. (Nominative case)
   (*b*) I don't know *what* you mean. (Objective case)
2. (*a*) I know *who* he is. (Nominative case)
   (*b*) I know *whom* I can trust. (Objective case)

PARSING PRONOUNS

Fully to parse pronouns means to tell their (1) Kind; (2) Antecedent (if there is one); (3) Gender; (4) Person; (5) Number; (6) Case and Why.

Written Parsing of Pronouns

These are some of the books which Fred sent me from the library.

Pron.	*Kind*	*Antecedent*	*Gender*	*Pers.*	*No.*	*Case*	*Construction*
These	demon.		neuter	third	plur.	nom.	subject of verb *are*
some	indef.		neuter	third	plur.	nom.	predicate nominative after intransitive verb *are*
which	rel.	*books*	neuter	third	plur.	obj.	object of verb *sent*
me	pers.		common	first	sing.	obj.	indirect object of *sent*

Exercises in Parsing Pronouns

Parse the pronouns in any group of five or ten successive sentences, pages 51 or 66-69, (*a*) orally in class; (*b*) written in class; (*c*) or as home work to be handed in.

Have the written parsing corrected in class by interchanging papers and marking them according to the teacher's oral parsing.

Continue practice till the class reaches the desired level of speed and accuracy (and so on for the other parts of speech).

3. The Adjective

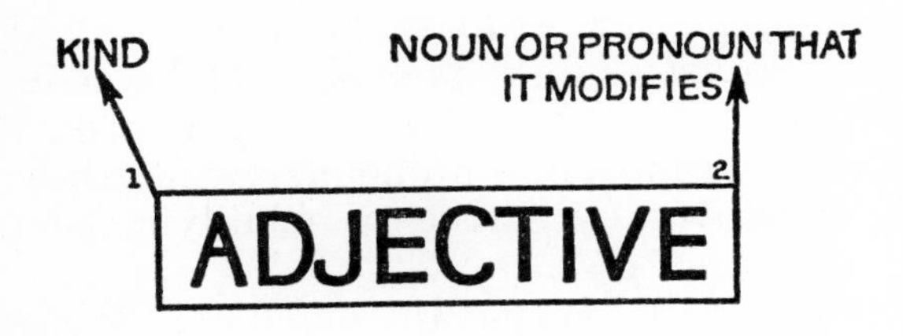

Adjectives are words that modify a noun or pronoun. Any word that modifies a noun or pronoun is an adjective, and any word that does not, is not an adjective.

(1) KIND

Adjectives are of two kinds or classes: descriptive and non-descriptive.

1. **Descriptive adjectives** are those which name qualities or characteristics of the object described so that we can see, hear, smell, taste, or feel it more definitely and vividly. Examples are adjectives like *tall, short, white, red, happy, loud, smooth, ugly, sweet, cold.*

Such adjectives have three forms, or degrees of comparison by which their meanings can be intensified, the positive, the comparative, and the superlative.

Positive	*Comparative*	*Superlative*
tall	taller	tallest
cold	colder	coldest

Positive	*Comparative*	*Superlative*
ugly	uglier	ugliest
soft	softer	softest
beautiful	more beautiful	most beautiful

Proper adjectives, which are derived from proper nouns, can be considered loosely as belonging to the descriptive group, but have no comparative or superlative forms.

2. **Non-descriptive adjectives** are those which merely point out or indicate number or amount, without describing the object they modify. Non-descriptive adjectives are of several subgroups or classes, such as adjectives of quantity, amount, and number, like *little, few, many, some, all, much, five, ten, first, second*; and the pronominal adjectives, which consist of the pronouns (personal, interrogative, demonstrative, relative, and indefinite pronouns), when these words turn into adjectives by virtue of modifying a noun or pronoun.

The definite article *the* and the indefinite articles *a, an,* belong to this non-descriptive group.

(2) TEST OF AN ADJECTIVE

In parsing adjectives there is only one test, but it must be strictly and literally applied: Does the word in question modify a noun or a pronoun?

Most nouns, particularly nouns of material, can be used as adjectives: an *oak* tree, a *silver* watch, *childhood* years, a *clay* pipe, *pipe* clay, a *gold* chain.

Conversely, adjectives easily become nouns when they are used in place of a noun instead of to modify a noun.

1. The *bravest* are the *tenderest.*
2. The *loving* are the *daring.*
3. To the *pure* all things are pure.

Occasionally, too, the difference between adjectives and adverbs, which is usually clear and definite, becomes hazy, and keen thinking is needed to keep them apart. Such is the case with the use of the predicate adjectives, where adverbs would naturally be expected, in such phrases as *turn pale* or *turn sour*, *shine bright*, *stand firm and sure*, *smell sweet*, *taste sour*, *ring clear*.

Again, *well* is usually an adverb, but is correctly used as an adjective in the following sentences:

1. I felt *well* yesterday.
2. You are looking *well* now.

Their power as descriptive adjectives outweighs their power as modifiers of the verb.

(3) PARSING ADJECTIVES

To parse an adjective is to tell (1) the kind (descriptive or non-descriptive); (2) the noun or pronoun it modifies.

Since an overwhelmingly large proportion of adjectives are in the positive degree, no reference need be made to the degree of comparison of an adjective, unless it is in the comparative or the superlative degree, when this fact should be pointed out.

Written Parsing of Adjectives

Soon o'er the yellow fields, in silent and mournful procession,
Came from the neighbouring hamlets and farms the Acadian women,
Driving in ponderous wains their household goods to the seashore.

Adjective	*Kind*	*Noun or Pronoun It Modifies*
the	definite article	*fields*
yellow	descriptive	*fields*
silent	descriptive	*procession*
mournful	descriptive	*procession*
the	definite article	*hamlets* and *farms*
neighbouring	descriptive	*hamlets* and *farms*
the	definite article	*women*
Acadian	descriptive (proper)	*women*
ponderous	descriptive	*wains*
their	non-descriptive (pronominal)	*goods*
household	descriptive	*goods*
the	definite article	*seashore*

4. The Verb

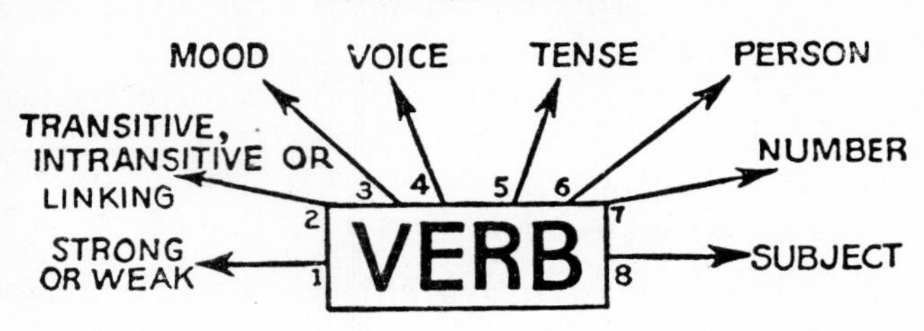

The verb is the most important and many-sided of all the parts of speech. It is always necessary. No verb; no sentence.

1. ACTION VERBS

Verbs are prevailingly the action words of a sentence, and can almost be defined as words that express action. To answer the question *Who does what?* is usually to put your finger on (1) the subject (the *who*); (2) the verb (the *does*), and (3) the object (the *what*).

Action words of this kind affirm or deny; they tell, declare, or assert something about their subject.

2. LINK VERBS

There are, however, in addition to the large number of action verbs, a small but important group that do not assert action, but serve merely to join the subject to the predicate; in other words, they are verbs that assert *being* instead of *doing*. Such verbs are really links, joining the subject to the complement.

The commonest and most important of these is the verb *to be*, which in its various forms, either as an independent or as an auxiliary verb, is the commonest verb in the language.

Other examples are *seem*, *appear*, *become*, *sound*, *feel*, *taste*, *smell*, *continue*, *remain*.

(1) STRONG (IRREGULAR, OLD) AND WEAK (REGULAR, NEW) VERBS

Both historically and actually, verbs are divided into two great classes according to the way they form their past tense and past participle.

1. Strong, or Irregular, Conjugation

Verbs that belong to this class form their past tense (*a*) without adding any letter and (*b*) usually by changing their vowels; and form their past participle (*a*) by adding *-n* or *-en* and (*b*) usually by also changing their vowels.

The principal parts of the fourteen strong, or irregular, verbs that cause the most trouble in speaking and writing are these:

Present	*Past*	*Past Participle*
begin	began	begun
break	broke	broken
come	came	come
do	did	done
eat	ate	eaten
give	gave	given
go	went	gone
lie	lay	lain
ring	rang	rung
run	ran	run
see	saw	seen
sit	sat	sat
take	took	taken
write	wrote	written

2. Weak, or Regular, Conjugation

Verbs in this group form their past tense and past participle (*a*) without changing their vowels and (*b*) by adding *-d*, *-ed*, or *-t* to the present tense. All new verbs which come into English follow this conjugation.

Examples are as follows:

Present	*Past*	*Past Participle*
walk	walked	walked
reach	reached	reached

Present	*Past*	*Past Participle*
love	loved	loved
decide	decided	decided
finish	finished	finished
die	died	died
dye	dyed	dyed
camouflage	camouflaged	camouflaged

(1) Special Class of Weak Verbs

The distinction between strong (irregular) and weak (regular) verbs is in the main easy to apply. There are, however. about sixty common verbs that are puzzling because they seem to show both strong and weak characteristics. Close attention will reveal that they belong to the weak group.

In general, the test of a weak verb is whether it adds a *d* or a *t* to form the past tense. If it does, even if it also changes its vowel, it is a weak verb. Contrast in this particular the strong verbs *bind, bound*; *fight, fought*; *find, found*; and *wind, wound*, with the weak verbs *bring, brought*; *catch, caught*; *sell, sold.*

Some of the most important of this special class of weak verbs are these:

Present	*Past*	*Past Participle*
bend	bent	bent
bet	bet	bet
bleed	bled	bled
bring	brought	brought
buy	bought	bought
cast	cast	cast
catch	caught	caught
cost	cost	cost
cut	cut	cut
feed	fed	fed
have	had	had
hurt	hurt	hurt
lose	lost	lost
make	made	made
read	read	read
say	said	said

Present	*Past*	*Past Participle*
seek	sought	sought
sell	sold	sold
send	sent	sent
set	set	set
sleep	slept	slept
tell	told	told
think	thought	thought

(2) TRANSITIVE AND INTRANSITIVE VERBS

Transitive verbs are those which take objects. The action passes over (transits) from the subject and lands upon the object.

The dog *bit* → the man.
The horse *ate* → the hay.
Children *love* → their mother.
This is the dog that *worried* → the cat that *killed* → the rat that *ate* → the malt.

Intransitive verbs are those which do not take an object.

Hey, diddle, diddle! The cat and the fiddle!
The cow *jumped* over the moon;
The little dog *laughed* to see such sport
And the dish *ran* away with the spoon.

Verbs are prevailingly transitive or intransitive. Even when they are not used in sentences, a genuine difference can be felt between such words, on the one hand, as *give, strike, throw, bear, see, set, lay,* and, on the other, *run, rise, live, go, come, wander, shine,* and *lie,* to say nothing of such non-action or link verbs as *be, seem, appear,* and *become.* In reality, however, as need arises, any transitive verb can be used intransitively and the intransitive verbs (except the verb *to be* and its equivalents) can be used transitively. When an intransitive verb is used transitively, it either (1) takes a cognate object, or (2) is used in a causative sense.

1. Cognate Object

Even a verb like *sleep, dream, live, run, fight,* can take as its object a noun with the same meaning as the verb, as, for example, *to sleep our last sleep, to dream a bad dream, to live a useful life, to give a costly gift, to fight a good fight.* This construction, in which the object is born from the verb itself, is called the *cognate* object, cognate meaning "born with", "akin".

2. Causative Verbs

Again, certain intransitive verbs can become transitive when they are used in the causative sense of causing or producing the action which they name. Examples are to *fly* a kite (to make a kite fly); to *walk* a horse (to make a horse walk); to *work* an employee hard; to *float* a raft down the river.

(3) MOOD

Verbs have three moods, or manners, in which they can make assertions and form sentences. They are the Indicative, the Imperative, and the Subjunctive. The first two of these offer little difficulty.

1. Indicative Mood

The indicative mood is the mood of all direct statements of fact and direct questions. More than nine-tenths of all the verbs in both speech and writing are in this mood.

2. Imperative Mood

The imperative mood is the mood of command. It has only one tense, the present, and only one person, the second. The subject is always *you*, either singular or plural, and since this fact is so well known, the pronoun is nearly always omitted.

3. Subjunctive Mood

The subjunctive mood, both in theory and in practice, is puzzling and subtle. Although comparatively rare, and gradually fading from use, it is too interesting and important to be ignored.

At present the subjunctive has three uses.

(1) Uncertainty

The subjunctive is used in uncertain conditions in order to emphasize their doubt much more strongly than the indicative mood would do. For example:

1. If it *turn* out as we hope, it will be a miracle.
2. If he *come*, I shall try to see him.
3. If it *rain* tomorrow, nobody could come.
4. If he *be* a man of his word, he will do what he promised.

In each of these sentences the indicative could be used, and its only effect would be to lessen the doubt and uncertainty suggested by the subjunctive. Incidentally, this use of the subjunctive is rapidly disappearing except on the part of the nicest speakers and writers.

(2) Conditions Contrary to Fact

A second use of the subjunctive is to express a condition contrary to fact:

1. If he *were* here, all would be well (but he isn't here).
2. If I *were* you, I shouldn't do that (but I am not you).
3. If it *were* in my power, I'd come to your aid (but it isn't in my power).
4. If you *had been* here, my brother *would* not *have died* (but you were not here).

This use of the subjunctive in unreal conditions is still both standard and necessary, and gives no signs of disappearing.

(3) Wish

The third use of the subjunctive is to express a wish:

1. Oh, that I *had* the power to help you!
2. God *bless* you!
3. Peace *be* with him!
4. Long *live* the king!

(4) *As It Were* and *Had Rather*

Two unrelated uses of the subjunctive are to be seen in the phrases *as it were* and *had rather*. *As it were* suggests that the statement with which it is used is not to be taken literally.

1. He seemed, as it were, in a kind of mental fog.
2. The very heavens, as it were, opened and flooded the earth.

The *had* of the phrases *had rather*, *had better*, *had as lief*, and *had as soon* is in the past subjunctive. These phrases have been in good use for hundreds of years and are still standard. *I had rather go* means *I should have* (or *hold*) *it more agreeable to go*. *Had* has the same meaning in the other phrases.

4. The Two Verbals: Infinitives and Participles

(1) The Infinitive

The infinitive is sometimes spoken of as a mood, although it does not have the power of asserting action as do the other moods. The infinitive is the noun form of the verb and is called a verbal. It can be used like other nouns as the subject of a verb, the object of a verb, the object of a preposition, and so forth.

The infinitive has three forms: (1) the root infinitive—*give, hear*, etc., (2) the infinitive with *to*, sometimes called the gerundial infinitive—*to give, to hear*, (3) the gerund—*giving, having given, being given, having been given*; *hearing, having heard, being heard, having been heard.*

Such words are double-natured: they have at the same time the uses of both verbs and nouns. On the verb side they may be modified by adverbs, and, if transitive take objects, if intransitive, are followed by predicate nouns or adjectives; on the noun side they can be used as the subject of a verb, the object of a verb, the object of a preposition, and can even be modified by adjectives.

Consider their double nature as revealed in the following sentences:

1. *Rowing* a heavy boat against the current is hard work.
   (As a verb, *rowing* governs the object *boat* and is modified by the

adverb phrase *against the current*; as a noun, *rowing* is the subject of the verb *is*.)

2. It is hard to avoid *hating* one's enemies.

   (As a verb, *hating* governs the object *enemies*; as a noun, *hating* is the object of the infinitive *to avoid*.)

3. Everyone dislikes *being* sick.

   (As a verb, *being* is completed by the predicate adjective [attribute complement] *sick*; as a noun, *being* is the object of *dislikes*.)

4. You can depend upon his *keeping* his word strictly.

   (As a verb, *keeping* governs the object *word* and is modified by the adverb *strictly*; as a noun, *keeping* is the object of the preposition *upon* and is modified by the possessive adjective *his*.)

5. She denied *having eaten* the apple.

   (As a verb, *having eaten* takes the object *apple*; as a noun, *having eaten* is object of the verb *denied*.)

6. The door showed no sign of *having been opened* recently.

   (As a verb, *having been opened* is modified by the adverb *recently*; as a noun, *having been opened* is object of the preposition *of*.)

(2) The Participle

The participle is the adjective form of the verb, and like the infinitive is called a verbal. At the same time, it shares in the uses of both adjectives and verbs.

Note the following forms of the participle: *giving, having given, being given, given, having been given, hearing, having heard, being heard, heard, having been heard.*

1. *Lifting* his hat politely, he bowed to the lady.

   (As a verb, *lifting* governs the object *hat*, and is modified by adverb *politely*; as an adjective, *lifting* modifies the pronoun *he*.)

2. *Being* the richest man in town, Mr. X subscribed largely to the new library.

   (As a verb, *being* is followed by the predicate nominative [attribute complement] *man*; as an adjective, *being* modifies the noun *Mr. X*.)

3. *Turning* pale with fright, the child burst into tears.
   (As a verb, *turning* is completed by the predicate adjective *pale*; as an adjective, *turning* modifies the noun *child*.)
4. The door *broken* yesterday has not yet been repaired.
   (As a verb, *broken* is modified by the adverb *yesterday*; as an adjective, *broken* modifies the noun *door*.)
5. *Having concluded* his address, he withdrew.
   (As a verb, *having concluded* takes the object *address*; as an adjective, *having concluded* modifies *he*.)

Note that the gerundial and participial forms are frequently identical and are therefore apt to be confused with each other. They must be distinguished by their function. If a verbal modifies a noun or pronoun, it is an adjective—that is, a participle. If the verbal is the subject of a verb, the object of a verb, the object of a preposition, or a predicate nominative (attribute complement), it is a noun—that is, the infinitive or gerund.

Exercises in Distinguishing Participles and Infinitives

Are the italicized forms participles (adjectives) or infinitives (nouns)?

1. *Forgetting* the past is sometimes a virtue.
2. *Laughing* at the funny expression, I turned to my sketch and began *working* in earnest.
3. *Having arrived* in the city only yesterday, he had not yet found a lodging.
4. The boy *standing* at the head of his class is my brother.
5. I am very proud of him for *standing* first.
6. And Arthur, *passing* thence, rode to the wood.
7. This is good only for *passing* the time.
8. He enjoyed *reading* your letter.
9. She always sings while *doing* her work.
10. He boasted of *having studied* all night.
11. Genius is an infinite capacity for *taking* pains.
12. The children stood *watching* them out of town.
13. By *praising* a man we sometimes injure him.
14. *Playing* baseball or football for money prevents a student from *representing* his school in athletics.
15. Although *closed* for repairs last week, the office will re-open today.

16. *Making* promises is not *keeping* them.
17. *Having been sent* by air mail, the letter reached him early yesterday morning.
18. "*Moving* pictures is a great nuisance."
    "You should say, '*Moving* pictures are a great nuisance,' shouldn't you?"
    "Say, you never cleaned house, did you?"
19. While I nodded, nearly *napping*, suddenly there came a *tapping*,
    As of someone gently *rapping*, *rapping* at my chamber door.
20. I had not yet heard of his *having been rejected*.

(4) VOICE

Transitive verbs, or verbs that take objects have two voices, the active and the passive.

The active voice of a transitive verb represents the subject as acting upon, or doing something to, the object. The line of action points from subject to object.

1. Heavy clouds hid → the sun.
2. Two people saw → him fall into the water.
3. Lightning struck → the house.

The passive voice reverses this situation. The line of action, instead of pointing forward from subject to object, points backward from predicate to subject. The subject receives the action, and is acted upon. The former object becomes the present subject.

1. The sun ← was obscured by heavy clouds.
2. He ← was seen to fall into the water by two people.
3. The house ← was struck by lightning.

(5) TENSE

Tense means time. There are only three possible times—present, past, and future. In the conjugation of the verb, however, there are six tenses instead of three. Tense in a verb, therefore, shows not only time but the state or kind of action as well—that is, whether or not it is ended or complete (perfected or perfect).

Present	*Present Perfect*
I write	I have written
Past	*Past Perfect*
I wrote	I had written
Future	*Future Perfect*
I shall write	I shall have written

In addition to these customary forms there are two other forms of conjugation which exist in order to give emphasis and show continued action in assertions:

Emphatic:	I do write	
(Action stressed)	I did write	
	I will write	
Progressive:	I am writing	I have been writing
(Action in progress,	I was writing	I had been writing
not yet finished)	I shall be writing	I shall have been writing

(6) PERSON AND (7) NUMBER

There are three persons of the verb, first, second, and third, corresponding to the three persons of the personal pronouns.

There are two numbers of the verb, singular and plural, corresponding to the two numbers of nouns and pronouns.

The verb takes both its person and its number from its subject, or, in other words, is said to agree with its subject in person and number.

(8) PARSING VERBS

Fully to parse a verb is to tell these facts about it: (1) Strong or Weak Conjugation; (2) Transitive, Intransitive, or Linking; (3) Mood (Indicative, Subjunctive, or Imperative); (4) Voice (Active or Passive); (5) Tense (Present, Past, Future, Present Perfect, Past Perfect, Future Perfect, etc.); (6) Person (First, Second, or Third); (7) Number (Singular or Plural); (8) Subject (which determines its Person and Number).

Written Parsing of Verbs

1. Never cross a bridge until you come to it.
2. He who fights and runs away
   May live to fight another day;
   But he who is in battle slain
   Can never rise and fight again.

Verb	*Strong or Weak*	*Trans. or Intrans.*	*Mood*	*Voice*	*Tense*	*Pers.*	*No.*	*Subj.*
1. *cross*	weak	trans.	imper.	act.	pres.	second	sing.	*you*[1]
come	strong	intrans.	indic.	act.	pres.	second	sing.	*you*
2. *fights*	strong	intrans.	indic.	act.	pres.	third	sing.	*who*
runs	strong	intrans.	indic.	act.	pres.	third	sing.	*who*
may live	weak	intrans.	subj.	act.	pres.	third	sing.	*he*
to fight	strong	intrans.	infin.	act.	pres.			
is slain	strong	trans.	indic.	pass.	pres.	third	sing.	*who*
can rise	strong	intrans.	indic.	act.	pres.	third	sing.	*he*
(can) *fight*	strong	intrans.	indic.	act.	pres.	third	sing.	*he*

[1]Understood.

Exercises

Using the sentences on pages 51 and 66-69, the class should be given enough practice in both the oral and the written parsing of verbs to insure reasonable familiarity with them.

5. The Adverb

VERB, ADJECTIVE, OR ADVERB THAT IT MODIFIES

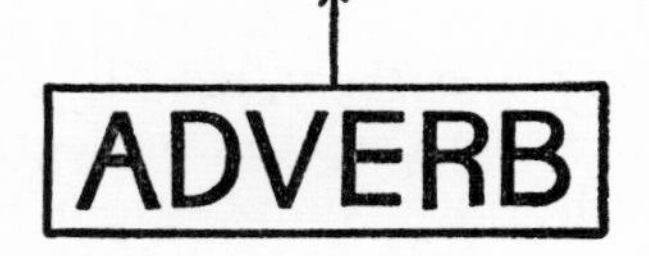

Along with the adjective, the adverb is one of the two parts of speech that modify. The difference between them consists in what they modify: adjectives modify nouns and pronouns; adverbs modify verbs, adjectives, and other adverbs. This is the sole test for an adverb, and is to be applied invariably to any adverb element—word, phrase, or clause.

Like adjectives, though to a less extent, adverbs are compared. In parsing an adverb, however, one need not mention the degree, unless it is in the comparative or superlative, in which case it should be commented on.

(1) DISTINGUISHING ADVERBS FROM ADJECTIVES

The ending *-ly* usually marks off the adverb from the adjective, but not every descriptive word ending in *-ly* is an adverb, for a number of common adjectives end in *-ly*, such as *cowardly*, *friendly*, *manly*, *womanly*, *silly*, *kindly* (also an adverb), *cleanly* (klĕn′lĭ, not klēn′lĭ), *lowly*, *sickly*, *timely*, *lovely*, *lonely*, *mannerly*.

Examine and discuss the shifting adverb or adjective tinge in the italicized words:

To play *safe*; to drink *deep* and to drink *deeply*; to stand *erect*; to look *good* and to look *well*; to arrive *safe* and to arrive *safely*.

1. Still water runs *deep*.
2. The sun shines *bright* on my old Kentucky home.
3. Velvet feels *smooth* and looks *rich* and *glossy*.
4. She grew *tall*. She grew *rapidly*.

(2) DISTINGUISHING ADVERBS FROM PREPOSITIONS

A preposition without its object becomes an adverb. Constant care, therefore, is needed to tell whether words like *in*, *up*, *out*, *within*, *without*, modify verbs and are therefore adverbs, or whether they take objects and are therefore prepositions. If they are prepositions, the phrase which they introduce may modify a verb and hence be an adverb phrase. See the section, The Preposition and Its Object, page 48.

(3) *THERE* EXPLETIVE

The word *there* has one important idiomatic use. This is to act as a kind of introductory word, occupying the rightful place of the subject before the verb, and thus letting the real subject come after the verb in a more prominent position for the sake of emphasis.

1. There is no telling when he will come.
2. There was no way to tell them apart.

In this convenient construction *there* is known not as an adverb but as an expletive, because it fills out the sentence while waiting for the subject. The pronoun *it* is used likewise in much the same way. Then *it* is an expletive rather than a pronoun.

(4) ADVERBIAL OBJECTIVE

There should be recalled at this point the adverbial use of a noun in the objective case to indicate length, measure, amount, etc. See Objective Case, (5) pages 19-20.

(5) PARSING ADVERBS

To parse adverbs is to point out the verbs, adjectives, or other adverbs which they modify, and thus show their adverbial use.

Written Parsing of Adverbs

1. Never have I seen so much power so easily controlled.
2. If I were running the world I would have it rain only between two and five a.m. Anyone who was out then ought to get wet.

	Adverb	*Verb, Adjective, or Adverb It Modifies*
1.	*never*	*have seen* (verb)
	so	*much* (adjective)
	so	*easily* (adverb)
	easily	*controlled* (participle)
2.	*only*	*between two and five a.m.* (adverb phrase)
	out	*was* (verb)
	then	*was* (verb)

6. The Conjunction

Conjunctions are words that connect words, phrases, and clauses. They are the coupling pins, as it were, of the train of thought, which hold it together, and enable it to add modifier after modifier and thought after thought until we have thoroughly and satisfactorily rounded out our meaning.

Conjunctions are of two classes: co-ordinating and subordinating.

(1) CO-ORDINATING CONJUNCTIONS

To co-ordinate means "to make or to keep equal"; thus co-ordinating conjunctions connect words, phrases, and clauses that are equal in rank.

There are three chief co-ordinating conjunctions: and, but, and **or.**

Co-ordinating conjunctions offer little difficulty either theoretically in parsing or practically in writing and speaking. All that is needed is to be able to recognize them on sight and, if they connect clauses, to be sure that the clauses are of equal rank.

A special group of co-ordinating conjunctions are the correlative conjunctions which are used in pairs to join "equals in rank", that is, the same parts of speech or their equivalent. They are

either . . . . . . *or*
neither . . . . . *nor*
both . . . . *and*
not only . . . . *but also*

These conjunctions stand at the beginning of each of the equal constructions they join. Be sure that the words between the correlatives

(a) include no words common to both expressions.
(b) include all words belonging only to the first expression

e.g., The arrows indicate the necessary corrections in the following:

(a) He is not only going to order the tickets but to pay for them too.
(b) He is unwilling to choose either his own ties or to let his mother buy them.

(2) SUBORDINATING CONJUNCTIONS

Subordinating conjunctions are both numerous and troublesome. They differ from co-ordinating conjunctions in several important ways.

1. As their name indicates, they introduce clauses of subordinate rank—in other words, clauses that depend for their full meaning upon the clause to which they are attached by the conjunction.

Consider how incomplete is the meaning of the following clauses, each a dependent clause introduced by a subordinating conjunction and left hanging in space without any main clause to depend from:

(1) If it doesn't rain soon ______.
(2) Although he promised to come ______.
(3) When I heard her sing ______.
(4) Because I wanted to read it too ______.
(5) Where the road crosses the creek ______.

2. Unlike co-ordinating conjunctions, subordinating conjunctions do not merely connect, but also form a part of the clause which they introduce.

3. Subordinating conjunctions properly introduce clauses, and rarely connect phrase with phrase or word with word as co-ordinating conjunctions do.

There are ten subclasses of subordinating conjunctions. It is troublesome to list them and learn them, but it is more troublesome not to do so, so frequent and important are they in speech and writing.

(1) **Time**

when, whenever, while, as, until, before, since, after, as soon as

I'll be ready when you come.

(2) **Place**

where, whence, wherever

Let's go where you saw the deer yesterday.

(3) **Manner**

as, just as, as if

Please do as I say.

(4) **Degree and Comparison**

as much as, so far as, as, than

He has known you longer than me = (he has known me)
He has known you longer than I = (I have known you).

(5) **Cause or Reason**

because, since, whereas, as, for

I believe it because you said it.

(6) **Result**

that, so that

He worked so hard that he saved a large sum for old age.

(7) **Condition**

if, unless, as if

I know you will help her if you can.

(8) **Concession**

though, although, even if

Though they are very rich, they do not put on airs.

(9) **Purpose**

that, so that, in order that, lest

He worked hard so that he would have enough for old age.

(10) **Noun clauses** introduced by *that* and many interrogative words like *how, what, when, where, why*.

That you don't agree is clear. (Subject)
I know why you don't agree. (Object)
The fact that you don't agree is clear. (Apposition with a noun in the nominative case)
We are faced with a real problem, how you might reach an agreement. (Apposition with a noun in the objective case)
The question is when you are going to reach an agreement. (Predicate nominative)

(3) PARSING CONJUNCTIONS

In parsing conjunctions there are two points of importance to be determined: (1) whether they are co-ordinating or subordinating; and (2) if subordinating, what kind of dependent clause they introduce—whether a noun, adjective, or adverb clause. It is not necessary to name the subclass to which subordinating conjunctions belong, such as time, place, manner, degree.

Written Parsing of Conjunctions

1. Knowledge comes but wisdom lingers.
2. Either you are mistaken or I am.
3. God made the country, and man made the town. (Cowper)
4. When I heard it, I was much surprised.
5. This is the place where he told us to come.
6. If you think so, you are mistaken.
7. He promised her that he would never leave her.
8. He ran so fast that he got out of breath.
9. Unless you go, we can't go either.
10. Though he is not rich, he is generous.

Conjunction	*Kind*	*Kind of Clause It Introduces*
1. *but*	co-ordinating	
2. *either...or*	co-ordinating (correlative)	
3. *and*	co-ordinating	
4. *when*	subordinating	adverb
5 *where*	subordinating	adjective
6. *if*	subordinating	adverb
7. *that*	subordinating	noun
8. *that*	subordinating	adverb
9. *unless*	subordinating	adverb
10. *though*	subordinating	adverb

7. The Preposition

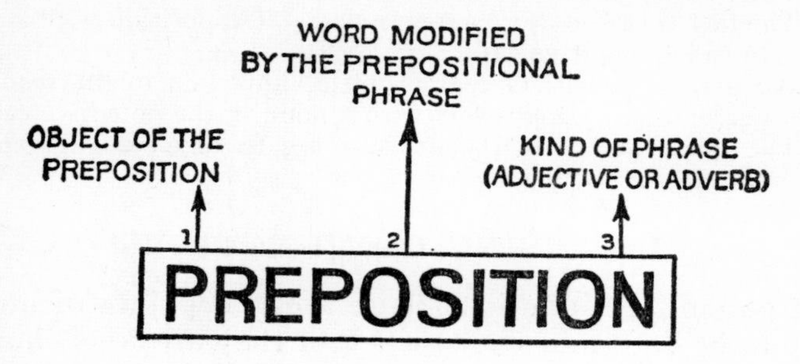

There are two essentials to be remembered in dealing with prepositions: (1) Prepositions always take an object; and (2) prepositions introduce and form a part of a small group of words, called a phrase, which usually modifies some other word in the sentence. If the phrase modifies a noun or a pronoun, it is an adjective phrase. If it modifies a verb, adjective, or adverb, it is an adverb phrase.

The commonest prepositions are these: *about, above, across, after, against, along, among, around, at, before, behind, below, beneath, besides, between, by, concerning, down, during, except, for, from, in, into, off, on, out, over, to, under, until, upon, up, with, within, without.*

(1) THE PREPOSITION AND ITS OBJECT

A preposition always takes an object.

Remove the object from a preposition, and the preposition turns into an adverb.

1. Stay in the house. (Preposition)
2. You may come in. (Adverb)
3. The dog ran down the street. (Preposition)
4. The ladder fell down. (Adverb)
5. "Get off the steps, I tell you. Get off." (First *off*, preposition; second *off*, adverb)
6. The wagon went *up* the hill. (Preposition)
7. We got *up*. (Adverb)

(2) PHRASES INTRODUCED BY PREPOSITIONS

The group of words introduced by a preposition acts together as a unit to modify some other part of the sentence; in short, the phrase does the work of either an adjective or an adverb. A preposition might be defined as a word placed before (*preposed*) a noun or its equivalent to make up an adjective or an adverb phrase.

(1) Adjective Phrases, Modifying Nouns or Pronouns

1. The house *by the side of the road* ______.
2. The face *on the bar-room floor* ______.
3. The girl *with the red hair* ______.

(2) Adverb Phrases, Modifying Verbs or Adjectives

1. ______ rode *at a rapid pace.*
2. Come *in a hurry.*
3. ______ stumbled *over the chair.*

The only way to tell whether a phrase is an adjective phrase or an adverb phrase is thus to see what it modifies. What the phrase does in the sentence determines its nature.

For further examples of prepositional phrases, see the sections on Phrases and Recognizing Phrases, pages 55-58.

(3) PARSING PREPOSITIONS

To parse a preposition is (1) to name its object; (2) to point out the word which the phrase modifies and thus determine whether the phrase is an adjective or an adverb phrase.

Written Parsing of Prepositions

1. Above all things be pleasant to those around you.
2. The house on the corner belongs to the man with the stick in his hand.

	Preposition	*Object*	*Word Modified by the Phrase*	*Kind of Phrase*
1.	*above*	*things*	*be*	adverb
	to	*those*	*pleasant*	adverb
	around	*you*	*those*	adjective

	Preposition	*Object*	*Word Modified by the Phrase*	*Kind of Phrase*
2.	*on*	*corner*	*house*	adjective
	to	*man*	*belongs*	adverb
	with	*stick*	*man*	adjective
	in	*hand*	*stick*	adjective

8. The Interjection

INTERJECTION

The interjection is the only part of speech that has no contacts with or relations to the other words in a sentence. Strictly speaking, therefore, interjections are hardly a part of speech at all. They are merely exclamations, expressing deep or sudden feeling. Examples are words like *oh, ah, bah, pooh, bravo, alas, hurrah, pshaw, hush, hello, amen.*

Many words and phrases can be used as exclamations and interjections; for example, *Horrors! Good work! Mercy on us! For shame! Oh dear me!*

It is only a step from phrases like these to longer exclamatory expressions such as

What a shame!
What a pity!
How very beautiful!
What a beautiful night!

The next step is the complete exclamatory sentence punctuated with an exclamation point instead of a question mark:

Isn't he a superb driver!
Did you ever see such a black cloud!
Wasn't that an exciting game!

PARSING INTERJECTIONS

Interjections need only to be recognized and pointed out. Since they have no grammatical connection with the rest of the sentence, no further parsing is possible.

Sentences for Parsing and Analysis

I

1. No bird soars too high if he soars with his own wing.
2. The guide pulled him from his blankets at dawn, and led him westward toward the distant line of foothills.
3. Such was the extremity of distress that the rats, who came to feast in those hideous dens, were eagerly hunted.
4. There was a young lady of Lynn,
   Who was so uncommonly thin
   That when she essayed
   To drink lemonade,
   She slipped through the straw and fell in.
5. I had a little doggy who went and bit a calf,
   And though he did it jokingly, I really couldn't laugh;
   I cut a little birch rod and took him down a peg:
   Because, you see, the calf he bit was one that's on my leg.
6. He that cannot think is a fool; he that will not think is a bigot; he that dare not think is a slave.
7. No man has a good enough memory to make a successful liar.
   —LINCOLN
8. If a man empties his purse into his head, no man can take it away from him.—FRANKLIN
9. A promise neglected is an untruth told.
10. A secret is your slave if you keep it, your master if you lose it.
11. An old-fashioned girl blushes when she is embarrassed; a modern girl is embarrassed when she blushes.
12. Ere the Christian could avail himself of this mishap, his nimble foeman sprang from the ground, and calling on his steed, which instantly returned to his side, he leaped into the seat without touching the stirrup and regained all the advantage of which the Knight of the Leopard hoped to deprive him.
    —SCOTT

CHAPTER IV

The Analysis of Sentences

Analysis versus Parsing

Parsing is concerned with the parts of speech and deals with words separately. Analysis is concerned with the parts of sentences, and deals with sentences as units. Parsing concentrates upon nouns, pronouns, adjectives, verbs, adverbs, prepositions, conjunctions, and interjections. Analysis concentrates upon subject, predicate, object or complement, and their modifiers, whether word, phrase, or clause.

Because analysis treats of matters like the kinds of sentences, modifiers of all kinds, and phrases and clauses as such, it is of direct use in learning to write. Especially is this true when it becomes necessary either to improve vague, weak sentences or to correct the scores of errors that will creep in despite our best efforts. Analysis thus conveniently bridges the gap between grammar and composition. Sentences are stubborn and tricky things, as every writer knows, and skill in analysing them helps us to handle them with greater ease and sureness.

Sentence Elements

Practically every element of sentence analysis is included in the tables on the following pages. To know what these terms mean and to be able to recognize the sentence functions which they name is to know the essentials of sentence analysis.

Sentence = subject plus predicate

Subject = {noun or its equivalent (word, phrase, or clause)} plus adjective modifiers {word, phrase, or clause}

Predicate = {
(1) transitive verb plus adverb modifiers {word, phrase, or clause} plus object
(2) intransitive verb plus adverb modifiers {word phrase, or clause}
(3) linking verb plus adverb modifiers {word, phrase, or clause} plus complement
}

Object = {noun or its equivalent} plus adjective modifiers {word, phrase, or clause}

Complement = {
(1) noun or its equivalent (word, phrase, or clause) plus adjective modifiers {word, phrase, or clause}
or
(2) adjective or its equivalent plus adverb modifiers {word, phrase, or clause}
}

Needed Grammatical Knowledge

1. The Four Kinds of Sentences: Simple, Complex, Compound, and Compound-Complex.
2. The Difference between Phrases and Clauses.
3. The Three Main Kinds of Phrases: Noun, Adjective, and Adverb.
4. Dependent Clauses and Independent Clauses.
5. The Three Kinds of Dependent Clauses: Noun, Adjective, and Adverb.

1. Simple Sentences

A simple sentence is one that contains one subject and one predicate and expresses one complete thought.

To analyse a simple sentence is to point out (1) the subject and the predicate; (2) their modifiers; and (3) the object or complement and its modifiers.

(1) SYMBOLS FOR WRITTEN ANALYSIS OF SIMPLE SENTENCES

Bare Subject, underlined once
Bare Verb, underlined twice
Bare Object, underlined three times
Adjective Modifiers (words or phrases), underlined with a wavy line
Adverb Modifiers (words or phrases), underlined with a broken line
Predicate Nominative or Noun Complement, not underlined.

1. Fine feathers do not make fine birds.
2. The girl on the corner is a friend of my sister's.
3. There[1] hath passed away a glory from the earth.
4. At Christmas he always sent all the sick people in the hospital beautiful flowers.
5. After a brief discussion the committee unanimously elected Mr. Glenn chairman.
6. Full many a gem of purest ray serene
The dark unfathomed caves of ocean bear.
7. Up and down the dreary camp,
In great boots of Spanish leather,
Striding with a measured tramp,
The Hidalgos, dull and damp,
Cursed the Frenchmen.

(2) COMMENTS ON THE USE OF THE SYMBOLS

Long experience has shown that these five symbols are the ideal number. They could easily be increased, but only with a loss in ease and effectiveness.

[1] Expletive (see page 42).

Both the indirect object and the objective complement, when a noun (see sentences 4 and 5), are to be underlined with three lines, just as the direct object is.

The predicate nominative (or noun complement after an intransitive verb—see sentence 2) is not underlined, thus marking it off from (1) the direct object, which is underlined three times, and (2) the predicate adjective (or adjective complement), which is underlined with a wavy line.

In underlining phrases, as distinguished from separate adjectives and adverbs, extend the line under the whole phrase, instead of breaking it up under each word.

The big, bad wolf is here. (Separate adjectives)

Who's afraid of the big, bad wolf? (Adverb phrase)

The cowboy was wearing a big, handsome, black hat. (Separate adjectives)

The man in the big, handsome black hat is a cowboy. (Adjective phrase)

(3) PHRASES

The chief trouble in analysing simple sentences comes in handling phrases. A phrase is a group of words (1) containing no subject or predicate and (2) performing the work of a single part of speech, usually a noun, an adjective, or an adverb.

1. Noun Phrases

A noun phrase is a phrase that is used like a noun. Its four commonest uses are the following:

1. The subject of a verb

   (*a*) To give cheerfully increases the pleasure of giving.

   (*b*) Your calling him a coward doesn't make him one.

2. The object of a verb

   (*a*) No one likes being a loser.

   (*b*) I hate having to resort to trickery.

   (*c*) They refused to accept charity.

3. In apposition with a noun
   (a) The phrase "On your toes" was often used by our coach.
   (b) His first ambition, to be the richest man in town, was realized.

4. Predicate nominative
   (a) Her chief fear was losing her hair.
   (b) My brother's hobby is collecting postage stamps.

Many of these are examples of the use of gerunds.

Exercises in Noun Phrases

Point out the noun phrases in the following sentences, and tell how they are used.

1. Sitting around a camp-fire and telling stories is great fun.
2. What confused me was your forgetting to bring the manuscript.
3. It is hard to teach an old dog new tricks.
4. The dog's barking in the house frightened the burglars away.
5. To give money is not always the best form of charity.
6. Your standing first in the class caused your parents great pleasure.
7. There is no use crying over spilt milk.
8. Writing an interesting story is a hard thing to do.
9. To win over such able opponents made me happy.
10. He resolved never to give up.
11. To jump across the ditch was impossible.
12. Your being late made us miss the train.

2. Adjective and Adverb Phrases

Phrases introduced by prepositions are the most numerous. Practically all such phrases either modify (1) a noun or pronoun and are hence adjective phrases, or modify (2) a verb, adjective, or adverb, and are hence adverb phrases. To find what they modify is the only way to tell them apart. The same phrase that is an adjective phrase in one sentence, because it modifies a noun or pronoun, may be an adverb phrase in another sentence because it modifies a verb, adjective, or adverb.

Adjective Phrases

1. The hat on the table is mine.
2. The house by the side of the road is clearly visible.
3. The man on the white horse is a good rider.
4. The stick in the corner fell down.

Adverb Phrases

1. Please put my hat on the table.
2. He got out of the car and stood by the side of the road.
3. He was mounted on a white horse.
4. The stick standing in the corner fell down.

See also the section on Phrases Introduced by Prepositions, page 49.

Exercises in Recognizing Phrases

I

Tell what the italicized phrases modify and thus show whether they are adjective or adverb phrases.

1. Just put your coat *in the hall*.
2. You will find the book *on the table in the parlour*.
3. Come *at the first possible moment*.
4. My bicycle is in the garage *across the street*.
5. You will find us waiting *for you*.
6. We once considered buying the house *with the green roof*.
7. A man of your standing should not stoop *to such tricks*.
8. There is always room *at the top for the best*.
9. Let's start *on our trip* early *in the morning*.
10. *Failure to convict* is no proof *of innocence*.

II

Point out the phrases introduced by prepositions and show them to be adjective or adverb phrases by telling what they modify.

If this exercise is assigned as written work, copy these sentences and underline adjective phrases with a wavy line and adverb phrases with a broken or dotted line. Do not mark your book.

1. A bird in the hand is worth two in the bush.
2. Under no circumstances will I agree to your proposal.
3. After supper we went to the best show in town.
4. One of the forts was laid in ruins.
5. A thing of beauty is a joy forever.
6. He was not of an age, but for all time.

7. Full well they laughed with counterfeited glee
At all his jokes, for many a joke had he.
8. Man's inhumanity to man
Makes countless thousands mourn.
9. There came to the beach a poor exile of Erin.
10. A clock of brass ticked on the mantel.

Simple Sentences for Analysis

Analyse the following sentences, using the symbols suggested on page 54.

1. A rolling stone gathers no moss.
2. Take things always by their smooth handle.
3. The weak in courage is strong in cunning.
4. The early bird catches the worm.
5. One man in his time plays many parts.
6. A highbrow is a person educated beyond his intelligence.
7. Drenched with rain, he rode at a gallop through the gate of the castle.
8. My heart is in the coffin there with Cæsar.
9. They wash, iron, cook, eat, and sleep in the same room.
10. After supper the cook retired to her room.

2. Complex Sentences

A complex sentence is one that contains one independent clause and one or more dependent clauses.

A dependent clause is one which does not make complete sense in and by itself, but which depends upon another clause for its full meaning.

Consider, for example, the incomplete, unfinished meaning of the following dependent clauses which have been cut away from their independent clauses and left hanging in the air.

1. Unless you will help me ——.
2. —— that you have been sick.
3. If you don't believe it ——.
4. —— who sold it to me.

Now match these dangling dependent clauses with the following independent clauses to which they belong and both the meaning and the grammatical construction are complete.

1. —— I have no one to turn to.
2. I am sorry ——.
3. —— ask your father.
4. I can't remember now the clerk ——.

A great deal of time and attention should be devoted to dependent clauses. Just as the phrase is the trouble spot of the simple sentence, so the dependent clause is the trouble spot of the complex sentence. To master dependent clauses is to go a long way toward mastering the analysis of sentences, and to be able to use dependent clauses properly in writing is to go far toward achieving an accurate and flexible style.

In written analysis the three different kinds of clauses may be indicated as follows:

Noun Clauses: enclosed in pointed brackets	< >
Adjective Clauses: enclosed in round brackets	( )
Adverb Clauses: enclosed in square brackets	[ ]

(1) PHRASES VERSUS CLAUSES

In distinguishing phrases from clauses there is one important point of likeness and one important point of unlikeness. The point of likeness is that both phrases and clauses are used as a single part of speech—either as noun, adjective, or adverb. The point of unlikeness is that the clause has a subject and predicate and that the phrase has none. Consider the difference as regards subject and predicate in the following parallel examples:

Phrases	*Clauses*
1. The man on the corner is my friend.	1. The man (that is standing on the corner) is my friend.
2. Please come at the first possible moment.	2. Please come [as soon as you possibly can].
3. Upon the arrival of the train the band struck up a lively tune.	3. [When the train arrived] the band struck up a lively tune.

(2) DEPENDENT CLAUSES

1. How Introduced

So important and varied are dependent clauses that it is advisable to notice in detail the ways they are introduced. Dependent clauses are usually introduced by either (*a*) subordinating conjunctions, or (*b*) relative pronouns.

(*a*) Subordinating Conjunctions (See Review of Grammar, pages 45-47.)

1. Time: *when, whenever, while, as, until, before, since, after, as soon as.*
2. Place: *where, whence, wherever.*
3. Manner: *as, just as, as if.*
4. Degree and Comparison: *as much as, so far as, as, than.*
5. Cause or Reason: *because, since, whereas, as, for.*
6. Result: *that, so that.*
7. Condition: *if, unless.*
8. Concession: *though, although, even if.*
9. Purpose: *that, so that, in order that, lest.*
10. The conjunction *that* introducing a noun clause.

(*b*) Relative Pronouns

The chief relative pronouns are *who* (obj. *whom*) *which, what, that.* They usually introduce adjective clauses.

Whether introduced by subordinating conjunctions, by relative pronouns, or in whatsoever way, dependent clauses are of three kinds:

(*a*) Noun Clauses
(*b*) Adjective Clauses
(*c*) Adverb Clauses

The way to distinguish them is the same as the way to distinguish (*a*) the parts of speech and (*b*) phrases: namely, to see what work they do in the sentence.

(*a*) Noun Clauses

A noun clause is a clause that is used like a noun—that is, in any of the five following ways:

1. The subject of a verb

<That he is mistaken> is evident.

2. The object of a verb

   They promised <that they would come>.

3. The object of a preposition

   Do you still agree with <what you said yesterday>?

4. In apposition with a noun

   The fact <that you agree> pleases all your friends.

5. Predicate nominative

   The question is <whether he has really been convinced>.

(*b*) Adjective Clauses

An adjective clause is one that modifies a noun or a pronoun.

1. Your opinion is the only thing (that matters).
   (Modifies the noun *thing*)
2. The book (which you lent me yesterday) is most interesting.
   (Modifies the noun *book*)
3. They were out of town during the time (you refer to).
   (Modifies the noun *time*, the relative pronoun being omitted)

(*c*) Adverb Clauses

An adverb clause is one that modifies a verb, adjective, or adverb.

1. He came [when you called].
2. [If you think so], go ahead.
3. [Although my hours have been shortened], I still have too much to do.
4. We ran so fast [that we got out of breath].
5. The situation is not so bad [as we had feared].
6. His condition is better [than we had even dared to hope].

See also the section on Subordinating Conjunctions, pages 45-47.

(3) RECOGNIZING CLAUSES

Using the pointed brackets < > for noun clauses, the round brackets ( ) for adjective clauses, and the square brackets [ ] for adverb clauses, point out the dependent clauses in the following sentences.

1. She learned to play the piano when she was still a little girl.
2. If you will come with me, I will take you to your room.
3. All things come to him who waits.
4. The fact that he believes it does not make it true.
5. He also serves who only stands and waits.
6. June is the month when days are longest.
7. He jests at scars who never felt a wound.
8. Although trifles make perfection, perfection is no trifle.
9. We asked what the price of the house was, but the owner said that it was not for sale.
10. I don't know what to tell her when she comes.

(4) ANALYSIS OF COMPLEX SENTENCES

After the dependent clauses have been marked as noun, adjective, or adverb clauses by means of the different brackets, further analysis of both the independent and the dependent clauses proceeds as in the simple sentence. That is, each clause is taken separately, and the subject, verb, object, or complement, and all modifying words and phrases, are marked as indicated on page 54.

1. Never put off till tomorrow <what you can do today>.

2. Have a heart (that never hardens), a temper (that never tires), and a touch (that never hurts).

3. No statue has ever yet been erected to a man (who was afraid of <what people might say>).

4. [If you would realize the state of the ant under your foot] think of your condition [were you under the foot of an elephant].

—PERSIAN PROVERB

5. There[2] was an old man of Tarentum
(Who gnashed his false teeth [till he bent 'em])
[When they asked him the cost
of <what he had lost>]
He replied, "<I can't say [for I rent 'em"]>.

[2] Expletive (see page 42).

(5) COMMENTS ON THE USE OF THE SYMBOLS

It will be noticed that neither co-ordinating nor subordinating conjunctions are marked. This in itself serves to distinguish them from other parts of speech which might be confused with them.

Notice, too, the use of the brackets, if there is more than one dependent clause in the sentence. There are several possibilities.

1. The dependent clauses may all be dependent on the same independent clause, in which case the brackets marking them off will neither overlap nor even partly coincide. For example:

(1) Tell me [when you can come] [if you don't mind].
(2) Have a heart (that never hardens), a temper (that never tires), and a touch (that never hurts).

2. One dependent clause may be dependent on another dependent clause, in which case the brackets of the inner clause will be included within the brackets of the clause on which it depends.

(1) They wired <that they could not stay [as long as they had expected]>.
(2) Here is the clerk (that promised us <that he would sell us the chairs at a 50 per cent. reduction>).
(3) This is the cat (that killed the rat (that ate the malt (that lay in the house (that Jack built)))).

Complex Sentences for Analysis

I

1. If a man empties his purse into his head, no man can take it away from him.
2. Never cross a bridge till you come to it.
3. A critic is a legless man who teaches running.

—CHANNING POLLOCK

4. I wonder why London cannot keep its own fools at home.

—GOLDSMITH

5. A specialist is a man who knows more and more about less and less.

—DR. WILLIAM J. MAYO

6. Lives of great men all remind us,
We can make our lives sublime.

—LONGFELLOW

II

1. The world is a comedy to those who think, a tragedy to those who feel.
2. A fool is one who is intelligent at the wrong time.
3. Nothing is particularly hard if you divide it into small jobs.

—HENRY FORD

4. The measure of a man's real character is what he would do if he knew he would never be found out.—MACAULAY
5. Music is the only language in which you cannot say a mean or sarcastic thing.—JOHN ERSKINE
6. Many would be cowards if they had courage enough.
7. The town was so small that when the train stopped, the engine was out in the country.
8. The man who cannot put fire into his speeches should put his speeches into the fire.

III

1. It was easy to teach the dog that he must come to me when I whistled.
2. We regret to inform you that we have no more straw hats in stock and that we shall not buy any others till next spring.
3. That is the desk where lost and found articles are restored to their owners.
4. Father said as he patted my shoulder, "Don't feel so discouraged because you failed."
5. He who knows only his side of the case knows little of that.
6. The smallest dewdrop that lies on the meadow at night has a star sleeping in its bosom.
7. Then let us say you are sad
Because you are not merry.

—SHAKESPEARE

3. Compound Sentences

A compound sentence is one that contains two or more independent clauses.

Independent clauses are joined by co-ordinating conjunctions, chief of which are *and*, *but*, and *or*.

Certain words seem to have a conjunctive quality or meaning and are sometimes known as conjunctive adverbs.

These are as follows:

also, furthermore, likewise, moreover, however, nevertheless, otherwise, still, accordingly, consequently, hence, then, therefore, thus.

It is best not to use them as co-ordinating conjunctions to join independent clauses. (See page 140)

(1) ANALYSIS OF COMPOUND SENTENCES

If none of the independent clauses of a compound sentence contains a dependent clause, such a compound sentence consists in effect of several simple sentences linked together by co-ordinating conjunctions. Analysis then proceeds as in the simple sentence:

1. The heavens declare the glory of God, and the firmament showeth his handiwork.
2. The rat, the mouse, the fox, the rabbit, watch the roots; the lion, the tiger, the horse, the elephant, watch the fruits.

(2) COMPOUND-COMPLEX SENTENCES

If one or more of the independent clauses of a compound sentence contain a dependent clause, such a compound sentence is in effect a linking of a simple sentence with a complex sentence or a linking of several complex sentences with one another. In order to distinguish this type of compound sentence from the preceding type, many teachers use the term "compound-complex sentence". In either case, such sentences offer no difficulties in analysis which have not already been touched on.

Examples of the analysis of compound-complex sentences are these:

1. Men must work, and women must weep,
   [Though storms be sudden and waters deep],
   And [the harbour bar be moaning].

2. He (who fights and runs away)
   May live to fight another day;
   But he (who is in battle slain)
   Can never rise and fight again.

Compound Sentences for Analysis

1. Cowards die many times before their deaths;
   The valiant never taste of death but once.
2. The hours of folly are measured by time, but the hours of wisdom no clock can measure.
3. Straws float upon the surface, but gold lies at the bottom of the stream.
4. Some are born great, some achieve greatness, and some have greatness thrust upon them.
5. Faithful are the wounds of a friend, but the kisses of an enemy are deceitful.
6. The curfew tolls the knell of parting day,
   The lowing herd winds slowly o'er the lea,
   The ploughman homeward plods his weary way
   And leaves the world to darkness and to me.

—GRAY

Sentences for Parsing and Analysis

I

1. From Clive's second visit to India dates the political ascendency of the English in that country.

2. The egg is smooth and very pale;
It has no nose, it has no tail;
It has no ears that one can see;
It has no wit, no repartee.

3. When wicked witches whisk switches, which witch whisks switches swiftest?

4. You never know what is enough unless you know what is more than enough.

5. The Night has a thousand eyes,
And the Day but one;
Yet the light of the bright world dies
With the dying sun.

II

1. Every man is an omnibus in which his ancestors ride.
—OLIVER WENDELL HOLMES

2. If it is not right, do not do it; if it is not true, do not say it.

3. He who loses wealth loses much; he who loses a friend loses more; but he who loses courage loses all.—CERVANTES

4. There was a young maid who said, "Why
Can't I look in my ear with my eye?
If I give my mind to it,
I'm sure I can do it,
You never can tell till you try."

5. He that is good at making excuses is seldom good at anything else.

III

1. 'Most any golfer, poor or rich,
Would never count the cost,
Could he but buy a golf ball which
Would bark when it is lost.

2. There are poor people in the mountains who live in such dilapidated shacks that every time it rains they have to go out and get in the sedan.—*The Literary Digest*

3. I usually get my stuff from an awful lot of people—who promised somebody else that they would keep it a secret.
—WALTER WINCHELL

4. "I can't decide whether I should go to a palmist or to a mind-reader."
   "By all means go to a palmist. It's evident that you have a palm."

5. *Etc.* is a sign used to make others believe that you know more than you do.

IV

1. What this country needs is a zipper olive bottle.
2. Be not merely good; be good for something.
3. I am an old man, and have known a great many troubles, but most of them never happened.—MARK TWAIN
4. It has been proved that pictures can be transmitted by radio.
5. When she opened those ruby lips of hers she spoke pure spearmint.—KAUFMAN & FERBER, *Dinner at Eight*

V

Passages for Parsing and Analysis

1. Whoever at fifty does not rate himself quite as low as most of his acquaintance would be likely to put him, must be either a fool or a great man, and I humbly disclaim being either.
   —JAMES RUSSELL LOWELL, *On A Certain Condescension in Foreigners*

2. Certain things are good for nothing until they have been kept a long while: and some are good for nothing until they have been kept and used. . . . Of those which must be kept and used I will name three—meerschaum pipes, violins, and poems.—OLIVER WENDELL HOLMES, *The Autocrat of the Breakfast Table*

3. I could not sleep when I got on such a hunt for an idea until I had caught it; and when I thought I had got it, I was not satisfied until I had put it in language plain enough, as I thought, for anybody to comprehend. This was a kind of passion, and it has stuck with me; for I am never easy now, when I am handling a thought, till I have bounded it north, and bounded it south, and bounded it east, and bounded it west.—ABRAHAM LINCOLN

4. I am sure that a man ought to read as he would grasp a nettle; do it lightly and you get molested; grasp it with all

your strength and you feel none of its asperities. There is nothing so horrible as languid study, when you sit looking at the clock, wishing the time was over, or that somebody would call upon you and put you out of your misery. The only way to read with any efficiency is to read so heartily that dinner-time comes two hours before you expected it.

—SYDNEY SMITH

NOTE: For additional sentences for parsing and analysis see Selections for Paraphrasing, pages 103-106 and Selections for Précis Writing, pages 110-116.

PART TWO

WRITING AND SPEAKING
PARAGRAPH AND SENTENCE

CHAPTER V

Writing the Paragraph

1. Independent Paragraphs

As a practical matter in writing, paragraphs may be divided into two classes: (1) independent or unrelated paragraphs, and (2) chain or related paragraphs. Their names suggest the difference between them.

An independent paragraph is one whose meaning is distinct and complete in and by itself. It is not connected with or related to any other paragraph. It stands alone, like a one-room cabin or like a single freight car on a side-track. It has its own subject or topic, which it develops as far as the writer wishes for his particular purpose. When the paragraph ends, if it has been successfully written, it leaves nothing more to be said at that time on that subject.

Independent paragraphs have many uses. They have increased greatly in numbers and variety as modern life has speeded up, and as the demand has grown for things that take less time and space than formerly. Long, detailed arguments and explanations have given place to succinct, one-paragraph articles which say keenly and convincingly all that need be said on some current topic.

Thus, in the light of the present and growing demands for paragraphs of this kind, but chiefly because ability to compose paragraphs forms a most important step in learning to write, a great deal of practice in independent paragraphs is necessary. Every day during the next month that the composition class meets, every pupil should write an independent paragraph either in class or at home. The more, the better. There is no way to learn to write except by writing, and the independent paragraph is the best place to start.

Chain, or connected, paragraphs are dealt with in Chapter IX, pages 165-188.

2. Writing from Topic Sentences

In order to keep definitely on the track of the paragraph idea, the first ten or twelve paragraphs should be written not from topics but from actual topic sentences. At the end of this chapter is a list of topic sentences which can be worked up into satisfactory independent paragraphs. They are divided, though not equally, between explanation, argument, description, and incident.

Look over the list carefully, and, as preparation for class do the following three things:

1. From the list choose one sentence from each of the groups—explanation, argument, description, and incident—which you would prefer to expand into a paragraph. The paragraph is to be not less than eighty words long, nor more than two hundred.

2. From these four sentences choose the one you feel you can develop most easily.

3. Think up some of the particulars and details that seem to belong to it. Try to think of at least five details. This may not be as easy as it sounds, for before you can write, you must think. Count the details on your fingers as you think of them, without writing any of them down on paper. Shut your eyes if you feel like it, and *force* your mind to *realize* or *see* the topic unfolding into a series of details and related sentence thoughts. Suppose, for example, that the sentence selected is this one:

> I recently visited a friend's room that showed many signs of carelessness and untidiness.

Before even such a simple paragraph topic as this can be developed, it is necessary to think up and think over the various details and particulars that serve to give a room an untidy appearance.

(1) AN UNTIDY ROOM

One class carried out the following plan. After writing the sentence on the board, the teacher asked the pupils to suggest details of untidiness. As different pupils named different details, he wrote each detail down in sentence form, numbering them in order. After every pupil had been given a chance to express himself, the list of numbered sentences on the board read after this fashion:[1]

Details of an Untidy Room

1. The soiled, tattered curtains hung crookedly.
2. The air was close and stale.
3. To one side there was a bookcase, in the wide-open door of which dangled a bunch of keys.
4. The window shades were faded.
5. Books and magazines were lying on a chair.
6. The table in the middle of the room was rickety.
7. Over the arm of a Morris chair was hanging a red sweater.
8. On the table were a baseball, a glove, a broken package of cigarettes, some ends of burned matches.
9. On the floor were an open shoe box, a pair of old shoes, and a soiled collar.
10. The bed was rumpled and littered with newspapers and clothes.
11. The walls were papered in ugly yellow.
12. There were no pictures on the walls.
13. There were no school or college pennants in the room.

After some discussion, it was decided to omit the last three details, because while yellow wallpaper and the lack of pictures and pennants might make the room look ugly and bare, they were not really signs of carelessness or untidiness.

Each pupil was then instructed to take the remaining ten

[1]C. J. Thompson, "Thought-Building in the Paragraph", *English Journal*, Vol. 5, 1916, pp. 610-619.

details and work them into a paragraph, changing the sentences or the order in which they came as each pupil saw fit.

One of the paragraphs that were written in this way follows. It is not a masterpiece, but it is a good average descriptive paragraph, having a clear topic sentence and seven sentences of details that bear directly on the topic.

An Untidy Room

Last spring I visited a student's room in which there were many evidences of carelessness and untidiness. The faded window shades and soiled, tattered curtains had been carelessly adjusted, as if with no thought of their appearance. Old and used smells filled the room. To the left there stood a bookcase, in the wide-open door of which dangled a bunch of rusty keys. Near the middle of the room, but against the farther wall, stood a rickety old table, on the bare surface of which there were a baseball and a glove, a broken package of cigarettes, some ends of burned matches, a chequered cap, a shaving set, and a brush and comb. On one arm of a Morris chair near the table dangled a wrinkled red sweater. On the bare floor, in front of the chair, near the table, lay an open shoe box, two discarded shoes, and a soiled collar. To the right stood a once well-made bed, littered with sections of a Sunday newspaper and with clothes.

(2) THE END-SENTENCE

You will notice that the last sentence merely adds one further detail—the untidy bed. There is no final sentence giving either a summary or the general impression or any application of the paragraph as a whole. No such sentence is necessary here, but a good end-sentence would certainly do no harm and might serve to give a more complete and finished effect. How would one of these do to round the paragraph off?

Certainly it was not the kind of room I should choose to live in.

Taken as a whole, it was about as unattractive a room as I ever saw.

If the room had been mine, I should have hated to have my mother or father see it in its present condition.

3. The Need for Details

The way in which the paragraph on the "Untidy Room" was written has been described at length because it makes clear how necessary it is to think up details and particulars before the topic sentence can be developed. That is the chief purpose of all independent paragraphs—to give details and particulars. Without details it is as impossible to write a paragraph as it is to build a brick wall without bricks or a frame house without planks. Without enough details our best efforts read strangely like the following composition which Henry Ward Beecher made famous:

Cows

The cow is an animal with four legs, two horns, and a tail. Cows give milk. I love good milk.

Once when a teacher left the choice of a subject to the class, a boy handed in the following theme.

An Unsuccessful Night Hunt

(Original Version)

On a cold wintry night last year, a few boys and I went possum hunting. While in the woods we built a large fire, and sat there to warm our cold bodies. After about an hour had passed we heard one of the dogs bark, and then after a few moments all of them began barking as fast as they could. We left the fire, and ran down through the woods where the dogs were, or at least, where we thought they were, but we did not find the dogs anywhere. We looked and listened for about an hour but could not find the dogs anywhere. Finally we left the woods, and went home. On our way we saw the dogs, and found out that they just had a fit instead of trailing a possum.

Notice how flat and tame this account is. The details, which are the only means by which we can realize the incident, are not only few but are also generalized and uninteresting. In fact the only details given are these:

Incident: An Unsuccessful Night Hunt

Details to make the reader realize the incident:

1. A cold night in winter.
2. A few boys went possum hunting.

3. We build a large fire in the woods.
4. At the fire we warmed our cold bodies.
5. After an hour one of the dogs barked.
6. Shortly afterwards all the dogs joined in.
7. We left the fire.
8. We ran through the woods to where we thought the dogs were.
9. We did not find them.
10. After an hour's looking and listening we still did not find them.
11. At last we went home.
12. On the way we met the dogs.
13. They had had a fit instead of trailing a possum.

The teacher read the theme aloud to the class the next day, and called attention to three things: (1) that the details were few and commonplace; (2) that there was an unfortunate instance of repetition in the fourth and fifth sentences; and (3) that though correct in spelling, punctuation, and sentence structure, the theme did not deserve a passing grade.

Then the teacher assigned the same subject to be written as a class exercise that day, cautioning the class to be sure to give enough definite details to enable the reader to see and realize what happened.

Among the paragraphs written in thirty minutes was the following. Contrast it, as to both the number and the interest of the details, with the original version.

An Unsuccessful Night Hunt

(Improved Version)

On a cold night last winter, a few boys and I went possum hunting. In hunting possums there is not much for the hunters to do until the dogs locate a trail. Walking along slowly, we began to grow cold, and when we came to a little hill with plenty of dry, dead pine branches on the ground, we stopped and built a fire. The warm blaze felt so good that we decided to stop there for a while. We were sitting around telling stories when we heard one of the dogs barking somewhere down by the foot of the hill. "Listen!" said Fred. All talking halted at once. In a few moments, all four of the dogs joined in, and it seemed to us as though they were going away from us. With a cry of "Possum!" we all ran as fast as we could down the hill. Jack stumbled over a log and fell, but was up again in a second. We reached the spot where we thought the dogs had been, but there was no sign of them. We listened for their barking. It had stopped. We looked for them for perhaps half an hour. By that time it was nearly midnight, so we started home. At the edge of the woods we met the dogs, tired out and panting. We all agreed that one of them had had a fit. When a dog is attacked with one of these fits, he usually starts running, with no evident aim or purpose. If there are other dogs around, they will join in after him and run until they are worn out. Our possum hunt had been a failure so far as hunting was concerned, but we all said that our little talk around the warm fire made up for the lack of possums. Then, too, we got plenty of exercise!

An analysis of the details in this theme gives the following result:

Details to make the reader realize the incident:

1. A cold night in winter.
2. A few boys went possum hunting.
3. Not much for possum hunters to do till the dogs strike a trail.
4. Walking slowly, we grew cold.
5. We came to a little hill covered with dry pine branches.
6. We stopped and built a fire.
7. We stayed by the fire warming.
8. We sat down and began to tell stories.
9. We heard one of the dogs bark near the foot of the hill.
10. "Listen!" said Fred.
11. We all stopped talking.
12. All four dogs joined in the barking.
13. They seemed to be going away from us.
14. We cried "Possum" and ran down the hill.
15. Jack fell over a log but was up again at once.
16. We reached the place where we thought the dogs were.
17. There was no sign of the dogs.
18. We listened for their barking.
19. They had all stopped barking.
20. We looked for them for half an hour.
21. By that time it was nearly midnight.
22. We started home.
23. We met the dogs at the edge of the woods.
24. They were tired out and panting.
25. We agreed that one of them had had a fit.
26. When a dog has a running fit, he starts running without aim or purpose.

27. Any other dogs near will join in.
28. They will run till they are tired out.
29. Our possum hunt had failed.
30. We had enjoyed our talk around the fire.
31. We had had plenty of exercise.

Here are thirty-one details instead of the original thirteen, and there are touches of interest here and there. Though the theme hardly deserves more than a B, it is a great improvement on the original; and this improvement is due almost entirely to the more successful use of details.

4. The Need of Details Again

So it is with all your writing. Even the simplest and most familiar paragraph topics have to be thought over and divided out into their appropriate details before being developed. Suppose your topic is as easy and commonplace as this one:

> Many improvements have been made in the town of —— during the last five years.

Do you know off-hand just what improvements have been made? It is clear that you must have this information before you can write a satisfactory paragraph on this topic. Ask your parents to mention all the improvements they can think of, and next day, with the teacher leading the discussion, make a complete list in class. It may prove surprisingly large.

Or imagine that your topic is this:

> The greatest need of our school is ______.

Two things will be necessary here: first, to decide exactly what *is* the greatest need; and secondly, to give detailed reasons to prove that this need is greater than several other rival needs that might be urged. Discuss this subject in class. Imagine that your class is the Board of Trustees, with power to act. What one thing does the school need most—a new building, more teachers, a new athletic field, a cafeteria, a library, a gymnasium? After this point is decided there comes the question, What reasons can you give to convince the other trustees or the voters of the school district that this need is greatest?

5. A Good End-Sentence

In fact, to have a clear topic sentence, and to give enough examples and details to develop it, are generally unfailing guarantees of a good paragraph; of a *good* paragraph, yes, but not of the *best* paragraph. One other thing is needed to raise "good" to "best".

This is to sum up, drive home, apply, or give the result or effect of the paragraph topic in a short, striking end-sentence. The closing sentence is to the rest of the paragraph what the snapper is to the whip. It gives it point and stingo. Without the snapper the whip doesn't crack; and without a forceful close the paragraph *does* crack,—in a different sense,—and much of the meaning leaks away.

Consider the excellence of the following italicized end-sentence which closes an article by Bruce Barton on automobiles: "The modern motor car has become intimately woven into our social and economic fabric. It has enriched the lives of our people. *It has transformed a nation into a neighbourhood.*"

We may not be able to write as good end-sentences as that, but we can at least keep from ending our paragraphs with sentences that are feeble, stringy, and sprawly.

To sum up, make each of your paragraphs measure up to the following triple test:

1. Does the opening sentence state the paragraph idea simply and definitely?

2. Are there enough details and particulars to make the paragraph idea clear and interesting?

3. Is the closing sentence good enough to deserve the place of honour at the end?

Paragraphs by Students Showing Use of Details

Here are five paragraphs by high-school students, one of explanation, one of argument, an editorial paragraph which is persuasion rather than argument, one of narration, and one of description. Each paragraph consists of details and particulars—that is, is built up in the same way that nine-tenths of all the paragraphs which you write will be built up.

(1) DETAILS USED TO EXPLAIN

You and Your Dog

It is no disgrace to be afraid of a dog, but it is a disgrace for a dog to be afraid of you. Cruelty to animals is the most depraved form of cowardice. It is one of the surest symptoms of an inferiority complex. The man who kicks a dog cannot hold his own in an equal struggle, so he chooses this means of venting his spleen. It has been said that a person's character may be judged by the kind of magazines he reads, the subjects of his conversation, and the behaviour of his dog. A better statement would be that a man's intelligence may be judged by his magazines and his conversation, but his character is best judged by the behaviour of his dog.

(2) DETAILS USED TO CONVINCE

A Word for Examinations

There are many reasons why examinations should be given. Examinations show certain specific things that a student has or has not learned. They sum up the course and give a clear idea of the subject as a whole because they force the student to make a comprehensive review of the course. In reviewing for the examination the student is required to learn any part or parts of the course that he may have slighted during the term. Some people write more clearly than they speak, and examinations give them a chance to make a better average. Examinations aid the instructor to grade these students fairly. All students have the same question, so that no particular student has an advantage over the rest. Since all students take the same examinations, a student can compare his grade with the grades of others and see how he stands in comparison with the rest of the group. The most conclusive argument for examinations is that no substitute has ever been found that can take their place in showing what a student has learned, what his average is when compared to the rest of the class, and in aiding the instructor to grade with regularity, impartiality, and fairness.

(3) DETAILS USED TO PERSUADE

Walk!

Let's go for a walk! Put on a pair of your most comfortable shoes and start on your way. It's a beautiful spring day, and the birds are there to welcome you. Perhaps you will walk in the woods, stroll along the lake-shore, or just tour your own town. These, of course, are only a few of the places you can visit, but look around and you will find many others close to you that offer varied attractions. You will not only find enjoyment, but will also get the invigorating exercise which is important to good health. It may be that you have been worrying about those extra pounds. What better reducing exercise could you find than walking? On the other hand, you could take baby brother or the family dog with you and thereby help to retain the good favour of the family. Today you have become so accustomed to the convenience of the automobile and the bus that walking seems out of the question. But if you did walk, think of the money you could save by not buying bus tickets or gasoline! Little savings like these mount up and help to buy that new hat or new golf club you have been wanting for so long. The next time you are bored and have that restless feeling, take a walk and see for yourself what satisfying results it will bring.

(4) DETAILS USED TO NARRATE

Treasure Hunt

It was very quiet. Softly he moved ahead until he reached the cavern entrance. With beating heart he leaned forward, scarcely daring to breathe. The shadowy and forbidding depths with the hint of things horrible and unseen gaped a horrid warning. But he had spent many years of unremitting search and constant toil for just such a moment as this. Besides, he did not lack courage. Weapon in hand he pressed onward with grim resolution and peered within. From the dim, shadowed depths came a yellow gleam—the glitter of yellow metal. Gold! Wherever he looked, the same yellow glimmer met his eye. The cavern was a veritable treasure trove. But as he leaned eagerly forward, as though to test the evidence of his senses, there came a weird, gurgling snarl from the black depths. In strangled accents came a voice: "I think it's the front tooth, Doctor."

(5) DETAILS USED TO DESCRIBE

Walking in the Rain at Night

The sharpest twinkle of a star or the brightest ray of the moon could not have penetrated the heavy clouds that night; it was only by the friendly but fragile beams the street light cast from under its little tin umbrella that I could see the rain dancing on the walk like a thousand-thousand diamonds which then ran together and made a shimmering, wrinkling, transparent sheet. Everything was very quiet and peaceful. I could almost count the sounds, the rain dripping from leaves and roofs, the merry gurgling of the water racing down the gutter, Paul's chatter, the splashing of our feet, and the sticky, pulling noise of tires on the wet pavement. I liked to see the cars pass because they always flung back a red streamer in a trembling zigzag down the street.

Topic Sentences for Writing Independent Paragraphs

I. Exposition

1. Swimming is excellent exercise for boys and girls.
2. Literary societies are beneficial to high-school pupils.
3. Everybody has a natural desire to be somebody else.
4. Birds are very interesting.
5. The eye sees easily and quickly what it is interested in.
6. Nicknames are earned in many ways.
7. Regular exercise is essential to health.
8. The training of a boy scout (girl guide) is a good preparation for citizenship.
9. Everyone should have a hobby.
10. Other people have had several ambitions for me.
11. In my opinion, the greatest invention is _____.
12. Believe it or not, the dictionary is an interesting book.
13. An invention I hope for but never expect is _____.
14. I think the finest human quality is _____.
15. Fashions in clothes (slang) change rapidly from year to year.
16. Boys gossip as much as girls do.
17. Campus slang is something to marvel at.

18. I think ____ is used oftener than any other word in the English language.
19. If I were teaching this class, there is one change I should certainly make.
20. My hobby is ____.
21. A good bird dog is probably the most intelligent of all animals.
22. Radio is a most interesting hobby.
23. A hard question to answer is, "Where do all the smart babies go?"
24. I would rather have a dog (cat) than a cat (dog) for a pet.
25. Man never stops in his search for more speed.
26. Plastics serve many everyday needs.
27. An orchestra (glee club) is a valuable asset to a school.
28. A house is not necessarily a home.
29. I have several reasons for wanting (not wanting) to go to the university.
30. The radio (telephone) has its disadvantages too.
31. A handicap is sometimes a blessing in disguise.
32. Words are like people.
33. A good friend and an old pair of shoes have much in common.
34. Cheap things are often expensive.
35. It takes real courage to go against popular opinion.
36. A valuable social asset is tact.
37. The more man learns about preserving life, the more he learns about destroying it.
38. Many birds are the farmer's friends.
39. Learning a language is very much like learning how to walk (swim, ski).
40. Sometimes the true worth of a man is not realized until after his death.
41. There are many ways of opening doors (closing windows, shaking hands).
42. ____ is sometimes not an admirable virtue.
43. Fashions in slang change rapidly.
44. You get what you pay for.

II. Argument

1. The greatest need of our school is ____. (Or exposition)
2. Although a dead language, Latin should not be dropped from the curriculum.
3. Boys should be required to study music.
4. All grades should be posted.
5. Every child should have an allowance.

6. Seniors in high school should be granted certain privileges.
7. A course in practical cookery would help most boys.
8. Children should (not) be told about Santa Claus.
9. It is wrong to keep animals in captivity.
10. It should be against the law to wear fur or feathers as ornament.
11. Monday would make a better school holiday than Saturday.
12. Students making a grade of A should be exempted from examination.
13. The study you like least may be doing you the most good.
14. Every child should be taught to swim.
15. A private house is (not) a better residence than an apartment.
16. Every student should join at least one club.
17. Weekly allowances should be earned.
18. All boys should learn a trade.
19. Every girl should learn how to make her own dresses.
20. Day-dreaming is (not) a waste of time.
21. Students should (not) be ranked on term reports.
22. Poverty is an aid (hindrance) to success.
23. High-school students should correspond with students in other lands.
24. One derives more pleasure from a play than from a motion picture.
25. The school day should begin at eight o'clock in the morning.

III. Description

1. One could tell it was Easter morning.
2. The two boys were arguing furiously.
3. His (Her) costume was the most original at the party.
4. Spring is here at last.
5. The baby lost his temper the other day.
6. I'd hate to have you see my top bureau drawer.
7. The queerest pet I ever had was ______.
8. Down the street dashed the runaway horse.
9. Not long ago I happened to be passing the engine house just as the fire alarm sounded.
10. I still remember my first visit to the museum.
11. The flower bed was a thing of beauty.
12. He was the queerest person I had ever seen.
13. It is very hard to be stern with a baby.
14. Yesterday was winter in her roughest mood.
15. My first night in the open was a delightful (not a delightful) experience.

16. It would be difficult to find two people differing more widely in appearance and disposition than ____ and ____.
17. There is one like him (her) in every class (at every party).
18. He was aptly nicknamed "Chubby".
19. We had never seen a house like that.
20. He was only a mongrel, but we loved him.
21. What fun it would be to furnish my room in my own way!
22. He (she) is the most attractive person I know.
23. One could not fail to notice him (her) in a crowd.
24. My den is cosily arranged.
25. Did you ever engage in a hand-to-hand encounter with a revolving door?
26. The bargain counter was a scene of wildest confusion.
27. Main Street on Saturday night is something to see.

IV. Narration

1. On account of the darkness and the rain I mistook the girl (boy) for my sister (brother).
2. Hurrying does not always save time.
3. It was the cleverest trick I ever saw played.
4. I had a very narrow escape the other day.
5. Practical jokes do not always have funny endings.
6. Did you ever try to get into the house without making a noise?
7. I overheard an interesting conversation yesterday on the street car.
8. The party was a great success.
9. If a girl ever asks you to teach her how to drive a car, don't accept.
10. I've had lots of hard luck lately.
11. Taking the cook's place for a day is no fun.
12. Everything went wrong that morning.
13. A soft answer turneth away wrath.
14. She fell back terrified as she opened the door.
15. I might have known that little brother could not keep a secret.
16. Although everyone laughed, it was not funny for me.
17. It is the unexpected that frequently happens.
18. I don't believe in ghosts, but ____.
19. Forgetfulness sometimes leads to much embarrassment.
20. Have I told you about my experience as a hitch-hiker?
21. That was one holiday that really went wrong.
22. He (she) and I were the best of friends until it happened.

23. Father warned us not to go, but, of course, we knew better.
24. We were certain that we had prepared a perfect alibi.
25. When the magician asked for a volunteer, I stepped forward eagerly.
26. I still don't quite understand how it happened.
27. I still remember my first visit to the dentist's.
28. He laughs best who laughs last.
29. Pride goeth before a fall.
30. There is an interesting story behind my most valuable photograph (coin, stamp).
31. This is the story of the big one that *didn't* get away.
32. Of course it was simply a case of mistaken identity, but neither of us is likely to forget the experience.

THE ROUND TABLE

1. If you were teaching composition, what grades would you give to the five paragraphs quoted under "Paragraphs by Students"? Hand in a slip with your grades on it and see how closely the members of the class agree with each other and with the teacher. In each case give reasons for the grade you have assigned.

2. Following closely the way in which the paragraph on the "Untidy Room" was planned and written, take the following topic sentence and work up the details in class:

It was evidently a home of wealth.

Consider this home from the outside point of view. You walk by the house and grounds, and as you pass you see various evidences that they cost a great deal of money. Think of the prettiest houses and yards that you have seen, and try to select the most striking features or details of each. Name them over in sentence form when the teacher calls for them in class and writes them upon the board. From the list on the board, choose the most vivid details and work them up into the best paragraph you can write.

After the last detail add a closing sentence of summary or comment like one of those suggested in connection with the "Untidy Room". Underline both this closing sentence and the topic sentence also in order to distinguish them from the sentences giving details.

3. Following the plan suggested in 1, take the opposite topic:

It was evidently a home of poverty.

Use the outside point of view entirely.

4. The two foregoing paragraphs were to be written from the out-

side point of view. Next, in imagination, go inside the two houses, and write two paragraphs using the same topic sentences:

It was evidently a home of wealth.
It was evidently a home of poverty.

5. Imagine that you are editor-in-chief of your high-school paper and that you are going to write a series of editorial paragraphs on desirable traits of character. Either as class work or as home work, write a paragraph about a page long on each of these topics, developing them in any way that seems to you most interesting and convincing: Courage, Enthusiasm, Determination, Sincerity.

6. Using the topic sentences suggested on pages 84-88, while studying the next several chapters, continue writing independent paragraphs, as the teacher directs, in class and as home work. Vary the topic sentences among the four groups—exposition, argument, incident, and description.

CHAPTER VI

Revising and Rewriting

1. The Necessity for Revising

When I say writing, O, believe me, it is rewriting that I have chiefly in mind.

—ROBERT LOUIS STEVENSON

Weigh well these wise words spoken by the gifted author of *Treasure Island*. They form the motto for this chapter and are a sure guide to better writing.

The sooner each beginning writer realizes that there is nothing sacred about his first draft, that, in fact, the first draft exists for the purpose of being torn to pieces and then put carefully back together in clearer, stronger form—the sooner he realizes this, the nearer he is to success. Like it or not, that is the only way.

(1) WHAT SUCCESSFUL WRITERS SAY ABOUT REVISING

Among successful writers the testimony concerning the need of revision is practically unanimous. Benjamin Franklin in composing his *Autobiography* wrote on only one half of each sheet of paper and left the other half for additions and corrections. Thomas Huxley, the English scientist and trained thinker, said, "Sometimes I write essays half a dozen times before I can get them into the proper shape." Cardinal Newman, the great English prelate and essayist, testified: "It is simply the fact that I have been obliged to take great pains with everything I have written, and I often write chapters over and over again, besides innumerable corrections and inter-linear additions."

The enormous pains the brilliant essayist Macaulay took with his writing have been set forth in detail by his nephew:

> The main secret of Macaulay's success lay in this, that to extraordinary fluency and facility he united patient, minute, and persistent diligence. . . . He never allowed a sentence to pass muster until it was as good as he could make it. He thought little of recasting a chapter in order to obtain a more lucid arrangement, and nothing whatever of reconstructing a paragraph for the sake of one happy stroke or apt illustration. . . . When at length, after repeated revisions, he had satisfied himself that his writing was as good as he could make it, he would submit it to the severest of all tests, that of being read aloud to others. . . . He could not rest until the lines were level to a hair's breadth, and the punctuation correct to a comma; until every paragraph concluded with a telling sentence, and every sentence flowed like running water.

If after a lifetime of thinking and writing such men as these still found it necessary to rewrite and to revise, the lesson for us is unmistakable: without vigorous and repeated revision, we cannot even hope to do good work.

2. The Way to Revise

In revising longer, assigned themes, there is a fairly definite procedure to follow which long experience has proved to be best.

(1) LET YOUR WORK GET COLD

For one thing, be sure to let at least one night go by between the first writing and the final revision. By all means correct and revise as soon as you have finished your first draft. In this way, you will find many mistakes. But do not stop there. Explain it as you will, you cannot then catch all of the blunders. Still less, while the glow of the effort of writing is yet upon you, can you improve and strengthen your sentences to top pitch. In this condition every writer tends to project upon his pages ideas that really exist only in his mind and which his pen has never transferred to paper at all. He cannot tell his good work from his bad. Let a night pass, however, and he sees everything in the clear cold light of the morning after, and mistakes and weaknesses fairly leap to the eye. That is why some themes that may seem impressive when we first write them dwindle to a strange level of dullness when we get them back from the teacher, so that we wonder at ourselves for ever having thought them good.

The ideal way to write is to start a theme three days before it is due. On the first day write the first copy out and revise it as best you can. On the second day revise it again more thoroughly. As the final and severest test, read it aloud to yourself and listen to it carefully. Your ear will catch monotony of sentence structure and weaknesses in punctuation and phrasing that your eye missed. Then write out your final copy carefully. Make it look as inviting as you can. On the next day, before you hand it in, glance through it once again as a final precaution. Many a ridiculous mistake has been caught and set right at the last minute.

(2) WHAT TO LOOK FOR

The mistakes that we make in writing are countless, but most of them can be classified under six heads. Look over the list carefully, for it is an important one.

1. Spelling and Capitalization
2. Punctuation
3. Grammar
4. Choice of Words
5. Sentence Structure
6. Paragraphing

Nine-tenths of all the errors that you will ever make from the time you start your next theme until you sign your last will and testament will fall under one or the other of these six classes.

As to the frequency of the different kinds of mistakes,

careful tabulation of many hundreds of themes shows that, excluding paragraphing, the mistakes of the average untrained writer are distributed as follows: Punctuation, 30 per cent; Choice of Words, 19 per cent; Sentence Structure, 19 per cent; Spelling, 18 per cent; Grammar, 14 per cent. In other words, the chances are that of every ten mistakes you make three will be errors in punctuation, two in the choice of words, two in sentence structure, two in spelling, and one in grammar. By comparing these figures with your monthly table of theme errors you can see in which department of writing you are individually strong and in which you are weak and need special coaching and care. Detailed instruction and practice in correcting these various types of errors are given in later chapters, particularly in the chapters on Punctuation, and on the Sentence.

(3) REVISE THREE TIMES, EACH TIME FOR A DEFINITE PURPOSE

1. **Read first for what are called mechanical or elementary mistakes.** Have your mind only upon blunders in (*a*) spelling and capitalization; (*b*) punctuation; (*c*) grammar; and (*d*) sentence structure with definite reference to the two worst sentence faults, the No-Sentence fault (see page 203) and the Comma Splice (see page 206). These four classes of errors belong together, and can be discovered and corrected at the same reading, though it will take all the care and concentration that you can muster.

2. **Look rapidly once again through the theme to see that the paragraphing is correct.** Should you combine several short paragraphs into one? Should you divide any of your longer paragraphs? The subject of paragraphing is discussed at length in Chapters V and IX. A fairly safe general rule is to be suspicious of any page you write that has more than two paragraphs (unless you are writing conversation), and to be equally suspicious of any page that contains no paragraph indentation at all. Of course sometimes you may

have three or more legitimate paragraphs to the page or may have a page and a half to one paragraph, but in most themes the odds will be against either chance.

3. These first two readings are concerned with correctness. Next comes effectiveness. After having revised for surface errors and paragraphing, **read the theme in order to judge what effect it will have on others.** If someone else had written it, how would it impress you? If it is argument, would it convince you? If it is exposition, does it seem complete and entirely clear? If it is description, is it vivid? If it is an incident, would it interest you? In the last analysis those are the qualities which make all written work good or bad and which, surface errors having been taken care of, determine whether or not you will amount to anything as a writer, either now or hereafter.

(4) READ YOUR WORK ONCE ALOUD

The last and severest test to which you should put your work is to read it aloud, listening critically the while. Listen for both faults and defects. A fault may be loosely defined as "something there which is wrong", and a defect as "something which ought to be there but isn't". Errors of both these kinds abound in writing, and strange to say the ear will detect many which the eye has overlooked. By reading aloud you can better test the flavour of such things as the beginnings and ends of your paragraphs and the quality of your sentence structure. Monotonous or babyish sentences entirely escape notice if read silently. By being read aloud, many a B theme has been turned into an A theme. It is one of the best ways to acquire efficient self-criticism.

3. The Importance of Outside Form

Do not underestimate the importance of the physical appearance of written work. How a theme looks as it is lifted from the pile, before even the first sentence is read, makes a great deal of difference. First impressions are strong. An attractive, careful piece of work starts off with everything in its favour, the teacher included. A slovenly, hasty, careless-looking theme has everything against it from the first word to the last, and must be of exceptional value or charm to overcome its physical handicap. The clothes our thoughts wear are as important as the clothes we ourselves wear.

There are three qualities which should unfailingly characterize every piece of home work you hand in during the school year: (1) Attractiveness, (2) Promptness, and (3) Correct Form.

The appearance of your work will be improved if you observe the following suggestions:

1. Rule a one-and-a-half inch margin at the left.
2. Unless otherwise instructed, write your name or pseudonym, the name of your class, and the date across the page near the top.
3. Centre the title. Do not place a period after it. Capitalize the first word in it and all other words except conjunctions, articles, and prepositions.
4. Leave a line between the title and the first line of the theme.
5. Write neatly and legibly. Use blue-black or black ink. Avoid flourishes.
6. Leave a wider space between sentences than between words.
7. Using figures, number each page in the upper right corner.
8. If you type your theme, (a) use a good grade of plain business paper; (b) double-space.

Without neatness your theme will almost certainly fail to receive a good grade. The easiest way to raise a grade from a D to a C or from a C to a B is to devote an extra fifteen minutes to recopying it in your best hand-writing.

As a final word on revision, keep in mind that no one who always has a thing done for him by someone else will ever learn to do that thing himself. If you rely on the teacher to find and correct your mistakes, you will never learn to correct them yourselves, and will be in a parlous state after graduation. If you can form in school the habit of intelligent self-criticism, you will have a lifelong friend to call on at need.

THE ROUND TABLE

1. After reading this chapter are you prepared to agree with the following statement of an experienced teacher: "In the last analysis the quality of a pupil's written work will depend upon his attitude toward revision"?

2. Thinking back over your written work of the last term, what proportion of your errors that the teacher found and corrected were due to real ignorance on your part and what proportion to haste and carelessness?

3. A good way to begin the habit of self-criticism is to ask the teacher to return one theme with the number and kind of mistakes indicated on the outside but not where the mistakes occur. Then try to find and correct every mistake thus made known. Suggest that this be done with an early group of themes.

4. As an interesting variation of revising your theme by reading it aloud to yourself, try this plan with a classmate: Let him read your theme to you and you read his theme to him. Wherever either of you halts or stumbles in his reading, there is likely to be need for revision, particularly in punctuation.

5. Choose a class committee of three and ask the teacher to submit to it the three or four best themes of every batch. Let the committee select the one best theme from those submitted by the teacher. Call it the Theme-of-the-Week, and have it read aloud to the class or posted on the room bulletin board or in the library. Get the other English classes to do the same thing, and exchange themes with them for purposes of pleasure and comparison.

6. Keep the different Themes-of-the-Week, and toward the end of the term make a class magazine from them, neatly bound and with a table of contents. Vary the contents of the magazine between short and long themes, explanations, incidents, verse, and so on. Exchange magazines with the other English classes.

7. As good training in criticism, try one or both of the following plans: (1) Divide the class into groups of four. Give each group the four themes of another group. Let each pupil in each group read in turn the four themes, correcting the mistakes, assigning a grade,

writing brief comments, and signing his initials. Each pupil is responsible only for his own grade and corrections. The teacher then collects the themes, corrects them, and grades them. The next day the more interesting themes are read aloud in class—comments, grades, and all.

(2) Divide the class into squads of five, with the best writer in each squad acting as captain. On theme day, let each squad gather in a different part of the room, and, working together, correct, revise, and grade their own themes during the class period. The teacher acts as referee in case of difference of opinion, and later gives a final grade to each theme.

8. Some writers, who are very much in earnest about their work, advise the following plan for beginners who really wish to learn: "Write out a first draft as well as you can. Then tear it up. Write out a second draft from memory and start your revising on that." As a variation of this, try the following plan in class, if the teacher approves: on some theme day, without previous notice to the class, let the teacher collect the themes as usual, and then have the class rewrite them from memory and revise them during the class period. Return the two versions for purposes of study and comparison. To repay the extra trouble, the teacher can either record the higher of the two grades or give a double grade averaged between the two.

9. For once copy a theme in your very best handwriting, as if competing for a $1,000 prize, and compare its looks with your average written work.

10. Ask the teacher to pass around the class the two best-looking and the two worst-looking themes in the next set she corrects. Glance through them without reading them and file the difference away in your memory.

11. Ask the teacher about your individual handwriting. Has it any peculiarities that you should correct? Is it better or worse than the average for the class?

12. Select whichever of the two following Error Tables the teacher prefers, and draw it off neatly in your notebook. Keep an accurate account of your mistakes week by week, both (*a*) for purposes of comparing your earlier and later themes for signs of improvement and (*b*) for discovering, by reference to the percentage table on page 93, which are your weakest points in writing.

PERSONAL ERROR TABLE I

Date	Type of Assignment	Grade or Mark	Misspellings	Incomplete Sentences	Comma Faults	Faulty Pronoun Reference	Faulty Verb Agreement	Dangling Modifiers	Total Mistakes	Comments

PERSONAL ERROR TABLE II

Date	Type of Assignment	Grade or Mark	Faulty Indorsement	Faulty Paragraphing	Faulty Sentence Structure	Faulty Capitalization	Faulty Punctuation	Misspellings	Faulty Grammar	Wrong Choice of Words	Total Number Mistakes	Number of Pages	Mistakes per Page	Comments

CHAPTER VII

Three Important Aids to Composition

1. Dictating 2. Paraphrasing 3. Précis Writing

1. Dictating

One of the greatest drawbacks in learning to write is that before we can write acceptably we *must* learn to write correctly. We cannot write pleasingly on any subject until we are able to avoid elementary blunders in spelling, punctuation, and sentence structure. Such higher qualities as interest, force, originality, humour, and charm are all based on a foundation of correctness and clearness.

One of the simplest and most direct aids to attaining correctness in the fundamentals is dictation. Dictation is easy to give, easy to correct, and always brings good results. It is surprising that more schools do not make use of it.

Short, interesting paragraphs should be used. The paragraphs should be varied between incident and description on the one hand and explanation and argument on the other. An occasional paragraph of conversation will give sureness and correctness in handling quotation marks and in making a new paragraph each time the speaker changes. By skilfully varying the kinds of paragraphs, one can cover almost any desired point in grammar and composition.

In giving dictation, one can use either complete paragraphs or a series of individual sentences. If a paragraph is to be dictated, the teacher will explain the paragraph first and, if necessary, give its context. Then he will read the paragraph aloud once to the class from beginning to end, with a short time allowed for questions and discussion. After that the actual dictating should begin—sentence by sentence, until the whole class has written it down. Then a minute or two should be given for each of you to read over your work and make any needed corrections. As the final step, the paragraphs should be immediately corrected in class. Each of you can either correct your own paper or exchange papers with the pupil next to you. If the paragraph is not too long, and if opportunity permits, the teacher can copy the paragraph on the board before the class assembles, drawing down a wall map or chart over it while dictating, and then removing the map when the time comes for correcting. In large classes and with long paragraphs, however, it will be easier for the teacher to read the paragraph over again, indicating orally all the sentences, and giving punctuation marks, difficult spellings, and so forth.

Dictation is the short cut to correctness in the composition course.

2. Paraphrasing

Dictation makes for correctness. Paraphrasing and précis writing give valuable training in (*a*) getting the thought from the printed page, and (*b*) rephrasing this thought in other and simpler words. To give this ability should be one of the express aims of the English course.

To paraphrase is to restate the thought of a selection more simply and clearly, to translate, as it were, difficult, involved language into simple, easy language.

A good paraphrase has three essentials:

1. It must be clear, definite, and easy to understand.
2. It must contain all the thought in the original passage.
3. It must not contain any thought that is not in the original.

Like a good witness, a good paraphrase tells the truth, the whole truth, and nothing but the truth.

The purpose of paraphrasing is first to make the reader dig down through language to the underlying thought and grasp the thought accurately and thoroughly, and, secondly, to reword the thought definitely and simply. This difficult task paraphrasing accomplishes with perfect efficiency. If a student can paraphrase a passage accurately, it is proof positive that he understands that passage thoroughly. The value of this training, in view of our natural tendency to loose reading and looser thinking, cannot be overemphasized.

The inescapable definiteness of paraphrasing is its chief benefit. It gives no chance for haziness or mistakes. It is as obvious as a sum in addition or subtraction. Either a paraphrase is accurate or it is inaccurate; and if it is written out on the board and discussed in class, both the writer of the paraphrase and everyone else can see where and why it is right or wrong.

The first assignments for paraphrasing should be short and not too hard—say a four-line stanza from a poem or a half-dozen lines of prose. Rarely should the length of a paraphrase exceed fifteen or sixteen lines of print. The important thing is not extent or amount, but accuracy and exactness in rewording the thought. After some practice is given, successive paraphrases should increase in difficulty rather than in length. The class texts in literature will furnish abundant material, and a wise choice of selections will throw much-needed light on certain obscure stanzas or difficult paragraphs which otherwise would go uninterpreted.

Consider the three following sentences, all of which are from a high-school course of study. The first sentence is from Lamb's essay on "Roast Pig", the second from Agnes Repplier's essay on "Children Past and Present", the third a stanza from Gray's "Elegy".

I

"Without placing too implicit faith in the account above given, it must be agreed that if a worthy pretext for so dangerous an experiment as setting houses on fire (especially in these days) could be assigned in favour of any culinary object, that pretext and excuse might be found in ROAST PIG." (52 words)

II

"We are not now alluding to those spoiled and over-indulged little people who are the recognized scourges of humanity, but merely to the boys and girls who have been allowed from infancy that large degree of freedom which is deemed expedient for enlightened nurseries, and who regulate their own conduct on the vast majority of occasions." (56 words)

III

But Knowledge to their eyes her ample page
Rich with the spoils of time did ne'er unroll;
Chill Penury repressed their noble rage,
And froze the genial current of the soul.
(31 words)

Now what, exactly, do these three sentences mean? They are neither particularly easy nor particularly hard. The best way to be sure of understanding them thoroughly is to paraphrase them. If some such paraphrases as the following are the result, it is certain that the sentences are clearly understood.

I

Without believing too strongly the story told above, it must be agreed that if a good excuse could be found for so dangerous a thing as burning a house down for the sake of anything to eat, that excuse would be ROAST PIG. (43 words)

II

We do not now mean those spoiled children who are pests to everyone, but only those boys and girls who from infancy have been given the amount of freedom usually thought wise and who are allowed to do as they please most of the time. (45 words)

III

But they never had a chance to be educated, and extreme poverty paralysed their poetic enthusiasm and creative instincts. (19 words)

In comparing these paraphrases with the original passages, observe that their main value consists in reproducing the thought accurately and simply, with special emphasis on *simply*. Except for the stanza from the "Elegy" there is no marked decrease in the number of words, but there is a great difference in simplicity. A paraphrase is not a summary, like the précis, but is a parallel version in simple words.

SELECTIONS FOR PARAPHRASING

Here are several typical selections for paraphrasing. Study the ones the teacher assigns till you have got their full meaning, and then put them into clear, simple words of your own. To do this accurately will not be easy.

1. Pride that dines on vanity sups on contempt.
2. Procrastination is the thief of time.
3. Cut your coat according to your cloth.
4. A man cannot speak but he judges himself.—EMERSON
5. To a shower of gold most things are penetrable.—CARLYLE
6. Sin has many tools, but a lie is the handle which fits them all.
   —OLIVER WENDELL HOLMES
7. Censure is the tax a man pays to the public for being eminent.
   —SWIFT
8. A man that is young in years may be old in hours, if he have lost no time.—BACON
9. He that hath wife and children hath given hostages to fortune.
   —BACON
10. To him whose elastic and vigorous thought keeps pace with the sun, the day is a perpetual morning.—THOREAU
11. Cowards die many times before their deaths;
    The valiant never taste of death but once.
    —SHAKESPEARE, *Julius Caesar*
12. Rightly to be great
    Is not to stir without great argument,
    But greatly to find quarrel in a straw
    When honour's at the stake.
    —SHAKESPEARE, *Hamlet*

13. Neither a borrower nor a lender be,
For loan oft loses both itself and friend,
And borrowing dulls the edge of husbandry.
—SHAKESPEARE, *Hamlet*

14. If a man does not keep pace with his companions, perhaps it is because he hears a different drummer. Let him step to the music which he hears, however measured or far away. . . .
—THOREAU

15. Revenge is a kind of wild justice, which the more man's nature runs to, the more ought law to weed it out; for as for the first wrong, it doth but offend the law, but the revenge of that wrong putteth the law out of office.—BACON

16. But the iniquity of oblivion blindly scattereth her poppy, and deals with the memory of men without distinction to merit of perpetuity.—SIR THOMAS BROWNE

17. I cannot praise a fugitive and cloistered virtue, unexercised and unbreathed, that never sallies out and sees her adversary, but slinks out of the race where that immortal garland is to be run for not without dust and heat.—MILTON

18. Death the Leveller

Sceptre and Crown
Must tumble down,
And in the dust be equal made
With the poor crooked scythe and spade.
—SHIRLEY

19. The Fate of the Humble

The applause of listening senates to command,
The threats of pain and ruin to despise,
To scatter plenty o'er a smiling land,
And read their history in a nation's eyes,

Their lot forbade: nor circumscribed alone
Their growing virtues, but their crimes confined;
Forbade to wade through slaughter to a throne,
And shut the gates of mercy on mankind.
—GRAY'S "Elegy"

20. Peacepoint

Were half the power that fills the world with terror,
Were half the wealth bestowed on camps and courts

Given to redeem the human mind from error,
There were no need of arsenals and forts.

—LONGFELLOW

21. It dropped so low in my regard
I heard it hit the ground,
And go to pieces on the stones
At bottom of my mind;

Yet blamed the fate that fractured, less
Than I reviled myself
For entertaining plated wares
Upon my silver shelf.

—EMILY DICKINSON

22. Outwitted

He drew a circle that shut me out—
Heretic, rebel, a thing to flout,
But Love and I had the wit to win:
We drew a circle that took him in!

—EDWIN MARKHAM

23. Erosion

It took the sea a thousand years,
A thousand years to trace
The granite features of this cliff,
In crag and scarp and base.

It took the sea an hour one night,
An hour of storm to place
The sculpture of these granite seams
Upon a woman's face.

—E. J. PRATT

24. The Influence of the Unseen

We can be but partially acquainted even with the events which actually influence our course through life, and our final destiny. There are innumerable other events, if such they may be called, which come close upon us, yet pass away without actual results, or even betraying their near approach by the reflection of any light or shadow across our minds. Could we know all the vicissitudes of our fortunes, life would be too full of hope and fear, exultation or disappointment, to afford us a single hour of true serenity.—NATHANIEL HAWTHORNE, *David Swan*

25. Old Age

But now let me tell you this. If the time comes when you must lay down the fiddle and the bow, because your fingers are too stiff, and drop the ten-foot sculls, because your arms are too weak, and after dallying awhile with eyeglasses, come at last to the undisguised reality of spectacles,—if the time comes when that fire of life we spoke of has burned so low that where its flames reverberated, there is only the sombre stain of regret, and where its coals glowed, only the white ashes that cover the embers of memory,—don't let your heart grow cold, and you may carry cheerfulness and love with you into the teens of your second century, if you can last so long.

—OLIVER WENDELL HOLMES, *Autocrat of the Breakfast-Table*

3. Prècis Writing

The word *précis* is from the French, and is pronounced *pray-see.* It is the French equivalent of the English word *precise,* and comes from two Latin words which mean "*cut off*" or "*cut short*". **A prècis is a summary, an abstract, a synopsis.**

The ability to make a clear, complete summary is in great demand today everywhere. Note-taking in school and college is only one form of summarizing. Book reports often give a synopsis of the plot. All newspaper reporters are called upon daily to give in a few sentences the substance of various addresses, speeches, and public meetings. The secretary of every organization, from the high-school English Club to the League of Nations, deals in summaries. The same is true of committees and committee reports. Bankers and business-men in general are constantly calling on subordinates and department heads for condensed reports concerning various projects and undertakings. The successful business lawyer is the man who has trained himself to disregard unimportant details and to give the essence of a problem in crisp, condensed shape. In fact, so universal is the world's demand for condensed knowledge and summarized facts that the ability to summarize is taken for granted among all successful men and women. To lack that ability is to live under a big handicap.

To make a good précis is not easy. The reason is simple. We must first think. In order to summarize any selection we have to understand it thoroughly, and to know not only its main idea but its secondary ideas as well. To do this we must read carefully and thoughtfully, forcing our minds to get the full meaning from every sentence. Sometimes this process is exceedingly difficult.

In the next place, after having absorbed the thought, we must produce it in our own words in much simpler and shorter form. As a rule, **a good précis will be only about one-third as long as the original.** If, for example, we are making a précis of a paragraph of 150 words, our précis should contain not far from 50 words, almost certainly not more than 60.

To be forced thus to phrase and to rephrase the thought until we have compressed it into the briefest possible scope is valuable training in itself. In the chapter on Revising and Rewriting, pages 90-98, and in the section on Wordy Sentences, pages 234-236, it will appear that one of the besetting sins of beginning writers is using too many words. We all should have a horror of being lengthy. Both writing and revising précis emphasize the necessity of being brief, and lead to clear, concise, direct phrasing. Thus the value of précis writing is threefold: it stimulates (1) intelligent reading, (2) clear thinking, and (3) concise writing.

In the first two of these particulars—namely, intelligent reading and clear thinking—précis writing is similar to paraphrasing. The difference between them lies in the fullness with which the thought of the original is reproduced. The paraphrase works with shorter units and expresses the thought fully in simpler parallel language. Usually a paraphrase is about as long as the original passage. The précis, however, does not parallel the thought, but condenses it into one-third its original length.

In making a précis, you will be helped by keeping the following directions in mind:

1. Read the selection carefully enough and often enough to grasp the leading thought or chief idea.
2. Give the selection a title which will indicate what it is about. This will serve directly to reveal the main thought.
3. Tabulate the main ideas.
4. Put the original aside and using your own words as far as possible, write a rough draft linking these essential ideas and omitting unimportant details. As a rule, omit figures of speech and most illustrations. Either omit quotations or change them into indirect speech. Use the third person.
5. Estimate the number of words in your rough draft. Your précis should be about one-third the length of the original.
6. Carefully revise your rough draft to make it crisper and more accurate, condensing if necessary by substituting word for phrase; word or phrase for clause; and word, phrase, or clause for sentence.
7. Check the accuracy of your work with the original. Count all your words and put the total at the end of your précis.
8. Write a fair copy of your précis.

SPECIMEN PRÉCIS

1. The Old Man and Death

A poor and toil-worn peasant, bent with years and groaning beneath the weight of a heavy faggot of firewood which he carried, sought, weary and sore-footed on a long and dusty road, to gain his distant cottage. Unable to bear the weight of his burden any longer, he let it fall by the roadside, and lamented his hard fate.

"What pleasure have I known since I first drew breath in this sad world? From dawn to dusk it has been hard work and little pay! At home is an empty cupboard, a discontented wife, and lazy and disobedient children! O Death! O Death! come and free me from my troubles!"

At once the ghostly King of Terrors stood before him. "What do you want with me?" Death queried in hollow tones.

"Noth—nothing," stammered the awed and frightened peasant, "nothing except for you to help me put again upon my shoulders the bundle of faggots I have let fall!" (158 words)—ÆSOP'S *Fables*

1. Précis

A poor old man was toiling home under a heavy load of firewood. Tired out, he dropped it, mourned his hard lot, and called on Death to set him free.

Immediately Death appeared and asked what he wanted.

The terrified peasant replied that he wanted nothing but help in restoring the load to his shoulders. (55 words)

2. The Main Essential

We may live without poetry, music, and art;
We may live without conscience, and live without heart;
We may live without friends, we may live without books;
But civilized man cannot live without cooks.

He may live without books—what is knowledge but grieving?
He may live without hope—what is hope but deceiving?
He may live without love—what is passion but pining?
But where is the man that can live without dining? (74 words)

—OWEN MEREDITH, *Lucile*

2. Précis

Civilized man can live without a great many desirable things, but not without cooks. He can live without books, hope, or love, but he must eat. (26 words)

3. Days

Daughters of Time, the hypocritic Days,
Muffled and dumb—like barefoot dervishes,
And marching single in an endless file,
Bring diadems and faggots in their hands.
To each they offer gifts after his will,
Bread, kingdoms, stars, and sky that holds them all.
I, in my pleachèd garden, watched the pomp,
Forgot my morning wishes, hastily
Took a few herbs and apples, and the Day
Turned and departed silent. I, too late,
Under her solemn fillet saw the scorn. (79 words)

—RALPH WALDO EMERSON

3. Précis

The Days file silently by, offering everyone the choice between valuable and worthless gifts. The poet chose a few worthless things. The Day departed with a scornful look. (27 words)

SELECTIONS FOR PRÉCIS WRITING

Write précis of the following selections. So far as possible follow the directions given above.

I

A Fox, being caught in a trap, was glad to bargain for his neck by leaving his tail behind him; but upon coming abroad into the world, he began to miss his tail so much that he almost wished he had died rather than come away without it. However, resolving to make the best of a bad matter, he called a meeting of the rest of the Foxes, and proposed that all should follow his example. "You have no idea," said he, "of the ease and comfort with which I now move about: I could never have believed it if I had not tried it myself; but really, when one comes to reason it out, a tail is such an ugly, inconvenient, unnecessary appendage, that the only wonder is that, as Foxes, we could have put up with such a thing so long. I propose, therefore, my worthy brethren, that you all profit by my experience, and that all Foxes from this day forward cut off their tails." Upon this, one of the oldest Foxes stepped forward, and said, "I rather think, my friend, that you would not have advised us to part with our tails, if there were any chance of recovering your own." (205 words)

—ÆSOP'S *Fables*

II

The great error in Rip van Winkle's composition was an insuperable aversion to all kinds of profitable labour. It could not be for want of assiduity or perseverance; for he would sit all day with a rod as long and heavy as a Tartar's lance, and fish all day without a murmur, even though he should not be encouraged by a slight nibble. He would carry a fowling-piece on his shoulder for hours together, trudging through woods and swamps, and up hill and down dale, to shoot a few squirrels or wild pigeons. He would never refuse to assist a neighbour even in the roughest toil, and was a foremost man in all country frolics for husking Indian corn or building stone fences; the women of the village, too, used to employ him to run errands, and to do such little odd jobs as their less obliging husbands would not do for them. In a word, Rip was ready to attend to anybody's business but his own; but as to doing family duty, and keeping his farm in order, he found it impossible. (184 words)

—WASHINGTON IRVING, *Rip Van Winkle*

III

Whenever he appeared in the streets and public places of Constantinople, Belisarius attracted and satisfied the eyes of the people. His lofty stature and majestic countenance fulfilled their expectations of a hero, and the meanest of his fellow-citizens were emboldened by his gentle and gracious demeanour. By the union of liberality and justice he acquired the love of the soldiers, without alienating the affections of the people. The sick and wounded were relieved with medicines and money, and still more efficaciously by the healing visits and smiles of their commander. He was endeared to the husbandmen by the peace and plenty which they enjoyed under the shadow of his standard. Instead of being injured, the country was enriched by the march of the Roman armies; and such was the rigid discipline of their camp, that not an apple was gathered from the tree, not a path could be traced in the fields of corn. (155 words)

—GIBBON, *Decline and Fall of the Roman Empire*

IV

We owe it, therefore, to candor and to the amicable relations existing between the United States and those powers [any European powers] to declare that we should consider any attempt on their part to extend their system to any portion of this hemisphere as dangerous to our peace and safety. With the existing colonies or dependencies of any European power we have not interfered and shall not interfere. But with the governments which have declared their independence and maintained it, and whose independence we have, on great consideration and on just principles acknowledged, we could not view any interception for the purpose of oppressing them, or controlling in any other manner their destiny, by any European power in any other light than as the manifestation of an unfriendly disposition toward the United States. (132 words)

—*From the Message to Congress of President James Monroe,* December 2, 1823

V

The thousand injuries of Fortunato I had borne as I best could; but when he ventured upon insult, I vowed revenge. You, who so well know the nature of my soul, will not suppose, however, that I gave utterance to a threat. *At length* I would be avenged; this was a point definitely settled—but the very definiteness with which it was resolved precluded the idea of risk. I must not only punish, but punish with impunity. A wrong is unredressed when retribution overtakes its redresser. It is equally unredressed when the avenger fails to make himself felt as such to him who has done the wrong. (107 words) —EDGAR ALLAN POE, "The Cask of Amontillado"

VI

The burden of our civilization is not merely, as many suppose, that the product of industry is ill-distributed, or its conduct tyrannical, or its operation interrupted by bitter disagreements. It is that industry itself has come to hold a position of exclusive predominance among human interests, which no single interest, and least of all the provision of the material means of existence, is fit to occupy. Like a hypochondriac who is so absorbed in the processes of his own digestion that he goes to the grave before he has begun to live, industrialized communities neglect the very objects for which it is worth while to acquire riches in their feverish preoccupation with the means by which riches can be acquired.

That obsession by economic issues is as local and transitory as it is repulsive and disturbing. To future generations it will appear as pitiable as the obsession of the seventeenth century by religious quarrels appears today. (157 words)

—RICHARD HENRY TAWNEY, *The Acquisitive Society*
By permission of G. Bell & Sons Ltd. and Clarke, Irwin & Co. Ltd.

VII

I was lowered one day in the bathysphere close inshore at Bermuda. At a depth of twelve fathoms we moved slowly out to sea, following the drifting barge overhead. A very large fish was holding all my attention, when suddenly I looked beyond and beneath it, and saw something long, thin, and black. It seemed to move slowly, but of this I could not be sure. I was seeing a real monster of the deep—a sea serpent! My face jammed against the quartz window; my telephoned reports became inarticulate and hysterical. The black object was so long that I could see neither head nor tail.

And then, as I followed its dimming length down and down into the blue depths, I happened to look back, and my sea serpent, my unbelievable eel or monster, expired after only ten seconds in my imagination: I was drifting over the Bermuda section of the trans-atlantic cable! (154 words)

—From *Half Mile Down*, copyright, 1934, by William Beebe. By permission of Harcourt, Brace and Company, New York.

VIII

In our time the writing and reading of detective stories has become a game between the author and his audience. It is a clever writer indeed who, in this sophisticated day, may hope to deceive the reader clue-hound. The harried author is himself no better than a fugitive, his cherished secret under his arm, seeking escape from his tireless admirers until such time as he has planned to unriddle his problem in his own way. But it is a pleasant chase, and the writer enjoys it, in anticipation, quite as much as do his relentless trackers. That the reader is always as clever a fellow as he thinks himself may be doubted, however, since his boast of triumph must find utterance after the revealed fact; and self-deception at that thrilling moment is easy to accomplish. It is difficult for an author, however ingenious, not to betray himself as he nears his conclusion; but by that time the chase is about over, and the reader may take small credit on the score of clairvoyance. Still, it is quite possible to place the finger of revelation upon a culprit as early as page 3, in a narrative of three hundred pages; Poe's feat of forecasting the events of *Barnaby Rudge* is famous. One wonders what he would have done with Mrs. Christie's *Murder of Roger Ackroyd* or Mr. Beeding's *Death Walks in Eastrepps*. Be all of which as it may, the ideal detective story of our time is a story in which, sleuth as one will in advance of the revelation, the author baffles at every turn and knocks one cold, at the end, with the simplicity and surprise of his solution. (280 words)

—VINCENT STARRETT, *Books Alive*

IX

As I sat below at the table plotting my noon position I suddenly had a feeling that something was wrong. A glance through the com-panion-way quickly changed my uneasiness to alarm, for there, directly behind and coming rapidly up to us, still in the first throes of birth, hung the largest waterspout we had ever seen. Its long black tentacle, suspended from the lowering tumultuous mother cloud, writhed and groped half-way to the sea, like the arm of a Gargantuan octopus seeking a grip upon an enemy. Our eyes clung to it fascinated as it reached down and down, sometimes retreating but always growing again. There became audible the distant roaring or sighing sound that first warns of approach to a waterfall when travelling downstream in a canoe. Underneath, at the surface of the sea, the sympathetic disturbance suddenly became more intense as the incipient whirl revolved faster and faster, throwing off bits of foam and loose water. A distinct bulge in the surface appeared, as if sucked by the parched column above, and rose higher every second. The spray and foam now began to be snatched upward, and before our eyes was formed a vapoury connection with the descending tube, linking cloud and sea. The connection established, more and more loose water shot whirling aloft, and the disturbed area at the base grew larger and more violent as it received the too heavy particles thrown away from the column by centrifugal force. The noise and tumult grew as the hissing of the column, the cry of the wind, and the crashing of the waters blended to form a fearsome roar. Augmented by more and more water, the lower half suddenly reached maturity and groped out to clasp hands with the upper, and the sea and sky were united by a spinning, weaving pillar of water. (308 words)

—From *10,000 Leagues Over the Sea*, copyright, 1932, by William Albert Robinson. By permission of Harcourt, Brace and Company, New York.

X

Suppose that a man tells you that he saw a person strike another and kill him; that is testimonial evidence of the fact of murder. But it is possible to have circumstantial evidence of the fact of murder; that is to say, you may find a man dying with a wound upon his head having exactly the form and character of the wound which is made by an axe, and, with due care in taking surrounding circumstances into account, you may conclude with the utmost certainty that the man has been murdered; that his death is the consequence of a blow inflicted by another man with that implement. We are very much in the habit of considering circumstantial evidence as of less value than testimonial evidence, and it may be that, where the circumstances are not perfectly clear and intelligible, it is a dangerous and unsafe kind of evidence; but it must not be forgotten that, in many cases, circumstantial is quite as conclusive as testimonial evidence, and that, not unfrequently, it is a great deal weightier than testimonial evidence. For example, take the case to which I referred just now. The circumstantial evidence may be better and more convincing than the testimonial evidence; for it may be impossible, under the conditions that I have defined, to suppose that the man met his death from any cause but the violent blow of an axe wielded by another man. The circumstantial evidence in favour of a murder having been committed, in that case, is as complete and as convincing as evidence can be. It is evidence which is open to no doubt and to no falsification. But the testimony of a witness is open to multitudinous doubts. He may have been mistaken. He may have been actuated by malice. It has constantly happened that even an accurate man has declared that a thing has happened in this, that, or the other way, when a careful analysis of the circumstantial evidence has shown that it did not happen in that way, but in some other way. (344 words)

—WM. PALEY

XI

Shadow is one of the easiest to perceive of all nature's beauties. As one may see the charm of a profile for the first time when looking at a silhouette, so one becomes aware of the perfection of a natural outline more quickly by seeing it drawn in one colour. It is much simpler to trace the fairy fretwork of a mountain ash when it lies on the grass in shadow than when the eyes are dazzled by the vivid green and clustering scarlet of berry and leaf against the sky. It has become a blue tree on the green canvas of a field. Without shadow things would seem unreal, unbreathing as figures in a dream—flat, unrelieved tapestry on the walls of the world. With it come reality and rounded loveliness. It is only the bare winter tree, the barren heart, that are shadowless. (145 words)

—MARY WEBB, "The Beauty of Shadow" from *The Spring of Joy*
By permission of the Trustees of the Mary Webb Estate and Jonathan Cape Ltd.

XII

Suppose it were perfectly certain that the life and fortune of every one of us would, one day or other, depend upon his winning or losing a game of chess. Don't you think that we should all consider it to be a primary duty to learn at least the names and the moves of the pieces; to have a notion of a gambit, and a keen eye for all the means of getting out of check? Do you not think that we should look with a disapprobation amounting to scorn, upon the father who allowed his son, or the state which allowed its members, to grow up without knowing a pawn from a knight?

Yet it is a very plain and elementary truth, that the life, the fortune, and the happiness of every one of us, and, more or less, of those who are connected with us, do depend upon our knowing something of the rules of a game infinitely more difficult and complicated than chess. It is a game which has been played for untold ages, every man and woman of us being one of the two players in a game of his or her own. The chessboard is the world, the pieces are the phenomena of the universe, the rules of the game are what we call the laws of Nature. The player on the other side is hidden from us. We know that his play is always fair, just, and patient. But also we know, to our cost, that he never overlooks a mistake, or makes the smallest allowance for ignorance. To the man who plays well, the highest stakes are paid, with that sort of overflowing generosity with which the strong shows delight in strength. And one who plays ill is checkmated—without haste, but without remorse. . . .

. . . Well, what I mean by Education is learning the rules of this mighty game. In other words, education is the instruction of the intellect in the laws of Nature, under which name I include not merely things and their forces, but men and their ways; and the fashioning of the affections and of the will into an earnest and loving desire to move in harmony with those laws. For me, education means neither more nor less than this. Anything which professes to call itself education must be tried by this standard, and if it fails to stand the test, I will not call it education, whatever may be the force of authority, or of numbers, upon the other side. (420 words)

—T. H. HUXLEY, *A Liberal Education*

CHAPTER VIII

Punctuation

> No man can write well who does not punctuate well; who does not vitally mean every punctuation mark as clearly and as vigorously as he means every word.
>
> —ARLO BATES, *Talks on Writing English*

(1) PUNCTUATION IN GENERAL

The writer's aim is always "Clearness first!" Communicating our thoughts and feelings to others is an uncertain business at best, and to keep from being misunderstood will tax all our ingenuity and effort. As the reader's eye races from word to word, he needs every particle of help we can give him. Of all aids to clearness, intelligent punctuation is one of the best.

(2) END PUNCTUATION

The two most important items of punctuation are the use of a capital letter to mark the beginning of a sentence and a period to mark the end. The capital and the period are, as it were, the headlight and the tail-light of the sentence, and without them a sentence would run wild in the dark. No other forms of punctuation can compare in importance with this use of the capital and period to mark the limits of the sentence. Sometimes, of course, one of the other two forms of end punctuation—the question mark or the exclamation mark—takes the place of the period. In fact, the same sentence, if given different end punctuation, will change its meaning:

> You don't believe me.
> You don't believe me?
> You don't believe me!

Here the period, the question mark, and the exclamation point each give a different turn to the thought.

(3) INTERNAL PUNCTUATION

In addition to end punctuation, there are several marks which are used to make clear the relation of phrases and clauses within the limits of the sentence itself. Chief among these internal marks of punctuation are the colon, the semicolon, and the comma. As we read, the eye and the mind working together, absorb the meaning not all at once but in little jets or spurts, as it were. Our progress is not by means of one sustained rush, like the flight of an arrow or a bullet, but is a kind of hop, skip, and a jump movement. Take the following simple example:

> About one o'clock today, on the way home to lunch, I saw the new fire engine come tearing by.

The way most people get the full meaning of this sentence is by four steps or stages: (1) about one o'clock today (2) on the way home to lunch (3) I saw the new fire engine (4) come tearing by. When the sentence is read in this way, there is no confusion or misunderstanding. All the details stand off clearly from one another, each detail following the preceding one logically and distinctly.

To bring about this desirable situation in every sentence is the purpose of all internal punctuation. By the use of comma and semicolon what is distinct in thought must be separated so that the reader can instantly grasp the separation, and what belongs together must be grouped so that the reader can easily grasp the grouped idea.

(4) PUNCTUATION AFFECTS MEANING

A change in punctuation changes the entire meaning of the following sentences:

1. Soldiers do not complain of hardships.
1*a*. Soldiers, do not complain of hardships.

2. Mr. Green, your next-door neighbour sent you these apples.
2*a*. Mr. Green, your next-door neighbour, sent you these apples.
3. Who said our guide is the best shot in the province?
3*a*. "Who," said our guide, "is the best shot in the province?"
4. Please phone Tom and say we can't come.
4*a*. Please phone, Tom, and say we can't come.
5. Woman! Without her, man would be a savage.
5*a*. Woman without her man would be a savage.

(5) THE IDEAL IN PUNCTUATION

Punctuation is both reasonable and logical. The system was not imposed upon writers by former pedants, who wished to make writing more difficult, but it was slowly evolved by the leading printers and publishers to make writing clear and easy to read, just as every province and city has established highway markers and traffic signals in order to guide and to aid traffic. Punctuation is as much a part of your writing as the letters with which you spell words.

It is easy to punctuate a good sentence which you understand thoroughly. What makes punctuation hard is either (*a*) lack of a clear understanding of the structure of the sentence to be punctuated or (*b*) the fact that the sentence itself is obscurely or awkwardly put together. If we write good clear sentences, punctuation is a comfort instead of an encumbrance. In the words of Professor Charles Sears Baldwin, "No one can punctuate with his hand until he has punctuated with his head."

THE TENDENCY TODAY TOWARD LIGHT PUNCTUATION

The trend in punctuation today is away from the heavy, close system of the past, with its complicated sentences and thick sprinkling of commas and semicolons, toward a simpler sentence structure with only the necessary punctuation marks to make the meaning clear.

(6) PRESENT-DAY USAGE OUR GOAL

In learning how to use these marks correctly and confidently, it is important to know not the practice of the past, but the standard usage of today. A recent important investigation[1] has made the actual facts of current usage available. A questionnaire on punctuation was sent to fifty-four leading book publishers, sixty-seven influential newspapers, and twenty-three important magazines. Their replies represent an authoritative cross-section of the standard usage of today. On this basis the following simplified treatment of punctuation has been put together. It represents the minimum requirements of standard modern punctuation.

(7) FREAKS OF PUNCTUATION

Try your hand on the following freaks of punctuation:

1. Every lady in this land
   Hath twenty nails upon each hand;
   Five and twenty on hands and feet;
   And this is true without deceit.

2. A funny little man told this to me:
   I fell in a snowdrift in June said he;
   I went to a ball game out in the sea;
   I saw a jellyfish float up in a tree;
   I found some gum in a cup of tea;
   I stirred my milk with a big brass key;
   I opened my door on my bended knee;
   I beg your pardon for this, said he,
   But 'tis true when told as it ought to be.

3. that that is is that that is not is not that that
   is not is not that that is that that is is not
   that that is not is not that it it is

4. It was and I said not but.

5. A Latin Example

The Oracle of Apollo at Delphi in ancient Greece was frequently consulted by kings and warriors as to the outcome of future events. Often cleverly worded, ambiguous answers were given. On one occasion a well-known Roman general sent to ask his fate in a war which

[1] Sterling Andrus Leonard, *Current English Usage*, published for the National Council of Teachers of English, 1932.

he was about to undertake. He received the answer: *Ibis, redibus. Nunquam in bello peribis.* (You will go, you will return. Never in war will you perish.) He embarked confidently for the war, only to fall in the first battle. His indignant widow reproached the oracle bitterly. The reply was that she had misread the message. The period was meant to come after *nunquam*, not after *redibus*.

PUNCTUATION TABLE

(Rules are further explained on the pages indicated in parenthesis.)

I. The Period

1. To mark the end of every sentence that is not a question or an exclamation (page 123).
2. After abbreviations (page 124).

II. The Comma

1. Between city and province (page 126).
2. Between the date and the year (page 126).
3. Before *but* and *for* in compound sentences (page 126).
4. To set off members of a series (page 127).
5. To set off a word in direct address (page 128).
6. To set off appositives (page 128).
7. To set off absolute phrases (page 128).
8. After *Yes* and *No* and mild exclamations (page 128).
9. To set off parenthetical sentence modifiers like *however, in fact, of course* (page 129).
10. To set off non-restrictive clauses (page 129).
11. After the greeting in friendly letters (page 134).
12. Before short quotations (page 135).
13. To wedge apart words or phrases which if read together would give a wrong meaning (page 135).
14. After a long, dependent adverbial clause coming first in the sentence (page 136).

III. The Semicolon

1. Between co-ordinate clauses not joined by *and, but,* or *for* (page 139).
2. Before *however* and certain other conjunctive adverbs when a complete independent statement is added to another complete independent statement (page 140).

3. Between long independent statements when either statement is punctuated with commas (page 140).

IV. Quotation Marks

1. Before and after a direct quotation (page 142).
2. To indicate the titles of articles, chapters, short stories, and single poems—but not the titles of books, magazines, and newspapers, which should be underlined (page 144).

V. The Apostrophe

1. To indicate the omission of a letter or a syllable (page 272).
2. To help form the plural of letters, figures, and words used without reference to their meaning (page 274).
3. To help form the possessive case of nouns and indefinite pronouns (page 274).

VI. The Dash

1. To mark a sudden change or an abrupt break in the thought.
2. Instead of commas, to enclose parenthetical expressions less closely connected with the thought.
3. Instead of the colon, before an informal list or enumeration.

VII. The Question Mark

1. After every direct question, whether quoted or not.

VIII. The Colon

1. After the greeting in a formal or business letter (page 146).
2. After such expressions as *these, the following, as follows,* to give notice of a list of particulars or examples (page 146).
3. To give notice of a formal quotation several sentences long (page 147).

IX. Underlining (Italics)

1. To indicate the titles of books, magazines, and newspapers (page 147).
2. To indicate words taken out of their context and used without regard to their meaning (page 148).
3. To indicate foreign words and phrases not yet felt to be a part of the language (page 148).

X. Exclamation Point

1. To indicate strong feeling after interjections and words or phrases meant to be understood as highly emotional.

XI. Parentheses

1. To enclose and separate interpolated material which is unexpectedly introduced and not grammatically connected with the rest of the sentence.

XII. Capital Letters

1. The first word in every sentence (page 152).
2. In the title of themes, stories, and books, the first word and all other words except the articles, prepositions, and conjunctions (page 153).
3. The first word of every direct quotation (*a*) which is introduced by *say* or its equivalent, and (*b*) which makes complete sense in and by itself (page 154).
4. Proper names (page 154).
5. Titles, degrees, and terms of family relationship when used with the names of persons (page 156).
6. Adjectives derived from proper names (page 158).
7. The first word of every line of poetry (page 158).
8. The pronoun *I* and the vocative interjection *O* (page 158).

1. The Period

(*Two Uses*)

(1) THE PERIOD AT THE END OF A SENTENCE

A period marks the end of every sentence that is not a question or an exclamation.

Two Danger Spots

The two chief violations of this rule, which are always considered serious, are these: (1) Punctuating a phrase or clause as if it were a sentence. See "The No-Sentence, or Period Fault", page 203 below. (2) "The Run-Together Sentence or Comma Splice". See pages 206-209.

These two offences against sentence unity should have been entirely weeded out of your writing by this time. As a test try the following eight sentences, and if you leave a single mistake uncorrected, glance at the two sections just referred to.

Test on the Period Fault and the Comma Splice

Name and correct the mistakes in these sentences:

1. It was a good many years ago, as men figure time. The place, an old, dilapidated shack near the rim of the desert.
2. My speech was over, I felt that I had failed.
3. This is still a good car, it can make sixty miles an hour on a paved road.
4. The sun's shining down so exceedingly hot causing me to faint.
5. His preparations for the night were very simple. The removal of his shoes and coat, in fact.
6. Notwithstanding the fact that it is doubtful whether a poet named Homer ever lived.
7. His desk was piled high with papers, before him were reports on three different cases.
8. "Watch the fullback," a man said, "he is going to try for a field goal."

(2) THE PERIOD AFTER ABBREVIATIONS

The second use of the period is to indicate abbreviations.

This usage concerns individual words instead of sentences and hence belongs rather to the field of spelling than to that of punctuation. It is usually ranked, however, as a rule of punctuation. It is still standard usage in this country, though some British and a few American publishing houses are showing a tendency to try to do away with it.

Examples

Professor White, but Prof. White; Doctor Wilson, but Dr. Wilson; Before Christ, B.C.; Anno Domini (in the year of Our Lord), A.D.

Mr. for Mister

Mrs. for Mistress or Missis

(But Miss without a period, for it is not an abbreviation)

R.S.V.P. *Répondez, s'il vous plaît* (Answer, if you please)

Y.M.C.A. Young Men's Christian Association

Exercises in All Uses of the Period

Supply any periods needed in these sentences and correct any errors in punctuation as between commas and periods:

I

1. The view was inspiring, the country club was on a hillside above a river that made a loop in the valley.
2. Little brown sausages and scrambled eggs made a good breakfast. Which we ate.
3. In the yard was a rabbit running wildly, it was afraid of me.
4. Propped against a china cow in a candy shop was a placard. Announcing a candidate for mayor of the city.
5. We gasped with amazement when we saw the steel worker drop a red-hot rivet to a man below him, it was the first time we had seen such a thing.
6. The tobacco leaves looked pale, they contrasted with the dark cedars and the pines near the field.
7. Two small boys ran down the road in the dust. Wheeling old automobile tires.
8. Close by the heap of soft coal grew a clump of goldenrod in bloom. Making a vivid contrast to the dark mound.
9. When he sat on the edge of the desk there was a great creaking, he was an unusually fat man.
10. The woman had wisps of stiff hair, kind eyes, and false teeth. Which she seemed to adjust by pursing her mouth.

II

1. The question was directed to Frederic J. Haskin, at Victoria, B.C.
2. Mrs. Jones always wrote R S V.P. at the bottom of her invitations, even those which she received herself.
3. What makes him so eager to put Ph D after his name?
4. Mr Allen advertised in the daily paper, asking that all books that had been borrowed from him "since 1898 A D" be returned.

2. The Comma

(*Fourteen Uses*)

The comma is the hardest of all punctuation marks to master, and for two reasons: first, it has almost as many uses as all the other regular marks put together; and secondly, some of its uses are not as clear and simple as those of the other marks. The period and the colon, for example, are as definite as the multiplication table. With intelligent practice and proper care no one need go astray on them. The comma, however, is a tricky and unruly member and must be constantly watched. If you can manage the comma, no other mark should give you any trouble.

The comma has eleven required uses and three preferred uses—fourteen in all.

1. Between city and province, state, or country.

Put a comma between the name of every city, town, or community and the state, or province, or country in which it is located.

Cincinnati, Ohio; Ottawa, Ontario; Paris, France.

2. Between the date and the year.

The Armistice took effect on November 11, 1918.
Shakespeare died at Stratford-on-Avon on April 23, 1616.
Julius Cæsar was born on July 12, 100 B.C.

3. Before *but* and *for* in compound sentences.

Note carefully that the only time a comma can be used to separate independent statements is in connection with one of the pure conjunctions *but*, *for*, or *and*. In all other cases either the period or the semicolon should be used. See below, under the Semicolon, pages 138-142, and the Comma Splice, pages 206-209.

Comma before *but* and *for*

1. The firemen worked hard and faithfully, but in spite of their efforts the house was destroyed.

2. The theatre was crowded as never before, for it had been announced that Charlie Chaplin was to appear in person.

Comma before *and*

The comma with *but* and *for* is required, and it is preferred with *and*.

1. (The sentence in the text immediately above.)
2. It kept getting darker and darker, and more and more people began to leave the grounds.

4. To set off the members of a series.

A series is three or more words, phrases, or clauses in the same construction. (Sometimes called *the red, white, and blue* construction.)

Words in Series

1. She was tall, graceful, and charming.
2. A narrow, winding, slippery road is doubly dangerous at night.
3. The whole family cooked, ate, and slept in one small room.

Phrases in Series

1. The stage setting for this scene consists of a piano and stool, a tall floor lamp, a leather sofa, and a small revolving bookcase.
2. In a large city you have your choice of travelling on the elevated, in a surface car, or on the subway.

Clauses in Series

1. It was evident that he had heard the rumour, that it had made him very angry, and that he was determined to learn the truth.
2. What you hear, what you read, and what you think all help to form your mental background.

The Comma before *and* in a Simple Series

The comma before *and* in a simple series is preferred by a large majority of the leading publishers of books and magazines, although newspaper usage is against it. So far as the best practice is concerned, therefore, we should continue to use it.

Preferred: Red, white, and blue are colours.
Permitted: Red, white and blue are colours.
Preferred: She was tall, graceful, and charming.
Permitted: She was tall, graceful and charming.

An important exception to this rule is the names of business firms and book publishers ending in *& Co.* or *and Company*. Usually no comma is used before the *and*. For example:

Harcourt, Brace and Company
Doubleday, Doran & Company

5. Direct address.

When any person or animal is spoken to directly by name, the name or title is set off by a comma.

1. Tom, ask your father whether you can have the car this afternoon.
2. Hurry, boys, or we'll be late.
3. Please lend me your knife, Fred.

6. Appositives.

1. Miss Wilson, our singing teacher, is going to a larger school next year.
2. I had never seen Mr. Gray, our coach, so excited before.
3. I at once called up Mr. Ransom, the motor car dealer.

7. Absolute phrases (always introductory and usually participial).

1. A large tree having blown down across the road, we had to detour through the woods.
2. Rain having fallen all the morning, the tennis matches had to be postponed.

8. *Yes* and *no* and mild exclamations like *oh* and *well* (but not *O*).

1. Yes, I'll be sure to tell him.
2. No, I don't see how I can possibly stay any longer.
3. Oh, excuse me. I didn't know that you had arrived.
4. Well, what can you expect from such a man?
5. Indeed, I never heard that before.

9. Parenthetical sentence modifiers like *however, in fact, of course.*

Other common sentence modifiers or transition words and phrases are *for example, nevertheless, indeed, no doubt, in short, as it were.* All such expressions must be set off from the rest of the sentence by commas.

1. He knew, of course, that the end was near.
2. They admit, in fact, that it cannot be done.
3. She continued, however, to insist that she was right.
4. For example, consider the modern ocean liner.

10. Non-restrictive clauses.

In order to understand non-restrictive clauses, we must first know what a restrictive clause is.

A. Restrictive Clauses

Modifying clauses are of two kinds, restrictive and non-restrictive. **A restrictive clause gets its name from the fact that it restricts or limits the meaning to one particular person, group, place, or thing.** Take, for example, the sentence:

The hat that you bought yesterday is very becoming to you.

The clause *that you bought yesterday* restricts the meaning of *hat* to one particular hat out of all the hats in the world, and is hence a restrictive clause.

The man who just spoke to me is our doctor.

Again, the clause *who just spoke to me* limits the idea *man* to one particular man out of all the men in town, and is hence restrictive.

Read the following sentences thoughtfully and notice how the clauses, all of which are restrictive, narrow and limit the idea to one particular person or thing out of all the possible persons or things in existence.

1. She borrowed a pencil from the boy who sat in front of her.
2. An amateur athlete is one who contests for pleasure, not for money.

3. The plumber who repaired the pipes this time is not the one that we had before.
4. A restrictive clause is one that restricts the meaning to one particular person, group, place, or thing.

If we were to try to suggest in a drawing what a restrictive clause does, we might represent it as a pointing finger

THE HAT
THAT YOU BOUGHT YESTERDAY
IS VERY BECOMING TO YOU
THE MAN
WHO JUST SPOKE TO ME
IS OUR DOCTOR
WHERE IS THE BOOK
I LEFT ON THE PIANO LAST NIGHT
LET ALL
WHO FAVOR THE MOTION
MAKE IT KNOWN BY RISING

that singles out one individual from all other similar persons or things and thus particularizes and identifies it.

Or we might represent a restrictive clause by a sharp-pointed wedge which narrows the idea to one alone out of the many possibilities.

This is not the knife | which I lent you yesterday. |

Is that the house | which was struck by lightning? |

Not all clauses, either restrictive or non-restrictive, are introduced by the relative pronouns *who*, *which*, and *that*. Many are introduced by subordinating conjunctions like *when*, *while*, *where*, *as*, *since*, *because*, *if*, *unless*, *although*.

Here are a few restrictive clauses introduced in this way. Notice that they are not set off by commas.

Restrictive Adverbial Clauses

1. He came when you called.
2. She listened to the radio while she was waiting for him.
3. We waited where you told us to.
4. Fold the paper just as I did.
5. I have not seen him since he left town.
6. The machine won't run till you repair it.
7. I can't go unless you go too.

Restrictive clauses, whether adjectival or adverbial, are so closely connected with the rest of the sentence that they cannot be cut away from it by any form of punctuation, not even commas.

B. Non-restrictive Clauses

Non-restrictive clauses do not restrict or limit the thought to any particular person or thing, but merely add another fact or idea to the one expressed in the main part of the sentence.

Examples

1. I am studying Latin, which is a hard subject.

Here the clause *which is a hard subject* does not single out any particular kind of Latin, but applies to Latin in general, to all Latin. It is hence a non-restrictive clause.

2. Printing, which is man's most important invention, was introduced into England in 1476.

Again, the clause *which is man's most important invention* does not limit the term *printing* to any particular kind, but applies to the idea of *printing* as a whole, adding the thought that it is man's most important invention. It is thus a non-restrictive clause and is set off by commas.

Think over the following sentences, and note how the clauses do not restrict or limit the nouns they modify, but merely give an additional fact concerning them. Each clause thus being non-restrictive is set off by commas.

1. The mayor's son, who has been away at college for four years, has just returned to town.
2. We started at once for the club-house, which was only six miles away.
3. My father, who was a minister, was both a scholar and a gentleman.

If we were to try to represent what these and all other non-restrictive clauses do in a sentence, we should have to use not a sharp wedge or a pointing finger, but a parallelogram of equal width at both ends.

Taking the two sentences above, we should have something like this:

I am studying Latin, [which is a hard subject].

Printing, [which is man's most important invention], was introduced into England in 1476.

The boxed-in, non-restrictive clauses could all be omitted from the sentences, and the meaning would still be complete and largely unchanged. Read the sentences without them. They are not essential to the meaning.

Restrictive clauses, however, are usually essential to the

meaning, and cannot be omitted without falsifying or destroying it.

In the light of what has been said of restrictive clauses study the following paired sentences. The clauses in them have been made as much alike as possible in order to emphasize the difference.

Non-restrictive	*Restrictive*
1. Unfortunately she has lost her handbag, which contained her diamond ring. (She had only one handbag.)	**1.** Fortunately she did not lose the handbag that contained her diamond ring. (She had several handbags.)
2. Jane Farley, who just went by, lives across the street from us.	**2.** The girl who just went by lives across the street from us.
3. Bill Gray, who failed to pass on four subjects, has been ruled ineligible for football.	**3.** No student who fails to pass on four subjects will be allowed to play football.

It is probable that most of the clauses which you write will be restrictive, not requiring commas. Before setting off a clause with commas, therefore, be sure that it is non-restrictive and hence needs to be set off.

THE ROUND TABLE

Recognizing Restrictive and Non-restrictive Clauses

In the following sentences distinguish between restrictive and non-restrictive clauses. Insert commas where necessary to set off non-restrictive clauses.

1. Jane Wilson who was elected May Queen this year is my best friend.
2. This is the best theme that you ever wrote.
3. Everybody who knows her was surprised at her sudden decision to become a trained nurse.
4. Chaucer who has been called the Morning Star of English poetry was a contemporary of Dante.
5. Some pupils never read a single book which they do not get from the school library.
6. Every duty which is put off returns with seven fresh duties on its back.

7. This man who is a stranger in the city wants to be directed to the best hotel.
8. Anyone who has ever tried to edit a school paper knows how much trouble it is.
9. Madame Curie who discovered radium is a Frenchwoman.
10. I shall never forget the man who sold me my first long trousers.
11. My older brother who has just turned twenty-one weighs only ten pounds more than I do.
12. The friends that we make in school and college last all through life.
13. Have a heart that never hardens a temper that never tires and a touch that never hurts.
14. He hurried home to see his brother who had been badly hurt in an automobile accident. (He had only one brother.)
15. He hurried home to see his brother who had been badly hurt in an automobile accident. (He had four brothers.)
16. Bill Brown who left town three years ago returned yesterday for a brief visit.
17. All the people who had been injured in the wreck were given first aid without delay.
18. The books which help us the most are those which make us think the most.
19. All who attended the concert agreed that it was highly successful.
20. The frame was made of aluminum which for this purpose is superior to steel.

11. After the greeting in friendly letters.

It will be remembered that the colon is used after the greeting in formal and business letters. See the first use of the colon, page 146, and Formal Letters, pages 374-377.

In friendly, informal, familiar letters, however, the comma is preferred to the colon, though the colon is still permissible. For example:

Dear Uncle Wat,	Dearest Mother,
Dear friend,	Dearest Sister,
My dear Miss Lucy,	Dearest old friend,

Three Additional Preferred Uses

The eleven uses of the comma just listed are thoroughly established, and seem fairly sure to remain standard for some time to come. The comma also has three other uses which can be described as preferred rather than required. We should know them and be able to employ them at need.

12. Before short quotations.

The colon is used to introduce long, formal quotations. See the third use of the colon, page 147. For short quotations only a sentence long, however, and in reported dialogue and conversation, the comma is preferred to the colon.

Examples

1. He quoted smilingly. "A stitch in time saves nine."
2. Let us say with the poet,

   "God's in his heaven—
   All's right with the world!"

   (*Note:* The colon could be used instead of the comma here.)
3. As Lowell strikingly said in "Democracy", "Compromise is a good umbrella but a poor roof."

13. To wedge apart words or phrases which if read together would give a wrong meaning.

This use of the comma is a general rather than a particular one, but is sometimes necessary unless we recast the entire sentence and remove the trouble in that way. Consider the sentence,

> As the frightened animals rushed by, the people on the corner shrank back in alarm.

Without the comma, *people* would seem to be the object of *by* instead of the subject of *shrank.*

Exactly the same confusion is avoided by the comma in the following sentence:

> Nearby, an old oak lifted its gaunt limbs to the skies.

The comma is needed to keep us from getting the wrong meaning. *Nearby an old oak, etc.*

Read the following sentences rapidly and see what a difference the comma makes:

Without: 1. I like to go to the mountains and to go to the seacoast is delightful too.

With: 1. I like to go to the mountains, and to go to the seacoast is delightful too.

Without: 2. She was always a little sentimental sister.
With: 2. She was always a little sentimental, Sister.

Without: 3. A few minutes before the first boat had started.
With: 3. A few minutes before, the first boat had started.

Comma before *for* as a Conjunction

Particular care is needed to keep the conjunction *for* from being confused with the preposition *for*. The conjunction takes the comma before it; the preposition never.

Preposition: 1. His father decided to send him to college for his education.
Conjunction: 2. His father decided to send him to college, for his education had not been completed.
Preposition: 3. They ran as fast as they could for the train.
Conjunction: 4. They ran as fast as they could, for the train was already starting.

In all the examples listed in this section, what the comma does is to act as a tiny wall or dam and thus keep the meaning from spilling over into the wrong part of the sentence.

14. After a long dependent adverbial clause coming first in the sentence.

Adverbial clauses are of many kinds. Read again at this point the sections on Adverbial Clauses, pages 61 and 62, and on Subordinating Conjunctions, pages 45-47.

When such clauses come first in the sentence the rule is as follows: (*a*) with short clauses no comma is required, though it is permitted; (*b*) with long clauses the comma is strongly preferred in order to make the reading easier and simpler.

Short Introductory Clauses: Comma permitted but Not Required

Permitted: 1. When father gave an order, we always obeyed.
Also Permitted: 1. When father gave an order we always obeyed.

Permitted: 2. While the sun was shining, we took several excellent pictures.

Also Permitted: 2. While the sun was shining we took several excellent pictures.

The former rule required the comma for short, introductory, adverbial clauses like these. Recent usage, however, is against requiring the comma.

Long Introductory Clauses: Comma Preferred

After long introductory clauses, however, the comma is still so overwhelmingly preferred that it may fairly be said to be required.

Preferred: 1. When I learned that the train was a local and took nearly all day to make the trip, I decided to go by bus instead.

Preferred: 2. While we were rushing around frenziedly trying our best to get the job finished before dark, Mother called to us that supper was ready.

Exercises in All Uses of the Comma

Supply commas wherever needed:

1. "Gertrude have you any nails in your shoes that could spoil the newly varnished floors in this house?" my sister asked the cook.
2. The day being cool the automatically controlled furnace began to warm the house.
3. Yes tapping the radio tube seemed to stop the whining in our set.
4. The covered brass bowl had a look of age; it had in fact been used long ago by a Chinese woman who had cherished the hand-stove.
5. The garage doors which were manipulated by a device that was electrically controlled were much too heavy to be rolled back by the little boy unaided.
6. She asked me excitedly "Can you find the ball in that long grass?"
7. After all the carpenters working on the porch were honest men.
8. Until she learns to put enough shortening in her batter and to keep the irons at the right temperature her waffles will stick to the waffle iron.
9. The muffins were left untouched for we disliked bread made with bran.

10. Is this book published by Little Brown and Company?
11. The rattling noise a very loud clamour of tin on cement was the result of the driver's upsetting a traffic sign.
12. The house having been insulated we were able to use the attic.
13. We thought however that we could get to our meals on time if our mother called us from the garden by blowing a policeman's whistle.
14. My dear Mr. Green
15. Was it Macbeth who said "All the world's a stage" or was it some other Shakespearean character?
16. His telegram was sent me on March 16 1946.
17. What bird is that that one with the green on the wings Kate?
18. The carpet-sweeper an elegantly polished implement of golden oak was bought in 1908.
19. The rain having blotted out his footprints a hunter lost his way in the swamp.
20. A man riding on a mule and followed by his wife on foot was asked why the wife was walking. He answered "She ain't got no mule."
21. In Copenhagen Denmark he secured a sailing vessel that had been used as a training ship.
22. The china figure a plump gentleman in yellow trousers and vest and black tail-coat displayed black spectacles on a round face.
23. The curtain which was made of a poor quality of theatrical gauze very soon looked as flimsy as a dishrag.
24. We like good reading for high schools deserve the best.
25. There were asters in bloom near the road and against the fence ironweed showed deep purple flowers.
26. The candle a taper of beeswax had a fresh fragrance like honey.
27. Oh Sarah I have come to borrow a number of that magazine which costs ten dollars a year.
28. Flipping the omelet over the boy at the stove looked playfully at the customer.

3. The Semicolon

(*Three Uses*)

> Ability to use the semicolon adds considerably to a writer's resources. —GEORGE L. SUMMEY, *Modern Punctuation*

The semicolon has three established uses, none of which gives any sign of losing ground, for the semicolon fills a place that no other mark does. Its use is a sign of a varied and usually a satisfactory sentence structure. Look through several of your back themes, and if you fail to find several semicolons to each theme, the chances are that your sentence structure will be choppy and monotonous, verging on the type called "Baby Sentences" and discussed on pages 230-231.

1. Use the semicolon between co-ordinate clauses which are not joined by *and, but,* or *for* and which are related in thought.

Remember that the comma can be used to join the parts of a compound sentence only when the parts are relatively short and are joined by a pure conjunction like *and*, *but*, or *for*.

In all other cases the clauses must be separated either by a period or, if short and closely connected in thought, by a semicolon. This use of the semicolon has been suggestively called the "half-period".

For and Comma

Right: He sat down by the side of the road, for he was very tired.

Period

Right: He sat down by the side of the road. He was very tired.

Semicolon

Right: He sat down by the side of the road; he was very tired.

Semicolon

1. The wind died down; the leaves fell silently through the still air to the earth.
2. The train jolted to an unexpected stop; the passengers sat up in their seats and looked questioningly at one another.
3. Night came down quickly over the little valley; here and there lights began to spring up in the cabins.

(Note that while the semicolon is correctly used in these three sentences, either the period or the *and*-comma could be substituted. The comma by itself, however, could not be used in place of the semicolon. This would turn the sentences into comma splices.)

2. Before *however* and certain other conjunctive adverbs when a complete independent statement is added to another complete independent statement.

See list of conjunctive adverbs on page 65.

Examples

1. He had worked hard all his life and had invested wisely; however, the bank failure swept his savings away.
2. She has frequently deceived me before; hence I cannot altogether believe her now.
3. You had better get a new tire for your left front wheel or have the old one retreaded; otherwise you will have a bad blowout some day.

This same principle of punctuation that requires the semicolon with *however* formerly required it with *yet*, and *then* and *so*. Now, however, usage is divided; and although the semicolon is to be preferred, the comma is permissible.

Yet, *Then*, and *So*

Preferred: 1. The rain began to fall faster and faster; yet the children did not come in.
Permitted: 1. The rain began to fall faster and faster, yet the children did not come in.

Preferred: 2. The boat began to leak worse and worse; then it turned over and sank.
Permitted: 2. The boat began to leak worse and worse, then it turned over and sank.

Preferred: 1. Just then the bell rang; so we all went in to dinner.
Permitted: 1. Just then the bell rang, so we all went in to dinner.

3. Between long independent statements when either statement is punctuated with commas.

The logic of this use of the semicolon is clear; it is to enable the reader to see instantly the relationship of the independent statements and to distinguish them from phrases or words within the statements themselves which are set off by commas. This use has been called the "double comma".

Take, for example, the following sentence:

> The road was winding, slippery, and steep, and the car we were driving was old, shaky, and none too powerful.

With only the comma after *steep* to divide the two independent clauses, the meaning is not clear till the end is reached; but if a semicolon is used instead, both relationship and meaning are instantly clear.

> The road was winding, slippery, and steep; and the car we were driving was old, shaky, and none too powerful.

Examples

1. (The sentence in the text, six lines above, beginning "With only the comma after steep," etc.)
2. The town had never been large, and of late years had lost instead of gained in population; but the climate was delightful, the people were both cultured and kind, and all in all it was a pleasant place to live in.

Exercises in All Uses of the Semicolon

Supply semicolons and commas wherever needed:

1. The men were kept busy carrying buckets of water to the newly planted cedars and Carolina cherry trees shrubbery must be kept alive at all costs.
2. We felt almost unnecessarily conscientious when we read the telegram for the fourth time however we all wanted to be sure to send it in the best form.
3. The letter startled me and made me tremble with joy I had been willed ten thousand dollars.
4. The big stone fireplace in the sun-room was beautiful and convenient consequently we had our steak dinners in this porch with the many windows.
5. He had missed his street car and it was raining so hard that he did not like the prospect of waiting on the corner he was therefore delighted when a friend invited him to ride in an automobile.
6. Brass andirons a gleaming fender a brass-bound fire screen all made the fireplace look ready for a hospitable blaze we were proud of our hearth.

7. Molly always said sentimentally "I do love an open fire" and smiled dreamily when winter was mentioned moreover she seemed to be taking credit for inventing open fires for her air was smug.
8. The rug on the floor was dyed a soft gray-blue all the curtains were made of gray linen.
9. Dahlias Michaelmas daisies and goldenrod were combined in the blue vase I thought how brightly the dahlias which were of a rich crimson glowed in contrast to the blue and gold.
10. We did not know trees could be fed therefore ours starved.

4. Quotation Marks

(*Two Uses*)

Quotation marks have two established uses:

1. **Before and after a direct quotation.**

A direct quotation is one that reproduces the actual words of the speaker or writer.

Examples

1. "The still, sad music of humanity" is one of Wordsworth's most famous lines.
2. The umpire jerked up his hand and called decisively, "You're out!"
3. The storekeeper said regretfully, "I don't believe I can let you have it for that price."

For other examples, see section 3 under Capitalization, page 154.

Notice in sentence 1 that there is no comma after the quotation. The reason is that the quotation is the subject of the verb *is* and hence cannot be separated from it in any way.

(1) DIVIDED QUOTATIONS

Divided quotations need special attention, for not only do they require two sets of quotation marks but the punctuation on both sides of the division must be carefully watched. Notice particularly the punctuation in the following sentences immediately preceding the second set of quotation marks.

1. "Not on your life!" shouted Tom. "You couldn't catch me in a hundred years."
2. "What do you mean," he interrupted, "by bothering me this way?"
3. "Let's not quarrel," she said earnestly. "We've been too good friends to get angry over such a trifle."
4. "I don't believe I can," she replied, "but I will do my best."
5. "I don't agree with you," said his friend; "however, I won't oppose you any longer."

(2) QUOTATIONS WITHIN QUOTATIONS

A quotation within a quotation takes single instead of double quotation marks.

"I don't think so," she answered. "What I understood your mother to say was 'Be sure to take enough blankets.' "

(3) WITH REFERENCE TO OTHER PUNCTUATION MARKS

The question of whether quotation marks are to be placed inside or outside other marks of punctuation can be simply stated as follows:

(*a*) Always put quotation marks *outside* the period and the comma if the sentence is complete or in conversation.

1. He answered, "I never heard that."
2. "It is hard to tell," he continued, "which side of the river the smoke is coming from."

(*b*) With other marks, such as the question mark, the exclamation point, and the dash, put the quotation marks outside them if they are part of the quotation, inside them if they are not part of the quotation.

1. She asked, "Will you come?"
2. Did he tell us he had "a nice house" or "an ice house"?
3. "How exciting!" he replied.
4. Did she say, "I will come"?
5. Tom said wildly, "But suppose the car is stolen ——"

(4) INDIRECT QUOTATIONS

Indirect quotations do not take quotation marks. An indirect quotation is one which does not give the exact words of the speaker or writer but only the general substance or idea. Indirect quotations are usually introduced by *that* or *whether*.

Indirect: 1. He said that he couldn't come tomorrow.
Direct: 1. He said, "I can't come tomorrow."
Indirect: 2. He replied that the car could make eighty miles an hour.
Direct: 2. He replied, "The car can make eighty miles an hour."

(5) CHANGE OF SPEAKER

In writing dialogue make a separate paragraph for every change of speaker. No matter how short it is, each speech requires a separate paragraph.

"Coming?" he asked.
"No."
"See you later then."

(6) QUOTATIONS OF MORE THAN ONE PARAGRAPH

When a quotation consists of more than one paragraph, put quotation marks at the beginning of each paragraph, but at the end of the last paragraph only.

2. To indicate titles of articles, chapters, sections, short stories, and single poems, but not titles of books, magazines, and newspapers, which should preferably be underlined instead of quoted. (See Number 1 under "Underlining", page 147.)

Examples

1. Gray's "Elegy" and Poe's "The Raven" have been called the best-known poems in English and American literature.
2. Huxley's "A Piece of Chalk", Lowell's "Democracy", and Emerson's "The American Scholar", all of which we consider essays, were first delivered as speeches.

3. "Punctuation" is the title of the chapter in this book which we are studying at present.

Exercises in the Use of Quotation Marks

Supply quotation marks as well as other punctuation marks wherever needed:

1. As children the two girls had written or rather had begun a romantic tale entitled Romona Heiress of Gonzales Court but the story was never published.
2. All that I ask is —— began the teacher but stopped suddenly.
3. Is this soup made of animals or not he inquired bitterly.
4. Yes she told him you can eat more noodles I suppose although I must tell you that you are too fat already.
5. Would you read any story with such a title as Little May asked Virginia scornfully.
6. A famous Russian story is The Cloak by Gogol.
7. My tooth broke off exclaimed Billy after the fight.
8. Fasten all the windows please exclaimed my mother sharply.
9. The skies they were ashen and sober says Poe of an October evening.
10. The butcher said he had no fresh shrimp for sale on Tuesday.
11. Come when you can he said we are always glad to see you.
12. His last words I replied were I shall never forget your kindness.
13. When you have put away the dishes added Mother dust the furniture.
14. Did she tell you she would pay back the four hundred dollars?
15. I have almost anything in season answered the grocer and I particularly recommend the celery.
16. Have you read the chapter entitled Revising and Rewriting I asked it contains some useful hints.
17. That's an evasion snapped the officer what I asked was where were you yesterday?
18. Jimmy Royce unable to hear well asked Mrs. Royce what she had decided to do.
19. Did the letter say come at once I asked.
20. Enough of this nonsense he exclaimed let us have the truth.

5. The Colon

(*Three Uses*)

The colon has three definite uses, for which no other punctuation mark will serve. There is little reason ever to make a mistake in employing it.

1. After the greeting in a formal or business letter.

This is the established usage among North American publishers and business houses. Practically four out of five of them use the colon after the greeting.

Examples

Closed Punctuation	*Open Punctuation*
The Cambridge University Press, Toronto, Ontario. Gentlemen:	Chatto and Windus 70 Bond Street Toronto, Ontario Gentlemen:

For other examples, see "The Business Letter", pages 360-362.

Note, however, that in friendly, personal letters the comma instead of the colon is preferred after the greeting:

Dear Father, Dearest Nan,
My dear Sister, Dear Tom,

See "The Informal Letter", page 378.

2. After such expressions as *these, the following, as follows,* to give notice of a list of particulars or examples.

Examples

1. Last month the kinds of books most in demand at the public library were these: adventure stories, detective stories, love stories, biographies, and plays.
2. A recent article in a sporting magazine listed the leading game birds of America as follows: the wild turkey, the wild duck, the bobwhite or quail, and the dove.

For other examples see the section on the sentence of announcement in developing a jointed subject, page 176.

Recall also, as is noted there, that if no such expression as *these, the following,* or *as follows* is used, no punctuation mark at all comes between the verb and the list that it introduces. For example, in the first sentence given above, if the word *these* is omitted the colon should be omitted too. Then the sentence would read:

> Last month the kinds of books most in demand at the public library were adventure stories, detective stories, love stories, biographies, and plays.

Note finally that in introducing a list, whether or not *these*, *the following*, or *as follows* is used, in no case can either the comma or the semicolon be employed.

3. To introduce a long, formal quotation.

Example

1. You are doubtless familiar with Macaulay's eloquent comment on the difference between the public and the private life of Charles I: "We charge him with having broken his coronation oath; and we are told that he kept his marriage vow! We accuse him of having given up his people to the merciless inflictions of the most hot-headed and hard-hearted of prelates; and the defence is that he took his little son on his knees and kissed him! We censure him for having violated the articles of the Petition of Right, after having, for a good and valuable consideration, promised to observe them; and we are informed that he was accustomed to hear prayers at six o'clock in the morning!"

Remember that the comma may be used to introduce a short, informal quotation.

6. Underlining (Italics)

(*Three Uses*)

Underlining a word in writing is a sign to the printer to set that word in italics. Since it will probably be some years before any of your work will appear in print, we shall here use the term *underlining* instead of *italics*.

Underlining has three well-defined uses.

1. To introduce the titles of books, magazines, and newspapers.

Notice the difference in usage between quotation marks and underlining as indicated both in this rule and in section 2 under "Quotation Marks", page 144. The titles of books, magazines, and newspapers are preferably underlined, while the individual parts or sections of a book, such as chapter headings, individual stories, individual poems, and so on, are put in quotation marks.

Examples

1. One of the best articles in the *Encyclopaedia Britannica* is by Theodore Watts-Dunton on "Poetry".
2. Did you read the editorial "What Are We Coming To?" in a recent issue of the *New York Times*?
3. Three of the most interesting novels ever written are Stevenson's *Treasure Island*, Conan Doyle's *The White Company*, and Dumas's *The Three Musketeers*.

2. To indicate words taken out of their context and used without regard to their meaning.

Examples

1. The three most commonly mispronounced words in English are *was*, *of*, and *what*.
2. Poe was fond of musical words like *Ulalume*, *Lenore*, *Annabel Lee*, and *Nevermore*.
3. It is hard to get the liquid *u* sound in such words as *suit*, *supreme*, and *supernatural*.

Notice the similarity between the wording of this rule and the rule for the use of apostrophe *s* in forming the plural number. That is, words taken out of their context and used without regard to their meaning (*a*) are underlined and (*b*) form their plural by adding apostrophe *s*. See page 274.

3. To indicate foreign words and phrases not yet felt to be a part of the language.

English is a most hospitable language, and welcomes words from all sources. Often such words are so commonly used that they lose their foreign flavour and are thus felt to be thoroughly Anglicized. Other foreign words, however, are used less frequently and are felt still to belong to their original language. Such words and expressions are to be underlined if you have any occasion to use them. A good rule is this: if the word is (*a*) preceded in the main part of the dictionary by two parallel lines, or if (*b*) it is given under "Foreign Words and Phrases", underline it.

Examples

1. The president is *ex officio* a member of the committee.
2. The cavalry had a hard time establishing *liaison* with the infantry.
3. The class took as their motto *ad astra per aspera.*
4. Louis XIV of France is credited with the famous saying, *L'état, c'est moi.*

Exercises in Underlining

Underline or use quotation marks where necessary, and supply any additional punctuation marks required:

1. Did you read Spotted Killers an article written by Hugh Prior in Field and Stream for May 1945?
2. After an attack of sciatica he could not drive his car and was hors de combat so far as the race was concerned.
3. He read Boswell's Life of Johnson recently.
4. The boys fought at every meeting until the coach managed to bring about a rapprochement.
5. He frequently overworked and and so.
6. Jack London's To Build a Fire is one of the best short stories listed on page 422 of Learning to Write.
7. The carpenter could not understand exactly what the term latch meant.
8. The innkeeper instructed the sign painter to leave a wider space between Coach and and and and and Horses.
9. Shakespeare's Hamlet is my favourite character. Macbeth is my favourite play.
10. In today's issue of the Tribune said my brother at the breakfast table there was an excellent editorial called The Same Old Game.

7. Footnotes, Reference, and Bibliographies

Many high schools are now requiring in the upper years either once or twice a year a long theme that involves considerable reading in the library. The teacher furnishes a list of references: notes are to be taken on the references and later worked up into a long paper, sometimes called a research theme.

Such material may either be quoted, that is, the actual words of the original may be given; or it may be cited, that is, the facts or ideas it contains may be reproduced in the student's own words. In either case exact reference to the source of the quotation or citation should be made.

References are of two kinds: (1) books and (2) magazines.

(1) BOOKS

The following items constitute a complete, exact reference to a book:

1. Name of the author exactly as it is given on the title page, followed by a comma.
2. Title of the book, underlined, followed by a comma.
3. Name of the firm publishing the book, followed by a comma.
4. Year of publication, followed by a comma.
5. Exact page (or pages) in the book where the information referred to is to be found, followed by a period.

The usual way to make a reference in a footnote is to put a small figure in an inverted caret (↓) at the end of the quotation or citation, and then to repeat the figure at the bottom of the page and follow it with the complete reference. For example:

> As a prominent teacher and writer has well said, "It is wrong to leave pupils so ignorant of mechanics that their letters prove them to be uneducated." ↓

(2) MAGAZINES

A reference to a magazine article follows the same form except that while the name of the magazine is underlined

↓ C. H. Ward, *What Is English?*, Scott, Foresman and Co., 1925, p. 25.

the title of the article is put in quotation marks. For example:

> Prior to the World War, nearly all of the colleges of the Middle West invested their endowment funds almost exclusively in farm real-estate first mortgages. ♆

Bibliographies

A bibliography is a list of the books and magazine articles, alphabetically arranged, which were used in preparing the paper. There are two differences between a reference in a footnote and a reference in a bibliography: (1) In a footnote a definite page reference is given, but not in the bibliography; (2) in a footnote the last name of the author is usually given last, but in the bibliography it is given first in order to make the alphabetical arrangement clear.

A brief sample bibliography on the subject "The Popular Ballad" might take the following form:

BIBLIOGRAPHY

Sandburg, Carl, *The American Songbag*, Harcourt, Brace and Company, 1927.

Sargent, H. C., and Kittredge, G. L., *English and Scottish Popular Ballads*, Houghton Mifflin Company, 1904.

Sharp, Cecil J., *One Hundred English Folksongs*, Oliver Ditson Company, 1916.

Magazines

Gerould, G. H., "The Making of Ballads", *Modern Philology*, Vol. 21, 1923.

Gordon, G. W., "Old Songs That Men Have Sung", *Adventure*, December 20, 1925.

Encyclopaedias

Child, F. J., "Ballad Poetry", *Johnson's Universal Cyclopaedia*, 1897.

♆ Harold T. Smith, "Endowment and Security", *Journal of Higher Education*, Vol. 4, 1933, p. 71.

Lang, Andrew, "Ballads", *Encyclopaedia Britannica*, eleventh edition.

Pound, Louise, "Ballad", *Encyclopaedia Britannica*, fourteenth edition.

Punctuation of References

Note that the system of punctuation advised here is to set off the different items of each reference by commas. This practice is clear, logical, and has the sanction of many of the leading colleges and universities. Some colleges prefer other systems, such as the colon between the author's name and the title of the book or the article. It is easier and more consistent, however, to use commas throughout.

THE ROUND TABLE

1. Make and bring to class five exact references as follows:
   (*a*) one citation from your English text
   (*b*) one quotation from some other of your textbooks
   (*c*) one citation from a recent magazine
   (*d*) one quotation from a recent newspaper
   (*e*) one citation from an important article in some encyclopaedia.
   Be sure to make the references (*a*) complete and (*b*) exact.
2. As directed by the teacher, prepare a bibliography of (*a*) books and (*b*) encyclopaedia and magazine articles on an assigned subject.

8. Capital Letters

(*Eight Uses*)

Capital letters have eight uses.

1. Capitalize the first word in every sentence.

Beginning the first word in every sentence with a capital letter is by all odds both the most important and the most frequent use of capitals. In fact, it is *the* basic rule of capitalization, just as putting a period at the end of every declarative and imperative sentence is *the* basic rule of punctuation. Whatever else is or is not done, these two rules must be unfailingly observed.

2. In the titles of themes, stories, and books capitalize the first word and all other words except the articles (*a*, *an*, *the*), prepositions, and conjunctions.

(1) THEME TITLES

Centre the title of the theme on the first line of the paper. Put no punctuation mark after it, unless the title is a question or an exclamation, when of course a question mark or an exclamation point will be necessary. Do not put quotation marks around the title. Some writers capitalize long prepositions like *concerning*, *underneath*, *notwithstanding*, and so on, and long conjunctions like *nevertheless*, *consequently*, *accordingly*, and *moreover*. Follow the teacher's directions on this point.

Leave one line vacant between the title and the beginning of the theme.

Here is a list of titles for themes. Write them out, (*a*) capitalizing them correctly and (*b*) centring them on the page. Leave a line between each title and the next, and make as attractive a display page as you can.

1. The most beautiful object I ever saw
2. Do animals think
3. A dog's love of motoring
4. What I have found out about tires
5. Some things which the modern child has never seen
6. Getting acquainted with the neighbour's dog.

(2) BOOK TITLES

The following is a list of well-known books and short stories illustrating the use of capitals in titles. Read them carefully until you see clearly the reason for each capital and each lower-case letter.

Mark Twain . . . . *The Adventures of Huckleberry Finn*
Thomas Bailey Aldrich . *The Story of a Bad Boy*
R. H. Dana. . . . . *Two Years before the Mast*
Rudyard Kipling . . . *The Man Who Would Be King*
A. E. W. Mason . . . *Fire over England*

3. Capitalize the first word of every direct quotation

(*a*) which is introduced by *say* or its equivalent, and

(*b*) which makes complete sense in and by itself.

This rule is the third most commonly violated of all the rules of capitalization. Notice carefully the wording. Every direct quotation must begin with a capital letter on two conditions: (1) the quotation must be introduced by *say* or one of its synonyms (and, we may add, be preceded by a colon or a comma); and (2) the quotation itself must make complete sense.

These two conditions are fulfilled in the following examples. Observe them.

1. Montaigne humorously remarked, "Nothing is so firmly believed as what we least know."
2. Algernon Sidney whimsically but truly remarked, "Liars ought to have good memories."

On the other hand, no capital letter is used (*a*) if the quotation is not a direct quotation or (*b*) if it is not introduced by *say* and does not make independent sense. The following quotations, for example, are not introduced by *say*. Neither do they make sense by themselves, but are run in with the rest of the sentence as a part of it. They do not, therefore, begin with capital letters.

1. Together we took the open road "over the hills and far away".
2. Byron describes a man who had "just enough learning to misquote."

4. Capitalize all proper names, such as the names of persons, places, countries, races, languages, organizations, and so forth, including the names and the titles of God.

(1) GEOGRAPHICAL NAMES

The names of all continents, oceans, countries, states, provinces, counties, cities, streets, rivers, lakes, and so forth, should be capitalized.

Europe	Quebec	St. Lawrence River
Atlantic Ocean	Dundas County	Lake Erie
France	Wentworth County	Main Street
United States	Hamilton	Portage Avenue
Ontario		

In regard to capitalizing such words as *county*, *river*, *street*, *college*, and so forth, when they are a part of proper names, usage is sharply divided between books and magazines on the one hand and newspapers on the other. About five out of every six publishers of books and magazines prefer to capitalize; about two out of three newspapers prefer not to capitalize.

Book and Magazine Usage	*Newspaper Usage*
Cook County	Cook county
Mississippi River	Mississippi river
Main Street	Main street

The usage for us to follow is clearly that of the best books and magazines. Capitalize, therefore, both parts of geographical names.

(2) NORTH, SOUTH, EAST, AND WEST

A special situation exists in regard to the words *north*, *south*, *east*, and *west*. When used to mean simply the points of the compass, or to indicate direction, they are common nouns and take a small letter.

Examples

1. The farther north you go, the colder it gets; the farther south you go, the warmer it gets.
2. The coast is a hundred and fifty miles due east from here.

When, however, these words refer to particular sections, or well-defined areas of Canada or the United States, they are capitalized.

Example

Although they have lived in the West all their lives, they have many friends and relatives in the East.

(3) NAMES OF ORGANIZATIONS, BUSINESS FIRMS, AND TRADE NAMES

Troublesome varieties of proper names are the organizations, business firms, and copyrighted trade names which have sprung up in such large numbers and which form no small part of the national advertising and national correspondence in this country. All such names are the property of the particular organization, industry, or business which has adopted them, and we must take care to spell, punctuate, and capitalize them exactly as they are given in the advertisement or on the official stationery.

Examples

Organizations	*Business Firms*
The Canadian Club	Parke, Davis and Co.
The Society for the Prevention of Cruelty to Animals	The Macmillan Company of Canada Limited

Trade Names

Eversharp Pencils
Ivory Soap

5. Capitalize titles and terms of family relationship when these are used as part of the names of persons or are used in place of the names. Academic degrees are always capitalized.

(1) TITLES AND TERMS OF RELATIONSHIP

(*a*) With the name or as the name:

King George	Professor R. G. Wilson
Doctor Osler	The Reverend S. T. Swinton

1. When I told Mother and Father, they were much surprised.
2. She is very much like Uncle Toby.
3. Would you come at once, Doctor?

(*b*) Without the name:

1. He was elected president of his class.
2. Please send for a doctor.
3. He is a professor in the provincial university.

Terms of family relationship are not capitalized when preceded by the definite or indefinite article or by *my*, *our*, *your*, *his*, *her*, *their*.

1. I live with my mother, but my father is sometimes away for months at a time.
2. I have an aunt living in Winnipeg.

(2) DEGREES

Degrees, whether or not used with the name of the person holding them, are capitalized.

1. I am going to take a B.A., but my brother is applying for a B.Sc.
2. Which do you prefer, the Master of Arts or the Master of Science?
3. Reverend Philip Gaines, D.D., LL.D.

THREE *Don't's*

Do not capitalize the names of (1) the seasons, (2) classes in school or college, or (3) studies, except the languages.

(*a*) SEASONS

The days of the week and the months of the year are capitalized, but not the seasons—spring, summer, autumn or fall, winter.

1. March, April, and May are usually considered the spring months.
2. That Sunday was the hottest day of the summer.

(*b*) CLASSES

School and college classes are not capitalized.

1. I hope to enter the freshman class at the university next year.
2. Her younger brother is in the fourth grade.
3. One of my cousins is in first year at high school.

(*c*) STUDIES

Among the studies and courses at school and college only the languages are capitalized.

1. Most girls find mathematics hard.
2. I am studying Latin in high school and expect to take up Greek in college.

6. **Capitalize adjectives derived from proper nouns such as those listed in Number 4 above.**
7. **Capitalize the first word of every line of poetry.**
8. **Capitalize the pronoun *I* and the vocative interjection *O* (but not the exclamation *oh* unless it begins a sentence).**

Exercises in Uses of Capital Letters

Supply capital letters and suitable punctuation marks where they are needed:

1. The quiet rain made us think of sandburg's poem fog for the shower came "on little cat feet".
2. I went to a meeting of the kiwanians in oshawa.
3. If you shop on bruce street be sure to see the dresses in cunningham's display window.
4. That child's name was actually lake huron.
5. The trees leaned to the north after the hurricane.
6. The tall girl easily opened the can with her strong hands and the little boy of eight exclaimed her strength is as the strength of ten.
7. His favourite resort in the west is banff.
8. Who could say which twin was my father and which was my uncle?
9. She wanted to study both french and spanish but her teachers warned her that since algebra was a required subject it would be difficult to take two languages and also history english and mathematics.
10. ernest thompson seton . . . wild animals I have known
    john buchan . . . book of escapes and hurried journeys
    h. g. wells . . . the shape of things to come

General Exercises in Punctuation

A

Write the following sentences and prose passage as the teacher directs, either as exercises to be handed in or as dictation in class. Supply all needed punctuation marks and capital letters. Some of the sentences are correct as they stand. Exchange papers and correct them in class under the direction of the teacher.

I

1. I beg your pardon sir
2. The librarian has just ordered the following books Scott's *Ivanhoe* Dickens's *A Tale of Two Cities* and Thackeray's *Henry Esmond*
3. I do not think she is at home however I shall phone her anyway
4. There are three things we can do keep on with the same plan give it up or make a new one.
5. It was hard pulling for the hill was long and steep
6. Mr. Stone the proprietor of the store ran to the window and shouted police.
7. Remember if you lose the bet will have to be paid.
8. Inside the rooms were painted a cool gray.
9. The road is steep for most of the route lies in the mountains.
10. It is very easy to confuse affect and effect.

II

11. Up above the big rock towered over us.
12. The chief forms of amusement are tennis golf and swimming.
13. You would enjoy meeting my mother who plays beautifully on the piano.
14. Before we could move the vase toppled over
15. The bible is the book of books.
16. He is our chief therefore we should loyally follow his wishes.
17. We were on the look out for a place that was high dry and sheltered.
18. Benjamin Franklin who was a friend of Thomas Jefferson was one of the most versatile men the United States ever produced.
19. When I was fifteen years old my father gave me three pure-bred Red Leghorn hens which were the start of my flock
20. When I was fifteen years old my father gave me the three pure-bred Leghorn hens which were the start of my flock.

III

21. Run here Mary your kitten has fallen into the bath tub.
22. Dr. Welborne our family physician is one of the most popular men in town.
23. Why didn't you tell me that your brother was sick
24. The question of expenses however is not what is bothering me.
25. We had better go at once hadn't we
26. At daybreak he woke us up and said its time to start if we expect to get to town in time to meet the bus
27. The following club members have resigned Mr. Wilton Mr James Mr. Simms and Mr. Anderson
28. Inside the piano was going at full blast.
29. A pupil who does not really study hard misses much that is of permanent value in after life.
30. General Lee who was an ideal gentleman was made president of Washington College after the Civil War

IV

31. I liked all the fellows but one in particular was the nicest chap I ever met
32. As soon as the bus comes in the station takes on new life.
33. Well if you can't I can
34. My favourite fruits are peaches grapes and cantaloupes
35. The six most important cereals are wheat corn oats rye barley and rice
36. Next year I shall begin the study of French, geometry, and Shakespeare.
37. It rained hard all the morning otherwise I should certainly have come
38. Our modern language teacher can speak three languages French Italian and Spanish
39. He was the best athlete in school in fact he made his letter in baseball, football, basketball, and track.
40. Two of the greatest bars to success are these fear of ridicule and fear of making a mistake.

V

41. Two of the greatest bars to success are fear of ridicule and fear of making a mistake.
42. Mark twains huck finn is a very interesting book it tells the story of a boys life on the mississippi river
43. When the coach told me I want you to play fullback tomorrow I could hardly keep from yelling for joy.

44. Pat our Irish setter was lying on the porch.
45. Poe who died at the age of forty is one of the most famous of American poets
46. Come around to the back door said the woman and I'll give you some food.
47. Three very desirable qualities are accuracy, promptness and dependability.
48. Everybody began to run down the street shouting stop thief
49. Tennis golf and swimming are my favourite sports.
50. Theres no use going any farther he replied lets return home

VI

51. The Union Station quick said the detective as he jumped into the taxi. "I've got to make the 12.20 train sure."
52. The policeman on the corner who had been watching the quarrel somewhat uneasily, now stepped forward and held up his hand.
53. There are as many is as ss in Mississippi.
54. The most useful tools are a screwdriver a pair of pliers a lug wrench and a jack.
55. No said the teacher you havent got it right yet.
56. "What has become of the library copy of Who's who?" I asked
57. He was a manly little fellow.
58. The boy obligingly said no, father let me get it for you then he ran quickly out to the car and brought back the missing package.
59. Having called the meeting to order the chairman asked someone to state the object of the meeting.
60. My father used to say to me pay as you go and if you can't pay don't go.

VII

the chub caught sight of this shape of doom rushing upon him through the golden tremor of the water he shot off in a panic seeking some dark crevice or some weed thicket dense enough to hide him but the loon was almost at his tail there was no crevice to be found and the weed thickets were too sparse and open to conceal him this way and that he darted doubling and twisting frantically around every stalk or stone but in spite of his bulk the loon followed each turn with the agility of an eel the loosened silt boiled up in wreaths behind his violent passage and the weeds swayed in the wake of the thrusting webs in less than a minute the chase the turmoil of which drove every other fish large or small in terror from the feeding ground came suddenly to an end rising abruptly with the fish gripped in his great beak the loon burst upon the surface sending shoreward a succession of circling ripples without ceremony he gulped his meal then swimming rather low in the water and with head thrust out before him he hurried to his nesting place on the islet as if he thought he had been too long away from his domestic duties

—SIR CHARLES G. D. ROBERTS, *Neighbours Unknown*

B

Punctuate and paragraph the following passages, paying special attention to the dialogue.

1. I approached a group of rowdy youngsters who were playing ball to ask the whereabouts of a short street in the neighbourhood I dunno one said ask the dope over there on the corner sat a small boy under a faded beach umbrella with a large sign reading all kinds information — 1¢ to 5¢ he was a homely child wearing glasses and a studious look and his nose might be called a topographical error Im looking for bird street I said he pulled out a large map and pointed out the location that will be one cent he replied seriously and added havent you any more questions mister well there is another bit of information I need I said with tongue in cheek where is the sacroiliac joint for several minutes he shuffled books of every description cook books almanacs a handbook of chemistry diseases of animals rogets thesaurus and finally to my surprise an ancient copy of grays anatomy after much search he found the answer and an illustration I gave him a quarter and he thanked me profusely Im studying for several professions he mentioned casually

—ERNEST W. PAGE in *The Reader's Digest*[1]

2. This is mr micawber said mr quinion to me ahem said the stranger that is my name mr micawber said mr quinion is known to mr murdstone he takes orders for us on commission when he can get any he has been written to by mr murdstone on the subject of your lodgings and he will receive you as a lodger my address said mr micawber is windsor terrace city road I in short said mr micawber with the same genteel air and in another burst of confidence I live there I made him a bow under the impression said mr micawber that your peregrinations in this metropolis have not as yet been extensive and that you might have some difficulty in penetrating the arcana of the modern babylon in the direction of the city road in short said mr micawber

[1]By permission of the author and *The Reader's Digest.*

in another burst of confidence that you might lose yourself I shall be happy to call this evening and instal you in the knowledge of the nearest way I thanked him with all my heart for it was friendly of him to offer to take that trouble at what hour said mr micawber shall I at about eight said mr quinion at about eight said mr micawber I beg to wish you good day mr quinion I will intrude no longer so he put on his hat and went out with his cane under his arm very upright and humming a tune when he was clear of the counting house

—CHARLES DICKENS, *David Copperfield*

3. A ride of two hundred and odd miles in severe weather is one of the best softeners of a hard bed that ingenuity can devise perhaps it is even a sweetener of dreams for those which hovered over the rough couch of nicholas and whispered their airy nothings in his ear were of an agreeable and happy kind he was making his fortune very fast indeed when the faint glimmer of an expiring candle shone before his eyes and a voice he had no difficulty in recognising as part and parcel of mr squeers admonished him that it was time to rise past seven nickleby said mr squeers has morning come already asked nicholas sitting up in bed ah that it has replied squeers and ready iced too now nickleby come tumble up will you nicholas needed no further admonition but tumbled up at once and proceeded to dress himself by the light of the taper which mr squeers carried in his hand heres a pretty go said that gentleman the pumps froze indeed said nicholas not much interested in the intelligence yes replied squeers you cant wash yourself this morning not wash myself exclaimed nicholas no not a bit of it rejoined squeers tartly so you must be content with giving yourself a dry polish till we break the ice in the well and can get a bucketful out for the boys dont stand staring at me but do look sharp will you

—CHARLES DICKENS, *Nicholas Nickleby*

THE ROUND TABLE

1. As advised in Chapter VII, dictation is a sovereign aid to attaining skill in punctuation. Every day that this chapter is being studied, a short passage from a story or essay selected from the class text in literature or from a current magazine might well be dictated in class.

2. Be particularly careful to avoid:

   (1) The comma splice (See pages 124 and 206-209)

(2) The no-sentence fault (See pages 124 and 203-206)
(3) Using any mark of punctuation
(*a*) between the subject and its verb
(*b*) between the verb and its complement
(*c*) between the last adjective of a series and the noun it modifies
(4) Using a colon, semicolon, or comma between the verb *are* or *were* and a following list of details and examples.

3. Look over your back themes, get the teacher to help you, and ask yourself two questions: (*a*) Is there any principle of punctuation that I do not understand or that I feel uncertain about? (*b*) What seem to be my weak points or prevailing errors in punctuation? Ask for class discussion in any usage you do not feel certain about.

4. Take a page of this textbook assigned by the teacher and explain all the punctuation marks on it, including paragraphing.

5. Do the same thing with a page from any good magazine.

6. In your last two themes draw a ring around every punctuation mark and capital letter and account for its use by stating the rule concerned.

7. Glance back through your last month's (or two months') themes to see what mistakes you made in punctuation. Ask for class discussion on any usage you do not feel certain about.

Answers to Freaks of Punctuation, Page 120

1.
Every lady in this land
Hath twenty nails; upon each hand
Five; and twenty on hands and feet;
And this is true without deceit.

2.
A funny little man told this to me:
"I fell in a snowdrift; in June," said he,
"I went to a ball game; out in the sea
I saw a jellyfish float; up in a tree
I found some gum; in a cup of tea
I stirred my milk; with a big brass key
I opened my door; on my bended knee
I beg your pardon for this," said he,
"But 'tis true when told as it ought to be."

3. That that is, is; that that is not, is not; that that is not, is not that that is; that that is, is not that that is not. Is not that it? It is.

4. It was "and" I said, not "but".

CHAPTER IX

Chain Paragraphs and Jointed Subjects—Simple Explanation

CHAIN PARAGRAPHS

The only real difference between independent paragraphs and chain paragraphs is that, as their names indicate, chain paragraphs are connected while independent paragraphs stand alone. On page 73 an independent paragraph was compared to a one-room cabin or to a single freight car standing by itself on a side-track. Chain paragraphs may be likened to different rooms in the same house connected with one another by halls and doors, or to freight cars in the same train joined together by couplings and coupling pins. Or, to change the figure, an independent paragraph stands alone with its arms folded; a chain paragraph places its hands on the shoulder of the paragraph in front of it, and they all march in the same direction.

WRITING ON JOINTED SUBJECTS

As was stated in Chapter V, the first fundamental in writing is ability to compose independent paragraphs. But we cannot stop there. Much of the writing that we shall be called upon to do both in school and afterwards in the world will consist not of single paragraphs but of a series of paragraphs dealing with the same subject and linked each to each.

So far as exposition and argument are concerned, the way to proceed is very definite and clear. For example, consider the following prescription for writing a four-paragraph theme of explanation. It has almost the value of an exact formula.

There are five necessary steps. To omit any one of them will not only keep you from doing your best work but will almost certainly result in weakness and failure. There is nothing magical in the five steps. They are simply the result of applying to the task of writing the same kind of intelligence and common sense that an architect uses in building a house or that an engineer uses in planning a bridge.

THE FIVE STEPS IN EXPLAINING

(*Before Beginning to Write*)

The First Step: Analysing the Subject into Paragraph Ideas
The Second Step: Choosing the Paragraph Ideas to Be Developed
The Third Step: Arranging the Paragraph Ideas

(*After Beginning to Write*)

The Fourth Step: Announcing the Paragraph Ideas
The Fifth Step: Connecting the Paragraph Ideas

1. The First Step: Analysing the Subject

(*Before Beginning to Write*)

Granted a suitable subject, the first thing to do is to divide the subject up into its parts or elements or points. Henry Ford stated a highly useful principle when he said, "Nothing is particularly hard if you divide it up into small jobs." He was not thinking of writing when he said it, but it holds good for writing themes as well as for making automobiles.

(1) SIZING UP A SITUATION

This first step of analysing the subject is absolutely imperative. Nor is it just one more troublesome process invented by composition teachers and textbook writers to take the joy out of life. The power to analyse, to get at the bottom of things, to size up a situation, to leave no essential factor out of account, to be able to tell the difference between the important, the unimportant, and the most important—this is a demand that the world of business makes on every successful man. The merchant, the banker, the lawyer, the head of any business or important department must have this ability to a marked degree or he will not go far or last long. Under the name of judgment it is the chief factor in business efficiency and material success in life.

The daily situations calling for analysis and decision are so common that we are hardly aware of how frequent they are. Is our next pair of shoes to be tan or to be black? Which moving-picture show shall we go to tonight? Do we want our father to buy a large, heavy car or to buy a smaller, lighter car and put the difference in price into new living-room furniture? Do we wish the family to go this summer to the beach or to the mountains? Which college have you decided to go to? And are your reasons good enough to convince your parents that you are right? Or are you considering whether to leave school and go to work instead of entering college? Are you satisfied with your choice of a profession, or after all should you be planning for something else?

Whether we are aware of it or not, we spend many of our waking moments analysing and deciding such matters as these. Thus when we analyse a subject before beginning to write, what we are really doing is simply utilizing in our writing whatever powers of analysis, decision, and judgment we are fortunate enough to possess.

(2) ANALYSING THE SUBJECT

Analysing the subject is not only the first step in point of time, but it is also the first step in point of importance. You cannot do anything with a subject until you have taken it apart and can thus consider each point individually. Of all the five steps it is the one most generally neglected by inexperienced writers, and to its neglect are due more weak themes than to any other single cause. If "Look before you leap" is a good rule, "Think before you write" is a better one.

Consider the six following subjects. They are all good ones, and every boy or girl in the class will have some ideas about them.

1. Causes of Student Failure in School
2. Qualities of Ideal Manhood
3. Bars to Success in Life
4. Leading Causes of Automobile Wrecks
5. The Advantages of Being a Boy (or a Girl)
6. Why Children Tell Falsehoods

Let us suppose that the first subject is the one assigned—Causes of Student Failure in School. Now the causes of failure are varied and numerous. Some are important, some are unimportant; some affect many students, some affect only a few students. It is clearly out of the question to write a short theme on all the causes or even on any large number of them. To try to do so would end only in naming the causes over without discussing them. In other words the result would be a list instead of a composition.

Let it be agreed, therefore, that we shall deal with only the four leading causes of failure.

In order to do this intelligently, however, we shall have first to jot down all the causes that we can think of and weigh them with one another to decide which are the most important. Suppose that the teacher calls for suggestions on this point from individual pupils. As the various causes are named, they are written down on the board for all to see.

If the class is really in earnest about it and everybody tries to think, the resulting list may take some such shape as the following, which was put together by a class of twenty-two students in twelve minutes' time.

Causes of Student Failure in School

1. Not enough study
2. Lack of interest in subject

3. Sickness
4. Too much participation in student activities
5. Worry
6. Too many outside social activities
7. Poor preparation in previous years
8. Having to do outside work to earn money
9. Carelessness
10. Mentally deficient
11. Inattention in class
12. Not knowing how to study
13. Inability to concentrate
14. Misbehaviour
15. Ill favour of teacher
16. Indifference as to passing
17. Bad companions
18. Dissipation
19. Timidity
20. Poor teaching
21. No ambition
22. Discouragement

In looking over the list, notice that each topic has been jotted down exactly as it was called out by the pupil. No effort was made by the teacher to improve the wording or to avoid duplication. For example, topics 2, 11, 16, and 21 are more or less alike—Lack of interest in subject, Inattention in class, Indifference as to passing, No ambition; as are also numbers 12 and 13—Not knowing how to study and Inability to concentrate. Never mind how helter-skelter or ragged the list of topics looks when you first jot it down. Order and smoothness will come with the second step of choosing and arranging the most suitable topics. The first essential is to get down on paper as long and as varied a list of related topics as you can possibly think up. Nobody can build a house without materials, and at this stage your only building materials are topic ideas.

In the next section we shall take the second steps of choosing and arranging the topics which we wish to develop.

Exercises in Analysis

1. What are some of the essential elements in the following qualities?

Good temper	Real patience
A high sense of honour	Loyalty

2. Suppose you were running for mayor of your town. What needed improvements as to buildings, paving, sewerage, parks, and so forth, would you advocate in your platform? Remember to make no recommendations that you would not be willing to defend and justify before the voters.

3. Suppose that the trustees of your school have $100,000 available for improvements and have appointed you to represent the student body as their adviser. What would you recommend that they should do with the money?

4. Glance again through the list of the Causes of Student Failure on page 168, and see whether you can make any important additions to the list.

5. With the whole class thinking together, and the teacher at the board, take the following two of the remaining subjects suggested on page 168 and analyse them fully in class:

Bars to Success in Life
Leading Causes of Automobile Wrecks

6. Analyse any one or two of the remaining subjects of those given on page 168.

7. For other opportunities for analysis, see the list of Jointed Subjects, pages 185-188.

Suggestions for Analysing and Developing a Subject

The following table includes nearly everything it is possible to do in exposition, or the explaining of ideas. The methods of the first column are best suited to formal essays. The next time ideas are slow in coming to you, run over this table for suggestions.

1. *Define*
2. *Classify*
3. Seek *Origin*
4. Discuss *Changes*
5. Treat *Historically*
6. Show *Cause and Effect*
7. Make a *Comparison* or a *Contrast*
8. *Illustrate* by examples
9. Make a *Hypothesis* (suppose conditions were otherwise)
10. Describe *Uses*
11. Describe your *Feeling toward the Subject*
12. *Criticize*, or go further, and
13. Assign a *Value*
14. Treat as a *Symbol*
15. Think of it as *Evolving, Growing, Having a Future*

2. The Second Step: Choosing the Paragraph Ideas

(Before Beginning to Write)

Analysis provides the working materials, and is thus the first step toward writing. The second step consists in looking through the suggested points and choosing the best of them for development into paragraphs. To do this is much easier than to provide the materials in the first place through analysis.

Consider the twenty-two causes for student failure in school which were listed on pages 168-169. They are of various kinds. Some are large, some small; some important, some unimportant; some duplicate others. Let us limit our choice to four, and let us try to choose wisely. After some discussion and argument the composition class that originally proposed the twenty-two topics decided to develop these four:

Not enough study
Too many outside social activities
Poor preparation in previous years
Not knowing how to study

This is a fairly satisfactory choice, though not everyone would agree on exactly these four. Other good topics that might well have been chosen are these:

Lack of interest in subject
Too much participation in student activities (with special reference to athletics)
Discouragement

These two groups of topics taken together, however, include the cream of the list and would satisfy nearly everybody.

(1) UNITY

Such examples as these illustrate the value of weighing and choosing our topics from a large list of mixed possibilities. If we have analysed thoroughly and chosen wisely, there is no doubt or guesswork about the result. We can feel sure that we have the best possible selection of paragraph ideas. We can also feel sure that every idea which we have selected in this way vitally belongs to the subject. No alien or foreign topic can creep in. In other words, so far as paragraph topics are concerned, what we write will have clear and complete unity. Our chosen ideas will bear directly upon our subject and upon nothing but our subject.

3. The Third Step: Arranging the Paragraph Ideas

(*Before Beginning to Write*)

The arranging of the topic ideas in the clearest and strongest order is the next step. Remember that the order of topics is always important. It always makes some difference, and sometimes makes a great deal of difference, which idea comes first, which comes second and third, and, above all, which comes last.

The safest working rule is to open with the idea that is second in importance, to close with the most important idea, and to put the others in between in the order of climax, or of increasing importance. If we let either (1) the index figures on the letter A or (2) the four "face" cards indicate the relative importance of the topic ideas, the formula for arrangement will be something like this:

First Paragraph . . . . A^2 or King
Second Paragraph . . . . A^4 or Jack
Third Paragraph . . . . A^3 or Queen
Fourth Paragraph . . . . A^1 or Ace.

(1) SPACING PARAGRAPH IDEAS

Along with planning the order of the paragraph ideas goes the need of devoting enough space to each idea in order to develop it properly. We must avoid at all costs writing ourselves out on the first two or three paragraphs, and then, since the theme has reached the required length, dismissing our last idea, important as it is, in a hurried sentence or two. That is almost exactly how *not* to write a good theme. Yet it is a danger we are all likely to fall into unless we do a little intelligent planning as to paragraph length at the same time that we plan the paragraph order.

This is very easy. All that we have to do in a short four- or five-paragraph theme is to reserve enough space for the all-important last paragraph, at least as much as we give to the first paragraph and probably a little more. An average four-paragraph theme, of the type we are considering here, will probably run to not much less than two pages or to not much more than three pages. That means that the average length of the paragraphs will come somewhere between one-half and two-thirds of a page, or at the outside between two-fifths and four-fifths of a page each.

A safe rule of thumb, if not followed too closely, is to make no paragraph less than half a page or more than a page long.

Keeping in mind this requirement of paragraph length as well as that of paragraph order, and applying both of them to the topic already chosen, we get some such result as this:

FOUR LEADING CAUSES OF STUDENT FAILURE

First Paragraph. . . . Poor preparation in previous years
(Length: three-quarters to one-half page)
Second Paragraph . . . Not knowing how to study
(Length: about one-half page)
Third Paragraph . . . Too many outside social activities
(Length: about one-half page)
Fourth Paragraph . . . Indifference and laziness
(Length: three-quarters to one-half page)

(2) CLEARNESS AND EMPHASIS

Choosing the topic ideas, as already noted, secures unity. Arranging the topic ideas before beginning to write secures both clearness and emphasis. It secures clearness, for when the topic ideas are thus weighed and considered in advance and as a consequence are arranged in the most suitable order their clearness is assured, since the inner essential of clearness *is* effective order.

Arranging the topic ideas according to the plan suggested likewise secures emphasis, for one-half of emphasis consists in putting important ideas in emphatic positions, and we have agreed to put the most important topic idea last (which is the most emphatic place) and the next most important topic idea first (which is the next most emphatic place). The other half of emphasis consists in giving sufficient space (or time) to the proper development of important ideas instead of letting them straggle along and tail off into nothingness after we have exhausted our energy in the first couple of paragraphs. By planning in advance, therefore, to make the last paragraph at least as long as the first paragraph, we avoid sacrificing our most important idea and thus give it emphasis by space as well as emphasis by position.

Exercises in Choosing and Arranging Topics

1. According to the method suggested, choose and arrange the four (or three, or five) best topic ideas from the class list made up in Exercise No. 5, page 170, on

    Bars to Success in Life
    Leading Causes of Automobile Wrecks

2. Choose and arrange the best topic ideas resulting from Exercise No. 6, page 170.

3. Read over the following suggested list of the Ten Marks of an Educated Man, from an article by Albert Edward Wiggam in the *American Magazine*. Choose and arrange the four or five marks you think most important. Be prepared to defend your opinions if necessary.

THE TEN MARKS OF AN EDUCATED MAN

(1) He keeps his mind open on every question until the evidence is all in.
(2) He listens to the man who knows.
(3) He never laughs at new ideas.

(4) He cross-examines his daydreams.
(5) He knows his strong point and plays it.
(6) He knows the value of good habits and how to form them.
(7) He knows when not to think and when to call in the expert to think for him.
(8) You can't sell him magic.
(9) He lives the forward-looking, outward-looking life.
(10) He cultivates a love of the beautiful.

4. Recently a group of 369 high-school boys and 415 girls were asked to check a list of "desirable qualities" in a father.

The quality which received the largest vote was "Spending time with his children".

The others were rated in the following order:

(2) Respecting his children's opinions.
(3) Being an active church member.
(4) Being a college graduate.
(5) Never nagging his children about what they do.
(6) Making plenty of money.
(7) Being well dressed.
(8) Being prominent in social life.
(9) Having a love of music and poetry.
(10) Owning a good-looking car.

Choose and arrange the four or five qualities you think most desirable.

4. The Fourth Step: Announcing the Paragraph Ideas in the First Sentence

(*After Beginning to Write*)

The most important part of skyscrapers and of railroad bridges is underground. In these structures, what we see depends for both its efficiency and its safety upon what we do not see. So it is with writing. The three important steps just described must all be taken before we begin to write at all. A thoughtful mental foundation must be laid.

After we have (1) analysed the subject, (2) chosen the best topic ideas, and (3) arranged them in the proper order, we are then ready to begin to write—and not till then. Since clearness and definiteness are our principal aims in this type of theme, the best way to start is with a sentence of enumeration, as it is called, which names over for the reader the topic ideas to be discussed. In this way the writer lets the reader know at the start (1) exactly what aspects of the subject are to be considered and (2) in what order they will be taken up. The value of an opening sentence of this kind in a theme of explanation is evident.

To illustrate exactly what is meant, glance back at the first topic outline of the Causes of Student Failure in School, on page 173, and let us suppose we are starting to write a four-paragraph theme based on it. The opening sentence would take some such form as this:

> The four leading causes of student failure in school are poor preparation in previous years, not knowing how to study, too much indulgence in outside social activities, and downright laziness.

You will note that this sentence is simply, almost barely phrased.

In case we wished to begin with a somewhat more elaborate sentence, we might open in this way:

> The reasons why students fail in school are both numerous and varied, but probably the four most important ones are these: students are poorly prepared in previous years, they do not know how to study, they indulge too much in social activities, and they do not spend enough time on their studies.

Another, less formal beginning would be this:

> I feel sure, from what I have seen, that most students fail in school because they come in poorly prepared, don't know how to study, waste time at too many parties, and were born lazy.

From these examples it will be seen that the opening sentence of enumeration can be either matter-of-fact and formal in tone, or more personal and informal if desired. In either case, attention should be paid to two particulars: (1) the sentence must name the topic ideas in exactly the order in which they will be developed later in the theme; and (2) there are only two correct ways to punctuate: (a) Use no punctuation mark at all after *are* if the topic ideas follow directly; (b) use the colon after such expressions as "——are these"; or "——are as follows"; or "——are the following"—as in the second of the illustrative sentences on the Causes of Student Failure in School. In no case use either the comma or the semicolon after *are* or whatever verb it is that takes the place of *are*.

Exercises in Naming the Paragraph Ideas in the First Sentence

Write two opening sentences of enumeration, one simple and formal and one more informal and personal, on each of the following subjects:

1. Bars to Success in Life.
2. Leading Causes of Automobile Wrecks.
3. The Advantages of Being a Boy (or Girl).
4. Why Children Tell Falsehoods.
5. The Marks of an Educated Man.

In accordance with this plan, be sure that the first sentence of every theme written on any of the jointed subjects suggested on pages 185-188 below announces the topic ideas in the order in which you will develop them. In spite of the definiteness of the form of these opening sentences, try to make them as varied and original as possible.

(1) WRITING THE THEME

After the four preceding steps have been taken, with the subject analysed and the topic ideas chosen, arranged, and named in the opening sentence, the actual writing of the theme begins in earnest. Each paragraph in turn, from the first to the last, is to be developed in detail as was explained in the chapter on the Independent Paragraph, page 73. Remember that there is no essential difference between the independent paragraph and the chain paragraph except that the former stands by itself and the latter belongs to a group. Each needs a topic sentence, or at least a definite topic idea; each must have enough definite details to make the topic idea clear or vivid to the reader; and each is the better for a short striking end-sentence which drives home and clinches the topic idea.

To each of our chain paragraphs, therefore, we must apply the same three questions as were applied to the independent paragraph:

1. Does the opening sentence state the paragraph idea simply and definitely?
2. Are there enough details and particulars to make the paragraph idea clear and interesting?
3. Is the closing sentence good enough to deserve the place of honour at the end?

There is, however, one important additional requirement that the chain paragraph must fulfil: it must be connected with what goes before, and must lead up to what comes after.

To meet this requirement is the purpose of the fifth and last step.

5. The Fifth Step: Connecting the Paragraph Ideas

(1) TRANSITION WORDS AND PHRASES

The word "transition" comes from the Latin, and means a "going over" or a "passing across". In a mental sense it means exactly what the Anglo-Saxon word "bridge" means in a physical sense. Both are means of getting from one thing to another thing. By the aid of bridges we pass over gaps in the ground, and by the aid of transition words and phrases we pass over gaps in the thought and follow easily the writer's ideas from paragraph to paragraph.

Transition words and phrases are not only bridges but guide-posts and road signs as well. They not only show the way but also carry us over. Thus in their double duty of directing mental traffic and of furnishing a bridge for it, transition words and phrases are of the greatest possible service in exposition and argument. They are "thought signals". The careful writer makes constant use of them. They are sovereign aids both to clearness of expression and to ease in reading.

A necessary step, therefore, in writing chain paragraphs is first to become keenly aware of the value and necessity of the various kinds of transition, and secondly to train ourselves to make regular and increasing use of them in writing.

Although our language has a great variety of transition expressions, their number is after all not so large that we cannot become thoroughly familiar with most of the good ones. The following list contains the commonest and best. Consider it carefully, for it is a most useful collection.

(2) TRANSITION TABLE

1. DEMONSTRATIVES: **this, that, these, those**
2. NUMERALS AND SYNONYMS FOR NUMERALS: **first, in the first place, to begin with, secondly, in the second place, lastly**
3. "AND" AND ITS SYNONYMS (continuing the same line of thought): **again, also, in the next place, once more, furthermore, moreover, likewise, besides, similarly, for example, for instance**
4. "BUT" AND ITS SYNONYMS (introducing opposed or contrasting thoughts): **but, then, nevertheless, still, however, at the same time, yet, in spite of that, on the other hand, on the contrary**
5. DEGREES OF CERTAINTY: **certainly, surely, doubtless, indeed, perhaps, possibly, probably, anyhow, anyway, in all probability, in all likelihood, at all events, in any case**
6. CONSEQUENCE OR RESULT: **therefore, consequently, accordingly, thus, as a result, in consequence of this, as might be expected, so**

All these connectives are satisfactory bridge words except two—*and* and *so*. The trouble with these words is that they have been worn out through being overworked.

(3) LINKING CHAIN PARAGRAPHS

As each paragraph idea is reached in turn, from the first one to the last one, we must make clear to the reader exactly how and in what order our paragraphs are being developed. In fact, we must not only make this so clear that our readers can easily follow the development, but we must make it so clear that our readers cannot possibly *fail* to follow the development. This sounds like a hard requirement, but in a theme of explanation it is a just one.

Two things are necessary: (1) at the beginning of each paragraph the paragraph idea should be clearly stated in the topic sentence, and (2) *some definite transition word or phrase* should be used to link the paragraph with what has gone before.

The first of these two necessities, that of the topic sentence, has been dealt with in detail in the section on Independent Paragraphs. To state the paragraph topic clearly and definitely is always helpful in explaining; it is more than helpful in the type of explanatory theme we are considering here—it is essential. Be sure, therefore, that the opening sentence of each paragraph states the paragraph idea simply and unmistakably.

The second necessity is definitely to link each paragraph with the preceding paragraph by means of a transition word or phrase like those suggested in the list on page 179. Theoretically this is an easy thing to do, but for some reason it is hard to form the habit of doing it regularly. All experienced writers know the value of it, and instinctively use transition words to guide and assist their readers from paragraph to paragraph.

ELEPHANTS MARCH LIKE THIS, AND SO SHOULD PARAGRAPHS

This definite linking of paragraph with paragraph is the fifth and last of the five steps in writing. If we now apply it to the illustrative outlines of the theme on the Causes of

Student Failure, the final result will be something like this. Transition words are italicized in order to call attention to them.

THE FOUR CHIEF CAUSES OF STUDENT FAILURE

First Paragraph The four leading causes of student failure in school are poor preparation in previous years, not knowing how to study, too much indulgence in outside social activities, and not studying hard enough.

Second Paragraph *In the first place*, poor preparation in previous years often brings about failures in such continuing subjects as English, history, mathematics, and the languages.

(This cause of poor preparation is developed in the rest of the second paragraph, about three-quarters of a page long.)

Third Paragraph *In the second place*, no small number of students fail because they spend too much time on outside social activities and pleasures.

(This cause is developed in the third paragraph, about one-half a page long.)

Fourth Paragraph *A third important cause* of student failure is not knowing how to study.

(This cause is developed in the fourth paragraph, about one-half a page long.)

Fifth Paragraph *The fourth and probably the chief reason why students fail* is simply that they do not study hard enough to pass.

(This cause is developed in the fifth and last paragraph, about three-quarters of a page long.)

Note how exactly this skeleton outline illustrates the five steps that have been dealt with in this chapter. It definitely accomplishes the following results:

1. Before it could be put into its present shape, real

preliminary thinking had to be done in (*a*) analysing the subject, (*b*) choosing and (*c*) arranging the topic ideas to be developed.

2. The opening sentence of enumeration names over the topics to be discussed.
3. The first sentence of each paragraph
   (*a*) states clearly the topic idea of the paragraph and
   (*b*) by means of definite transition words links its paragraph with the preceding paragraph and advances the thought development one distinct stage.

To sum up, in the five sentences of this skeleton outline there is present every necessary element for writing an adequate explanation of the proposed subject. In addition, it meets all the demands of unity, clearness, and emphasis. Moreover, it has the clearness of an architect's plan and the efficiency that comes only from intelligent thinking. In short, it offers an ideal pattern for explaining.

STUDENT ESSAYS

The Four Essentials of Greatness

(The way this theme was put together offers an interesting exercise both in independent paragraphs and in jointed subjects. Each of the four paragraphs was written by a different student, the first and last by girls, as it happens, and the second and third by boys. The paragraphs were written independently of each other as supposed editorials for the school paper. The following week the teacher and the class put them together, chose the title, and wrote the part of the theme that is printed in italics, namely, the sentence of enumeration and the transition phrases connecting the paragraphs. Thus four independent paragraphs on kindred subjects were linked into one connected treatment.)

No man can be considered truly great who lacks courage, enthusiasm, determination, or sincerity.

To begin with, courage is such a simple word and yet such a necessary quality. Are you courageous? Have you, as a school boy or girl, the spirit to overcome your obstacles both in your school and outside activities without help? Have you, as a businessman, the moral courage to be strictly honest with all your competitors and your clients? Are you, the parents of the nation, strong enough to raise your children to be worth-while citizens by allowing them to make their own decisions when necessary or do you choose the easier way and decide for them? Have you, as a Christian, the fearlessness that is necessary to do what you know is right? Courage is bravery in both the physical and moral sense; it is that quality of mind which meets danger and opposition with firmness and intrepidity. Without it one loses everything; with it one conquers his world.

In the next place, enthusiasm is necessary for one's complete success in any undertaking. Under its powerful influence men often accomplish astounding things in many fields of endeavour. It is human nature for people to be enthusiastic over things not in their line of duty rather than over things which they must do, but there are a few people who are more fortunate in this respect. These few usually are brilliant successes in their particular vocations. Without enthusiasm all progress in the scientific field, in religion, in civilization, would be greatly retarded if not stopped altogether. Without enthusiasm there can be no great athletes, no great writers, no great scientists, no great nation.

In addition to courage and enthusiasm, determination is also necessary. To hang on although believing you are beaten, to keep trying because you don't want to admit defeat—these are two elements of determination. Nothing succeeds like success and nothing fails like failure. No man has probably ever scaled the heights who has not had the sickening feeling that his work was all in vain and wondered why he kept struggling when the odds were so much against him. I read something once which particularly impressed me—"What is a failure?"

> "It is only a spur to the man who receives it right
> To go in and fight once more.
> If you've never failed, it's an even guess
> You never have won a high success."

The grit to come back and lick the thing that licked you—that's determination.

The last and most important characteristic of all is sincerity. Sincerity is one of the most beautiful words in the English language. It carries with it a multiplicity of associations; nobility of spiritual qualities, genuineness, steadfastness, and permanence. It is the pure gold ingredient of friendship, the bed rock upon which friendship is built. The man who has a reputation for sincerity is indeed fortunate. His opinions are valid, his advice is sought, and he is highly esteemed. As a friend he is without parallel. His frankness may hurt, but he is genuinely interested in you, and his advice is worth twice that of an obsequious flatterer. His sincerity includes not only meaning what he says but being honest in behaviour. His business life is beyond reproach, and he is honest in all dealings with his fellow men. His character rings true and mellow like an old Chinese gong which has stood the test of ages.

THE ROUND TABLE

1. The aim of this whole chapter on Chain Paragraphs and Jointed Subjects is to give the ability to accomplish the five steps in writing, in the order named, and consequently to enable the student to draw up complete skeleton outlines like the one quoted.

With this outline as guide, prepare similar outlines, one or two at a time, on the remaining subjects referred to in previous sections of this chapter.

2. Using the subjects in the list on pages 185-188, the teacher should assign as many (*a*) skeleton outlines and (*b*) complete themes as may be needed in order to give the whole class almost automatic ease in handling jointed subjects.

3. Note the fact that the proof of a satisfactory theme is the ability of anyone to get a clear understanding of the thought development from hearing the key sentences read aloud. Each day themes are to be handed in, several pupils should be asked to read the key sentences to the class. Pay particular heed to clearness and definiteness both of language and of transition.

4. The pupils themselves should correct one another's themes once each week. The following plan has been found to work well:

(*a*) Redistribute the themes when they are handed in so that each pupil will have someone else's theme.

(*b*) Ask that each pupil (1) try to correct all mistakes in spelling, punctuation, grammar, paragraphing, and sentence structure; (2) write a general comment or opinion on the theme as a whole; (3) give the theme a grade and sign and date it. If desired, this can be done in class the day the themes are handed in.

(*c*) Redistribute the themes again, and have a second pupil do the same three things that were done by the first pupil.

(*d*) The teacher will then glance over the themes finally, correcting them in red pencil or ink, grade them, and hand them back to be looked over again by the writer and the two pupils who corrected them.

Jointed Subjects for Themes

Not all the subjects which are listed below lend themselves to the method of development advocated in this chapter. Although the fundamental procedure of analysis, selection, and arrangement will remain largely unchanged, it is often effective to vary the introductory and concluding paragraphs. "Suggestions for Analysing and Developing a Subject" on page 170 offer many hints as to how such variety may be obtained. The following suggestions for varying the introductory paragraph will be found especially useful:

1. Use a striking example which illustrates the subject. If this example employs dialogue it is likely to be even more effective.
2. By reference to recent events show that the subject is timely.
3. Describe your feeling toward the subject.
4. Suppose that conditions were otherwise.
5. Make a comparison or a contrast.
6. Define any term in the subject which requires explanation.

When a separate concluding paragraph is desired, the following suggestions offer possibilities:

1. Summarize or re-state the main ideas. This method is especially useful in argument.
2. Consider future trends.
3. Assign a value.
4. Suppose conditions were otherwise.
5. Make a comparison or a contrast.
6. Use a striking example.

For additional suggestions see the chapter on "The Personal Essay", pages 476-486.

SCHOOL LIFE

1. Sicknesses High-School Boys and Girls Are Subject To, and How They Can Be Avoided
2. How to Develop a Vocabulary

3. What We Can Learn from the Dictionary
4. Traits of a Good Athlete
5. Why Go to College?
6. Pros and Cons of Examinations
7. Pros and Cons of School Athletics
8. Interesting School Traditions
9. Advantages (Disadvantages) of a Large School
10. How to Be Unpopular
11. If I Were a Teacher
12. Our Most Valuable School Organizations
13. School Pests
14. Why Join a Hobby Club?
15. Why Students Leave School

FAMILY LIFE

1. A Good Time Today versus a Good Time in My Grandfather's (Grandmother's) Day
2. Sounds That Keep Me Awake at Night
3. Guests I Have Insulted
4. My Faults According to My Family
5. Practical Ways High-School Students Can Economize
6. The Essentials of a Good Living-Room
7. Trials of an Only Daughter (Son)
8. Tragedies of My Childhood
9. Advantages (Disadvantages) of Being the Youngest
10. Ambitions My Family Have for Me

COMMUNITY LIFE

1. The Chief Needs of Our Town
2. What Our City (or County or Provincial) Taxes Buy for Us
3. The Prevention of Unnecessary Noises
4. The Chief Amusements of Our Locality
5. Some Interesting Local Superstitions
6. The Three (Four) Most Beautiful Spots near ——
7. What Laws Affect Me Directly
8. Advantages of a Community Centre
9. What Our Community Offers to the Tourist

OUT-OF-DOORS LIFE

1. Native Wild Flowers
2. How Animals Protect Themselves
3. Useful Trees of My Locality
4. Useful and Harmful Birds

5. Bird Enemies
6. How Seeds Are Scattered
7. Fish That Are Found in My Locality
8. Hunting versus Fishing As a Sport
9. How to Train a Dog
10. Habits of My Neighbour's Dog
11. The More Intelligent Insects
12. Instances of Memory in Animals
13. What Flowers Bloom First, and Where
14. Tricks of Horses (Dogs)
15. Pets of Which My Family Did Not Approve
16. Pets I Have Loved and Lost
17. Camera versus Gun
18. How Animals Prepare for Winter
19. Birds I have Studied
20. Forest Protection

MISCELLANEOUS

1. Why Some Girls Are So Popular (Unpopular)
2. Why People Buy the —— Automobile
3. Four Great Leaders
4. The Essential Qualities of a Good Farmer
5. Advantages (Disadvantages) of Farm Life
6. Qualifications for Leadership
7. Traits of Character I Most Admire
8. Traits of Good Sportsmanship
9. The Beach versus the Mountains
10. Reading a Newspaper and Reading a Magazine
11. Things in Modern Life That I Am Dissatisfied With
12. Ghosts I Should Like to Meet
13. Some Uses of Electricity
14. My Debts—Other Than Financial
15. My Favourite Magazine—and Why
16. Four Wonders of the Modern World
17. Collecting Stamps (or Picture Post Cards)
18. Things I Like to Eat
19. Careers Others Have Chosen for Me
20. My Boyhood (Girlhood) Ambitions Five Years Ago
21. What I Have Learned from People Who Dislike Me
22. If I Had Three Wishes
23. Things I Hate to Do
24. Things about Girls (Boys) That Irritate Me
25. The Five Books I Would Take with Me if I were to Live Alone on a Desert Island

26. How to Drive Safely
27. Living Men and Women Who Are Doing Things That Are Worth While
28. How to Use a Dictionary
29. Radio Entertainers I Like Best
30. Animal Traits in Human Beings
31. Human Traits in Animals
32. Fears of Childhood
33. Advertising Signs Seen on a Trip
34. Forms of Stinginess
35. My Pet Superstitions
36. Hobbies That Are Worth While
37. The People Who Come into a Drug Store
38. Three Books I Want to Own, and Why
39. Characteristics of the Days of the Week
40. Harmful (Beneficial) Recent Inventions
41. How the Days of the Week Got Their Names
42. The Cleverest Ads I've Noticed Lately
43. Things Which No Longer Shock the Public
44. The Disadvantages of Having Ears
45. Nicknames of History
46. Mistakes of Women about Small Boys
47. What Some Outsiders Think of School
48. Poisons in Common Use Today
49. The Best Cartoon I Remember
50. People Who Bore Me
51. The Art of Hitch-Hiking
52. People I Have Copied
53. Heroes of the Sport Page
54. Things I Should Like to Forget
55. Red-Letter Days in My Life
56. Vocations Which Interest Me
57. The Uses of Adversity
58. Why I Chose ——— as a Hobby

CHAPTER X

Oral Composition

Oral Composition is the most direct approach a school can make to the needs of real life.

—C. H. WARD

1. The Speaker and the Modern World

Depending upon what profession we enter, probably all of us after graduation will speak from a hundred to a thousand times more than we write. We sometimes call certain of the high-school courses practical and certain others theoretical. Whether or not this distinction is wise, one fact is certain: the English language is the only thing in the entire course of study that every one of us will have to use, every day, during the rest of his life. The ability to write well and the ability to speak well, taken together, are the most definitely and unfailingly useful of all our acquirements.

Make no mistake about it. Whether you like it or not, you are going to be called on frequently in later life to speak in public—sometimes with previous notice, sometimes without. As was said in the first chapter: "As life is constituted today, this is inevitable. The only way to avoid it is to sink so low in the business and social scale that nothing you can do or say will make any difference to anybody else."

Do not underestimate the meaning of this situation to you personally, and the importance of doing all you can while in school to help prepare yourself to meet it. Concerning the close relationship between your speaking in school and your speaking in the world, Leverett S. Lyon of the University of Chicago has pointed out: "If a student, using material with which he is familiar, can get a desired result *here* and *now* with *this* audience, he can, using material with which he is *then* familiar, get a desired result *then* and *there* with *that* audience." This statement is fundamentally true. Although there is a tremendous difference between the high school and the university of hard knocks, as the world has been called, the same qualities that enable you to succeed in school will carry you to success in the world.

2. What to Speak On

Both the success and the pleasure of oral composition depend in no small degree on having a suitable subject. The best subject for you is the one you know most about and are most interested in, no matter what it is. Do not be afraid that your audience will not like it too. If you are enthusiastic about it, they will become enthusiastic also. At the end of this chapter are ten suggested types of subjects. They comprise nearly all the possible varieties. Look through the list and choose the five kinds of subjects you think you could do best with. You will not like them all, but some of them should certainly appeal to you.

Possibly the two easiest types will be numbers 1 and 2, Incident and Simple Explanation. As for the first, interesting things are happening around us or to us every day; and as for the second, there is sure to be something that each of us knows better how to do or to make than does anyone else in class. All of the topics contain possibilities; excellent talks have been made on all of them.

3. Delivery

Much more than half the effectiveness of any speech comes from the way it is delivered. Exactly the same talk given by one speaker will be interesting and convincing, and given by another speaker will be boring and weak. Call to mind the speakers whom you like best, and in all probability you will find that what you like is not what they say so much as the way they say it. Delivery is all-important.

One's delivery depends upon a number of factors, and is as subtle and complex as personality itself. In fact, at bottom, delivery is simply personality speaking, and a strong, pleasing, sincere personality is nearly always a guarantee of a strong, pleasing, sincere speech.

(1) BEARING

How you stand and bear yourself is an important element in your delivery. You should try to stand straight without seeming stiff or wooden, and at the same time to be at ease without seeming slouchy or careless. The natural constraint that we all feel when facing an audience sometimes makes us sprawl against the teacher's desk, rock on our toes, twist and squirm about, and take strange attitudes. Unless it makes you self-conscious, it will help you to practise speaking at home before a large mirror, particularly after having had the benefit of the criticisms and suggestions of teacher and classmates. One way to insure that you will make a good speech in public is to have made that speech many times in private.

As you stand before the class, look directly toward them, not at the floor or the ceiling or out of the window. It is best not to gaze directly into the eyes of those on the first row or two lest you become too conscious of them and forget those in the back of the room. Look rather at the last row, speaking by turns to the student in the right-hand rear corner, in the centre of the back row, and in the left-hand rear corner. If you can hold the attention of the back row, as a matter of course you will interest everybody in between. Pause, change position slightly, and address a different part of the back row when you pass from one topic to another in explaining, or from one incident to another in telling a story. Remember that your audience have no paragraph indentations before them to indicate breaks in the thought.

(2) VOICE

Your voice is the most important physical trait of your personality. Much more depends upon it than you realize. Call to mind several people whom you do not like, and you will be almost sure to find that they have disagreeable voices. As Robert Quillen puts it in one of his *Letters from a Bald-Headed Dad to His Red-Headed Daughter*: "Many a girl who seems to have a fortune in her face and figure is revealed as a bankrupt when she opens her mouth. Speech reveals far more than the meaning of words. It reveals home influence, early environment, breeding, character. It is a window you open to show strangers your history."

Study your own voice carefully and critically. Listen to it as you would to the voice of a stranger whom you are anxious to size up. Is your voice pleasant or unpleasant? high? harsh? whining? nasal? hoarse? breathy? monotonous? What, if anything, is the matter with it? Seek the criticism of fellow students and ask the teacher privately for a frank opinion of it. Some voices are by nature better than others, but all voices, whether good, bad, or indifferent, can be greatly improved by care and practice.

Next only in importance to the quality of the voice itself comes the way you use it. For practical speaking purposes, an average voice well used is as effective as a good voice poorly used. As you speak, have constantly in mind not the people nearest you but those farthest from you, in the extreme rear of the room. You will not need to shout. An overloud voice is always disagreeable. But you must make a conscious effort to have your voice carry over the heads of the front half of the room and prolong itself until it reaches the rear wall. Most beginning speakers have two prevailing faults: (*a*) they speak too fast, and (*b*) they speak too low. Try to avoid both of these mistakes. It is a good rule to have it understood in class that if anyone cannot hear the speaker, he should rise quietly in his seat for a moment or raise his hand. This will not disturb the speaker and will let him know when he should raise his voice a little. Try also not to keep the same tone and the same speed all the time. Vary the pitch of the voice, and also its force and rapidity of utterance. Monotony of either pitch or rate is deadly.

(3) ENUNCIATION

Enunciation refers to the distinctness or indistinctness with which you utter your words. Good enunciation means speaking words clearly and crisply; it means giving full tone value to all syllables, especially to the final consonants of each word, with direct reference to troublesome sounds like final *-gth, -th, -g, -gs, -ing, -k, -ks, -t, -st, -sts, -d,* and *-en.* We should avoid slurring and blunting, and not say *an', san',* and *thousan'* for *and, sand,* and *thousand*; or *fer* or *fuh* for *for*; or *I saw 'im* and *I heard 'um* for *I saw him* and *I heard them*; or *whut* and *wuz* for *what* (*whŏt*) and *was* (*wŏz*); or *didjer, meetcher,* and *dontcher* for *did you, meet you,* and *don't you*; or *Uhmurricun* for *American*; or *fif, govermunt,* and *kep* for *fifth, government,* and *kept*; or *comin'* and *goin'* for *coming* and *going.* We will not continue such confused enunciation as makes possible a quip like the following: "Use *fortify* in a sentence." "That's easy. This suit cost me *fortifi'* dollars." Nor will we blunt, swallow, or otherwise maim such long-suffering words as *literature, record, round, children, arctic, history, sophomore, absolute, recognize, candidate, finally,* and *quarterly.* We will pronounce differently *affect* and *effect*; *real* and *reel*; *poplar* and *popular*; *pillow* and *pillar*; *statue, stature,* and *statute.*

To make everybody in the class understand what we are saying, we shall have to speak more slowly, more loudly, and more distinctly than at first would seem necessary. On these points the criticism of teacher and classmates will be most helpful. To acquire a good clear enunciation will take real effort and continued practice on our part. When we are tempted to give up trying and wonder if it is worth the trouble it takes, we should think of George Bernard Shaw's vigorous words in the first act of *Pygmalion*: "Remember that you are a human being with a soul and the divine gift of articulate speech; that your native language is the language of Shakespeare and Milton and the Bible; and don't sit there crooning like a bilious pigeon."

(4) PRONUNCIATION

Unlike enunciation, pronunciation is not concerned primarily with distinctness of utterance, but with (*a*) the proper placing of the accent and (*b*) giving the correct sound to the different letters and syllables of a word. Pronunciation is concerned with individual words, and enunciation with phrases and groups of words. Good pronunciation and good enunciation usually go hand in hand, for the person who is careful about the one is likely to be careful also about the other. It is entirely possible, however, to enunciate a word clearly and at the same time to mispronounce it, or to pronounce a word correctly and to enunciate it indistinctly. Mistakes in pronunciation come from ignorance; mistakes in enunciation, from carelessness.

Rightly or wrongly the world of society attaches great importance to pronunciation, for pronunciation is one of the readiest means of judging a person's education and culture. One of the surest ways to excite ridicule is to mispronounce a word in company. The smiles may be politely concealed while the unfortunate mispronouncer is present, but they will come out after he has gone. If you like to be laughed at, there is no better way than to be guilty of such pronunciations as *ellum* for *elm*, *drownded* for *drowned*, *genuīne* for *genuĭne*, *defi′cit*, for *def′icit*, *hospit′able* for *hos′pitable*, *mischee′vous* for *mis′chievous*, *alloomni* for *alumni*, and other similar unfortunate slips.

This question of pronunciation will matter tremendously to you in after life. As someone once expressed it, we should take the best of care both of our teeth and of our pronunciation, and for the same reason: every time we open our mouths, somebody gets an impression. A later chapter[1] in this book is devoted to pronunciation, and goes into this fascinating subject in detail. For the present, take full advantage of the work in oral composition in order to find out your prevailing mispronunciations and how to correct them. To do this you will need to pay close heed not only to the criticism of your own talk but to the criticisms of the talks of the other speakers as well.

(5) USE OF NOTES

In making the talk you should get along without notes if possible. If, however, the subject is a complicated one, with a large number of points or subdivisions, or if you feel nervous and need the notes to give you confidence, you should be allowed to have them. Often the mere fact that notes are available if needed will enable a speaker to go through the entire talk without having to refer to them at all.

If notes are used, they should be few and unobtrusive. Best for the purpose are cards or slips of paper three by five inches, with the notes written across the short way so that the cards can be held conveniently in the hand. In addition to a brief list of the topics to be followed, a good opening and a good closing sentence might be written out for safety's sake, though they should not be read from the card if you can remember them. By all means avoid memorizing your talk. To do so is to deliver a declamation, not make a speech, and destroys both the spirit and the benefit of what you are trying to do. It is better to fail outright than not to make a fair-and-square attempt.

If the idea of standing up before the class and speaking to them makes your heart play leapfrog, remember two things: (1) your audience is usually friendly and easily interested in what you are interested in; (2) though you may not realize it, every member of the class is just as scared as you are when his time comes to speak. Unfortunately there is no

[1]Chapter XVII.

way of avoiding a feeling of restraint and embarrassment in making a speech in public. Even trained and experienced speakers suffer from it to a certain extent. The best way to lessen it is to choose as good a subject as you can, and become so absorbed in it that you will forget yourself in your effort to share it completely with others.

All criticism of class talks should be helpful and constructive. When any member is giving a talk the ideal attitude is for the whole class to consider itself a committee of friends to help that member improve his bearing and voice, and to correct his mistakes—in short, to help him learn to do well the same thing that every member of the class in turn is trying to learn this year. Both frankness and kindness are needed; either without the other is unavailing. To pick flaws only, without a word of praise, is discouraging; to praise indiscriminately, without noting faults, is actually harmful. A good plan is to devote the first part of the criticism to commending the good points of the talk, the middle part to pointing out mistakes and corrections, and the last part to any related matters or general observations suggested either by what was said or by the way it was said.

Since only one student can speak at a time, every student, depending upon how large the class is, has a chance to profit by the criticism concerning other speakers twenty or thirty times oftener than by the criticism of his own speech. A good course in oral composition will eliminate most of the commonest errors in grammar and pronunciation if a class takes the work seriously and really tries. This is too valuable a chance to miss.

In detail, it has been found that marked and permanent improvement is made in the sixteen following troublesome verbs which cause more than four-fifths of all our verb errors:

do	run	sit	begin
see	come	set	ring
break	go	lie	take
give	eat	lay	write

Study their principal parts and practise on them till they are thoroughly familiar to you. See pages 31-33.

In the oral composition class also, everyone has a good chance to meet and conquer these seven prize speech demons:

but what (for **but that**)
***everyone—they**
between you and I
***these kind**
kind of a
***like for as**
***best of any**

*There is a tendency in current colloquial usage in favour of the four starred forms, but standard literary usage is still decisively against them.

Finally, as time goes on, we can learn to bring under control the four artful annexers *and*, *and then*, *and so*, and *and-er*.

These are no light achievements.

6. Desirable Techniques in Speeches for Special Occasions

The following is a summary of points to be remembered when making public addresses for special occasions.[1]

1. To keep in mind the main purpose of the speech
2. To stay within the time limit
3. To know the facts and to state them clearly
4. To direct all efforts toward promoting a feeling of friendliness and ease
5. To begin interestingly and to close gracefully
6. To give definite and concrete reasons for one's advocacy of a cause
7. To stimulate desirable emotions, as loyalty, justifiable pride, enthusiasm for or interest in a cause or activity, without disparaging or stirring antagonism toward other persons or causes
8. To introduce light touches and amusing anecdotes when appropriate
9. To express appreciation when it is due, and to do so without flattering and in other than a stereotyped way

[1] *An Experience Curriculum in English*, pp. 183, 184.

Suggestions for Subjects of Talks before the Class

(See also the lists of subjects, pages 185-188, 452-453, and 487-497.)

1. Incident or Story

Personal experiences; stories of the family; legends of the province or the neighbourhood; folk tales; incidents in the lives of famous men and women; retelling of short stories or chapters from novels or of stirring narrative poems like "Herve Riel", "Tam o' Shanter", "John Gilpin's Ride", "The Pied Piper of Hamelin", "The One Hoss Shay", "The Blind Men and the Elephant", "The Skeleton in Armour", "Horatius at the Bridge", "The Highwayman", and so forth.

2. Explanation of a Process, or How to Do or to Make Something

There is some one thing that you know more about than anyone else in class. No matter how small or trivial it may seem, explain it in detail. Use a blackboard sketch or drawing if it will make the explanation clearer or will give you confidence.

3. Current Event

Interesting side-lights on travel, invention, discovery, current history, and so forth, taken usually from good magazines.

4. Book Report

Not to be confined to a mere retelling of the plot. Properly used, a great aid to the course in Supplementary Reading and a direct stimulation to wider and more intelligent class reading. If two students report on the same day, one can deal with the author and his works in general, and the other discuss the particular book or story chosen.

5. Argument

(*a*) Informal symposium: a kind of "talk-around" in which several students argue informally on various phases of the assigned subject.

(*b*) Debate: a formal debate especially prepared by four (or six) students with first-round arguments and rebuttal in regular debate form; presided over by a student elected or appointed from the class, with the class as a committee of the whole to vote on (1) the winning side and (2) the best individual debater; will require the whole of one or two periods.

6. Description of a Famous Picture, with either a large copy, if available, displayed on the wall, or a small copy passed around the class. The pictures in this book on pages 439-441 are good examples.

The picture can be introduced by a short account of the artist's life and achievement. If two students report on the same day, one can discuss the artist and the other the picture. Occasionally a picture or a replica of a famous statue, or even an unusually good cartoon, can be used.

7. Magazine Day

A favourite magazine is brought to class, passed around, and its features, departments, policy, and standing discussed.

8. Myths

Many of the Greek, Roman, and Norse myths not only are exceedingly interesting in themselves but also throw much needed light on literature.

9. My Hobby

An attractive, highly personal type of subject. It can be treated either seriously or humorously, and in either case can be made most interesting, though it requires some experience and self-confidence.

10. My Jonah

Like "My Hobby", a very personal type of subject. It is nearly always treated humorously and with mock despair. If it succeeds, it succeeds astonishingly well. There is no middle ground.

THE ROUND TABLE

1. Do you think oral composition is a more complete expression of yourself than written composition?
2. One convenient way of choosing a critic is to start at the top of the class roll and proceed alphabetically downward for the speakers and to start at the end of the roll and proceed alphabetically upward for the critics. Thus everyone can keep up easily with who is to speak next and who is to act as critic.
3. List five of the worst prevailing faults of yourself and of your schoolmates in enunciation.
4. What are the ten words most commonly mispronounced in school? Make a composite list in class.
5. Start a permanent list in your notebook for your personal use of words you have discovered you are mispronouncing. This should be kept up during your entire school and college course.
6. Which two of your schoolmates, one boy and one girl, have the pleasantest speaking voices? Who has the pleasantest speaking voice you ever heard?

7. If, instead of one student's reporting each day, a whole period is devoted to oral composition, an interesting series of related reports can be made on such projects as the following:

(1) A Study of Home (or County) Industries
(Each student treating a different industry)

(2) Men and Women Who Have Done Most for the Town in the Last Twenty-five Years
(Material from personal interviews as well as other sources)

(3) Men and Women Who Are Doing (Have Done) Worth-While Things in Our Day

(4) Notable Movements of Our Time
(For example, Red Cross, Boy Scouts and Girl Guides, World Peace, Society for Prevention of Cruelty to Animals, Pure Food, Playgrounds, Reforestation, Equal Suffrage.)

CHAPTER XI

The Sentence: Making Sentences Unified

A sentence is easier to twist and turn than a rubber band.
—J. W. LINN

Said a wise author, "Do not have too much respect for a sentence the first time you write it."

As was said in Chapter V, the paragraph is such an important unit in writing that with it practice in writing should begin. Correct paragraphing can come only from thoughtful planning. In other words, good paragraphs are the result of foresight or prevision. On the other hand, the sentence, which is the unit of both thought and speech, is in a very special sense the unit for revision.

Most writers have the habit of driving ahead with their first draft as fast as they can. If the right word or the right phrase will not come promptly, many leave a blank space and go ahead anyhow. The chief thing is not to lose motion, but to keep on putting ideas and details down as rapidly and as long as they come into the mind. As was noted in the chapter on Revision, the result is that sentences are frequently both faulty and fragmentary. After we have finished a paragraph or a theme comes the need of going back over it and correcting and tightening it. Each sentence must be read over carefully to see first that it *is* a sentence and then to see whether it is doing the work it is supposed to do. Is it unified? Is it clear? Is it emphatic? Are there too many sentences of the same length and pattern? Are there mistakes in grammar? These and a hundred other questions crowd in upon the writer who is honestly trying to improve his writing and bring it up to the highest level of correctness and effectiveness within his present powers.

The ways in which a sentence may go wrong are almost as numerous as the sands of the sea. This and the following chapters illustrate and give directions for correcting the commonest mistakes. Learn to recognize these main sentence sins and the remedy for each.

Following is an outline of these four important chapters. The outline is not as complicated as it seems at first. Familiarize yourself with it at the outset and refer to it often by way of review.

CHAPTER XI

Making Sentences Unified

1. Avoiding the No-Sentence, or Period Fault
2. Avoiding the Run-Together Sentence, or Comma Splice
3. Avoiding the Cat-and-Dog Sentence

CHAPTER XII

Making Sentences Clear

1. Getting the Main Thought into the Main Clause
2. The Proper Placing of Modifiers
3. The Proper Use of Reference Words
4. Avoiding Faulty Change in Grammatical Construction (Parallel Structure for Parallel Ideas)

CHAPTER XIII

Making Sentences Emphatic

1. Avoiding Baby Sentences
2. Avoiding Wordy Sentences
3. Putting Something before the Subject

CHAPTER XIV

Making Sentences Pleasing

1. Variety
2. The Short, Memorable Sentence
3. The Balanced Sentence

Making Sentences Unified

Unity in the sentence requires (1) that each sentence shall be a complete statement, with a subject and a predicate, instead of being a fragment or a part of a sentence; (2) that there shall not be too many ideas crowded into any one sentence; and (3) that the ideas in the same sentence shall be akin to and consistent with each other.

Of the many sins against the sentence, by far the two worst are (1) the No-Sentence, or Period Fault, and (2) the Run-Together Sentence, or Comma Splice. The No-Sentence violates a fundamental rule of grammar. Both the No-Sentence and the Comma Splice violate unity. The Cat-and-Dog Sentence violates unity.

(1) THE NO-SENTENCE, OR PERIOD FAULT

Both grammar and unity require that a sentence shall be a complete statement, with a subject and a predicate, instead of being a fragment of a sentence like a phrase or a clause.

A Phrase Used As a Sentence

Wrong: 1. He formed the habit of reading a great deal. Thus storing his mind with much valuable information.

Right: 1. He formed the habit of reading a great deal, thus storing his mind with much valuable information.

Wrong: 2. Most pupils go to high school and live at home. In this way combining the unusual advantages of both school and home.

Right: 2. Most pupils go to high school and live at home, in this way combining the unusual advantages of both school and home.

Also Right: 2. Most pupils go to high school and live at home. In this way they combine the unusual advantages of both school and home.

A CLAUSE USED AS A SENTENCE

Wrong: 3. There is a teacher I shall always remember. Because she had a sweet voice and a pleasant smile.

Right: 3. There is a teacher I shall always remember, because she had a sweet voice and a pleasant smile.

Wrong: 4. The accused declared that he was not guilty. That if given a chance he could prove an alibi.

Right: 4. The accused declared that he was not guilty, and that if given a chance he could prove an alibi.

In order to avoid the No-Sentence fault, or to correct it if it somehow slips in among respectable sentences, one needs the following knowledge gained from grammar and analysis:

(1) Clear understanding of what constitutes a subject and what constitutes a predicate.

(2) Clear understanding of the asserting power of the finite verb as distinguished from infinitives and participles.

(3) Clear understanding of (*a*) the incompleteness of thought in dependent clauses such as "because she had a sweet voice and a pleasant smile" (sentence 3 above) and "that if given a chance he could prove an alibi" (sentence 4 above); (*b*) the incompleteness of thought in phrases such as "thus storing his mind with much valuable information" (sentence 1 above) and "in this way combining the unusual advantages of both school and home" (sentence 2 above).

Review the definitions and examples of phrases and clauses in the section on Analysis, pages 55-62. If you do not feel sure of these distinctions, ask for class practice and discussion of doubtful points.

To correct the No-Sentence fault, all that is usually necessary is to employ a comma instead of the offending period that shuts the helpless clause or phrase off from the rest of the sentence on which it depends. This is the case with most of the examples given above. Notice, however, that sometimes other steps are advisable. Sentence 2, for example, can be split into two sentences by substituting the finite verb *combine* for the participle *combining*.

Among recent writers there is a growing tendency to use

fragmentary sentences, especially in building up the details of a descriptive paragraph. Sinclair Lewis, for example, in *Main Street* describes a house by means of the following phrases, which he punctuates as sentences:

> A concrete sidewalk with a "parking" of grass and mud. A square smug brown house, rather damp. A narrow concrete walk up to it. Sickly yellow leaves in a window with dried wings of box-elder seeds and snags of wool from the cotton-woods. A screened porch with pillars of thin painted pine surmounted by scrolls and brackets and bumps of jigsawed wood. No shrubbery to shut off the public gaze. A lugubrious bay-window to the right of the porch. Window curtains of starched cheap lace revealing a pink marble table with a conch shell and a Family Bible.

Likewise Percival Christopher Wren uses periods instead of dashes or semicolons to set off the words and clauses in the following paragraph from *The Desert Heritage*:

> Life's an amazing thing. Life. Fate. Destiny. The Providence that shapes our ends. God's will. Whatever you choose to call it.

Mr. Lewis and Mr. Wren are both successful and distinguished fiction writers, and have as much right as anyone else to take liberties with sentences. The reason they can afford to do so is that they know words and their ways. Entirely different, both in motive and in effect, is such an accumulation of sentence fragments and miscapitalizations as the following, which was written by a college freshman who ought not to have been passed out of high-school English:

> A four story structure surrounded by an Athletic field, tennis court, and Gymnasium. The Riverside Park on the banks of the James, an ideal amusement. Consisting of a club house, bathing beach, ball grounds and a large lawn covered with trees and flowers; The Public Library, and Various Churches.

If you find yourself leaning toward a fragmentary style, adopt this working rule: Write only complete sentences with obvious subjects and predicates, until you have your first book published. Then let your conscience be your guide.

Exercises in the No-Sentence Fault

1. In the passages quoted from Mr. Lewis and Mr. Wren on page 205, how many of the word units punctuated with periods are (*a*) complete sentences, (*b*) clauses, (*c*) phrases, (*d*) words?

2. One teacher uses the following plan in dealing with the fragmentary style in themes. She allows the students to write an occasional impressionistic paragraph composed of the shreds and patches of sentences, but only on condition that the writer put a star (*) after each incomplete sentence to show that he is writing no-sentences from choice, not from ignorance.

3. Copy and correct the following sentences. Do not limit yourself merely to changing the period to a comma if you can find a better way.

(1) It was a good many years ago, as men figure time. The place, an old, dilapidated shack near the rim of the desert.
(2) The sun's shining down so exceedingly hot causing me to faint.
(3) The boys, Philip Ray, a miller's son and Enoch Arden, a poor, rough sailor lad.
(4) His preparations for the night were very simple. The removal of his shoes and coat, in fact.
(5) Notwithstanding the fact that it is doubtful whether a poet named Homer ever really lived at all.
(6) The cornerstone of the building which had been put in place with elaborate ceremonies.
(7) The final score being nothing to nothing, much to the sorrow of the crowd.
(8) Making both incisions a fourth of an inch long and one inch broad, thus enabling the wound to bleed freely.

4. How would you punctuate the following extract from a recent editorial in a prominent newspaper?

> "As regarded by its devotees, mathematics is considered not only as the essence of fidelity, but as possessing an unending charm of grace and symmetry. An elegance that is clear, warmless, exact. So unyielding and precise as to arouse one's awe. So relentless in its virtue of universal and indomitable accuracy as to challenge every one's admiration."

(2) THE RUN-TOGETHER SENTENCE, OR COMMA SPLICE

The second grave sentence fault is the Run-Together Sentence, or Comma Splice. It consists of joining (splicing) two sentences by means of a comma. Examples of the comma splice abound not only in the writing of high-school and college students, but also, unless they are very careful workmen, in the work of professional writers as well. The comma is the trickiest of all punctuation marks, and seems to have a special knack of slipping in between two sentences, where it has no right to be.

Wrong: 1. I do not care for any more fruit, I have had enough.
Wrong: 2. I felt sure that he would come, I never knew him to break a promise.
Wrong: 3. I took my watch to the jeweller's to be fixed, he found a good deal of dust in it.
Wrong: 4. "He put the canary on a twig in the cedar tree," I said, "it just stood there without trying to fly."

There are four ways of correcting the comma splice, any of which will do the work. Which one is best in any given case will depend upon the closeness or kinship of the ideas expressed in the two spliced sentences. The four ways are these:

I. Make two sentences, using a period instead of a comma.
II. Use a semicolon instead of a comma.
III. Add a conjunction between the sentences.
IV. Reduce one of the sentences (usually the first) to the level of (*a*) a phrase or (*b*) a clause.

If we apply these remedies in turn to the four offending sentences quoted above, we get the following results. The starred sentences are best.

Right: 1. I do not care for any more fruit. I have had enough. (I)
Also Right: 1. *I do not care for any more fruit; I have had enough. (II)
Also Right: 1. *I do not care for any more fruit, for I have had enough. (III)
Also Right: 1. I do not care for any more fruit, having had enough. (IV*a*: second sentence reduced to a phrase)
Also Right: 1. I do not care for any more fruit, because I have had enough. (IV*b*: second sentence reduced to a clause)

Right: 2. *I felt sure that he would come. I never knew him to break a promise. (I)

Also Right: 2. I felt sure that he would come; I never knew him to break a promise. (II)

Also Right: 2. *I felt sure that he would come, for I never knew him to break a promise. (III)

Also Right: 2. I felt sure that he would come, never having known him to break a promise. (IV*a*: second sentence reduced to a phrase)

Also Right: 2. I felt sure that he would come, because I never knew him to break a promise. (IV*b*: second sentence reduced to a clause)

It will be noted that in these first two type sentences any one of the four methods of correction can be used, though not with equal effectiveness. In the third and fourth sentences, however, not all the methods can be applied.

Right: 3. I took my watch to the jeweller's to be fixed. He found a good deal of dust in it. (I)

Also Right: 3. I took my watch to the jeweller's to be fixed, and he found a good deal of dust in it. (III)

Also Right: 3. *When I took my watch to the jeweller's to be fixed, he found a good deal of dust in it. (IV*b*: first sentence reduced to the rank of a clause)

Right: 4. "He put the canary on a twig in the cedar tree," I said. "It just stood there without trying to fly." (I)

Also Right: 4. "He put the canary on a twig in the cedar tree," I said, "but it just stood there without trying to fly." (III)

Also Right: 4. *"When he put the canary on a twig in the cedar tree," I said, "it just stood there without trying to fly." (IV*b*: first sentence reduced to a clause)

These four sentences clearly illustrate the comma splice and the four ways of curing it. The comma fault is so definite that it can be readily detected, and the cure is so simple that it can be easily applied, but to do so will require watchfulness in revision.

Exercises in the Comma-Splice Fault

Try each of the four methods of correcting the following comma splices and choose the one best suited to each sentence:

1. My speech was over, I felt that I had failed.
2. Some of the children were well-dressed, others were wearing old, ragged clothes.
3. This is still a good car, it can make sixty miles an hour on a paved road.
4. "It must be murder," the detective pointed out, "a man can't shoot himself twice through the heart either by accident or on purpose."
5. The sky is blue, between the leaves of the chestnuts rises the green spire of St. Margaret's Church.
6. The bird dogs are the staunchest allies to the hunters, they not only locate the birds but also retrieve them after the killing.
7. We had that experience once, we don't want it again.
8. His desk was piled high with papers, before him were reports on three different cases.
9. "Watch that halfback," Don shouted, "he is going to try for a field goal."
10. A pig is like a person, it must have fresh air and exercise to develop properly.

3. The Cat-and-Dog Sentence

A third violation of unity occurs in what may be called the Cat-and-Dog Sentence. This type of error is not nearly so serious as either the no-sentence or the comma splice, but is both common enough and important enough to need a word of caution. It occurs when two ideas that have not the slightest bearing on each other are included in the same sentence, usually held loosely together by the artful annexer *and*, although they may be no more comfortable in each other's company than a strange cat and a strange dog in the same room. A good example is the familiar one about the Chinese:

> Gunpowder was invented by the Chinese, who are very fond of rice.

Other Examples of Cat-and-Dog Sentences

Faulty: 1. Jane was an only child and was sent to the university to study medicine.

Better: 1. (*a*) Jane was an only child. She was sent to the university to study medicine.

Faulty: 2. The Eskimos live chiefly on blubber and fish, and are not of a high order of intelligence.

Better: 2. (*a*) The Eskimos live chiefly on blubber and fish. They are not of a high order of intelligence.

Or, if it is the writer's belief that the Eskimos' diet lowers their intelligence, the two following combinations are permissible, but not otherwise:

Also Better: 2. (*b*) The Eskimos, who live chiefly on blubber and fish, are not of a high order of intelligence.

Also Better: 2. (*c*) The Eskimos, who are not of a very high order of intelligence, live chiefly on blubber and fish.

The safest rule with such sentences as these is to split the unfriendly ideas apart and put each in a sentence by itself.

General Exercises in Making Sentences Unified

Revise the following where necessary, avoiding all No-Sentence Faults, Comma Splices, and Cat-and-Dog Sentences. Five of the sentences are correct.

1. When I bought the radio I paid $25.00 down, the rest is to be paid in monthly instalments.
2. "The delay in publication," he said, "was due to an acute shortage of paper."
3. No one likes him very much. Except, of course, his brother.
4. Do not delay, send your order now.
5. The brakes having failed, the car crashed into the barrier.
6. Bill Winston is the best punter on the team, and is particularly fond of chewing gum.
7. At this point where their footsteps might be expected to be no longer visible.
8. In the late afternoon Jimmy arrived, a bulky parcel in his arms.
9. Were you ever lost in the woods, if so you know how I felt.
10. Tell him to hurry, we must not miss that train.

11. It was an unhappy experience. One which I should not care to repeat.
12. What a tall building!
13. The language of the Spaniards is very soft and musical, and many of them in this country become fruit sellers.
14. Some of the sentences in this exercise are correct, others are not.
15. He travelled across Canada last summer. Thus obtaining material for his book.
16. "We will ship your order next week," he said, "that's the best we can do."
17. I have just read an interesting story by Rudyard Kipling. The title of which is "They".
18. Tom makes good grades in history, and last week his father bought a new car.
19. Bob said that he would come soon. Also that he would bring Douglas with him.
20. I screamed, "Fred, don't leave me here, nobody will ever find me!"
21. Good marks do not come of their own accord; they must be earned.
22. I made a mistake common to most beginners, I looked at the audience.
23. We clutched desperately at the ladder. Each of us trying to displace the other.
24. Mother sent us for various medicines. Boric acid, liniment, and iodine.
25. Dawn at last, now I could investigate those weird sounds.

CHAPTER XII

Making Sentences Clear

Clearness within the sentence depends upon many things, but chiefly upon position, or the order of words. If the word order is right, clearness usually follows as a matter of course.

Clearness will be discussed under the four following heads:

1. Getting the Main Thought into the Main Clause
2. The Proper Placing of Modifiers
3. The Proper Use of Reference Words
   (1) Pronouns
   (2) Participles
4. Avoiding Faulty Change in Grammatical Construction

1. Getting the Main Thought into the Main Clause

One of the ever-present problems in writing clear-cut sentences is putting the main thought in the main clause. A complex sentence consists of one independent clause and one or more dependent clauses. The laws not only of good writing but of common sense as well require that the leading idea shall be carried by the independent clause. To do this is not hard if two conditions are met: (1) if the sentence is relatively short, consisting, say, of only two clauses; and (2) if we take time to think the sentence through before beginning to speak it or to write it down.

For example, the relative importance of the main thought and of the secondary or modifying thought in the following four sentences is clear. In each, the modifying thought is in the dependent clause and the main thought is in the independent clause. The main thought is capitalized in order to call attention to it.

Correct: 1. When I look upon the tombs of the great, EVERY EMOTION OF ENVY DIES IN ME.

Correct: 2. If a man empties his purse into his head, NO MAN CAN TAKE IT AWAY FROM HIM.

Correct: 3. Before I ask you to be my friend, I WILL BE OPEN AND SINCERE WITH YOU.

Correct: 4. Although Greece is a small country, IT HAS PRODUCED MANY GREAT MEN.

The trouble comes when we begin a sentence without knowing how it will end, and therefore slip into the fault of putting the secondary or modifying thought in the independent clause and tacking on the main thought in a trailing dependent clause or phrase. In the following sentences, for example, the main thought, which is again capitalized, is banished to the dependent clause or phrase.

Faulty: 1. I had acquired a liking for the law; SO I DECIDED TO GO TO COLLEGE.

Faulty: 2. They were just turning the corner, WHEN THEY HEARD THE NOISE OF A SHOT.

Faulty: 3. He was weakened by age and disease, DYING BEFORE ANY OF THE OTHERS.

Faulty: 4. The distinguished visitor advanced to the front of the platform WHEN THE WHOLE AUDIENCE ROSE AND CHEERED.

The remedy in all such cases is simple: reverse the situation and put the secondary or modifying thought in the dependent clause, and give the main thought to the main clause:

Correct: 1. As I had acquired a liking for the law, I DECIDED TO GO TO COLLEGE.

Correct: 2. Just as they were turning the corner, THEY HEARD THE NOISE OF A SHOT.

Correct: 3. Weakened by age and disease, HE DIED BEFORE ANY OF THE OTHERS.

Correct: 4. When the distinguished visitor advanced to the front of the platform, THE WHOLE AUDIENCE ROSE AND CHEERED.

Exercises in Getting the Main Thought into the Main Clause

Improve the following sentences by putting the main thought in the independent clause and the secondary or modifying thought in a dependent clause:

1. We were driving slowly down a little side road in the woods when we saw a deer with a lovely little fawn.
2. I was about to enter the house when I heard someone cry, "Fire!"
3. She was looking at the new car with great interest when the salesman came up and asked what she thought of it.
4. I was walking down the street when I heard the fire-bell ring.
5. The line was frayed by hard use, breaking when he attempted to lift the pike into the boat.
6. It is raining hard, and I can't see how to drive.
7. He mixed the two chemicals together, thus causing an explosion which blew him through the window.
8. The proprietor was closing up the store last night when he was held up by a burglar.

2. The Proper Placing of Modifiers

Between the time of King Alfred and that of Chaucer, the English language lost most of its inflections—that is, lost those word changes which show such facts as number, case, person, tense, and so forth. In particular, except in pronouns, the ending that showed the objective case was worn away, so that no way remains of telling from the way a noun looks whether it is the subject or the object of a verb. Adjectives likewise lost all outward indications of whether they modify a singular or a plural noun and whether that noun is masculine, feminine, or neuter. For all genders and both numbers only one form remained.

As a result of such changes as these, the order of words in an English sentence has become of the greatest importance. As was pointed out in the section on Parsing, page 14, *The dog bit the boy* means one thing, while *The boy bit the dog* means something entirely different, though no change in the words themselves has taken place, but only a change in their position. And to continue the illustration, no living person could tell the meaning of such word orders as these:

Bit the dog the boy.
Bit the boy the dog.
The dog the boy bit.
The boy the dog bit.

Thus out of the six possible combinations, those five words can be arranged in one way only in order to bring out the desired meaning, namely, *The dog bit the boy.*

It is the same way with modifiers. For both clearness and effectiveness, the position of all modifiers must be carefully attended to. It usually makes a big difference where you put them.

Kinds of Modifiers

On the basis of complexity, **modifiers are of three degrees: words, phrase, and clauses.** Whether a modifier is a word, a phrase, or a clause, however, it does the same work in the sentence and should be *put as close as possible* to what it modifies.

Examine the following four sentences. They illustrate both the two kinds of modifiers, adjective and adverb, and the three degrees of modification, word, phrase, and clause.

Adjective Modifiers

Word	*Phrase*	*Clause*
1. The *corner* house is mine.	The house *on the corner* is mine.	The house *that is on the corner* is mine.
2. The *long-haired* dog is a setter.	The dog *with the long hair* is a setter.	The dog *that has long hair* is a setter.

Adverb Modifiers

Word	*Phrase*	*Clause*
3. He came *unwillingly.*	He came *against his will.*	He came *although he was unwilling.*
4. The dog ran *fast.*	The dog ran *at a rapid rate.*	The dog ran *as fast as he could.*

Notice the use of modifiers in the following sentences.

Absurdities are due to the fondness that modifiers always display for their nearest neighbours:

1. Only he lost his hat (nobody else did).
   He only lost his hat (nobody stole it).
   He lost only his hat (and nobody else's).
   He lost his only hat (he never had but one).
   He lost his hat only (but saved his shoes and clothes).
2. Lost: A silk umbrella by an old gentleman with a carved ivory head.
3. Wanted: Gentleman wishes room and board with garage space for wife in refined private home.
4. Wanted: Double bed wanted cheap by an elderly lady with wooden head and foot, wire springs, and mattress.
5. The captain's wife wore a diamond pin in her hair which had been bought in Paris.
6. He struck the gold-fish bowl with his head, which was fortunately empty.

In such extreme cases as these the error is both clear and easy to correct. The misplaced modifier must be moved and put in the right place, immediately touching what it modifies, so that nothing can come between them and divorce them.

(1) FOUR TROUBLESOME WORDS

Only, *Not*, *Nearly*, *Almost*

Certain adverbs need careful watching, or they will insist on straying off and attaching themselves to the wrong word. The outstanding offender is *only*, as can be seen from the first sentence above, but *not* and *nearly* are almost as bad. When we say, "I nearly picked up a dozen nails in our driveway," we mean we picked up *nearly a dozen*, that is, nine or ten; when we say, "We *almost got home* by ten o'clock," we probably mean that we got *almost home* by ten o'clock; and when we say of a person who has died suddenly, "Why, I *only saw him last week*," we certainly mean that we *saw him only last week*. There is one position and one position only in which *only*, *not*, *nearly*, and *almost* can be depended on to do their full duty—that is, immediately in front of the word or group of words they are expected to modify.

(2) MORE TROUBLE MAKERS

Either—Or, Neither—Nor, Both—And, Not Only—But Also

The four most important correlatives are those mentioned above, *either—or, neither—nor, both—and, not only—but also.* The proper place for these conjunctions is immediately before the word they introduce, and the important thing is to see that the words they introduce are the same part of speech. Carelessness in this respect results in a good deal of loose writing. (See pages 44-45.)

Faulty: 1. Either you can take the bus or go on the trolley.
Better: 1. You can either take the bus or go on the trolley.
Faulty: 2. She said that she could neither be comfortable in the town nor in the country.
Better: 2. She said that she could be comfortable neither in the town nor in the country.
Faulty: 3. The whole family both complained of the climate and of the neighbours.
Better: 3. The whole family complained both of the climate and of the neighbours.
Faulty: 4. Not only did I feel that she was leading him on but also that she was laughing at him behind his back.
Better: 4. I felt not only that she was leading him on but also that she was laughing at him behind his back.
Also Better: 4. I felt that she was not only leading him on but also laughing at him behind his back.

(3) THE SPLIT INFINITIVE

Some years ago most of the books on standard usage contained express warnings against splitting infinitives, that is, against putting an adverb between the *to* and the verb. Such expressions as *to clearly understand, to devotedly serve, to firmly believe,* were frowned upon. More recently, under the present pervasive relaxing of rules and standards, more and more writers are allowing themselves to split infinitives wherever they feel inclined. Though many successful authors do so, splitting infinitives still suggests either careless writing or indifference to the best usage.

There is nothing to be gained by splitting infinitives in such cases as the following:

Loose: 1. To eventually succeed is better than not to succeed at all.
Better: 1. Eventually to succeed (or, to succeed eventually) is better than not to succeed at all.
Loose: 2. To entirely conceal one's feelings is almost impossible.
Better: 2. Entirely to conceal one's feelings (or, to conceal one's feelings entirely) is almost impossible.

On the other hand there is one reason in favour of splitting infinitives that cannot be denied. If an adverb is put between the *to* and the verb, it cannot by any possible chance modify anything but the infinitive. Sometimes, though very rarely, it may be necessary to thus split an infinitive in order to avoid ambiguity. Consider the following sentences:

1. To fail occasionally is better than never to try.
   (Does *occasionally* modify *to fail* or *is*?)
2. To lose one's temper often signifies lack of self-control.
   (What does *often* modify?)
3. To attend unfailingly helps to establish a reputation for reliability.
   (Does *unfailingly* modify *To attend* or *helps*?)

If the adverbs are inserted in the infinitives, there can be no doubt of the meaning:

1. To occasionally fail is better than never to try.
2. To often lose one's temper signifies lack of self-control.
3. To unfailingly attend helps to establish a reputation for reliability.

Such cases as these, however, occur very seldom. It is best not to split infinitives except where necessary to clearness.

Exercises in the Proper Placing of Modifiers

Revise those of the following sentences which contain misplaced modifiers. Three of the sentences are correct.

1. She lived in the fear of being permanently discharged for three years.
2. I have read the diary that my sister wrote many times.
3. I neither like history nor mathematics.
4. He not only is dishonest but cowardly as well.
5. He invited us either to come on Friday or on Saturday.
6. His father told him never to be late.
7. The child tried to swallow the pill three times.
8. He said on New Year's he would turn over a new leaf.
9. Mrs. Jones not only invited my sister but also my brother and me.
10. All men are not white.
11. Many students provided the books which were required voluntarily.
12. He said that he could just remain for an hour.
13. Finally a young man approached the chair in a brown fedora in which Mr. Lane sat.
14. We neither admire his achievements nor envy his popularity.
15. People who are blindly prejudiced in most cases cannot be forced to change their opinions.
16. I was thankful that we only had an hour to wait.
17. In the final battle of the campaign the guerrilla leader was again defeated and killed.
18. I was quite sure that he had no chance of passing soon after he began to write.
19. Either he returned late last night or early this morning.
20. Every student is not good in English.
21. Not only is he a brilliant student, but also a concert pianist.
22. He said that he intended to address the parcel to his brother on the front verandah.
23. Remember to read the poems assigned carefully.
24. When we arrived at the school, not all the boys were there.
25. The telephone rang just as we opened the door with shrill insistence.

3. The Proper Use of Reference Words

(*Pronouns and Verbals*)

(1) PRONOUNS

A pronoun is like a mirror. A mirror reflects whatever is nearest it. So, too, a pronoun insists on referring to whatever noun is nearest it, regardless of logic or meaning. To pronouns, provided that the number and gender are satisfactory, all antecedents look alike. Of all the parts of speech, therefore, pronouns are among the hardest to manage. Loosely handled, they cause a large number of errors.

Mistakes in pronouns fall under three clauses: (1) wrong reference, (2) ambiguous reference, and (3) no reference. (1) In wrong reference, the pronoun refers to the wrong antecedent; (2) in ambiguous reference, the pronoun refers to too many antecedents; and (3) in no reference, the pronoun has no antecedent to refer to.

1. Wrong Reference

In instances of wrong reference, the pronoun refers to the wrong antecedent, usually because the wrong antecedent stands between the pronoun and its rightful antecedent. Amusing results often follow mistakes of this kind.

1. He pulled out an old handkerchief, blew his nose, and then put it in his pocket.
2. The captain of the ship swam ashore, and so did the cook. She was insured for fifty thousand dollars, and was heavily loaded with pig-iron.
3. The Woman's Missionary Society met Wednesday evening with Mrs. ——. Miss Minerva —— read a paper on "Personal Devils". Sixteen were present. (*From a county newspaper*)
4. Last night I lay in a gondola on the Grand Canal at Venice, drinking it all in, and life never seemed so full before.
5. If fresh milk disagrees with the baby, it should be boiled.

Anyone, Anybody, Everyone, Everybody—THEY!

An important variety of wrong reference is the use of a plural pronoun to refer to a singular antecedent. The four worst trouble makers are *anyone, anybody, everyone,* and *everybody.* Each of these is definitely singular in form, and should therefore be referred to by a singular pronoun. Thus, *If anybody calls, ask him to wait* is right, but *If anybody calls, ask them to wait* is wrong. For two reasons, however, it is very hard to keep from using a plural pronoun to refer to *anyone, anybody, everyone,* and *everybody.* In the first place, all four of these words, although singular in form, are plural in effect. *Everyone* and *everybody* are equivalent to *all*; and *anyone* and *anybody* likewise mean any possible one, hence every possible one, hence all. In the second place all four words are of common gender—that is, they refer indifferently to males and females alike. There is, however, no common singular personal pronoun in English, but only *he, she,* and *it.* When, therefore, we refer to *anyone* or *everyone* by a singular personal pronoun, we have to choose between the sexes, and say either *he* or *she,* although in the first instance *anyone* or *everyone* may be thought of as neither masculine nor feminine but as both. These two reasons make it much easier and more natural to say *anyone—they* or *everyone—they* than to say *everyone—he* or *anyone—he.* Everybody, authors and teachers included, would like to use *they, their,* and *them* to refer to these words instead of using *he, his, him* or *she, her, her.* It may be that the two reasons mentioned above will gradually establish the plural pronoun reference as correct. In fact, in loose, colloquial usage the plural pronoun seems already fairly well established. So far as we are concerned, however, we should in serious writing continue to use the inconvenient, but correct, singular.

Loose: 1. Every member of the camping party must bring their own bedding.

Better: 1. Every member of the camping party must bring his own bedding.

Loose: 2. Anyone can do this if they try.
Better: 2. Anybody can do this if he tries.
Loose: 3. If everybody has finished their work, they may go home.
Better: 3. Whoever has finished his work may go home.
Also Better: 3. All who have finished their work may go home.

2. Ambiguous Reference

Ambiguous means "doubtful", "uncertain", and comes from a Latin word that means to wander around. **In cases of ambiguous reference the pronoun refers not to one antecedent but to several antecedents, and confusion results.**

1. When anyone passed he gave him a kick.
2. The man was driving an old ox when he became angry and kicked him, hitting his jawbone with such force as to break his leg.
3. When Will saw his father he asked him to go to the bank and cash a cheque for him, but he said he was too busy.

The confusion among pronouns and antecedents in sentence 3 is so great that the best remedy is to quote what was said. The sentence would thus read as follows:

When Will saw his father he said, "Please go to the bank and cash a cheque for me," but his father said that he was too busy.
Also clear: When Will saw his father, Will asked him to go to the bank and cash a cheque for him, but his father said he was too busy.

3. No Reference

In cases of no reference, the pronoun has no antecedent to refer to, but is loosely used to refer to a whole clause or to a preceding idea. This type of error, although very common, is both hard to detect and hard to correct. It is already winning its way in colloquial usage.

Loose: 1. We do not tear your clothes with machinery.
We do it carefully by hand. (*Laundry advertisement*)
(Grammatically, the only word in the sentence that could correctly serve as the antecedent of *it* is *machinery*. Such reference is absurd. Equally absurd is the loose reference of *it* to the idea of tearing your clothes. The sentence should read:

Better: 1. We do not tear your clothes with machinery. We do our work carefully by hand.
Loose: 2. A crowd of us went deer hunting last week and killed four of them.
Better: 2. A crowd of us went deer hunting last week and killed four deer.

The Orphan "Which"

The worst offender in the no-reference type of pronoun errors is the relative *which.* It is easy to add a final clause to a sentence by means of a *which* that does not refer to any definite antecedent but to the general idea or action conveyed in the sentence. While convenient, this usage is slipshod, and is usually a sign of loose thinking. It is permissible in informal conversation, but not in serious writing.

Loose: 1. I stuck my head out of the window, which was a foolish thing to do.
Better: 1. I foolishly stuck my head out of the window.
Also Better: 1. Sticking my head out of the window was foolish.
Also Better: 1. It was foolish of me to stick my head out of the window.
Loose: 2. Her father was one of the meanest and most influential men in town, which made the policemen unwilling to summon her for breaking traffic laws.
Better: 2. The fact that her father was one of the meanest and most influential men in town made the policemen unwilling to summon her for breaking traffic laws.
Also Better: 2. Her father was one of the meanest and most influential men in town, and this fact made the policemen unwilling to summon her for breaking traffic laws.

(2) VERBALS

Along with pronouns another source of constant trouble is the verbal. This is so because the verbal functions as two parts of speech at the same time. (For illustrations and examples, see the chapter on the Review of Grammar.) On the one hand the participle, the gerund, and the infinitive are verbs and (*a*) if transitive take objects; (*b*) if linking take complements and (*c*) are modified by adverbs. At the same time the participle is an adjective and as an adjective must have a noun or pronoun to modify. The gerund and the infinitive are used as nouns, but as expressions of action should be closely related to the person or things performing this action. In connection with this last necessity trouble comes. We start a sentence with a participial phrase but when we come to the independent clause we do not provide the participle with anything to modify; or we begin with a gerundial or infinitive construction and provide the gerund or the infinitive with no "agent" and thus we leave the verbals dangling helplessly in space. For this reason this error is known as the hanging or the dangling participle gerund, or infinitive.

The error can be most clearly seen in such humorous instances as the following, in which the participle, having nothing to modify, lays fast hold on the nearest noun and thus makes merry with the meaning.

Dangling Participles

1. Entering the churchyard, a large white tombstone is seen.
2. Crossing the field, a deep ditch is seen.
3. Having eaten our lunch, the steamboat departed.
4. Wearing a pale blue skirt and white suède shoes, father looked at her in admiration.

If the error is as ridiculous as these, it can be easily detected and remedied. When, however, there is nothing funny or unusual about the dangling participle, it often escapes notice.

Faulty: 1. Being always a good student, the teacher felt sure he would pass.
Better: 1. Since he was always a good student, the teacher felt sure he would pass.
Faulty: 2. Having very little to do, there was a good chance to read as much as we wanted to.

Better: 2. Having very little to do, we had a good chance to read as much as we wanted to.

Also Better: 2. Since we had very little to do, we had a good chance to read as much as we wanted to.

Dangling Gerunds

Like participles, gerunds should always be so used that their connection with the words to which they refer is unmistakable.

Faulty: On entering the room, an overturned chair was seen.
Better: On entering the room, we saw an overturned chair.
Faulty: After listening intently, a faint groan was heard.
Better: After listening intently, I heard a faint groan.

Dangling Infinitives

Faulty: To play bridge well a good hand is needed.
Better: To play bridge well, one needs a good hand.

Exercises in the Proper Use of Reference Words

Classify the mistakes in the following sentences as (1) wrong reference; (2) ambiguous reference; (3) no reference; (4) dangling participle; (5) dangling gerund. Then correct the mistakes. Four sentences are correct as they stand: two in A; two in B.

A

1. After bolting my sandwich, the train pulled out.
2. The men went deer hunting, but were unable to find any.
3. When you fill the coffee cup, be sure not to spill any of it on the tablecloth.
4. In talking to Jones recently, he told me about his narrow escape.
5. Mary asked Lucy where her tennis racquet was.
6. I did not sleep very well the night before, which made me late for breakfast.
7. If a fact does not fit your theory, discard it.
8. While using the typewriter yesterday morning, the ribbon broke.
9. She often became angry, but it was soon over.
10. If anyone has found a gold fountain pen, he should leave it at the office.

11. Having purchased my camera from a reliable dealer, it has given excellent service.
12. The man told his neighbour that he had caught his boy in his strawberry patch the day before, and that if he did it again he thought that he ought to punish him.
13. We heard the aeroplane engine start, but were disappointed to learn that it was not going up.
14. He became quite ill, caused by the rolling of the boat.
15. A typewriter is a valuable aid. Most professional writers use them.
16. If anyone does not wish to contribute, they should state their objections now.
17. Carrying my limp form, John and I soon reached the house.
18. After reading the essay, a summary should be made.
19. Having recovered the ball on a fumble, Queens soon scored again.
20. The spokesman assured us that everyone was willing to do their duty.

B

1. When you read very hard, it makes your eyes smart by bedtime.
2. While running the rapids, a rock overturned our canoe.
3. Having worked so hard, it was a pity he failed.
4. It was a rule of the camp that everyone should be in his room by ten o'clock.
5. Upon going to bed, the light should be turned off.
6. He told his brother he would soon hear from him.
7. The popcorn came in a paper bag and we ate it.
8. In writing narration, unusually long paragraphs should be avoided.
9. He did not finish the book, which was due to his lack of perseverance.
10. There go the Joneses in their new car; she is driving as usual.
11. She removed the papers from the shelves and dusted them.
12. Being quite sure that the answer was correct, Bob smiled quietly to himself.
13. You must be careful in handling a revolver. They are dangerous.
14. In the poem it says that all men are equal.
15. Opening the door, a strange sight met his eyes.
16. Yesterday he lost his pen, which prevented him from writing the test.

17. In choosing a person to play the part, she should be attractive in appearance.
18. His forehead was bleeding, caused by a sharp blow from a stone.
19. Standing there in the moonlight, nothing more was said by our visitors.
20. By reading aloud, many themes can be improved.

4. Avoiding Faulty Change in Grammatical Construction

Use parallel structure for parallel ideas

One prevalent danger in writing is an unconscious tendency to change constructions midway in a sentence. A famous piece of advice given by Lincoln was, "Don't swap horses in the middle of a stream." An equally good rule in writing is, "Don't change constructions in the middle of a sentence." If there are two or three ideas of parallel rank in one sentence, these parallel ideas should be expressed in parallel form. Such sentences as the following show various shades of this type of error:

Faulty: 1. He said that he would return soon and for us to work hard while he was away. (Two parallel ideas, the first expressed in a *that* clause and the second in a *for to* phrase)

Faulty: 2. Football teaches a boy quickness, courage, and what to do in an emergency. (Three parallel ideas, the first two expressed as nouns and the third in a *what* phrase)

Faulty: 3. I like taking a long walk in the country and also to ride in a good automobile. (Two parallel ideas, the first expressed in a gerund, or infinitive in *ing*, and the second in the infinitive with *to*)

Faulty: 4. When we finally reached the beach, a beautiful sunset was seen. (Faulty change from the active voice of the first clause to the passive voice of the second clause)

The remedy in all such cases is to give parallel forms to the parallel ideas. There are usually two ways of doing this:

(1) change the wording of the first idea so as to make it like the wording of the second idea; or (2) change the wording of the second idea so as to make it like the wording of the first idea. Thus the four sentences above can be improved as follows:

Better: 1. He said that he would return soon and that we must work hard while he was away. (Both parallel ideas in parallel *that* clauses)

Better: 2. Football teaches a boy quickness, courage, and resourcefulness. (Three parallel ideas in parallel noun form)

Better: 3. I like taking a long walk in the country and also riding in a good automobile. (Both parallel ideas in parallel gerund phrases)

Also Better: 3. I like to take a long walk in the country and also to ride in a good automobile. (Both parallel ideas in parallel infinitive phrases)

Better: 4. When we finally reached the beach, we saw a beautiful sunset. (The active voice of the first clause correctly continued in the second clause)

Exercises in Correcting Faulty Change in Grammatical Construction

In the following examples of mixed structure, try making (1) the first idea similar in form to the second; and (2) the second idea similar in form to the first. Choose the better form.

1. He decided to go west this summer and on going to Europe next winter.
2. His high grades were due partly to his own hard work and partly because he had a quick mind.
3. At first he thought that she was proud, conceited, and that she had a hard heart.
4. He had trained himself in writing correctly and to speak as correctly as he wrote.
5. The audience are requested to be in their seats when the curtain rises and that they should not interrupt a number by applauding.
6. In the engineering course students learn the use of a transit and how to survey land.
7. The standing of a student depends both upon his mind and how hard he studies.

8. Although we had fixed the tents and the beds very carefully, an uncomfortable night was spent by all of us.
9. Anyone who wishes to learn the violin must begin young, for you cannot really master it after you are grown.
10. From my window I could look out on the valley, and in the distance beautiful blue mountains could be seen.
11. Since it was beginning to rain, and the evening being cool, we decided to remain at home.
12. He promised to cut the lawn at once and that he would rake it later.
13. I like playing baseball better than to take part in such indoor sports as badminton.
14. We could see the flickering gleam of the lightning, but no sound of thunder could be heard.
15. In the fair grounds were many people, some throwing confetti, some blowing horns, and others walked up and down the midway.
16. He was not informed of the purchase they had made and that he would have to accept delivery.

CHAPTER XIII

Making Sentences Emphatic

As compared with the whole composition or the paragraph the sentence is a very small unit. Sentence emphasis, therefore, resolves itself chiefly into a question of emphasis by position. The different sentence elements such as subject, verb, object, and the various modifying words and phrases must be shifted around till the unimportant ones are tucked away in the middle of the sentence, and the important word or phrase is placed at the end.

You can make your sentence structure more effective if you

(1) Avoid Baby Sentences
(2) Avoid Wordy Sentences
(3) Vary the Sentence Structure
    (1) by putting the important idea last
    (2) by using inverted order
    (3) by using both periodic and loose sentences
    (4) by putting something before the subject.

1. The Baby Sentence

You will remember that back in first-grade days all the sentences in your primer consisted of tiny, simple statements, one to each sentence. The sentence order was always the same, Subject, Verb, Object or Complement, like this:

> I have a dog. My dog's name is Don. Don sees me. Don runs to meet me.

We may smile at these baby sentences, but even high-school pupils in weaker moments have been known to revert to earlier habits and hand in a paragraph that reads after this fashion:

> Ellen was a beautiful maid. Her cheeks were tinged by the sun. She lived on an island. This island was in Loch Katrine. It was a very beautiful island.

In such exaggerated sentences as these the childishness and weakness of the sentence structure can be readily seen. The remedy, likewise, is simple: combine the short, monotonous, simple sentences into larger complex sentences. The four statements about the dog could be put together thus:

> When my dog Don sees me, he runs to meet me.

The four statements about Ellen and her island might be combined in either of the two following ways:

> Ellen was a beautiful maid who lived on a lovely island in Loch Katrine; *or,* On a beautiful island in Loch Katrine lived a lovely maid whose name was Ellen.

Consciously as we write and revise we should try to keep from writing too many short simple sentences or too many compound sentences held together by *and's* and *but's* and *so's.* It is a sign of growing maturity and mental development to increase our average of complex sentences wisely linked together by such connectives as *when, where, since, because, although, if, unless, so that,* and so forth.

In particular, two childish sentence patterns are to be avoided, the *and* habit and the *so* habit.

(1) THE *AND* HABIT

Just one step removed from the kindergarten stage of "I have a dog", "My dog's name is Don", comes the practice of linking simple sentences in twos and threes by means of the much overworked *and.*

Faulty: 1. I have a dog, and he is a setter.
Better: 1. I have a dog. He is a setter.
Also Better: 1. I have a setter dog.
Also Better: 1. My dog is a setter.

Faulty: 2. The lifeguard was a big, fine-looking fellow, and his name was William.

Better: 2. The lifeguard, whose name was William, was a big, fine-looking fellow.

Also Better: 2. The lifeguard was a big, fine-looking fellow named William.

The trouble with such sentences as these is that the two ideas linked by *and* are not equal in value—in other words, are not co-ordinate. One of the two ideas is distinctly secondary to the other and therefore should not be joined to the main idea by *and*, which shows equality of value. Instead, the secondary idea should be expressed in a modifying word, phrase, or clause which gives the exact relationship and the relative importance of the two ideas expressed. Thus, in the sentences quoted, "I have a dog and he is a setter", the two ideas (1) that I own a dog and (2) that this dog is a setter are wrongly co-ordinated. If the fact that I own a dog is uppermost in the writer's mind, the best way to put it is, "I own a setter dog", while if the fact that this dog is a setter is uppermost, the best way to put it is, "My dog is a setter."

(2) THE *SO* HABIT

Equally prevalent and equally slipshod with the *and* habit is the *so* habit.

Faulty: 1. The cook is sick, so we shall either have to go out for dinner or cook it ourselves.

Better: 1. The cook is sick; consequently we shall either have to go out for dinner or cook it ourselves.

Also Better: 1. Since the cook is sick, we shall either have to go out for dinner or cook it ourselves.

Faulty: 2. She was very tired after her long trip, so she went to bed early.

Better: 2. She was so tired after her long trip that she went to bed early.

Also Better: 2. Because she was very tired after her long trip, she went to bed early.

While the *and* and *so* habits are very similar, the *so* habit is easier to correct than the *and* habit for the following reason: almost any relationship between ideas may be loosely expressed by *and*, and hence the exact relationship must be discovered before the weakness can be corrected. On the other hand, *so* expresses only two relationships: (1) usually cause or reason; (2) sometimes result. To correct the loose use of *so*, therefore, is simple. There are three ways of doing it:

(1) Instead of *so* use *consequently*, *therefore*, or *hence* preceded by a semicolon.

(2) Begin the sentence with *since* or *because* and omit *so*.

(3) If the relationship is result, use *so* in the first clause as a modifier followed by *that* to introduce the second clause. For example:

Faulty: We were tired by the time we reached Richmond, so we decided to spend the night there.

Better: We were so tired by the time we reached Richmond that we decided to spend the night there.

Let it be noted that there is nothing inherently or grammatically wrong with either the *and* or the *so* habit. They are natural and convenient ways to express our random thoughts. They are permissible in conversation and in informal personal letters. They are as easy-going as a pair of old shoes. In themes, however, and in serious writing they should not be used.

Exercises in Correcting the "And" and the "So" Habit

Improve the following sentences either by substituting a better connective for "and" and "so" or by recasting the whole sentence.

1. Everyone was nice to us, so we enjoyed our visit very much.
2. John came home and the dog was dead.
3. The visitor arrived promptly at six o'clock and then he went to his room.
4. Our auto broke a rear spring under the heavy load, so we had to postpone our trip till later.

5. I have a dog, and it is partly white and partly black.
6. The tire was almost entirely worn out, so we decided not to have it vulcanized.
7. The Thomsons didn't have enough money to pay cash for their new radio, so they bought it on the instalment plan.
8. These negro boatmen are very skilful, and launch their boat through the surf with little difficulty.
9. He was getting angry at her teasing, so she decided to stop.
10. At the end of the midway is a small grandstand, and this is always crowded at night.

2. Wordy Sentences

Wordiness is the foe both of emphasis and of effectiveness. Using too many words will make even good ideas waver and stumble along instead of forging straight ahead. No sentence can be either striking or pleasing that is rambling and wordy. Experienced critics estimate that 30 per cent. of the words in the average high-school and freshman theme could be profitably omitted.

One trouble with detecting and remedying wordiness is that it is a general rather than a specific fault. The No-Sentence blunder, for example, and the Misplacing of Modifiers, are both very obvious errors, and can be spotted almost as clearly as a mistake in multiplication. Wordiness, however, is vague and pervasive. Unless it is flagrant it is hard to put your finger upon it and say, "Here lies the fault." Consider the fuzzy, confused effect of such writing as this:

> I think one's home town should be very closely connected with one's self. It should be something, which, as we grow older, we will look back upon the pleasant memories connected with our home town. (35 words)

This passage has faults other than wordiness. It is confused and repetitive. If, however, we cut down the number of words as much as we can, we shall find that we have cut out the confusion and the repetition at the same time:

> Our home town should be so closely connected with us that, as we grow older, we will look back upon it with pleasant memories. (24 words)

Wordy: 1. It was with great difficulty and effort that I wrote my theme last night. (14 words)
Better: 1. I had great difficulty in writing my theme last night. (10 words)
Wordy: 2. There is quite a good bit of labour and expenditure of money involved in the laying out and keeping up of a golf course. (24 words)
Better: 2. It takes much labour and money to lay out and keep up a golf course. (15 words)
Wordy: 3. She spoke to me when we met each other yesterday in a very cool way. (15 words)
Better: 3. She greeted me yesterday very coolly. (6 words)

Exercises in Improving Wordy Sentences

Trim and tighten the following sentences into as few words as possible:

1. There is nothing which is more refreshing than a drink of iced lemonade.
2. In the English room is a small reference library containing books to be used in connection with the parallel reading of this course.
3. Without a single opposing vote she was unanimously selected as the prettiest girl in school.
4. He succeeded in landing the fish in a way that was really skilful.
5. The main and principal purpose is to increase the general health of the province as a whole.
6. May I have the pleasure of having an interview with you?
7. There were two great universities which were developed in England during the Middle Ages.
8. In making chocolate cake, the first thing to do is to get your ingredients gathered together.
9. There are many purposes that the radio is used for at the present time.
10. When the mayor went out of office, he was made the recipient of a beautiful silver pitcher.
11. The wonderful choice of words in "The Raven" is unsurpassed in its superb selection of diction.
12. There are a good many reasons why we should have a new athletic field, and among them the three most important are these:
13. A night that is lighted by the moon is best for rowing on the lake.

14. The old, worn-out, thin, trembling horse plodded slowly and wearily along.
15. The far-famed and world-renowned mountains of British Columbia are very beautiful.
16. To read too many books that are sad and depressing is not good for the mind.
17. Those of the human family who are domiciled in vitreous places are admonished against hurling petrified substances.
18. After you have collected your thoughts together, repeat again what was said by the garrulous, talkative, and loquacious old man.
19. I should like to say that there were three of us who helped the policeman, and that John was an instrumental factor in recovering the purse which had been stolen.
20. It was the general consensus of opinion that the vocal selection rendered by Miss Ermia Jones left much to be desired.

3. Something before the Subject

As was pointed out in the section on the Proper Placing of Modifiers, the paramount thing in an English sentence is the order of words. For a thousand years the established order has been Subject—Verb—Object or Complement. This order is drilled into us from childhood to old age hundreds of times every day, until it becomes a fixed part of our speech consciousness.

Any change, therefore, from this order is unusual and attracts attention to itself. The surest way, then, to emphasize a word or a phrase is to take it out of its expected place and put it somewhere else. Remember that a sentence is easier to twist and turn than a rubber band. Remember also that to change the order of words is always to change the emphasis on ideas.

The two most important places in the sentence are the beginning and the end, with the end far outranking the beginning. The problem, therefore, of calling attention to an important idea usually resolves itself into how the word or the phrase carrying the important idea may be put at the end of the sentence.

The effect of this simple fact upon sentence structure is fundamental. Granted that you write with a fair degree of grammatical correctness, nothing will improve your style as much as wise attention to the way your sentences end. The influence of the order of words in the sentence will be discussed in these divisions:

(1) Putting the Important Idea Last
(2) Using Inverted Order for Emphasis
(3) Using the Periodic Sentence
(4) Putting Something before the Subject

(1) PUTTING THE IMPORTANT IDEA LAST

Read the following paired sentences carefully and notice how the emphasis focuses on the end idea, when as in the second of each pair you are kept waiting for it.

Exercises in Sentence Emphasis

1. (*a*) What we really are depends on our heart, not on our head.
1. (*b*) What we really are depends not on our head, but on our heart.
2. (*a*) And my heart shall nevermore be lifted from out that shadow
   That lies floating on the floor.
2. (*b*) And my heart from out that shadow that lies floating on the floor
   Shall be lifted—nevermore.
3. (*a*) But these three, faith, hope, love, now abide; and love is the greatest of these.
3. (*b*) But now abideth faith, hope, love, these three; and the greatest of these is love. (Revised Version)
4. (*a*) I think that you are mistaken, however.
4. (*b*) I think, however, that you are mistaken.

As we read these sentences, we see the distinct change in emphasis produced by changes in the word order. Always remember that the end of the sentence is the place for the important idea. **Specifically, avoid closing with a weak**

qualifying phrase like *I suppose, however, in my opinion, it seems to me.*

Try the effect of putting some other idea in the end position.

1. A pupil should feel that to hand in dishonest work is beneath him.
2. Bottle tops or buttons may be used if checker men are not available.
3. However, I believe I can graduate if I can pass geometry.
4. The thing that people fear most is being laughed at.
5. Most of the workmen are foreign born, I am told.
6. I must have jumped ten feet when I heard the snake hiss.
7. He could never be guilty of dishonesty, even when it was to his own advantage.
8. I shall go on without him if he does not come soon.
9. The car hit an oily patch and skidded badly as we made a sharp turn around the corner.
10. Anything is worth doing well if it is worth doing at all.
11. He has never been accused of lack of frankness, whatever other faults he may have.
12. Mount Everest has become famous throughout the world because of its height and rugged beauty.

(2) USING INVERTED ORDER FOR EMPHASIS

One striking way to secure emphasis is to invert the usual word order—that is, to turn the sentence exactly around and begin with the object or modifier of the verb and end with the subject.

Read the following sentences in the inverted order, then turn them around to the natural order, and notice how their emphasis evaporates.

1. Blessed are the peacemakers.—MATTHEW v. 9
2. Never again will you catch me doing that.
3. How great a matter a little fire kindleth.
4. How are the mighty fallen!
5. Now is the accepted time.
6. Gone are the days when my heart was young and gay.
7. Silver and gold have I none; but what I have, that give I thee. —ACTS iii. 6

The inverted sentence is an unusual way of securing emphasis. It differs from the more common method of putting the most important idea last in that it gives special stress not to the sentence end but to the sentence beginning. Instead of a spotlight in the rear, it carries, as it were, a headlight in front. On this account it is sometimes called the Display Sentence.

Most exclamatory sentences are cast in the inverted order. We say "What a beautiful day!" or "What a sad death!" instead of saying, "The day is very beautiful" or "The death is very sad." It is a good rule to have at least one inverted or one exclamatory sentence to every page. Form the habit of doing this and you will add to your style a touch of both vividness and variety.

(3) USING LOOSE AND PERIODIC SENTENCES

For the third time in this chapter let us remind ourselves that the normal order of words in the English sentence is Subject—Verb—Object or Complement. According to whether (*a*) this order is kept, or (*b*) the verb is withheld until the end, sentences are classified as (1) Loose and (2) Periodic.

1. Loose Sentences

A loose sentence is one which unfolds in the natural order of Subject, Verb, Complement, adding one detail after another until the meaning is complete. A loose sentence can be stopped in one or more places before the end is reached and still make sense. Loose sentences are natural, easy, and effective, if they are not used to the exclusion of other kinds of sentences such as the periodic, the exclamatory, and the inverted sentence.

Following are two typical loose sentences. The figure in parentheses after each sentence gives the number of places at which the sentence could be stopped before the end. Find these places and verify the fact that the sentences could be stopped there.

1. The ship finally crept into port, with her crew utterly worn out, her rigging caked with ice, and her hull leaking in several places after her long battle with November gales. (4)
2. The car nearly turned over, after sideswiping the wagon and skidding across the road into the bank. (3)

2. Periodic Sentences

A periodic sentence is one which, instead of unfolding its meaning as it goes, withholds its meaning until the end is reached. It cannot be stopped before the close and still make sense. It accomplishes this by withholding the verb, always the key word of the sentence, as long as possible, usually till just before the end or by withholding in a similar way a complement or object. An easy way to remember the periodic sentence is to remember that its meaning is not complete until the period is reached.

In order either to write periodic sentences or to make loose sentences periodic, all that is needed is to put the modifying phrases and clauses first and thus save the end place for the verb. For example, the two loose sentences quoted above can be turned into periodic sentences as follows:

1. With her crew utterly worn out, her rigging caked with ice, and her hull leaking in several places after her long battle with November gales, the ship finally crept into port. (The four prepositional phrases put first; the meaning incomplete till the end)
2. After sideswiping the wagon and skidding across the road into the bank, the car nearly turned over. (The two prepositional phrases put first; the meaning incomplete till the end)

Read carefully the six following sentences and compare them. The first three are loose and the second three periodic. All six are by established writers, and are effective instances of good sentence craft.

Loose Sentences

1. On the other side he looked down into a deep mountain glen, wild, lonely, and shagged, the bottom filled with fragments

from the impending cliffs, and scarcely lighted by the reflected ray of the setting sun.—IRVING, *Rip van Winkle*

2. And the little pale, round-shouldered dealer stood almost on tiptoe, looking over the top of his gold spectacles, and nodding his head with every mark of disbelief.
—STEVENSON, "Markheim"

3. The old philosopher is still among us in the brown coat with the metal buttons and the shirt which ought to be at wash, blinking, puffing, rolling his head, drumming with his fingers, tearing his meat like a tiger, and swallowing his tea in oceans.—MACAULAY on Johnson

Periodic Sentences

1. When all the preparations were done and the holy evening come, a sweet enchantment would sink down over them.
—SELMA LAGERLÖF, "A Christmas Guest"

2. Past the mocking bareness of the benches, past the blackboard where the flag, loosed from three of its tacks, hung limp and dispirited, he made his way to the shaky little pulpit.
—BARRET WILLOUGHBY, "The Devil Drum"

3. But when Albert Edward with his usual politeness had closed the door behind the vicar and the two church-wardens he could not sustain the air of unruffled dignity with which he had borne the blow inflicted on him.
—SOMERSET MAUGHAM, *The Verger*

All six of these sentences are good. Each accomplishes effectively what the author wished it to accomplish. The loose sentences are easy, natural, and vivid. Vivid too are the periodic sentences, which give the impression of more care and thought than do the loose sentences and which, since they suspend their full meaning till the end, produce a definite effect of focused emphasis.

Two important principles follow from these facts: (1) either the loose or the periodic sentence is good if it is well written; (2) neither the loose nor the periodic sentence is good if it is used to the exclusion of the other. To get the best effect they should be mixed. Too many loose sentences give the impression of careless, slipshod thinking; too many periodic sentences give the opposite effect of an over-careful, artificial style. Since, however, the universal tendency of beginning writers is to use only loose sentences, the point for us to work on consciously and carefully is how to increase our use of periodic sentences.

There is only one way to do this, but it is both easy and effective: *Put something before the subject.*

(4) PUTTING SOMETHING BEFORE THE SUBJECT

Unless we watch our sentences very carefully, we are likely to begin ten out of ten of them with the subject. It is almost impossible for an inexperienced writer to begin a sufficient number of his sentences with something other than subject when he is writing his first draft. In revising, however, anyone can notice whether too many sentences begin with the subject.

The best general rule is to begin from at least a third to a half your sentences with something other than the subject. After your first draft has been corrected for such elementary errors as grammar, spelling, punctuation, and so on, read each paragraph over carefully to see how your sentences begin. By transferring modifying words, phrases, and clauses to the front of the sentence, you can increase the proportion of something-before-the-subject sentences, greatly to the benefit of the variety and vividness of your style.

Consider the following paragraph from one of the best known of American stories, "Rip van Winkle". It has five sentences, only two of which begin with the subject. Of the other three sentences two begin with adverbial phrases and one with an adjective phrase. These before-the-subject phrases are italicized in order to emphasize them. If you will change them to positions after the verb (indicated in the text by carets), you will notice a decrease in effectiveness.

> *In a long ramble of the kind on a fine autumnal day,* Rip had unconsciously scrambled ^ to one of the highest parts of the Kaatskill Mountains. He was after his favorite sport of squirrel shooting, and the still solitudes had echoed and reechoed with the reports of his gun. *Panting and fatigued,* he

threw himself, ∧ late in the afternoon, on a green knoll, covered with mountain herbage, that crowned the brow of a precipice. *From an opening between the trees* he could overlook ∧ all the lower country for many a mile of rich woodland. He saw at a distance, the lordly Hudson, far, far below him, moving on its silent but majestic course, with the reflection of a purple cloud, or the sail of a lagging bark, here and there sleeping on its glassy bosom, and at last losing itself in the blue highlands.

This paragraph was written over a hundred years ago. Here is a paragraph from "The Talk of the Town" taken from the *New Yorker*. Of its ten sentences five begin with something before the subject. As you read, notice the monotony that would follow from taking the italicized expressions and putting them in the places indicated by carets.

Field Trials for Spaniels

At intervals after Labour Day every year, about thirty-five hundred pheasants are set loose ∧ on the island in batches of five hundred by the English Springer Spaniel Field Trial Association. *By the time of the trials*, the birds are presumably sufficiently acclimated ∧ to behave naturally. The dogs compete in pairs, and each dog has two men with him, a "handler" (sometimes the owner and sometimes a trainer) and a "gun". The gun does nothing but shoot the bird when the dog locates and flushes it. He remains as unobtrusive as possible while the handler, who wears his dog's number on an armband, gives all the orders. *Behind the dogs and men are* two judges ∧. *To their rear* are the steward of the beat (a sort of general manager), a man with a big sign bearing the dogs' names and numbers, and the gallery, generally numbering about a hundred and fifty ∧. The dogs start off together on parallel courses and one of them usually flushes a bird in fifteen or twenty minutes. His gun shoots it, his handler gives orders, the dog retrieves it, and his judge takes notes. *When each entrant has got a* bird, the "series" is over ∧.

An examination of the work of most careful writers such as Macaulay, Carlyle, Stevenson, and others, will show that a large proportion of their sentences do not begin with the subject. Recent writers, too, vary their sentences skilfully between putting the subject first and putting something before the subject. An interesting, mature style cannot be attained in any other way.

Exercises in Putting Something before the Subject

Try several arrangements of the following sentences, in each case putting something before the subject:

1. The man behind the gun is in the last analysis the one who wins the war.
2. He crept downstairs very early in the morning and lighted the fires.
3. The regiment proudly marched into the cheering city with flags flying and drums beating.
4. Pluck is better than luck, say what you will.
5. Don't let him argue you into signing the petition whatever you do.
6. Determination is better than brilliance in the long run.
7. I knew we were going to be good friends as soon as I saw him smile.
8. The mountains rise far ahead on the southern horizon. They look like a blue mist from this distance.
9. My friend gave up duck hunting in disgust, after nearly freezing in the cold wind and bogging down several times in the sticky marsh mud.
10. The doctor at last decided reluctantly to operate after having tried every other remedy.
11. The piping call of a curlew came faintly from the chilly grey sky.
12. The last of these reasons is undoubtedly the strongest.
13. A truck ran into a new Cadillac not five minutes before you arrived.
14. The soldiers continued to file by one after another in never-ending procession.
15. Mr. Milton has to catch the 7.55 train every morning, no matter how late breakfast is or how sleepy he feels.

CHAPTER XIV

Making Sentences Pleasing

Making sentences Unified and Clear is a duty: ***You must.***
Making sentences Emphatic is a responsibility: ***You ought.***
Making sentences Pleasing is an ideal: ***You will if you can.***

Making sentences pleasing depends upon a multitude of things. As much as anything else it depends upon the choice of words. Words and their ways form the subject of the next several chapters. So far as structure is concerned, however, sentence effectiveness may be considered under three heads:

1. Variety
2. The Short, Memorable Sentence
3. The Balanced Sentence

1. Variety

Sentences may be divided according to three principles:

I. According to Grammar
  (1) Simple
  (2) Complex
  (3) Compound
  (4) Compound-complex
    (See pages 53-58.)

II. According to the Order of Words
  (1) Loose
  (2) Periodic
    (See pages 239-241.)

III. According to the Length

Of course these divisions are not exclusive, but overlap each other. We may have, for example, a short, loose, simple sentence or a long, periodic, complex sentence, and so on.

The important point is that although there are many kinds of sentences and although each kind is good in itself, no kind is good if it is used too much. Both simple and compound sentences need a fair proportion of complex sentences to set them off to the best advantage; short sentences should be varied with long, and loose sentences should be interspersed with periodic. In fact, writing a paragraph is not unlike making a cake: good materials are of course necessary, but it is equally necessary to blend the materials in the right proportion.

With this in mind each writer as he revises, should look over his work a paragraph at a time, and ask himself such questions as these:

1. What is my favourite kind of sentence? (The answer will probably be the short simple or the short compound.)

2. Do I use this kind of sentence too much, and thus neglect other and possibly better sentence forms?

3. Has my sentence structure enough variety to avoid monotony?

4. What is my average sentence length?

As regards sentence length, it is interesting to note how widely the practice of different writers varies. Some of the best of the older essayists, like Carlyle, Ruskin, and Stevenson, have an average sentence length of something like thirty words; Macaulay averages from twenty to twenty-five; Emerson, close to twenty; college freshmen, about fourteen. Your own average will probably not be far from twelve words, or say, roughly, a line and a half to two lines. If this is true, and you find that you are prone to write too many two-line sentences, vary them by an occasional one-line sentence, and a more than occasional three- or four-line sentence.

HELPS IN REVISING FOR SENTENCE VARIETY

1. Diagnose your own sentence structure and find what kind of sentence you use too much and what kinds you use too little. The teacher's aid on this point will be most helpful.

2. Frequently put something before the subject. On the average, see to it that from a third to a half of your sentences begin with something before the subject.

3. Occasionally use the inverted sentence. Of your something-before-the-subject sentences, put at least one on every page in the inverted order, that is, Complement—Verb—Subject.

4. Try the effect of having at least (*a*) one exclamatory sentence and (*b*) one interrogative sentence on every page.

5. Vary your sentence length purposely. On the average, for every five sentences that are two lines long, have one sentence that is one line long and two sentences that are three or four lines long.

2. The Short, Memorable Sentence

"An epigram," said Arlo Bates, "is a notion rounded like a snowball for throwing." This both defines and illustrates what a short, memorable sentence should be.

In our writing we should try our best to make an occasional sentence like that—pithy, pungent, striking. The ideal place for such a sentence is either at the beginning of the theme, in order to attract the reader at the outset, or at the end of each paragraph, in order to round off and drive home the paragraph idea.

Here are interesting examples of pungent, striking sentences, "notions rounded like snowballs for throwing".

1. Good libraries are not made; they grow.
2. A fool is a man who is intelligent at the wrong time.
3. Education is the cheap defence of nations.
4. Unto the pure all things are pure.
5. A sword, a spade, and a thought should never be allowed to rust.—JAMES STEPHENS

6. You can't tell whether an author is alive until he is dead. —WALTER RALEIGH
7. There never was a good war or a bad peace.
8. Poetry is the record of the best and happiest moments of the happiest and best minds.—SHELLEY
9. Pessimism is only the name that men of weak nerves give to wisdom.—MARK TWAIN
10. Logical consequences are the scarecrows of fools and the beacons of wise men.—T. H. HUXLEY

Bring in two similar examples that you have found in your reading, and comment on them in class.

3. The Balanced Sentence

Often sentences gain point and pungency if they are balanced. A balanced sentence is one which sets similar or contrasted ideas over against one another in matched and paired clauses and phrases. The paired clauses and phrases not only match each other in thought but are parallel in structure as well. This similarity of structure gives tremendous emphasis to the parallel ideas. A good balanced sentence is hard to write, but is exceedingly effective. Experiment with trying to make at least one good balanced sentence in your next theme.

Read the following balanced sentences more than once, noticing how the thought is paired and the expression is parallel.

1. If you call a man friend, do not doubt him; if you doubt him, do not call him friend.
2. When reason is against a man, he will be against reason.
3. Character is what we are; reputation is what people think we are.
4. As we account for every idle word, so must we account for every idle silence.—BENJAMIN FRANKLIN
5. A gentleman is unselfish because he never remembers himself, and courteous because he never forgets himself.
6. Some books are to be tasted, others to be swallowed, and some few to be chewed and digested.—FRANCIS BACON

7. There were gentlemen and there were seamen in the navy of Charles II; but the seamen were not gentlemen and the gentlemen were not seamen.—MACAULAY
8. A cynic is one who never sees a good quality in a man, and never fails to see a bad one.—HENRY WARD BEECHER
9. Parents spend half their time worrying how a child will turn out, and the rest of the time wondering when a child will turn in.
10. The notice which you have pleased to take of my labours, had it been early, had been kind; but it has been delayed till I am indifferent, and cannot enjoy it; till I am solitary, and cannot impart it; till I am known, and do not want it.
—SAMUEL JOHNSON to the Earl of Chesterfield

THE ROUND TABLE

(*Based on the four preceding chapters*)

1. In a drive against sentence errors, one teacher proposed to the class to list the six mistakes they made oftenest, and to centre attention on them. Here is the list they settled on.[1]

(1) Error in the use of the apostrophe
(Proposed by the teacher)

(2) Error in the use of quotation marks
(3) The comma fault
(4) Any grammatical error
(5) Any error in sentence structure
(6) The use of *which* without an antecedent
} Proposed by the class

Discuss this list in class and either adopt or improve it.

2. (*a*) Take your last theme and draw a ring around every *and* and every *so* which connects clauses. Revise the sentences so as to substitute other and more exact connectives. Then notice the improvement. (*b*) Write at least one theme without using a single *and* or a single *so* to connect clauses.

3. Take any of your themes with a grade of C and condense it into two-thirds of its present length.

4. Examine your last two themes for the proportion of loose and periodic sentences. Be prepared to give the figures in class, and to discuss them in the light of what other students are doing in this regard.

5. Look over your last two themes and see whether you have used a single (*a*) inverted, (*b*) exclamatory, or (*c*) interrogative sentence.

6. Count the sentences in your last theme and see how many begin with the subject and how many with something other than the subject.

[1]Margaret Bell Merrill, "Charting Errors in English," *English Journal* Vol. 8, 1919, page 227.

7. Examine at least two of your themes for the proportion of sentences (*a*) under two lines long and (*b*) over two lines long.

8. Have the teacher assign to the class five of the older authors and five of the more recent authors represented in the class literature text to discover their average sentence length. Divide the passages up among the class so that no assignment will be too long.

9. As a class exercise write an independent paragraph on one of the subjects suggested on pages 84-88 above. Let the paragraph consist wholly of short, simple sentences of the Subject-Verb-Complement type. Next day rewrite the paragraphs using as many kinds of sentences as possible, such as the exclamatory, the interrogative, and the inverted. Do not leave a single sentence that begins with the subject. Compare the versions.

MISCELLANEOUS SENTENCE ERRORS FOR CORRECTION

(*Based on the four preceding chapters*)

A

Name and correct the errors in the following sentences. Two of the sentences are correct.

1. If you will turn to the appendix, the example I quoted will be found.
2. I am sure everyone had a good time and enjoyed themselves all day.
3. He borrowed the clothes with which he disguised himself from a friend.
4. If you told someone that you lived in a cubicle, they might not know what you meant.
5. After some discussion we decided not to drive any farther that night. The road being slippery and dangerous when it strikes the mountains.
6. After visiting the circus he had only ten cents left.
7. If there is any pupil in the class who can answer this question, I wish they would do so.
8. The private saluted the lieutenant, which he returned.
9. Everyone should do their own thinking.
10. The school-house needs to be painted badly. Its lack is an eyesore.
11. It seemed as if every time he looked at a donkey he brayed.
12. If you fail in school it will not be because the course is too hard, but will be due to your lack of study.

13. The speaker talked both longer and more rapidly than we had expected.
14. After wandering around for an hour, the right road was found.
15. One cannot remember everything the teacher tells you.
16. The mills refused to raise wages, which is why they struck.
17. He told his brother he would soon get a letter.
18. Depressions are responsible for disorder, loss of wages, and they stir up trouble and hard feelings.
19. Whenever he met the principal he always greeted him cordially.
20. The examination was a hard one, some of the pupils wrote good papers, however.

B

Name and correct the errors in the following sentences. Two of the sentences are correct.

1. Every pupil in the school is asked to come to the meeting if they possibly can.
2. After the accident, glass was scattered around. Because the windshield had been broken.
3. Not one of the girls would tell their age.
4. At eighteen we are told that Keats was already a great lyric poet.
5. The customer bought the car, but it was sold by him soon afterwards.
6. In gym it teaches you to march in correct time and to hold yourself erect.
7. Playing tennis is more fun than to play golf.
8. Everyone expressed their regret at having to leave early.
9. We usually spend our holidays in either Haliburton or in Muskoka.
10. No man would work hard to make a living if he could get one in any other way.
11. It felt cold when I left the house, which led me to wear my coat.
12. The doctor saw the minister going into his house.
13. Being very costly, the book had a limited sale.
14. A general course is somewhat different, you may choose any two subjects besides history and English, these are compulsory.
15. Everybody thought he would become a great writer after reading his first novel.

16. If one will study hard in high school and college the chances are they will amount to something in later life.
17. He just had two dollars to show for the month's work.
18. The superintendent told the principal that he was right.
19. Saturday can either be used for work or for recreation.
20. He frequently forgot his glasses, which greatly hampered his work.

PART THREE

VOCABULARY BUILDING

CHAPTER XV

The Word

Language is primarily the thing we think with; it is more than mere communication.

—HAROLD E. PALMER

Sentences are made up of ideas, or rather of the relationships between ideas. Each idea in turn is conveyed by a word, so that with the word we reach the starting-point of both speech and writing. In the last analysis our powers of both thought and expression depend upon the number, exactness, and effectiveness of the words we have at our command, or rather upon the number, exactness, and effectiveness of the ideas behind our words.

The English language is almost incredibly large. The latest complete dictionary[1] contains 605,000 words. Of this tremendous number even an educated person probably will never come in contact with more than 3 per cent., about 18,000 words in all, and most people meet only a third or a sixth of that number. It is supposed that the average child of six or seven knows between 500 and 1,200 words; the high-school graduate between 3,000 and 5,000; and the college senior adds between 1,000 and 2,000 more. In nothing do people vary more than in their store of mental ideas and the words that express them.

It was said on page 4 that learning to write is learning to grow up. It is equally true that learning to appreciate good literature is learning to grow up. Thus a vital element in growing up is increasing one's vocabulary. To increase one's vocabulary is to deepen and enrich one's inner life. Our

[1]The Merriam-Webster, Second Edition, reprinted 1944.

whole mental life is based on the number of our thoughts, and in order to express our thoughts and feelings we must have words. One's word hoard bounds and encloses his mental stature as his skin bounds and encloses his body. If we lead narrow lives we shall need only a small vocabulary, but if we feel keenly and think deeply, we shall need an ever-increasing store of words. As Emerson well said, "I learn immediately from any speaker how much he has already lived, through the poverty or splendour of his speech." One measure of a man is his vocabulary.

1. Our Three Vocabularies

We do not actually use more than a small proportion of the words we know. Every person has three vocabularies, one within the other, like wheels within wheels. First there is our active, or *speaking vocabulary*. This consists of the relatively small number of words we habitually employ from day to day in the ordinary course of business and pleasure. Second comes our *writing vocabulary*. This is made up of additional words of a more thoughtful and dignified type, for if we are writing an essay on a literary subject, such as a play of Shakespeare, a novel of Dickens, or on a technical

OUR THREE VOCABULARIES

subject like the radio or the aeroplane, we call in a number of words we should ordinarily have no occasion to use.

Third comes our *reading* or *recognition vocabulary*, much the largest of the three. By means of it we read and understand the various books and magazines that we turn to for information or pleasure as the months and years go by. If we like to read, and read widely enough and long enough, we may acquire an unusually large and rich reading vocabulary.

The relative size and relationship of these three vocabularies may be suggested by the arrangement of three concentric circles.

2. Increasing One's Vocabulary

The chief difficulty does not lie in getting new words into our outermost circle. If we read a good deal and have a fair degree of mental curiosity, we can't keep new words out. The main trouble comes in getting a new word first from the outermost circle into our writing vocabulary and then from our writing vocabulary into our active, speaking vocabulary. This is no mean achievement, and requires considerable originality and independence. George Herbert Palmer, in his suggestive essay on language, *Self-Cultivation in English*, urges us (1) to learn and (2) to learn how to use two new words every week. "A word used three times," he suggests, "slips off the tongue with entire naturalness. Then it is ours forever, and with it some phase of life which had been lacking hitherto. For each word presents its own point of view, discloses a special aspect of things, reports some little importance not otherwise conveyed, and so contributes its small emancipation to our tied-up minds and tongues."

(1) WAYS TO INCREASE ONE'S VOCABULARY

If we are mentally alert and lead wide-awake lives, there is no way of keeping our vocabularies from developing. Each new idea, each fresh experience, each additional fact, each unknown thing we come in contact with, adds new words. Our bodies stop growing while we are still in college, but our minds, unless we put them to sleep with the drug of routine, keep on developing as long as we live.

In detail, however, there are many ways in which we may re-enforce and stimulate this important process of acquiring new words. Seven of these are as follows:

1. Wide, intelligent reading.
2. Intelligent listening, especially to speeches, sermons, oral reports, addresses by visiting speakers, and class lectures.
3. Careful, idiomatic translating from whatever foreign language we are studying, with special reference to Latin.
4. Paraphrasing.
5. Verse writing.
6. Developing an active interest, if possible a passion, for new words, and collecting them eagerly.
7. Habitual and friendly use of word books, with special reference to the dictionary.

The last two of these belong together, and call for further attention. Each is of critical importance. It will not do us much good to meet new words either by way of the ear or by way of the eye, unless we look them up in a good dictionary and thus master them thoroughly. The origin and habits of words form one of the most fascinating studies in the world.

(2) WORD BOOKS

Special books on the study of words exist in large numbers. Many of them are interesting, and all of them are useful. Best for your purposes at present are these:

I. For Your Own Library and Personal Use

(To be within reaching distance at all times as you read and study)

1. A good, recent dictionary of the size and completeness of Webster's *Collegiate Dictionary*, fifth edition.

II. For the School Library

(To be available for consultation when needed)

1. The latest complete dictionary, such as the Merriam-Webster *New International,* second edition, and the *Shorter Oxford Dictionary.*
2. Crabb's *English Synonyms.*[1]
3. Roget's *Thesaurus of English Words and Phrases.*[1]
4. Brewer, E. Cobham, *Dictionary of Phrase and Fable,* rev. ed., J. B. Lippincott Company.

III. For Proper Names

5. *Century Dictionary and Cyclopedia*: Proper Names, vol. 9, D. Appleton-Century Co.
6. *Gayley,* C. M., ed., *Classic Myths in English Literature* (both classic and Old Norse mythology), Ginn and Company.
7. Bulfinch, Thomas, *The Age of Fable,* T. Y. Crowell and Company.

By all means buy a good, recent dictionary for your personal use. A dictionary should be indispensable in the study of English. Since whatever dictionary you get will serve through all four years of high school, the cost per year is less than that of nearly any other book you buy. And see to it that your dictionary is always within reaching distance as you read and write. This may sound like a trivial direction. It is not. It is essential. People are so constructed that when a new or a doubtful word is met, there is a fleeting impulse to look it up. If, IF the dictionary is within three feet at that very moment, we may obey the impulse and look it up. But if the dictionary is at school, or upstairs, or in the next room, or *even across the room we are sitting in,* the odds are that we shall never look that word up at all. Human nature is that way.

THE ROUND TABLE

1. List ten words that you know the meaning of, but which you have never used in either writing or speaking.

2. A week from today, bring to class a list of all the new words you have come in contact with during that week. Keep a careful account,

[1]Now available in inexpensive, revised editions published by Grosset and Dunlap.

look up all the new words, and be prepared to explain them to the class—spelling, pronunciation, meanings, and derivation. It will be interesting to compare the size and quality of the different lists.

3. What dictionary do you use? What is its date?

4. How near to you is the nearest dictionary (*a*) when you are studying in school and (*b*) when you are studying at home?

5. If no dictionary is near at hand as you study and read, what means, if any, do you take to investigate unknown words as you meet them? If a dictionary is not within reading distance, the next best thing is to have a small notebook and a pencil at your elbow, and jot down all new or doubtful words as you meet them. Some such plan is the only way. Otherwise you will never do anything about it, and will miss many chances of enlarging your mental horizon.

6. Following are some of the most useful vocabulary tests. They may be ordered through the Vocational Guidance Centre, Ontario College of Education, Toronto, Ontario.

1. *Thorndike Test of Word Knowledge*
   Publisher—Teachers College, Columbia University, New York City
   4 Forms—A, B, C, D—Time up to 30 minutes
   Type— word sameness—multiple choice
   Norms— Grades 4A-9A inclusive)
   and College Graduates)

2. *Michigan Vocabulary Profile Test* (E. B. Greene)
   Publisher—World Book Co., Yonkers-on-Hudson, New York
   2 Forms Am, Bm. (no time limit)
   Type— multiple choice
   Vocabulary in sections, as follows:
   Human Relations, Commerce, Government, Physical Sciences, Biological Sciences, Mathematics, Fine Arts, Sports
   Norms— Percentile ranks for High School Grades and College

3. *English Vocabulary Tests for High School and College Students* (W. T. Markham)
   Publisher—Public School Publishing Co., Bloomington, Illinois
   2 Forms, I, II (no time limit)
   Type— multiple choice, (word sameness)
   Norms— Median Scores for Grades 9, 10, 11, 12

4. *Clinton General Vocabulary Tests*
   Publisher—Coop. Book Store, Corvallis, Oregon
   2 Forms—A, B. (no time limit)

Type— Multiple choice (word sameness)
Norms— Number of words for each year of High School and College and vocabulary in 1000's of words.

5. *Cooperative Vocabulary Test*
   Publisher—Cooperative Test Service, New York
   Form Q, non-timed (10-30 minutes)
   Type— word sameness (multiple choice)
   Norms— Grades 7-16.

6. *The Inglis Tests of English Vocabulary*
   Publisher—Ginn and Company, New York
   Forms A, B, C.
   Type— multiple choice
   Norms— Percentiles—9th Grade to College Graduate level.

7. *Sentence Vocabulary Scale* (C. S. Holley)
   Publisher—The Public School Publishing Co., Bloomington Illinois
   Forms—Gr. III-VIII, Gr. VII-XII
   Type— sentences (multiple choice answers)
   Norms— Grade Scores

CHAPTER XVI

Spelling

1. Using the Dictionary

Three essential pieces of information about every word are (1) its spelling, (2) its pronunciation, and (3) its meanings. A fourth item, sometimes necessary, usually interesting, always helpful, is its derivation or origin. Only the first two, spelling and pronunciation, can be taken up in this book.

The dictionary is the great source book for all information of this kind, a treasure house of untapped richness.

(1) SPELLING

Correct spelling is of fundamental importance both in school and after graduation. Almost any other kind of mistake has a better chance of passing unnoticed than has a misspelled word. In school, it is your grades that suffer; in the world, it is your chance of a job that pays the price of ignorance. When notice is given of an opening, every business house receives a flood of written applications. On the average, three-fourths of these are thrown into the wastebasket on the score of bad handwriting and poor spelling. Only the good spellers have the chance of a personal interview. Promotion likewise usually goes to those who are best trained in the spoken and written word. No business concern wants an ignorant executive or department head. You can stay on the bottom and not know your native tongue, but you will have a back-breaking time getting to the top if you are ignorant of how most educated people spell and pronounce.

(2) SPELLING DEMONS AND TROUBLE SPOTS

Long experience has shown that most of our spelling ills come not from difficult words but from a relatively small number of fairly easy words, not over several hundred in all, that give trouble to everybody alike. Believe it or not, the three words most commonly misspelled by college freshmen are *too*, *its*, and *their*. A well-known teacher and writer says: Dictate to every ninth-year class in American high schools this sentence, "The next grammar lesson would be too long for one day, but it is all right for two days."[1] You will get these results from every thousand pupils:

grammer, 238 times
to for *too*, 261 times
alright, 342 times
all other misspellings, 47 times

The ten words most often misspelled by high-school graduates in the official College Entrance Examinations over a period of almost a decade were these, in the order given:

1. too
2. its
3. believe
4. together
5. their
6. principal
7. committee
8. therefore
9. separate
10. pleasant

An examination of our Provincial Departmental Examinations would probably give much the same evidence.

The practical lessons for all of us in the light of such facts as these are, first, to find our own particular trouble makers in the general list of spelling demons given on pages 277-281; and secondly, to find our own particular trouble spots in the different words we misspell and to cure these spots by emphasizing them in some striking way. For instance, on our personal list of misspellings that we are directed to keep (page 276, question 1) we might underline twice in red the offending letter or draw a red ring around it. One student taught himself to spell *separate* by writing the first *a* in red pencil about four times as tall as the other letters—

[1]C. H. Ward, *What is English?*, p. 251.

sepArate. Any device is a good one—the more absurd the better—that fixes your attention unwaveringly on a trouble spot and helps you to avoid it henceforth and forevermore.

2. Four Useful Rules

(1) DROPPING FINAL *E*

Words ending in a final *e* drop the *e* before suffixes beginning with a vowel, but retain the *e* before suffixes beginning with a consonant.

COMMON SUFFIXES BEGINNING WITH A VOWEL

-able	-ible
-al	-ic
-ation	-ing
-ed	-ian
-er	-ous

COMMON SUFFIXES BEGINNING WITH A CONSONANT

-ful
-less
-ment
-sion, -tion
-some

Examples

come +ing =coming
fame +ous =famous
sale +able=salable
guide +ing =guiding; +ance =guidance
hcpe +ing =hoping; +ful =hopeful
shame+ful =shameful; +less =shameless
move +ing =moving; +ment=movement

Exceptions

Words ending in *-ce* or *-ge* before suffixes beginning with *a* or *o* keep the final *e* in order to preserve the soft sound of the *c* and *g*.

change +able=changeable
courage+ous =courageous
peace +able=peaceable

THE ROUND TABLE

Using as many of the common vowel and consonant suffixes as possible, form derivatives from the following words, retaining or omitting the final silent *e* according to the rule:

1. adore
2. desire
3. fascinate
4. force
5. grieve
6. hope
7. like
8. love
9. move
10. notice
11. outrage
12. rescue
13. service

(2) DOUBLING A FINAL CONSONANT

Double the final consonant when adding a vowel suffix to words ending in a single consonant preceded by a single vowel

(a) in all words of one syllable

(b) in words of more than one syllable when accented on the last syllable.

Examples

stop (word of one syllable)+*ed* (suffix beginning with a vowel)= *stopped* (final consonant doubled)

slap (word of one syllable)+*ing* (suffix beginning with a vowel)= *slapping* (final consonant doubled)

begin (word accented on last syllable)+*ing* (suffix beginning with a vowel)=*beginning* (final consonant doubled)

occur (word accented on last syllable)+*ed* (suffix beginning with a vowel)=*occurred* (final consonant doubled)

THE ROUND TABLE

1. Add *-ed* and *-ing* to the following words and either double or do not double the final consonant:

1. jab
2. pin
3. cut
4. suffer
5. merit
6. equip
7. enter
8. forget
9. omit
10. offer
11. control
12. differ
13. refer
14. profit
15. remit
16. occur

2. Add *-ing* to the following words:
pin, pine; tap, tape; feel; help; rout; differ; shin, shine; prefer; camp; look

3. Explain and justify by the rule the following spellings:
sloping; hating; grinning; planning and planing; canned and caned; ceiling; equalling; referring, reference; developing; offered; forgetting

(3) *IE* OR *EI*?

When *ei* and *ie* have the sound of long *e* use *i* before *e* except after *c* or "For the sound of *ee* call the POLICE" will help you to remember the rule.

Examples

e after c	*i after l (and other letters)*
deceive	believe
receipt	relieve
perceive	pierce
ceiling	yield

Exceptions

There are seven exceptions to this rule: *either, neither, financier,* **leisure,* **seize, species,* and **weird.* Only the three starred words are likely to be misspelled. If, then, we learn these,—*leisure, seize,* and *weird,*—the police will take care of the rest.

THE ROUND TABLE

Insert correct form (*ie* or *ei*) in the following words:

1. ach ve	7. f nd	13. bel f
2. conc ve	8. l sure	14. p ce
3. gr f	9. hyg ne	15. br f
4. dec t	10. s ze	16. c ling
5. ch f	11. th f	17. y ld
6. n ce	12. w rd	18. dec tful

(4) *Y* TO *I* BEFORE *ES*

Words ending in -*y* preceded by a consonant change the -*y* to -*i* before adding -*es*. This rule applies to forming both (*a*) the plural of nouns ending in -*y* and (*b*) the third person singular of verbs ending in -*y*. In both cases, if the -*y* is preceded by a vowel instead of a consonant, simply add -*s*.

Examples

Nouns ending in *-y* preceded by a consonant:

ally + es = allies
berry + es = berries
lady + es = ladies

Verbs ending in *-y* preceded by a consonant:

try + es = tries
deny + es = denies
marry + es = marries

Y preceded by a vowel:

chimney + s = chimneys
allay + s = allays
valley + s = valleys

THE ROUND TABLE

Apply the rule in adding *-es* to the following nouns and verbs ending in *-y*:

Nouns

1. boy
2. essay
3. fairy
4. hobby
5. journey
6. key
7. melody
8. mercy

Verbs

1. carry
2. buy
3. defy
4. delay
5. employ
6. hurry
7. satisfy
8. say

Note that *day+ly*=daily; and that *gay+ety*=*gaiety* (preferred over *gayety*).

3. The Division of Words (Syllabication)

In addition to getting all the letters in a word right, there are two other points we need to know about spelling: (1) how a word is divided—in other words, its syllabication; and (2) whether a compound word is hyphenated or not.

All words except monosyllables are divided into two or more syllables. Thus words have natural joints, as it were, and can be properly divided only at a joint. When we come to the end of a line in writing, having started on a word of several syllables, the impulse is to continue to write up to the half-inch margin at the end of the line, and then to divide the word exactly at that point, regardless of whether or not a syllable division occurs there. This sometimes leads to just as actual mistakes as if the word had been misspelled.

The dictionary, in spelling a word, indicates either by the accent or by spacing and by a very short dash where the syllables come. Whenever we divide a word, we must be sure we are doing so correctly. *Combination*, for example, divides itself into *com-bi-na-tion*, and we can divide it at any of these places. *Filling* is divided *fill-ing* but *fillet* and *filly* are *fil-let* and *fil-ly*. Other tricky divisions are *sign-ing* (but *sig-na-ture* and *sig-nal*), *ful-fil*, *car-ry*, *pen-ny*, *dis-charge*, *sing-ing*, *sin-gle*, *na-tion*, *shad-ow*.

A syllable formed by a single letter, whether at the beginning or the end of a word, should never be divided, as *alone*, *about*, *busy*, *many*.

It is best never to divide a proper noun, especially if it is the name of a person.

Do not divide a hyphenated word except at the hyphen.

THE ROUND TABLE

Write the following words in list form, dividing them into syllables as you think they should be divided. Verify your divisions from the dictionary, correcting any mistakes and learning the correct forms:

1. referring	7. reluctant	13. forever
2. interference	8. terribly	14. galloping
3. solving	9. interrupt	15. forcibly
4. salvation	10. trickling	16. telling
5. bodily	11. processes	17. helping
6. abiding	12. recitation	18. chemical

4. Compound Words

(1) THE USE OF THE HYPHEN

Another troublesome problem in spelling is when and when not to hyphenate. When two words are often used together, there are three possibilities: (1) the words may remain separate and distinct, as is the case with *Red Cross*, *red pepper*, and *red tape*; (2) the words may be hyphenated, as *red-handed*, *red-hot*, and *red-letter*; (3) or they may have become one word and thus be written solid, as *redbird*, *redcap*, and *redhead*. Nearly all compound words go through these three stages. The oftener compound words are used the closer does the connection become. Moreover, the growing tendency today is for all compound words to be written solid. These three stages shift with time and use, and there is no way of telling in advance which stage a word is in. Many good spellers, who rarely have to go to the dictionary for any other reason, have to consult it constantly to settle this matter of compound words.

Here are some common compound words which illustrate the three stages of union. It is important that you know them.

1. *Two Separate Words*	2. *Hyphenated*	3. *One Word*
all right	high-strung	highway
high school	so-called	classroom
class day	first-class	textbook
post office	left-handed	schoolmate
school bus	self-denial	bookmark
school year	self-reliance	today
no one	self-respect	tomorrow
per cent	good-bye	tonight
will power	well-bred	baseball
good night	old-fashioned	handbag
some day		cannot
		daylight
		typewriter
		oneself

(2) THE PLURAL OF COMPOUNDS

Notice that there is some variation in forming the plural of compounds.*

When *man* or *woman* is the first element and serves to denote the sex of the whole, both elements take the plural form: *men-servants*, *women writers*; but the first element is unchanged in a word like *girl friends*.

Combinations like *the Johnson children*, *the Smith brothers*

*Based on *Essentials of English Grammar*: Jespersen.

are treated as compounds; but we say *the sisters Dodson* and *the brothers Smith* when the surname comes last.

Usage is divided between *Lord Chancellors* and *Lords Chancellor, Governor-Generals* and *Governors-General.* The tendency of usage seems to favour the making of the second element plural: *court-martials, postmaster-generals.*

Similarly, *the Miss Browns* is likely to prevail as a more natural plural than *the Misses Brown.*

A title before a name is generally unchanged: *two Mr. Bertrams*; *Gonerils, Regans,* and *Lady Macbeths.*

Compounds that denote units of measurement are treated as single words: *handfuls, spoonfuls, mouthfuls.*

Compounds containing a preposition or adverb inflect the first element: *sons-in-law, lookers-on, goings-on.* But if the first part is the base of a verb, the word is generally inflected as a whole: *draw-backs, go-betweens, lock-outs.*

An exception to the general rule here is the plural of *good-for-nothing,* which is *good-for-nothings.* As *good* is an adjective, the form *goods-for-nothing* would suggest a wrong idea.

(3) COMPOUND WORDS USED AS ADJECTIVES

When two words are used together as an adjective preceding the noun they modify, they regularly take the hyphen. Thus, *well known, high school, worth while, post office, class day,* when used as adjectives, all take the hyphen; as, a *well-known* man, a *high-school* game, a *worth-while* book, *post-office* regulation, *class-day* exercises, and so forth.

Notice, also, that most of the hyphenated words in column two above are adjectives.

FRACTIONS

Write fractions with the hyphen when used as compound adjectives.

NUMBERS

All numbers from 21 (twenty-one) to 99 (ninety-nine) are hyphenated:

thirty-six, forty-four, fifty-five, eighty-seven

THE ROUND TABLE

Copy the following sentences and with the aid of the latest dictionary write the italicized compound words correctly.

1. The crow is a large *black bird,* much larger than the regular *black bird.*
2. Please go to the *post office* and send this package to the *book keeper* by *parcel post.*
3. My father sent me a *night letter* on my *birth day.*
4. Please show *common sense* in the use of the *semi colon.*
5. Please bring me my *walking stick* from the *bed room.*
6. What *wave length* does your local *radio station* use?
7. How many men are on the *rail road's pay roll*?
8. Have you ever seen a *touch down* made from the *kick off*?

5. Homonyms or Doublets

One particular source of trouble in English is the large number of homonyms or doublets that our language contains. The word *homonym* comes from two Greek words, *homos,* meaning "the same", and *onoma* meaning a "name". **Homonyms, therefore, are words having the same pronunciation but differing in origin, meaning, and usually in spelling.** It is estimated that probably about one in twelve of all our mistakes in spelling comes from these troublesome homonyms or doublets.

Doublets

1. break (Can you break it?)	brake (To put on brakes)
2. coarse (A load of coarse gravel)	course (He took the proper course)
3. fair (Fair play)	fare (Good fare)
4. great (A great man)	grate (Put coal on the grate)
5. heal (To heal one's wounds)	heel (He bruised his heel)
6. missed (Sorry to have missed you)	mist (Fog and mist)
7. pain (To suffer pain)	pane (Broke the windowpane)
8. week (Twice a week)	weak (A weak voice)

The method of treating homonyms varies. On the whole it seems best, however, to realize that there are many troublesome doublets, and that one should couple them together frankly at the outset, and try to distinguish them in spelling, in meaning, and in use.

THE ROUND TABLE

1. Distinguish the following homonyms by using them correctly in phrases or short sentences:

(1) alter altar	(7) canvas canvass	(13) red read
(2) bare bear	(8) dear deer	(14) stake steak
(3) base bass	(9) feet feat	(15) stationary stationery
(4) berry bury	(10) flea flee	(16) sun son
(5) berth birth	(11) here hear	(17) there their
(6) bread bred	(12) lie lye	(18) who's whose

2. Give the other doublet for the following homonyms, and distinguish each from the other:

(1) flare	(8) plain	(15) sweet
(2) hail	(9) pour	(16) time
(3) insight	(10) principal	(17) veil
(4) key	(11) roll	(18) wave
(5) load	(12) seed	(19) wreak
(6) maze	(13) slow	(20) you
(7) pearl	(14) style	

3. Distinguish the following triple homonyms by using them in phrases or short sentences:

(1) rode road rowed	(3) sow sew so	(5) to too two
(2) seas sees seize	(4) site cite sight	(6) seer sear sere

6. The Apostrophe

The apostrophe has three very definite and important uses: (1) to mark the omission of a letter or a syllable; (2)

to help form the plural of letters, figures, and words used without reference to their meaning; and (3) to help form the possessive case of nouns and indefinite pronouns.

(1) APOSTROPHE TO MARK OMITTED LETTERS

In the constant effort to take short cuts in speech, we often leave out a letter in certain words, and thus contract them from two syllables into one. Thus instead of saying *are not*, we leave out the *o* and say *aren't*; or instead of *they are* we say *they're*; and for *it is*, we say *it's*. **In all such cases the apostrophe must be used to mark the place of the omitted letter.**

Here are some of the commoner contractions. The four most troublesome ones are starred.

can't	I'll	wasn't
couldn't	I've	weren't
doesn't	isn't	*who's
don't	*it's	won't
hasn't	o'clock	wouldn't
haven't	shan't	*you're
he's	*they're	we're

Note particularly the four starred forms. They give trouble because they are easily confused with resembling forms. *It's* is the contraction for *it is*, and not the possessive of *it*. (*It's* late; *it's* never too late to mend, etc.; but, The dog came back without *its* collar; This tree has lost *its* leaves.) Similarly, *who's* is the contraction for *who is*, and must not be confused with *whose*, the possessive of *who*. (*Who's* there? *Who's* that at the phone? But *whose* hat is this? I've just seen the man *whose* car was wrecked yesterday.) Likewise *they're* is the contraction for *they are*, and must be distinguished from the possessive *their*. (*They're* here, but *their* baggage did not come.) *You're* is the contraction for *you are*, and must not be confused with the possessive *your*. (*You're* sure that *your* train is on time?)

(2) APOSTROPHE TO FORM THE PLURAL OF LETTERS AND FIGURES

For the sake of clearness and convenience, apostrophe *s* (*'s*), instead of simply *s*, is usually added to form the plural of letters, figures, and words used without regard to their meaning.

Examples

1. The most troublesome figures to write clearly are *5*'s and *7*'s.
2. Unless you dot your *i*'s and cross your *t*'s, your *i*'s will look like *e*'s and your *t*'s will look like *l*'s.
3. The reason you got the wrong answer is that you mixed up your +'s and —'s.

(3) APOSTROPHE TO FORM POSSESSIVE

('*s* and *s*')

(1) The Possessive Case of Nouns

1. If the noun is in the singular number, add apostrophe *s* (*'s*).

The man's hat; a boy's book; father's watch; a lady's fan.

This is the simple, invariable rule in forming the possessive singular, and present usage applies it even when the noun ends in an *s* sound:

Keats's life; Burns's poems; Jones's wife; Dickens's novels; James's sister.

Only in extreme cases, where there is a multiplication of hissing *s*'s, is the apostrophe alone without the *s* used to form the possessive singular: Ulysses' wanderings; Sophocles' dramas; Edgar Lee Masters' poetry; for goodness' sake.

Hence, ninety-nine times out of a hundred, to form the possessive singular, add '*s*.

2. If the noun in the plural number ends in *-s* or *-es*, to form the possessive simply add the apostrophe.

Take, for example, the s-plurals *sailors, trees, foxes, boys*. The s-ending is a part of the plural number.

To form the possessive, simply add the apostrophe.

sailors' togs; trees' leaves; foxes' holes; boys' clothes.

3. If the noun in the plural does not end in *-s* or *-es*, to form the possessive add apostrophe *s* ('*s*).

men's failures; women's work; mice's nests; brethren's society; children's games; oxen's horns; deer's enemies; heathen's idols; seraphim's wings; alumni's choice; alumnae's wishes.

(2) The Possessive Case of Pronouns

The indefinite pronouns, however, many of which end in *one, body, else,* form the possessive by adding apostrophe *s* ('*s*).

no one's business; everybody's belief; one's wish; another's work; someone's hat; nobody's land; everyone else's opinion; somebody else's seat.

The apostrophe is never used, in any circumstances, to form the possessive of personal, relative, or interrogative pronouns:

yours	ours
his, hers, its	theirs
whose	whose?

THE ROUND TABLE

1. Using very short sentences, or even phrases, form the possessive case of the following nouns:

(1) cat	(4) brother	(6) Daisy
cats	brothers	(7) father-in-law
(2) gentleman	brethren	(8) somebody
gentlemen	(5) Tom	(9) nobody else
(3) woman	Thomas	(10) Holmes
women		(11) alumnus

2. Copy the following sentences and insert apostrophes wherever needed. Do not write in your book.

(1) "Whos there?" a mans voice called. "I wont open the door till Im certain you arent a thief."
(2) If were to be there by four oclock, wed better be starting now.
(3) Why didnt you let me know you couldnt come? Its too late to borrow anyone elses car now.

(4) It wont be long now. Theyre about ready to start.
(5) Your *n*s and your *u*s look exactly alike.
(6) Whose hat is that on the table?
(7) This paper is ours, not theirs.
(8) Its no use to complain. Anybodys guess is as good as anybody elses.

7. A Final Word

In all of your efforts to improve your spelling, never forget that you must be your own doctor, nurse, and druggist. Each one must diagnose and prescribe for himself—and then faithfully take his own medicine. No two people are troubled by exactly the same words.

It follows from this that while books and teachers can point the way, you alone can cure your spelling ills. Keep a list in your English notebook of your own misspellings gleaned from themes, dictation, reports, quiz papers, or from any source whatsoever. This list, together with a similar list of your mispronunciations, should be unfailingly kept up to date and frequently reviewed. If you make these lists complete and study them faithfully, they may well prove in later life to be the most directly practical and helpful thing you got from school this year.

THE ROUND TABLE

1. In your English notebook keep a personal Stop-Look-and-Listen list of all words which you misspell, either from ignorance or from carelessness.

2. Select two captains, and let each captain choose in turn a member of the class until the whole class is divided into two sides. On four different days, with or without notice, let the teacher choose and dictate fifty of the words from the list of demons given on pages 277-281. After the dictation let the sides exchange papers and correct them in class. Give prizes (actual or imaginary) to the winning side and to the two best spellers.

3. Try this eleventh-year spelling test either at home or at school:

pronunciation	accidentally	February
dining	therefore	anniversary

perhaps	movable	referring
affect	already	writing
description	altogether	beautiful
definite	describe	conscience
separate	occurring	constitution
running	twenty-four	ied

4. Here is a list of fifty-five simple, familiar words. Theoretically you knew them all before entering first-year high school. Look at them carefully and suspiciously. Do not scorn them because they are short and deceptively simple. Are you willing to look on these words as forming a special group of Inexcusables, and to agree with the teacher (1) that one misspelled word from this list will reduce any theme to a C grade, and (2) that two or more misspellings from it will automatically give a theme a failing grade?

Inexcusables

1. across	12. does	23. meant	34. studied	45. used to
2. almost	13. doesn't	24. minute	35. studying	46. usually
3. already	14. etc.	25. ninth	36. sure	47. whether
4. all right	15. forty	26. o'clock	37. surprise	48. which
5. always	16. fourth	27. off	38. their	49. wholly
6. among	17. having	28. quite	39. till	50. who's
7. around	18. hoping	29. really	40. together	51. whose
8. before	19. isn't	30. seems	41. too	52. woven
9. busy	20. its	31. sense	42. tries	53. writer
10. coming	21. itself	32. speech	43. truly	54. writing
11. divide	22. led	33. stopped	44. until	55. yours

Words Easily Misspelled

(Correct Forms to Be Established)

(*Arranged in Groups of Ten*)

I	II	III
1. abbreviation	11. acquaintance	21. all right
2. absence	12. across	22. altar
3. acceptable	13. address	23. alter
4. accessible	14. adjourn	24. altogether
5. accidentally	15. adjustable	25. alumna (ae)
6. accommodate	16. advice (*noun*)	26. alumnus (i)
7. account	17. advise (*verb*)	27. always
8. accumulate	18. aggravate	28. amateur
9. acknowledge	19. agreeable	29. among
10. achievement	20. alliteration	30. amount

IV

31. analysis
32. anybody
33. anyone
34. apiece
35. apparatus
36. apparent
37. arguing
38. argument
39. assassination
40. ate

V

41. athletics
42. author
43. automobile
44. awkward
45. bade
46. baggage
47. balance
48. ballad
49. banana
50. baring

VI

51. barring
52. becoming
53. before
54. beginning
55. believe
56. benefited
57. biscuit
58. boundary
59. bouquet
60. breadth

VII

61. breathe
62. breeches
63. budget
64. buoy
65. buoyant
66. burglar
67. bus
68. busy
69. business
70. cafeteria

VIII

71. calendar
72. cannot
73. capital (*adj*., chief; *noun*, city, wealth)
74. capitol (state-house building)
75. career
76. careless
77. ceiling
78. cemetery
79. changeable
80. changing

IX

81. chaperon
82. chauffeur
83. chief
84. clothes
85. coherence
86. column
87. comely
88. coming
89. commit
90. complexion

X

91. comrade
92. conceit
93. confident
94. conscience
95. conscious
96. contempt
97. contemptible
98. controlled
99. corps
100. council

XI

101. courteous
102. courtier
103. criticism
104. criticize
105. cupola
106. customary
107. dealt
108. deceive
109. decent
110. decided

XII

111. decision
112. defendant
113. definite
114. dependent (*adj*.)
115. descendant
116. descent
117. describe
118. desert
119. desirable
120. dessert

XIII

121. develop
122. dining
123. disagreeable
124. disappear
125. disappoint
126. disastrous
127. discipline
128. dissatisfied
129. dissipate
130. divide

XIV

131. divine
132. doctor
133. does
134. doesn't
135. don't
136. drudgery
137. drunkenness
138. eighth
139. embarrass
140. emigrant

XV

141. eminent
142. enunciation
143. envelop (*verb*)
144. envelope (*noun*)
145. equipped
146. etc.
147. everybody
148. everyone
149. everything
150. everywhere

XVI

151. exaggerate
152. excitement
153. exhaustion
154. existence
155. expense
156. extraordinary
157. extravagant
158. fascinate
159. fiery
160. finally

XVII

161. foreign
162. forehead
163. formerly (not formally)
164. forty
165. fourth
166. friend
167. fulfil
168. gaiety
169. generally
170. goddess

XVIII

171. governor
172. government
173. grammar
174. granite
175. grandeur
176. grievance
177. grievous
178. guarantee
179. harass
180. having

XIX

181. height
182. hoping
183. humble
184. humour
185. illegible
186. immensely
187. incidentally
188. inexcusable
189. infinitive
190. innocence

XX

191. inoculate
192. interrogative
193. isn't
194. isolate
195. it's
196. its
197. itself
198. judgment
199. knew
200. laid

XXI

201. led
202. legend
203. legible
204. leisure
205. lightening
206. lightning
207. loose
208. lose
209. lovable
210. maintenance

XXII

211. mattress
212. meanness
213. meant
214. medicine
215. metaphor
216. mileage
217. misspell
218. miscellaneous
219. mischievous
220. mosquito

XXIII

221. necessary
222. nickel
223. niece
224. ninety
225. nobody
226. nothing
227. no one
228. noticeable
229. noun
230. obliged

XXIV

231. obstacle
232. occasion
233. o'clock
234. occurred
235. off
236. omitted
237. oneself
238. optimism
239. paid
240. parallel

XXV

241. pastime
242. pastoral
243. peaceable
244. permissible
245. perseverance
246. personification
247. perspiration
248. pessimist
249. picnic
250. picnicking

XXVI

251. piece
252. pleasant
253. possess
254. practice (*noun*)
255. practise (*verb*)
256. precede
257. preceding
258. preparation
259. principal (*adj.*, most important; *noun*, head, chief, capital wealth)
260. principle (*noun*, guiding rule)

XXVII

261. privilege
262. probably
263. proceed
264. procedure
265. prodigy
266. professor
267. profited
268. pronunciation
269. quiet (still)
270. quite (entirely)

XXVIII

271. quiz
272. quizzes
273. really
274. receive
275. recommend
276. referred
277. relieve
278. religious
279. remembrance
280. renaissance

XXIX

281. renascence
282. repetition
283. restaurant
284. rhythm
285. salary
286. scarcely
287. schedule
288. seize
289. sense
290. separate

XXX

291. shining
292. siege
293. sieve
294. simile
295. skein
296. somebody
297. someone
298. sophomore
299. speech
300. stationary (not moving)

XXXI

301. stationery (writing supplies)
302. stopped
303. stretched
304. studying
305. successful
306. superintendent
307. superstitious
308. sure
309. surprise
310. syllable

XXXII

311. synonym
312. tariff
313. tendency
314. there
315. their
316. theirs (not their's)
317. they're
318. till (but until)
319. together
320. too

XXXIII

321. tragedy
322. tries
323. truly
324. umbrella
325. undoubtedly
326. unnecessary
327. unnoticeable
328. until (but till)
329. using
330. usually

XXXIV

331. valet
332. vengeance
333. verify
334. village
335. villain
336. visible
337. weather
338. weird
339. welfare
340. whether

XXXV

341. wield
342. who's (who is)
343. whose (belonging to whom?)
344. won't
345. writer
246. writing
347. written
348. yield
349. yours (not your's)

CHAPTER XVII

Pronunciation

Pronunciation is to the spoken word what spelling is to the written—a sure proof either of knowledge or of ignorance. There is no way to cover up a mistake in pronunciation. It is obvious to everybody, and is usually greeted by others with an inward smile of amusement, surprise, or pity, according to circumstances. In sheer self-defence we must learn to speak correctly.

Mistakes in pronunciation are due to three causes: (1) slovenly enunciation; (2) wrong placing of the stress or accent; (3) wrong sounding of a letter, either vowel or consonant.

1. Slovenly Enunciation

Careless, hasty enunciation is responsible for a good many of our mispronunciations. Instead of giving each word its individual, rightful place, we run them into each other like a collapsing telescope.

The following anecdote is an amusing illustration of how easy it is to misunderstand indistinct enunciation. Three ladies were talking about a conversation they had overheard between a man and his wife.

"They must have been to the circus," said Mrs. S., "because I heard her mention 'a trained deer.'"

"No, they were talking about going away," answered Mrs. B., "for she said, 'Find out about the train, dear.'"

"Both of you are wrong," exclaimed Mrs. C. "They were discussing music, for she spoke of 'a trained ear' as distinctly as could be."

Just then the woman herself appeared, and they appealed to her to settle it.

"I spent last night in the country," she explained with a smile, "and simply asked my husband if it had rained here last night."

As an exercise in enunciation, try reading this incident aloud several times, bringing out unmistakably what each of the ladies said.

THE ROUND TABLE

1. For good practice in enunciation read the following sentences aloud clearly and slowly, bringing out the meanings distinctly:

(1) She has lost her earring.—She has lost her hearing.
(2) He lives in a nice house.—He lives in an ice house.
(3) Let all men bend low.—Let tall men bend low.
(4) He saw two beggars steal.—He sought to beg or steal.
(5) This hand is clean.—This sand is clean.
(6) He would pay nobody.—He would pain nobody.
(7) That lasts till night.—That last still night.

2. For further practice in enunciation, try the following tongue-twisters. Some are old and familiar; some are new.

(1) The sea ceaseth, and it sufficeth us.
(2) Strange strategic statistics.
(3) Sarah in a shawl shovelled soft snow slowly.
(4) She sells sea shells.
(5) The Leith police dismisseth us.
(6) Surly Shirley sold silly shilly-shally Sally shiny satin slippers.
(7) Shook's snapshot shop shall show some sharp snapshots soon.
(8) Does Daisy's daily dozen delay Daisy's lazy dozing, or does Daisy's lazy dozing delay Daisy's daily dozen?
(9) When wicked witches whisk switches, which witch whisks switches swiftest?
(10) Are our oars here?
(11) Many a wit is not a whit wittier than Whittier.
(12) His suit showed spots of suet and soot.
(13) Truly rural.
(14) Tie twine to three tree twigs.
(15) The old cold scold sold a school coal scuttle.
(16) Shy Sarah saw six Swiss wrist watches.
(17) Does this shop stock short socks with spots?

(18) The sixth sheik's sixth sheep's sick.
(19) She stood at the door of Burgess's fish-sauce shop welcoming him in.
(20) Lemon liniment.

2. Wrong Accent

The accent is a very important part of English pronunciation. We may sound each letter and syllable in a word correctly, and yet put the stress or voice emphasis on the wrong syllable.

Study the two columns and fix the right accents firmly in your mind by saying the words over aloud several times with unusually strong stress on the accented syllable.

Accent the First Syllable	*Accent the Second Syllable*
ad′mirable	acces′sory
ap′plicable	address′
com′parable	adult′
con′versant	ally′
de′ficit	condo′lence
de′monstrate	defect′
des′picable	detour′
dis′putable	discharge′
ex′quisite	diverse′
for′midable	entire′
har′ass	excess′
hos′pitable	finance′
il′lustrate	grimace′
in′famous	indis′putable
in′teresting	inex′orable
in′ventory	inex′plicable
lam′entable	inquir′y
mis′chievous	irrep′arable
or′chestra	irrev′ocable
pos′itively	mishap′
pref′erable	moustache′
pri′marily	muse′um
rep′utable	pretence′
the′atre	research′
ve′hement	resource′
	robust′
	romance′

Sometimes the same word is accented differently if it is used as different parts of speech. Thus, as a noun, *survey* has the accent on the first syllable, *sur'vey*; as a verb, it has the accent on the last syllable, *survey'*. The word *accent* is used similarly: *ac'cent* is the noun; *accent'*, the verb. *Expert* as a noun is *ex'pert*; as an adjective it is *expert'*. *Absent* as an adjective is *ab'sent*; as a verb it is *absent'*.

THE ROUND TABLE

1. Read the following sentences aloud, accenting strongly the correct syllables:

(1) If you *absent* yourself from class, you will be marked *absent*.
(2) If we wish to *progress*, we shall have to make better *progress* than we are doing now.
(3) Please *record* this statement in the *record*.
(4) I *object* to being made the *object* of ridicule.
(5) The loser said he would *contest* the judges' decision in the last *contest*.
(6) The foreman said it was not his habit to *increase* wages if the workman demanded an *increase*.
(7) She disliked to *perfume* her handkerchief with even the most delicate *perfume*.
(8) Please *accent* the syllable on which the *accent* belongs.
(9) If you wish *expert* advice, you had better go to an *expert*.
(10) If you *extract* the flavour of the vanilla bean, it is called vanilla *extract*.

2. Read the following aloud and then check your pronunciation of the italicized words with the dictionary.

An old man with a *flaccid* face and *dour* expression *grimaced* when asked if he were *conversant* with *zoology*, mineralogy, or the *culinary* art. "Not to be *secretive*," he said, "I may tell you that I have given *precedence* to the study of *genealogy*. Since my father's *demise* it has been my *vagary* to remain *incognito* because of an *explicable*, *lamentable*, *irreparable* family *schism*. It resulted from a *heinous* crime committed at our *domicile* by an *impious* scoundrel. To *err* is human, but this affair was so *grievous* that only my inherent *acumen* and *consummate* tact saved me."

—SOURCE UNKNOWN

(1) DIACRITICAL MARKS

(*Key to the Symbols Used in Pronunciation*)

At the bottom of each page of the dictionary is a running list of common words with appropriate marks showing how the various letters—vowels, consonants, and diphthongs—are sounded. These are called diacritical marks, and to become thoroughly familiar with them is the first thing to learn about your dictionary, for the pronunciation of a word is given in parentheses immediately following each word.

THE ROUND TABLE

1. Do you pronounce *was*, *of*, and *what* correctly? If you are in earnest about pronunciation, you will make an immediate start on these three words. They look easy, but it will take all your care and effort to conquer them.

2. Probably the most variously pronounced word in English is *quinine*. One dictionary gives five pronunciations. Look them up. Which is the favoured pronunciation in your community?

3. What is the difference in your dictionary between the dash and the hyphen marking the division of syllables?

4. What is the difference in your dictionary between the primary (or chief) accent in a long word and the secondary (or light) accent?

5. If two pronunciations are listed as allowable, how can you tell which is preferred?

6. The following are good words to practise your pronunciation on. Try them first without and then with the dictionary.

suite	Asia	cents	Arctic
mauve	ere	film	elm
spavin	bade	Italian	library
tirade	decade	umbrella	pianist
won't	discern	white	

4. Proper Names

In both pronunciation and meaning proper nouns stand in a class by themselves and need special attention. Proper names from foreign languages, especially Greek, Latin, French, German, Italian, and Spanish, follow the laws of their own languages unless they have been in common use in

English long enough to become Anglicized. We must be extremely careful, therefore, to be sure we pronounce such names correctly.

Following are several proper names which are more or less commonly mispronounced.

(1) PLACE NAMES

Abitibi (ăb-ĭ-tĭb′-ĭ)
Argentina (är′jĕn-tē′nȧ)
Azores (ȧ-zōrz′)

Banff (bămf)
Bombay (bŏm-bā′)
Buenos Aires (bwā′nōs ī′rās)

Calgary (kăl′-ga-rĭ)
Cataraqui (kăt′-a-ră-kwi; kăt′-a-raw′kwĭ)
Chicoutimi (shĭ′-ko͞o′-tĭ-mĭ)

Esquimalt (ĕs-kwē′-mawlt)

Genoa (jĕn′ō-ȧ)
Gloucester (glŏs′tẽr)

Himalaya (hĭ-mä′lȧ-yȧ; less correctly him′ȧ lā′-yȧ)
Houston (hūs′tŭn)

Iowa (ī′ō-wȧ; not wā)

Kapuskasing (kăp′-us-kā′-sĭng)

Leicester (lĕs′tẽr)
L'Orignal (lor-nĕl′)
Los Angeles (lōs ăng′gĕl-ĕs or lŏs ăn′jĕl-ĕs or ēz)
Louisiana (Lo͞o-ē′zĭ-ăn′ȧ)
Louisville (lo͞o′ĭs- or lo͞o′ĭ-vĭl)

Madawaska (măd-a-wŏs′-ka)
Manitoulin (mă-nĭ-to͞o′-lin)
Miami (mī-ăm′ĭ)
Mojave (mō-hä′vȧ)

Nanaimo (nă-nī′-mō)
Nassau (năs′ô)
New Orleans (ôr′lē-ȧnz)
Newfoundland (accent either first or last syllable, not the second syllable; but Newfound′land dog)

Okanagan (ō-ka-nah′-gan)
Omaha (ō′mȧ-hô)

Penetanguishene (pĕn-e-tan′-gwĭ-shēn′)
Pompeii (pŏm-pā′yē; -pē′ī)
Port Said (pōrt sä-ēd′)

Quebec (kwĭ-bĕk′)
Quinte (kwĭn′-tĭ)
Quito (kē′tō)

Rainier (rā-nēr′)
Restigouche (rĕs′-tĭ-go͞osh)
Rio de Janeiro (rē′ō dā zhȧ-nā′rō)
Rio Grande (rē′ō grän′dȧ)
Rouen (ro͞o′än′)
Rouyn (ro͞o′-on)

Saguenay (săg′-e-nā)
Saskatchewan (săs-kăch′ē-wŏn)
Sault Ste. Marie (so͞o sānt-ma-rē′)
Sioux Lookout (so͞o)

The Pas (the pah)
Timagami (tē-mä′ga-mĭ)
Tours (to͞or)
Tucson (to͞o-sŏn′)

Uruguay (ū′ro͝o-gwā; o͞o ro͞o-gwī′)
Utah (ū′tô; ū′tä)

Worcester (wo͝os′tẽr)

Yosemite (yō-sĕm′ĭ-tē)

(2) FAMOUS PEOPLE

Beerbohm (bēr′bōm)
Beethoven (bā′tō-vĕn)
Boccaccio (bôk kät′chô)
Boswell (bŏz′wĕl)
Brahms (brämz)
Brontë (brŏn′tĭ)
Buchan (bŭk′ăn)
Chopin (shô′păn′)
Clough (klŭf)
Corot (kô′rō′)
Dante (dăn′tē; Italian pron., dän′tā)
de la Mare (dē lȧ mâr′)
Debussy (dēbü′sē′)
Don Juan (dŏn′ jŭ′ăn; Sp., dôn hwän′)
Don Quixote (dôn kwĭk′sôt; Sp., dôn kēhō′tā)
Dvorak (dvôr′zhäk)
Freud (froit)
Froude (frōōd)
Gandhi (gän′dē)
Gauguin (gō găn′)
Goethe (gû′tĕ)
Gogh, van (vän kôk′)
Hohenzollern (hō′ĕn-tsôl′ērn)
Jung (yŏŏng)
Kublai Khan (kōō′blī kän′)
La Verendrye (la vā′rän′drē′)
Leacock (lē′kôk)
Leeuwenhoek, van (vän lā′vĕn-hŏŏk)
Lowell (lō′ĕl)
Masaryk (mä′sȧ-rēk)
Maugham (môm)
Maurois (mô′rwä′)
Mayo (mā′ō)
Medici, de (dā mĕd′ē-chī)
Morse (môrs)
Nietzsche (nē′chĕ)
Nobel (nô-bĕl′)
Paderewski (pȧ′dĕ-rĕf′skē or rĕs′kē)
Pasteur (päs tûr′)
Pepys (pēps; pĕps; pĕp′ĭs)
Petrarch (pē′trärk)
Plato (plā′tō)
Proust (prōōst)
Rabelais (rȧ′b'lĕ′)
Ravel (rȧ vĕl′)
Robespierre de (dē rô′bĕs′pyâr′)
Sienkiewicz (shĕn-kyā′vĭch)
Strachey (strāchĭ)
Synge (sĭng)
Tchaikovsky (chī-kôf′skĭ)
Vermeer (fĕr mār′)
Vespucci (vĕs-pōōt′chē)
Vinci, da (dä vīn′chē)
Wagner (väg nēr)
Wycliffe (wĭk′lĭf)
Xerxes (zûrk′sēz)
Zweig (tsvīk; tsvīg)

(3) CLASSICAL NAMES

Achilles (ȧ-kĭl′ēz)
Aeolus (ē′ō-lŭs)
Ceres (sē′rēz)
Circe (sûr′sē)
Erebus (ĕr′ē-bŭs)
Hades (hā′dēz)
Hebe (hēbē)
Lethe (lē′thē)
Niobe (nī′ō-bē′)
Penelope (pē-nĕl′ō-pē)
Pleiades (plē′yȧ-dēz or plī′ȧ-dēz)
Psyche (sī′kē)
Satyr (săt′ēr or sā′tēr; distinguish from *satire*, săt′īr)
Ulysses (ū-lĭs′sēz)
Zeus (zūs′ or zōōs′)

THE ROUND TABLE

1. What is the most amusing blunder you have made (or heard) recently in the pronunciation of a proper name?

2. What is meant by saying that a word or pronunciation has been *Anglicized*?

3. Look carefully through the lists of proper names above and check your knowledge of them in the following particulars:

How many (*a*) did you know both the pronunciation and the meaning of? (*b*) were you doubtful about? (*c*) were altogether unknown to you?

4. *An Experience Curriculum in English* advises the following common-sense attitude in this difficult matter of correct pronunciation: "Minor variations in sounds or stresses grow up through adaptations to different physical or mental environments. . . . Such differences are desirable. They indicate life. Dictionaries should be followed with a judicious ear turned toward the habits of speech of the cultured people of the section concerned."

Additional Words Often Mispronounced

Test yourself carefully on this list and master it thoroughly.

I

1. alias (ā′lĭ-ăs)
2. ally (ally′)
3. amateur (ăm′ȧ-tûr′)
4. Appalachian (lā′)
5. apparatus (rā′)
6. athlete (ăth′lēt)
7. auxiliary (ôg-zĭl′yȧ-rĭ)
8. aye, ay (ever, ā)
9. aye, ay (yes, ī)
10. bade (băd)

II

11. bicycle (sĭk'l, but motor sīk'l)
12. bouquet (bo͞o-kā′; bō-kā′)
13. chastisement (chăs′tĭz-mĕnt)
14. column (kŏl′ŭm, not yŭm)
15. coupon (ko͞o′, not kū)
16. creek (kreek, not krĭk)
17. culinary (kū′lĭ-nĕr′ĭ)
18. data (dā′ or dä′)
19. desert (waste of sand, dez′ert)
20. desert (worthiness, dezert′)

III

21. dessert (sweets, dezert′)
22. diphtheria (dĭf-, not dĭp-)
23. docile (dŏs′ĭl; dō′sīl; dŏs′īl)
24. dour (do͞or)
25. draught (drȧft)
26. droll (drōl)
27. encore (äng′kōr)n.
28. envoy (ĕn′voi)
29. err (ŭr)
30. facile (făs′ĭl)

IV

31. forehead (fŏr′ĕd)
32. fragrant (frā′grănt)
33. genuine (jĕn′ū-ĭn)
34. gratis (grā′)
35. hearth (härth)
36. height (not heigh*th*)
37. heinous (hā′nŭs)
38. humble (sound the *h*)
39. imbecile (ĭm′bē-sĭl; ĭm′bē-sīl)
40. joust (jo͞ost or jŭst)

V

41. lenient (lē′, not lĕn′)
42. literature (lĭt′ẽr-ȧ-tûr, not -choor, -cher, or -toor)
43. longitude (lŏn′jĭ-tūd)
44. long-lived (līvd, lĭvd)
45. mineralogy (răl′, not rŏl′)
46. motorcycle (sīk l, but bicycle, sĭk l)
47. nape (nāp)
48. neither (nē′ther or nī′ther)
49. often (do not sound the *t*)
50. parliament (pär′lĭ-mĕnt)

VI

51. partner (not pardner)
52. penalize (pē′nal-īz)
53. perfume (*verb*, pẽr fūm′)
54. perfume (*noun*, pûr′fūm)
55. precedent (*noun*, prĕs′ē-dĕnt)
56. precedent (*adj*., prē-sēd′ĕnt)
57. quoit (kwoit or koit)
58. respite (rĕs′pĭt)
59. route (ro͞ot)
60. salient (sā′lĭ-ĕnt)

VII

61. senile (sē′nīl; sē′nĭl)
62. short-lived (līvd, lĭvd)
63. sleek (rhyme with leak)
64. soften (do not sound the *t*)
65. status (stā′)
66. subtle (sŭt′′l)
67. unprecedented (unprĕs′ē-dĕn′tĕd)
68. usually (sound the a)
69. version (vûr′shŭn)
70. wont (accustomed, wŭnt)
71. zoology (zō-ŏl′ō-jĭ, not zo͞o-ŏl′ō-jĭ)

CHAPTER XVIII

The Standing of Words

1. Speech Levels of Degrees of Dignity

A teacher of composition in correcting a student's expository theme once changed "had a hunch" to "had an idea". In explaining the reason afterwards, and in discussing the choice of words in general, the teacher gave this illustration: "*Father*, *papa*, and *dad* are equally correct. So are a dress suit, a baseball uniform, and a pair of pyjamas. It all depends."

Consider the difference between saying "to act unwisely" and "to play the fool"; "to lose one's mind" and "to go bughouse"; "I can't agree with you" and "Oh, yeah?" These expressions show a fundamental difference both in motive and in purpose, and this difference is double-edged. It extends behind the words, from within the mind of the speaker, and it also projects in front of the words, into the mind of the hearer.

Whether, therefore, any particular expression is suitable depends upon the purpose and occasion it is used for. In the complicated business of communicating our ideas to others, we need different varieties of speech. Good writers and speakers are careful not to mix up these varieties.

The dictionary recognizes five prevailing classes of words: (1) Standard or current speech (indicated by an absence of any of the four following labels); (2) Colloquial, abbreviated *Colloq.*; (3) Dialect, abbreviated *Dial.*; (4) Obsolete, abbreviated *Obs.*; and (5) *Slang.*

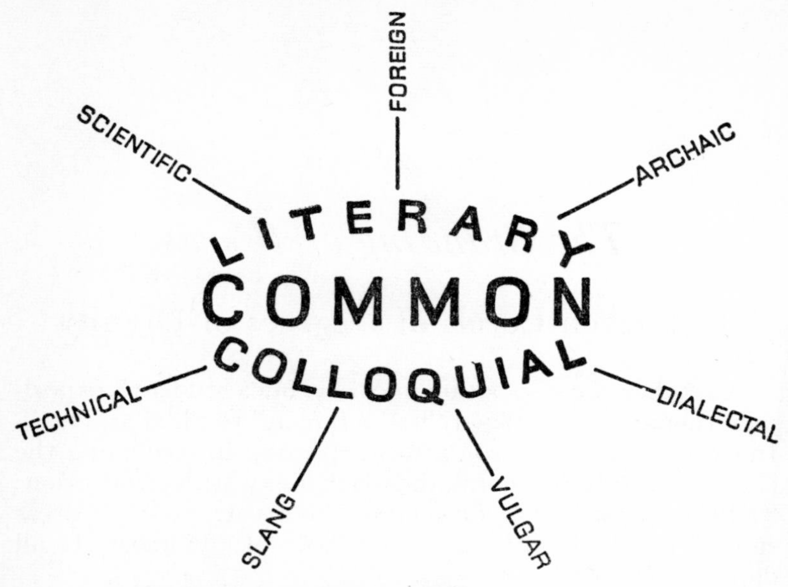

THE MAKE-UP OF THE ENGLISH VOCABULARY[1]

For our immediate purpose in this chapter, we need to familiarize ourselves with only three basic varieties of speech: (1) literary and formal; (2) familiar, informal, colloquial; (3) dialect, slang, and illiterate. We should, however, not only know these groups passively in theory, but also be able to distinguish them actively in our speaking and writing.

Consider the examples given in the following table.

Although these three standards of usage cannot always be kept clearly apart, and although there are many words which could possibly be ranked either as formal or familiar on the one hand, or as colloquial or slangy or dialect on the other, yet the three standards are fairly definite and distinct, and should be kept apart in our writing. **As a practical point, we should be on our guard in two particulars: (1) we**

[1]Through the courtesy of the *Shorter Oxford Dictionary.*

Permissible		*Not Permissible*[1]
1. *Literary, Formal*	2. *Familiar, Informal, Colloquial*	3. *Dialect, Slang, Illiterate*
abundance	plenty of, a great deal of	heaps, lots
father	papa, daddy	pop, pap, the old man
weary, fatigued	tired, worn out	all in
banquet	meal	grub, eats, a feed
masticate	chew	chaw
oration	speech, talk	spiel, bull, hot air
appropriate, seemly	fit	O. K.
impecunious	poor	broke
pusillanimous	cowardly	yellow
is not, are not	isn't, aren't	ain't
mendicant	beggar	bum

should not use stiff, formal language when easier, shorter words would serve. At all costs we must avoid trite expressions and fine writing. One of the best rules ever framed is the old familiar one, "Use the simplest words the subject will bear." (2) **On the other hand, we should not fall into the opposite and commoner error of writing beneath the dignity of our subject or of our readers.** We wish to be easy and natural in our writing as in our speech, but we should avoid the over-use of slang, of abbreviated words, of colloquial, and of dialect words. Our everyday speech is full of them, but we should keep the worst of them out of our written work, especially out of our serious explanatory themes. Few of us ever want to "talk like a book", but many of us will be helped by trying sometimes to write like a book.

THE ROUND TABLE

Degrees of Dignity: Up and Down in Formality

1. Divide a sheet of paper into three columns and head them as follows: I. Literary, Formal; II. Familiar, Informal, Colloquial; III. Dialect, Slang, Illiterate.

[1]Except in unusual circumstances, such as a dialect story.

Put each of the following words either into column one or into column three, and underline the word.

2. If the word belongs in column one, fill in columns two and three with appropriate synonyms coming down in dignity. If the word belongs in column three, fill in columns two and one with appropriate synonyms going up in formality. If you cannot fill in both columns, fill in at least one column.

(1) demise
(2) slumber
(3) swipe
(4) doc
(5) simpleton
(6) duds
(7) residence
(8) pay cheque
(9) inebriated
(10) stuck-up
(11) rube
(12) erudite
(13) skinny
(14) scram
(15) frugal
(16) cop
(17) automobile
(18) guy
(19) eccentric
(20) steed
(21) demented
(22) countenance
(23) corny
(24) contumacious
(25) mad

2. Standard Usage

(*Good Use*)

"Good English is that form of speech which is appropriate to the purpose of the speaker, true to the language as it is, and comfortable to speaker and listener. It is the product of custom, neither cramped by rule nor freed from all restraint; it is never fixed, but changes with the organic life of the language." (*An Experience Curriculum in English*, page 242)

The sole test of a word is usage. Standard usage, or, as it usually is called, Good Use, has three requirements. It must be (1) reputable, (2) national, and (3) current. Or, to express it differently, **Standard usage is the practice of reputable speakers and writers, of national renown, at the present time.** Note that the requirements are three and that each one is necessary. In this respect words are like three-legged stools: it takes all three supports to keep them from falling over.

(1) REPUTABLE USAGE

The first requirement is that a word shall be employed by reputable speakers and writers. This is not only the first but is also the fairest standard. It is the great body of trained speakers and writers, those who know language best and love it most, who mould fashions and set standards in speech. We others are glad to follow their example and do our part toward keeping our mother tongue strong, beautiful, and undefiled.

There are three prevailing ways in which we are in danger of violating reputable usage, and we should guard against each of them consciously and carefully. These violations are (1) Illiteracies, (2) Colloquialisms, and (3) Slang.

1. Illiteracies

On the lowest level of all, far beneath the surface of respectable speech, come what have been conveniently called ***illiteracies***. These consist of flagrant mistakes in grammar, and the use of wrong and wholly unauthorized words and turns of expression. Examples are such words as *disremember*, *anywheres*, *nowheres*, *complected*, *learn* for *teach* (as, "He learned me arithmetic"), and the convenient but impossible *ain't*; such expressions as *between you and I*, *that there*, *this here*, *this away*, *that away*, *them books*, *these kind*, had *of* come, couldn't *of* gone; double negatives like *didn't have no*, *won't never*, *can't hardly*; such verb blunders as *drownded* for *drowned*, "I *give* him the book" (past tense), "He *come*, *done*, *seen*, *run*" (for *came*, *did*, *saw*, *ran*), "They *have went*, *have came*, *have did*, *have saw*" (for *have gone*, *have come*, *have done*, *have seen*). Such mistakes as these are among the gravest and most regrettable sins against reputable usage. Every possible effort, both in school and out of school, must be continuously made to root them out forever.

THE ROUND TABLE

From your observation and experience, name (*a*) any illiteracies you may have trouble with; (*b*) any illiteracies in the speech of your school or community.

2. Colloquialisms

The word *colloquial* comes from two Latin words meaning "to talk with". Colloquial, therefore, means about the same thing as does "chatty" or "conversational". It suggests the informal, free-and-easy conversation between friends when they are off their dignity. **A colloquialism, therefore, is a word or turn of expression suitable for informal conversation, but hardly dignified or formal enough for a serious speech or essay.** The dictionary marks such words as this *Colloq.* as a sign to us to be careful how we use them for literary purposes.

Examples of easy colloquial speech are such words as *folks*; *a raise* (for an advance in salary); He comes *of a Sunday*; It was hard *to get going*; *Wait a bit*; *Well, why not?*; *mighty* and *awfully* in the sense of *very, exceedingly*; *so long* (for *good-bye*); *carryings-on*; *to take back* (recall); all such abbreviations and clipped forms as *Jap, auto, movie, knickers, maths, photo, prof, cap, ad, exam, phone, isn't, aren't, I'd, don't, won't, shan't.* Their name is legion.

Remember, as is explained in the section on Levels in Speech, that although colloquial words are not suitable for formal purposes, like sermons and essays, they are entirely fitting in conversation and informal writing—personal letters, for example. Moreover, the general tendency today, even on the part of the best writers and speakers, is toward a much easier and more familiar style than used to be considered proper. To call a word *colloquial*, therefore, does not necessarily condemn it, but simply puts us on guard to be careful in our use of it and not to employ it on serious, dignified occasions.

3. Slang

> Our slang's piquant as catsup; I decry it
> Not as a condiment but an entire diet.
>
> —WILLIAM LYON PHELPS

If you know the meaning of *piquant*, *decry*, and *condiment*, and will ponder the meaning of the quotation of

William Lyon Phelps, you will need little further direction on the subject of slang.

Slang is one of the commonest and most striking forms of language activity. Its aptness is almost irresistible, and for a short time the latest slang is in everybody's mouth.

Slang is violently figurative, usually in metaphor (see page 343). It consists either in coining new words or in taking a common word or expression and by a sudden twist giving it an unexpected meaning and thus applying it figuratively to a new situation. Often slang exhibits considerable humour and ingenuity. Everyone can recognize the force and the fun in instances like the following: *to pussyfoot, bonehead, chiseller, jitterbug, lounge-lizard, horse-opera, punch-drunk, yellow streak, to bark up the wrong tree, to bring home the bacon, a sucker list, to hornswoggle, to get cold feet, to face the music, joy ride, to rubber-neck, to rib.*

Just as often as not, however, slang is tame and objectionable. Poor slang has nothing in its favour but its newness, and when its novelty wears off there is nothing at all left to recommend it, not even a pleasant memory. How stale and flat seem now such expressions as the following, each of which at one time had its day—with the emphasis, fortunately, on the past tense: *skiddoo*; *Oh you kid!*; *Oh yeah?*; *Are you telling me?*; *hotcha*; *so's your old man*; *nertz*; *shoo-fly*; *you said a mouthful*; *says you?*

There is no denying that clever slang is fresh and piquant. If skilfully used, it adds zest and humour to informal speech. You have only to read the baseball, football, and boxing columns in any newspaper to have daily proof of humanity's fondness for racy metaphors and fresh slang.

Probably the greatest objection to slang is the practical one that it tends to become a "verbicide" or word-killer. We fall into the habit of letting a convenient slang term express a dozen different meanings or shades of meaning, instead of trying to say what we mean in other and more exact words. Thus we both limit the number of words we use, or ought to use, and also weaken the skill and precision of the words we do use.

To sum up, slang is a good servant but a bad master. Keep two rules concerning it constantly in mind. **(1) Discriminate. Use only the best and cleverest slang. (2) Don't overdo the matter,** for two reasons: (*a*) Good taste demands moderation. A touch of artistic make-up may render an attractive face more attractive. Too much make-up spoils even the attractiveness that was there originally.

(*b*) Don't let your use of slang starve your growing vocabulary. Again, like strychnine, a little stimulates; a great deal kills.

THE ROUND TABLE

1. What are the two cleverest slang expressions you ever heard? The two most objectionable?

2. Of all the more or less current slang of the day, do you think any has a chance of being taken permanently into the language? If so, which?

3. Bring to class the slangiest write-up you can find describing a sports contest—baseball, football, or any game. Rewrite part of it in literary style.

4. Read aloud in class what Holmes's *Autocrat of the Breakfast Table* says about slang. The passage is found in Chapter XI and occupies one full page immediately following "The Deacon's Masterpiece". It begins: "I have known several genteel idiots whose whole vocabulary had deliquesced into some half dozen expressions."

(2) NATIONAL USAGE

The second requirement of standard usage is that a word shall be *national*, that is, in good use throughout the country as a whole—north, east, south, and west. To be thoroughly national a word must (1) not primarily belong to another language, (2) not be peculiar to any particular trade or class, or (3) not be peculiar to any particular section or part of the country. Violations of these three requirements are (1) Foreign Words, (2) Technical Terms, and (3) Localisms, Provincialisms, or Dialect Words.

1. Foreign Words

Some writers have the fad of flavouring their style with an occasional expression from a foreign language—usually Latin or French. **The best practice is not to use a foreign word when an English word can be found to do the work.**

Convenient foreign expressions, which most people would understand, whether or not they would use them in their own writing, are these: *ad infinitum*, *quid pro quo*, *per se*, *prima facie*, *entre nous*, *esprit de corps*, *élan*, *cortège*, *un fait accompli*, *motif*, *laissez-faire*, *savoir-faire*, *raison d'être*, *tout ensemble*.

2. Technical Terms

Most trades, professions, classes, and ranks of society, as well as fads, games, and sports, have developed their own particular vocabulary of technical terms which the members or devotees use when talking to each other. Doctors and lawyers discuss professional matters in terms that mean little to the man in the street.

Examples of words that would require definition and explanation before they would be clear to the average man are, in football, *a safety*, *a touchdown*, *eligible to receive a pass*; in baseball, *an infield fly*, *a squeeze play*, *a sacrifice hit*; in tennis, *a foot fault*, *a let*, *a cross-court volley*; in golf, *a birdie*, *a chip shot*, *a slice*, or *a pull*; in the stock market, *a bull*, *a bear*, *a stop order*.

3. Localisms, Provincialisms, Dialect Words

The third violation of the requirement that words should be national is the **use of words and expressions that are peculiar to a certain part or section of the country.**

Professor Alexander of Queen's University records the existence of six Nova Scotia localisms, variants of the word *see saw*. Commonly known in Ontario as a teeter-totter this device is known in Nova Scotia as one of: *tilt*, *teeter*, *tinter*, *tilting board*, *tippin board*, and *sawman*.

There are many examples to be drawn from usage in different sections of the United States.

Examples in New England are *clever* in the sense of *good-natured, kind, calculate* for *think* or *expect, to home* for *at home*, and *visit with* for *to go to see* or *to pay a call on*; in the West, *loco* for *crazy, two bits* for *quarter, wrangle* for *to herd* or *round up livestock, pack* for *carry*, and *make a bed down* for *make up a bed*; in the South, *guess so* and *reckon so* for *think* or *suppose, evening* for *afternoon*, and *you all* in the sense of a group plural for *you*.

All such expressions, while primarily local in origin and use, are apt to spread beyond the boundaries of their particular section and to be used anywhere in informal or conversational talk. They thus give a colloquial, racy tang to both speech and writing that is meant to mirror the local colour of the different sections.

THE ROUND TABLE

1. What are the two most convenient foreign expressions you know or have come into contact with most frequently in your reading?
2. Name five technical terms connected with cooking, hunting, fishing, gymnastics, boxing, swimming, scouting, moving pictures, the radio.
3. Name several of the most characteristic localisms of your community or county.

(3) CURRENT USAGE

The third requirement of standard usage is that a word shall be in use at the present time. It is the accepted usage of today that counts, not that of the past or of the future. It is thus possible to err in two ways: (1) to use words that have passed out of active service and are now archaic or obsolete, and (2) to use newly coined words (neologisms) that have not yet made a place for themselves in the language. This process of dropping off words that have outlasted their usefulness and of taking on new words as the rapid changes of modern life create a demand for them is one of the signs that language is still a live and growing function of human society.

1. Archaic or Obsolete Words

Archaic means "antiquated, old-fashioned", and *obsolete* means "no longer in use, outworn". The terms are thus synonyms, although *obsolete* is the stronger of the two and suggests the quality of being not merely old-fashioned but of being both old-fashioned and laid aside. Neither term is a synonym for *old*. Most archaic and obsolete words are old, but age alone does not make a word either archaic or obsolete. Many of the oldest words in the language are still as vigorous and as necessary as they were a thousand years ago. Examples are the words for family relationship like *father*, *mother*, *husband*, *wife*, *son*, *daughter*, *sister*, *brother*, and so on; the numerals *one*, *two*, *three*, and so on; the pronouns *I*, *you*, *he*, *who*, *which*, and so on; the prepositions *for*, *from*, *by*, *with*, *in*, *at*, *to*, and so forth; the articles *a*, *an*, and *the*; and many of the words that we *have* to use in common speech every day of our lives. Such words can never become obsolete or even archaic.

Many other words, however, do outwear their usefulness, and after a longer or shorter period of increasing neglect are cast up like bits of driftwood on the banks of time as the great living stream of language flows on. Among the more interesting and significant of these are the following. We should know the meaning of each of them, for they not only have had a long and honoured history, but are still used to add a quaint flavour to poetry and stories of the long ago. Such are *yclept* (called, named); *dight* (clad); the two old *-n* plurals, *shoon* (shoes) and *kine* (cows); various exclamations and interjections with which people of several hundred years ago used to flavour their conversation, such as *haply*, *mayhap*, *in sooth* (truth), *forsooth*, *peradventure*, *prithee*, *perchance*, and *anon*; *eke* (also); the two old words for think or suppose, *ween* and *wot*; *eld* and *yore* (age, time long past);

swain and *wight* in the sense of person; the two old impersonal verbs which formerly took the dative case, *meseems* and *methinks*, both meaning *it seems to me*; *quoth* (said); and the old third person singular verb ending *-eth*, which Coleridge makes such effective use of in "The Rime of the Ancient Mariner", as witness the famous stanza,

> He prayeth best who loveth best
> All things both great and small;
> For the dear God who loveth us
> He made and loveth all.

2. New Words (Neologisms)

Every new invention, every fresh discovery, every advance of science, and every great crisis in world history and world thought calls new words into being. Think of the many word changes that came about when gunpowder took the place of the bow and arrow, and practically abolished hand-to-hand fighting in war. Consider, too, the host of new words made necessary when electricity displaced steam as our major labour-saving power. The two World Wars created a separate vocabulary of their own. The amazing popular spread of four great recent inventions, the automobile, moving pictures, radio, and aeroplanes, causes us to speak a language that would be absolutely unintelligible to our great-grandfathers.

Three Doors for New Words

1. slang

New words are constantly knocking at the door of our word house. Sometimes they are admitted, and sometimes not, depending on whether they fill a real need. Much of our slang springs up like mushrooms almost overnight, flourishes vigorously for a brief while, and then goes quickly out of fashion. Occasionally, however, a good wholesome slang word sticks, and eventually becomes entirely respectable. *Highbrow* is a case in point.

2. SHORT CUTS

We are always looking for the shortest way of expressing our thoughts, and uniformly prefer a word of one or two syllables to a word of three or four syllables. That explains how *cab* and *bus* and *pants* came into the language, and also why *phone* and *taxi* give every evidence of replacing the longer *telephone* and *taxicab*. That is also the reason that a number of new verbs, coined from existing nouns, are waiting around on the outside of standard usage, watching only for a chance to slip in. Examples are *to suicide* and *to burgle* or *to burglarize* for *to commit suicide* and *to commit burglary*; *to railroad* in the sense of *to put through in great haste* or *wrongly*; *to enthuse*; *to wire* meaning *to telegraph*; and *to picturize* meaning *to make a moving picture out of a play or a novel*. The best of these is *to wire*, and is almost sure of becoming standard. Probably the most objectionable is *to enthuse* for the longer *to become enthusiastic*. One hates to think of ever adopting *enthuse* into the family, but the saving pull of two syllables over seven syllables may some day bring it about.

3. NEW WORDS FOR NEW THINGS

Entirely different from the various kinds of tramp words, upstarts, and camp followers, which constantly hang around the outskirts of language, are the hundreds of words that are called into being to supply a real need and that thus become a permanent part of the nation's vocabulary. For example, the third edition of Webster's *Collegiate Dictionary* (1927) has six full pages of new words, approximately 350 in all, which had recently come into favour by the year 1927, the year in which that edition was issued. Among the commonest and most useful of these new words admitted in 1927 and 1934 are these:

(1) Admitted in 1927

1. ace
2. aerodrome
3. to camouflage
4. a close-up
5. decode
6. jazz
7. middy blouse
8. no man's land
9. novocaine
10. profiteer
11. reel (in moving pictures)
12. Rotarian
13. Schick test
14. slacker
15. soviet
16. static
17. swagger stick
18. tank
19. tune in
20. wheel base

(2) Admitted in 1934

1. aerial (in radio)
2. Armistice Day
3. balloon tire
4. beauty shop
5. blood pressure
6. community chest
7. a complex
8. contract bridge
9. crossword puzzle
10. daylight saving
11. Diesel engine
12. flu
13. free verse
14. girl scout
15. highbrow
16. insulin
17. intelligence test
18. jaywalker
19. League of Nations
20. racketeer
21. rayon
22. Rhodes scholarship
23. shell shock
24. smoke screen
25. spiritual (Negro hymn)
26. tail spin
27. thermos bottle
28. zero hour

Even more interesting are the following words. They are among the new words, about 470 in all, which were given recognition in the fifth edition of the Webster-Merriam *Collegiate Dictionary*, issued in 1941.

(3) Admitted in 1941

1. air-condition
2. axis
3. black-out
4. blitzkrieg
5. bobby pin
6. bulldozer
7. candid camera
8. C.I.O.
9. commercial (in radio)
10. cyclotron
11. escapism
12. fifth column
13. Gestapo
14. Lucite
15. microfilm
16. mosquito boat
17. neoprene
18. newscast
19. nylon
20. occupational therapy
21. photo finish
22. plastic (noun)

23. quisling
24. sanforize
25. softball
26. sulphanilamide
27. sustaining programme
28. Technicolor
29. telecast
30. tommy gun

The words on these three lists are both significant and typical. Some of them show the direct influence of the World Wars; some reflect great new industries; several important ones are concerned with mankind's constant efforts to fight disease and to prolong life; others name new inventions or improvements in existing inventions; three are from new games; others mirror experiences from science, gangdom, and music. It is not too much to say that a complete account of the origin and development of these words, together with that of the other new words in the latest dictionary, would be a fairly comprehensive history of North American civilization for the last two decades.

THE ROUND TABLE

1. Think of three words that became obsolete and three words that came into use when gunpowder practically abolished armour and hand-to-hand fighting.

2. Can you think of any other new words that have come into the language through World War II, the automobile, moving pictures, radio, the aeroplane, advances in preventive medicine?

3. In this connection name five words you know and use that you would have to explain to your great-grandfather.

4. How many of the words in the three lists above are unknown to you? Discuss this matter in class.

5. What is the meaning of the following interesting new words: sprung rhythm, radiothermy, collage, octane rating, televise, radar?

6. There is an old proverb, "Give him an inch and he'll take an ell." What kind of word is *ell* and what does it mean?

7. Bring to class two obsolete words, two provincialisms, two colloquialisms, two slang words, and two bookish words. Discuss the lists in class.

8. What are the last two new words you have heard? Where did you hear them and what do they mean? Exchange experiences in class.

9. After you finish this chapter, your vocabulary should be larger by a dozen or so new terms, if you did not know them before. They are

as follows. Be prepared (*a*) to define them and (*b*) to give two examples of each:

Standard Usage or Good Use
National Usage
Reputable Usage
Current Usage
Foreign Words
Technical Terms
Localisms or Provincialisms
Dialect Words
Archaic Words
Obsolete Words
Neologisms

Trouble Spots in Current Usage

CORRECT FORMS TO BE ESTABLISHED

Affect, effect. *Affect* is a verb and means "to influence", and *effect* means "to accomplish, to bring about".

The mercury in a thermometer is affected by both heat and cold.
His unusual determination enabled him to effect his purpose.
If the troops effect an entrance into the fort, it will affect the result of the entire war.

As a noun, *effect* means result. *Affect* is not used as a noun.

Aggravate. Means "to increase, to make worse".

Right: His illness was aggravated by an improper diet.

Aggravate in the convenient sense of "annoy, vex, exasperate" has not yet become standard English, and should be avoided.

All-around. Wrongly used for *all-round.*

Right: He is a good all-round athlete.

Alright. There is no such word. The correct phrase is *all right,* two separate words. Compare its antonym, *all wrong.* Contrast *although* and *always* which are written as one word.

Among, between. *Among* is used in referring to more than two, *between* in referring to two.

Wrong: The property was shared equally between the five children.
Right: The property was shared equally among the five children.
Right: There is little to choose between the two men.

Anybody, anyone, everybody, everyone. Remember that each of these words is preferably followed by a singular pronoun (*he* or *she*) rather than by the plural (*they*).

Any place, some place, no place, every place. Do not use for *anywhere, somewhere, nowhere, everywhere.*

Right: We could not find him anywhere.

Aye (**ay**), pronounced (1) ā and (2) ī. These are really two different words, though they are spelled alike. 1. *Aye* (ā) is poetic and archaic. It means "ever, always, continually".

Right: Forever and aye (ā) ; aye-lasting; For aye unsought-for.

2. *Aye* (pronounced ī) means "yes, yea". It is used in voting by word of mouth and by sailors in reply to an order by the mate or the captain.

Right: Those in favour make it known by saying aye (ī). The ayes have it. "All hands on deck." "Aye, aye, sir."

Balance, remainder. *Balance* means "the amount remaining after realizing assets and meeting obligations". It should not be confused with *rest* or *remainder*.

Right: At the end of the month he had a substantial balance in the bank.
Right: She spent the remainder of the week at her home.

Beside, besides. *Beside* means "by or at the side of"; *besides* means "in addition to, moreover".

Right: He laid the second book beside the first.
Right: He receives his travelling expenses besides his regular salary.

Blame it on. Use *blame* or *blame for*.

Colloquial: They blamed it on him.
Better: They blamed him for it.

But that, but what. After *doubt*, *but what* is wrong, and *that* is preferred to *but that*.

Wrong: There is no doubt but what you were there.
Right: There is no doubt that you were there.

Can't seem. Say *seems unable*.

Wrong: He can't seem to understand what he reads.
Right: He seems unable to understand what he reads.

Claim, declare. Correctly used, *claim* means "to demand as a right", not "to say" or "to declare".

Right: He claimed the land.
Right: He declared that he had been misquoted.

Could of. There is no such phrase. It is an illiterate spelling of the careless pronunciation of "could have".

Wrong: He never could of done it.
Right: He never could have done it.

So also in regard to *may of*, *might of*, *must of*, *should of*, *would of*.

Differ with, differ from. Unlike things *differ from* each other. Two people who do not agree *differ with* (or *from*) each other.

Right: A tennis ball differs from a baseball.
Right: Father and mother differ with each other on the subject of dancing.
Right: I differ with you in your belief that the twins differ from each other in looks.

Different from. *Different from* is preferred in American usage, and commoner in Canadian usage, although *different to* is permissible in British usage.

Right: The future will be different from the past.
Right: The trip was different from what I had expected.

Due to. *Due to* is not to be used instead of *because of* or *on account of* to introduce a phrase modifying a verb.

Wrong: Due to lack of study he failed to pass.
Right: Because of lack of study he failed to pass.
Also Right: His failure was due to lack of study.
Wrong: We reached home after dark due to a flat tire.
Right: We reached home after dark on account of a flat tire.

Either, neither. Each of these words is singular.

Right: Neither of the boys is here.
Right: Is either of you going to the theatre?
Right: Neither Ethel nor James has arrived.

Enthuse. A colloquialism. The correct form is "to become enthusiastic".

Etc. This is an abbreviation of two Latin words, *et cetera*, meaning "and other (things), and the like". Since *etc.* is an abbreviation, it must be followed by a period. Since *etc.* means "and others", it is wrong to say *and etc.* The word is never to be spelled *ect.* Someone has suggestively defined it as "a little word we use to make others think we know more than we do".

Everybody, everyone, anybody, anyone. Remember that each of these words is preferably followed by a singular pronoun (*he* or *she*) rather than by the plural (*they*).

Farther, further. *Farther* and *further* are in most cases interchangeable, but very careful writers like to make the following distinction: *farther* applies to actual, physical distance and *further* to quantity or degree. In other words, *farther* applies to movements of the body and *further* to movements of the mind.

Right: The farther north you travel, the colder it gets.
Right: We can go further into the plan next week.

Fewer, less. Although carelessly used as synonyms, in careful usage *fewer* refers to number and *less* to amount or quantity.

Right: There are fewer people in town in summer than in winter.
Right: He has less money than his brother.

Firstly. *First* is itself an adverb as well as an adjective, so that there is no need for *firstly* at all, and most careful writers and speakers prefer not to use it.

Right: First, secondly, thirdly, etc.

Fix. A colloquialism for *repair*, *prepare*, or *arrange*.

Colloquial: I will fix supper.
Better: I will prepare supper.
Colloquial: He fixed the tire.
Better: He repaired the tire.

Funny. Means "laughable, humorous". It should not be loosely used for "strange, odd, queer".

Colloquial: I saw a funny automobile accident yesterday.
Better: I saw an unusual automobile accident yesterday.

Hardly, scarcely. No negative should be used with these

words. *Hardly* means "with difficulty", and *scarcely* means "barely, only just".

Right: I could hardly hear him.
Right: The car could scarcely climb the hill.

Healthy, healthful. *Healthy* means "in good health, well and strong"; *healthful* means "causing health, good for the health".

Right: A healthy family; a healthy animal; healthful food; healthful surroundings.

Imply, infer. *Imply* means "to express indirectly" or "to hint"; *infer* means "to surmise" or "to conclude".

Right: In his speech he implied that the judge had been prejudiced.
Right: From the tone of his letter I inferred that he did not care to return.

In, into. As a rule, use *into* to express motion from outside to within.

Right: Throw that gum into the basket.

Ingenious, ingenuous. *Ingenious* (ĭn-jēn′yŭs) means "talented, intelligent, clever"; *ingenuous* (ĭn-jĕn′ū-ŭs) means "frank, sincere, outspoken".

Right: It takes an ingenious man to make a good inventor; it takes an ingenuous man to be honest and straightforward at all times.

Inside, outside. Need not be followed by *of*.

Right: He remained inside the house.

Is when, is where. These convenient but slipshod expressions should not be used in defining nouns.

Wrong: Camouflage is when you make something look like something else.
Wrong: Botany is where you study about flowers.
Right: Camouflage is the act of making something look like something else.
Right: Botany is the study which teaches us about flowers (or, is the science dealing with plants).

Its, it's. *Its* is the possessive case of *it*. *It's* is the shortened form of *it is*.

Right: The puppy is chasing its tail. The tree is losing its leaves. This sauce has lost its flavour.

Right: It's time to go. It's too late now. It's too high a price. It's my fault, not yours.

Kind of (a), sort of (a). There are three different errors we may fall into in using *kind of* and *sort of*.

(1) Using *kind of a* and *sort of a* instead of *kind of* and *sort of*.

Wrong: I do not like that kind (sort) of a car.
Right: I do not like that kind (sort) of car.

(2) Using *kind of* and *sort of* (then usually pronounced *kinder* and *sorter*) as adverbs meaning "somewhat, in a way, rather".

Colloquial: He was feeling kind of bad.
I can't help kind of liking him.
Better: He was feeling rather bad.
I can't help liking him somewhat.

(3) Using *these kind* and *these sort* for either *this kind* (*this sort*) or *these kinds* (*these sorts*).

Wrong: She does not care for these kind of books.
Better: She does not care for this kind of books.
Wrong: These kind of flowers do not smell sweet.
Better: This kind of flowers does not smell sweet.
Also Better: These kinds of flowers do not smell sweet.

Lay, lie. *Lay* is a transitive verb, taking an object, and means "to put, to place". Its principal parts are *lay, laid, laid*. *Lie* is an intransitive verb, and means "to rest, to recline, to remain in a flat position". Its principal parts are *lie, lay, lain*.

Right: If you lay the mattress on the porch, it will lie in the sun and dry out.

Right: Lay your book on the table. I laid mine there as soon as I came in yesterday. It has lain there ever since.

Like. *Like* should not be used for "as, as if", with a subject and a verb. *Like* is a preposition, not a conjunction, and should be followed by a noun or pronoun in the objective case.

Wrong: It looks like it will rain.
Right: It looks as if it will rain.
Wrong: Do like I do.
Right: Do as I do.
Right (*like* followed by a noun): She plays bridge like an expert.
Right (*like* followed by a noun): He handles his horse like a professional.

Likely, liable. *Likely* implies a probability, usually favourable. *Liable* suggests an unpleasant possibility. *Liable* also can be used to suggest obligation, responsibility, or susceptibility.

Right: It is liable to rain and spoil the picnic.
Right: He is likely to succeed.
Right: One is liable to arrest for exceeding the speed limit.

Locate. Should be used transitively.

Colloquial: They located in northern Ontario.
Right: They settled in northern Ontario.
Right: He located his store in London.

Lots of. Colloquial for *much* or *many.*

May, can. *May* implies permission to do a certain thing, while *can* implies power or ability. Careful speakers and writers keep these uses apart.

Right: He always does the best he can.
Right: A fast aeroplane can fly faster than two hundred miles an hour.
Right: May I borrow your pencil?
Right: May I come to see you tomorrow?

Myself. Myself has two standard uses: (1) to emphasize *I* as a subject, as in the expressions, "I saw him myself; I myself will guarantee this"; (2) to serve as reflexive object in such sentences as "I fell down and hurt myself; I overslept myself this morning". It is best, however, not to use *myself* simply as a substitute for *I* or *me.*

Colloquial: My brother and myself went hunting yesterday.
Better: My brother and I went hunting yesterday.

Colloquial: Will there be room for Alice and myself?
Better: Will there be room for Alice and me?

O, oh. A good working rule for keeping these troublesome words apart is this: *O* (1) is generally used in calling or speaking to someone directly (nominative of address); (2) is never followed by any mark of punctuation; (3) is always capitalized.

Oh (1) is an exclamation used by itself; (2) is not capitalized unless it begins a sentence or a line of poetry or a direct quotation; (3) is usually followed by either a comma or an exclamation point.

Right: This is the truth, O King.
Right: To your tents, O Israel.
Right: Oh! what a beauty (or Oh, what a beauty!).
Right: Oh, for the wings of a dove!

Off of. The *of* is unnecessary. Say *off*, not *off of*.

Wrong: Take the dishes off of the table.
Right: Take the dishes off the table.

Party. Means "a group, body, or association of persons", not "an individual or a single person". Its use in the latter sense is particularly objectionable.

Right: A party of sailors boarded the train.
Wrong: The party I went to see this morning had already left his office.
Wrong: Did you succeed in selling your party an automobile?
Right: Telegram to conductor: "Hold connecting train for a large party." (Twenty-five people arrive.)

In law it is correct to refer to one person as "a party" in the sense of "a party to the suit, the party of the first part", and so forth; but except in a legal document do not use *party* for *person*.

Plan on. The verb *plan* should be followed by a direct object.

Right: He planned spending (to spend) a week in the country.

Possessive before infinitive in -ing (gerund). Infinitives in *-ing* (gerund), like *being*, *falling*, *losing*, *jumping*, and so forth, are verbal nouns. When preceded by a pronoun or a noun, therefore, the pronoun should always and the noun should usually be in the possessive case, showing possession of the action named in the infinitive in *-ing* (gerund).

With Pronouns

Wrong: You can depend upon him being there.
Right: You can depend upon his being there.
Wrong: They insisted on me staying.
Right: They insisted on my staying.

With Nouns

Loose: I never heard of a man losing his temper as often as you do.
Better: I never heard of a man's losing his temper as often as you do.

Posted. Should not be used for *informed.*

Colloquial: He promised to keep us posted on the latest news.
Better: He promised to keep us informed about the latest news.

Principal, principle. *Principal* is either an adjective or a noun, most often an adjective. As an adjective it means "first in importance, leading, main".

Right: The principal thing is to be clear.
Right: The principal parts of a verb are the present infinitive, the past tense, and the perfect participle.

As a noun, *principal* has two important uses: (1) to mean "leader, directing head", as, "the principal of the school"; (2) to mean "a capital sum placed at interest or owed as a debt", as, "We should invest our principal safely and try to live off the interest."

Principle is never an adjective but always a noun, and means "a fundamental rule, a general truth", as "the principle of gravitation"; "He is a man of the highest principles."

Proved, proven. *Proved* is the preferred form of the past participle.

Quite. Means "entirely, wholly, altogether".

Right: I am not quite sure. You are quite right.
Right: Have you entirely recovered from your cold? No, not quite.
Loose: I felt quite sick last night.
Loose: She is quite pretty, isn't she?

Quite a (*an*) is loosely used to mean "somewhat, very, of considerable size, extent, number, etc."

Colloquial: quite a lot, quite a few, quite a number, quite sick, quite a little, quite a long time. Do not overuse these expressions.

Raise, rise. *Raise* is a transitive verb and means "to lift up, to cause to rise". Its principal parts are *raise, raised, raised. Rise* is an intransitive verb and means "to get up". Its principal parts are *rise, rose, risen.*

Right: He rose early and ate breakfast alone.

As nouns:

Right: a rise in prices; a rise in salary.
Colloquial: a raise in wages.

Reason is because. Since a noun clause is needed, say "the reason is that. . . ."

Wrong: The principal reason for his failure was because he did not study.
Right: The principal reason for his failure was that he did not study.

Set, sit. *Set* is a transitive verb and means "to put, to place, to cause to sit". Its principal parts are *set, set, set.*

Right: Please set this vase on the mantelpiece.
Right: Set the pitcher on the table.

Sit is an intransitive verb and means "to be seated, to rest, to remain in repose". Its principal parts are *sit, sat, sat.*

Set, however, in an intransitive sense, instead of *sit,* is correct in two special cases: (1) The sun sets; the setting sun; and (2) The hen sets; the setting hen (in the sense of "brooding over eggs").

Right: The hen is setting on her nest.
Right: The hen is sitting on her perch.

Shall, will. The proper use of *shall* and *will* marks the difference between the most careful and the less careful users of English. The difference is easy to explain, but hard to put into practice.

I. SIMPLE FUTURITY

1. In the first person *shall* denotes simple futurity.
2. In the second and third persons *will* denotes simple futurity.

II. DETERMINATION OR WILLINGNESS

3. In the first person *will* denotes willingness or determination.
4. In the second and third persons *shall* denotes determination.

There is really only one trouble spot—*shall* in the first person to express simple futurity. The other three uses take care of themselves. We should learn, therefore, to say "*I shall*" unless we mean "I am willing" or "I am determined".

(1) I Will

1. I will go in spite of what you say. (Determination)
2. I will give him a chance to get even. (Willingness)
3. If it takes all afternoon, I will not stop before I work this example. (Determination)
4. I will swap you my knife for it. (Willingness)

(2) I Shall

All of the following sentences are correct. Consider them carefully and read them aloud several times in order to get used to hearing yourself say *I shall*. In no sentence could you substitute "I am willing" or "I am determined" for *I shall.*

1. I shall be sorry to see you go.
2. I shall expect you, then, at nine in the morning.
3. I shall be glad to hear from him at any time.
4. We shall never get there in time if we don't go faster than this.

Shape. Should not be used to mean *condition* or *manner*.

Colloquial: He survived the experience in good shape.
Better: He survived the experience in good condition.

So. (1) Remember that *so* as a conjunction should be used with caution and not allowed to displace other and more exact connectives. (2) *So* should not be used for *very*.

Colloquial: We were so happy to receive your letter.
Better: We were very happy to receive your letter.
Also Better: We were so happy to receive your letter that we read it to the neighbours.

(3) *So* should not be used for *so that*.

Colloquial: I will leave the key so you can enter the house.
Better: I will leave the key so that you can enter the house.

Species (specie). *Species* in the sense of "sort, kind, variety" is both singular and plural.

Right: This species, that species, these species, those species.
Right: I have not seen this species of bird before.

Specie is not the singular of *species*, but is another word meaning "coin in bulk, usually of gold or silver".

Right: The express car was carrying a valuable shipment of gold specie.
Right: Large sums are more conveniently paid by cheque or in paper money than in specie.

Stop. A colloquialism when used in the sense of *stay*.

Colloquial: While there we stopped at the hotel.
Better: While there we stayed at the hotel.

Transpire. *Transpire* comes from two Latin words, *trans* (through) and *spirare* (to breathe). Its strict meaning is "to become known, to leak out". Many people use it in the looser, colloquial sense of "to happen, to occur, to take place". Avoid this use so far as you can.

Right: What happened that night never transpired.
Right: It transpired that there had been a secret treaty between the two countries all the time.
Loose: A peculiar accident transpired yesterday.
Better: A peculiar accident happened yesterday.

Try to (and). *Try to* is standard usage; *try and* is informal and colloquial.

Right: I shall try to come.
Colloquial: I shall try and come.
Right: Try to do better if you possibly can.
Colloquial: Try and do better if you possibly can.

The same situation exists in regard to *sure to* and *sure and*.

Unique. Unique means "single, sole, without a like or an equal". It should not be loosely and weakly used for "very unusual, notable, rare". It should not be compared, as *more unique, most unique*.

Loose and weak: I had a most unique experience the other day.
Loose: This is the most unique novel I ever read.
Right: The Egyptian sphinx is unique.
Right: The Grand Canyon is unique; there is no other like it.

Ways. Do not confuse the plural form with the singular.

Colloquial: He is a long ways from home.
Right: He is a long way from home.
Right: We can find ways of getting there.

Without. *Without* is a preposition and cannot be used in the sense of "unless, if not".

Wrong: I cannot go without you give me the money.
Right: I cannot go unless you give me the money.

Exercises in Detecting Trouble Spots in Current Usage

Choose the correct or preferred word or expression in each of the following sentences, and justify every choice.

1. Do not act (like, as) he does.

2. We shall discuss the subject (further, farther) tomorrow.
3. The lawyer (effected, affected) a reconciliation between his clients.
4. He is quite different (than, from) his brother.
5. (Is, are) either of them going with you?
6. John hopes to use the (balance, remainder) of his holidays for study.
7. (Fewer, less) students attended last week's game.
8. Father and (I, myself) are going fishing today.
9. (Its, it's) unfortunate that you cannot come with us.
10. He differed (from, with) his brother about the proper use of leisure time.
11. A severe storm (transpired, occurred) last night.
12. The speaker (asserted, claimed) that he had been misquoted.
13. I will (fix, repair) the mower tomorrow.
14. In his address the candidate (inferred, implied) that his opponent was dishonest.
15. The dance will take place (inside of, inside) the pavilion.
16. Although we looked (everywhere, every place) for the book we could not find it.
17. Jim said that he was in good (shape, condition) for the deciding game.
18. Will you come a little (ways, way) with us?
19. Do you plan (spending, on spending) the holidays in town?
20. I should not care to buy that (kind of a, kind of) bicycle.
21. We decided to (settle, locate) in the West.
22. Let everyone who dislikes the plan state (his, their) objections at once.
23. Every afternoon at two o'clock Aunt Lizzie (lay, laid) down for a nap.
24. (Due to, because of) the storm, we were unable to attend the concert.
25. Father objected to (us, our) remaining until after dark.
26. This pencil is so dull that I (can hardly, can't hardly) write with it.
27. (May, can) we visit you tomorrow?
28. He assured us that soon everything would be (alright, all right).
29. Bob was the first to leap (off, off of) the roof.
30. He distributed the money (among, between) the four of us.
31. Little David's (ingenious, ingenuous) habit of speaking his mind frequently embarrassed his parents.
32. We urged him to keep all his (principle, principal) in the bank.
33. Throw the scraps (in, into) the basket.

34. No one (became enthusiastic, enthused) about the plan.
35. He said that he would (try and, try to) do the work at once.
36. If he does not attend classes more regularly he is (liable, likely) to fail.
37. I do not doubt (that, but what) you are right.
38. The reason we arrived late was (because, that) we had tire trouble.
39. The speaker appeared to be well (posted, informed).
40. During their holiday in the country they lived in (healthful, healthy) surroundings.
41. It is (odd, funny) that no one has offered to help him.
42. She said that the (person, party) near the door had given her the details.
43. Sometimes Johnny's persistent questioning can be most (aggravating, exasperating).
44. We (stopped, stayed) in Windsor over night.
45. Because of his generosity the old man had (many, lots of) friends.
46. Mary assured us that the officer was (quite, very) handsome.
47. (Oh, O) Julius Caesar! thou art mighty yet!
48. This is a most (unique, unusual) painting.
49. We (shall, will) miss your letters.
50. I am (very, so) sorry to learn that you cannot come.
51. His unfortunate experience had a marked (effect, affect) upon him.
52. She remained near the window (so, so that) she could hear.
53. After the cloudburst the river began to (rise, raise).
54. You (should have, should of) arrived yesterday.
55. (Beside, besides) his salary he has a substantial income from investments.
56. A comma splice (occurs when, is when) two sentences are separated by a comma.
57. The radio (stands, sets) in the corner of the room.
58. We were (kind of, rather) sorry to see him go.
59. These (kinds, kind) of apples are difficult to obtain.
60. He triumphantly asserted that he had (proved, proven) his opponent wrong.

CHAPTER XIX

The Power of Words

Style is the use of words for their melody, power, and charm.
—JOHN MACY

Effective Words

We may write correctly so far as the laws of grammar and good use go, and yet write so feebly and uninterestingly that no one wants to read what we write. **To write effectively, then,—clearly, strongly, vividly,—is our second, and chief, aim.**

Like correctness, power or effectiveness of language is a highly complex quality, and results from fulfilling many other requirements. We shall consider here only the four leading ones, as follows:

1. The Exact Word: Synonyms
2. Connotation, or the Suggestive Power of Words
3. The Specific Word
4. Idioms

The next chapter will deal with three others:

1. Figurative Language
2. The Avoidance of Trite, Hackneyed Language
3. The Avoidance of Fine Writing

1. Exactness

(*Synonyms*)

People sometimes say of a good writer, "He clothes his thought in fitting words". This figure of clothing thought in words is a true one. A thought is formless and bare as it lies idle in the mind. It is not ready to appear in public till it has been given suitable dress in language.

Our words should fit our thoughts as a glove fits the hand or as the skin fits the body. To express it differently, we must use words that are neither too large nor too small, and neither too weak nor too strong. The search for exactly the right word is a task worthy of our best efforts. And the price of success is neither luck nor talent. It is eternal vigilance, and the infinite capacity for taking pains.

Take, for example, the two common words *large* and *small*. They are in almost constant use. Let us consider their possibilities.

(1) LARGE

When we wish to convey the idea of size or bigness, most of us are content to rely on two old stand-bys, *big* and *large*. To add to the idea of size, instead of using a stronger word, we merely add modifiers, and say *very large* or *great big* or *truly big*. There are, however, a half-dozen other words existing for this exact purpose and waiting to be called into service: *extensive*, *huge*, *vast*, *gigantic*, *immense*, and *tremendous*. Think of the relatively weak muscle of *big* or *large* as compared with *immense* or *tremendous*.

The mere size denoted by the word, however, is only half. The other half is the suitability of the word for its idea—that is, what it suggests to the imagination. Thus, if in addition to size, we wish to convey the suggestion of solidity and immovableness, we can use the word *massive*; or if we want to suggest clumsiness or awkwardness, we may employ *bulky* or *unwieldy*. If we are concerned with bigness of soul, we may need a word like *liberal*, *generous*, *munificent*, or *princely*. If it is internal bigness instead of external bigness we are thinking of, we need a word like *roomy*, *spacious*, *capacious*, or *commodious*.

Thus instead of the two words *big* and *large*, we can at need call upon any of a score of others to do our bidding and express our idea exactly and forcibly.

(2) SMALL

There is even a larger group of words available to convey the idea of smallness. First there are *small*, the opposite of *great*, and *little*, the opposite of *big*. Then, increasing in force, we have *diminutive*, *minute*, *tiny*, *wee*, *miniature*, *microscopic*, and *infinitesimal*. This group of seven concern the idea of size alone.

If to the idea of smallness we wish to add the suggestion of lack of power because small, we have *weak* and *feeble* to choose between. Or, if we wish to suggest that the smallness is due to lack of growth or development, we have a whole group of synonyms at our disposal—*slight*, *undersized*, *undeveloped*, *wizened*, *puny*, *stunted*, *dwarfed*, and *runty*. If the matter under discussion is of small importance, we can call it *trivial* or *trifling*. And finally, if it is a question of a person of small nature and a little soul, or the deeds done by such a one, we can avail ourselves of *mean*, *petty*, *illiberal*, *ungenerous*, or *sordid*.

The general situation in regard to synonyms is well illustrated by the two foregoing groups. Sometimes synonyms may be very close, and their meanings may be almost identical, only a small fraction of each word differing in meaning or in suggestion from the other. *Weak* and *feeble* are cases in point. Again, synonyms may be fairly distinct, and only a small proportion of the meanings may be the same. *Miniature* and *stunted* are examples. These differences may be suggested objectively as follows, the shaded parts of the

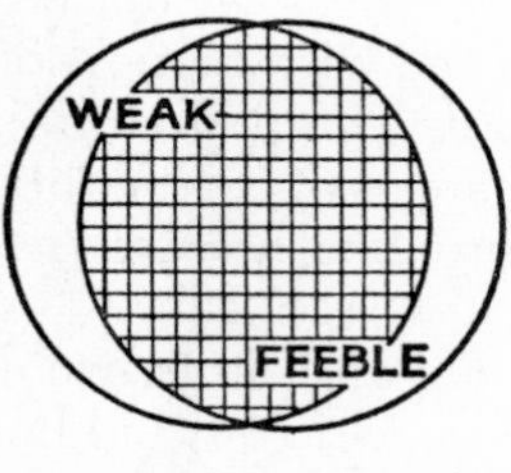

CLOSE SYNONYMS

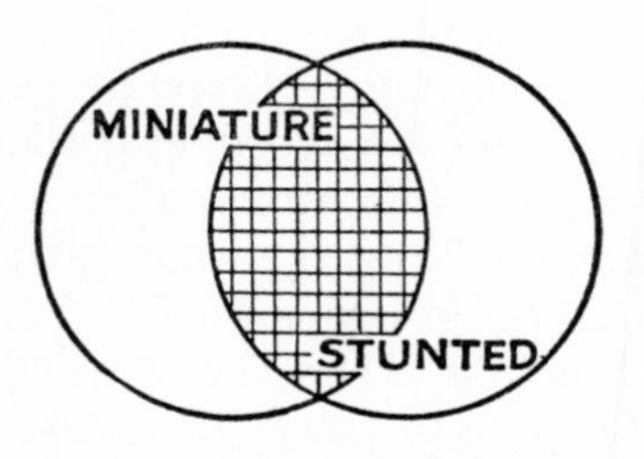

DISTANT SYNONYMS

circles indicating what the words have in common and the unshaded parts what they have individually.

THE ROUND TABLE

1. As directed by the teacher, give two synonyms for each of the following words:

(1) correct (*adj.*)	(8) ugly	(15) courage
(2) pale	(9) occupation	(16) frighten
(3) kill	(10) gay	(17) funny
(4) error	(11) fix (*verb*)	(18) love
(5) gain	(12) shine	(19) mysterious
(6) clear (*adj.*)	(13) kind (*adj.*)	(20) obtain
(7) pretty	(14) allow	

2. What is the difference between a *facsimile* and a *copy*?

3. Show that you understand the following words by completing the phrase:

(1) Flock of ____	(5) Drove of ____
(2) Bevy of ____	(6) Herd of ____
(3) Brood of ____	(7) Litter of ____
(4) Covey of ____	(8) Pack of ____

4. As directed by the teacher, study the following groups of synonyms until you feel that you understand the differences between them in both meaning and suggestion. Then (1) indicate which of them you have ever used in writing or in speaking; and (2) write a sentence containing one of the words in each group that you have never used before.

(1) Abhor, detest, dislike, hate, loathe
(2) Aged, ancient, antique, old, venerable
(3) Air, bearing, carriage, demeanour, mien
(4) Akin, alike, identical, similar, same
(5) Answer, rejoinder, repartee, reply, response, retort
(6) Attempt, endeavour, strive, try, undertake
(7) Baffle, balk, bar, check, fail, frustrate, hamper, hinder, impede, prevent, retard, thwart
(8) Candid, frank, impartial, open, sincere, straightforward, truthful, unprejudiced
(9) Caution, discretion, prudence, care
(10) Churlish, gloomy, gruff, ill-natured, morose, sour, sullen, surly
(11) Empty, fruitless, futile, idle, unavailing, useless, vain
(12) Enduring, lasting, permanent, perpetual, endless
(13) Faithful, loyal, staunch, trustworthy, trusty, reliable
(14) Grief, melancholy, regret, sadness, sorrow

(15) Home, house, dwelling, domicile, residence, habitation
(16) Pleasant, agreeable, delightful, enjoyable (*Loose and inexact*: nice)
(17) Polite, courteous, civil, gentlemanly
(18) Put out, vexed, annoyed, exasperated, provoked, irritable, angry, mad (*Incorrect*: aggravated; *slang*, sore)
(19) Quarrel, disagreement, dispute, wrangle, broil, row, fuss, feud
(20) Raise, lift, heave, hoist, rear, elevate, exalt
(21) Reprove, rebuke, reprimand, admonish, chide, upbraid, reproach, scold, berate (*Slang*: get after)
(22) Smell, odour, scent, fragrance, aroma, perfume, stench, tang
(23) Stay, tarry, linger, stop, sojourn, remain, abide, live, reside, dwell, lodge
(24) Throw, pitch, hurl, fling, cast, toss, flip, sling, heave, launch, propel
(25) Wise, learned, erudite, sagacious, sapient, sage, prudent, discreet

5. As directed by the teacher, learn the difference between the following pairs of tricky words until you are able to use them correctly in sentences:

(1) ability, capacity
(2) accede, exceed
(3) admittance, admission
(4) all ready, already
(5) allusion, illusion
(6) anxious, eager
(7) audience, spectators
(8) avenge, revenge
(9) avocation, vocation
(10) bring, take
(11) character, reputation
(12) childlike, childish
(13) cite, site
(14) complacent, complaisant
(15) compliment, complement
(16) connote, denote
(17) contagious, infectious
(18) continual, continuous
(19) council, counsel
(20) credible, creditable, credulous
(21) custom, habit
(22) decided, decisive
(23) defective, deficient
(24) delusion, illusion
(25) demean, lower
(26) deprecate, depreciate
(27) disinterested, uninterested
(28) eligible, illegible
(29) eminent, imminent
(30) ensure, insure
(31) enunciation, pronunciation
(32) equable, equitable
(33) error, blunder
(34) exceptional, exceptionable
(35) expect, suppose
(36) formally, formerly
(37) human, humane
(38) imaginary, imaginative
(39) induction, deduction
(40) invent, discover
(41) judicial, judicious
(42) knowledge, wisdom
(43) last, latest
(44) learn, teach
(45) loath, loathe

(46) lose, loose
(47) luxuriant, luxurious
(48) majority, plurality
(49) momentary, momentous
(50) moral, morale
(51) mutual, common
(52) observance, observation
(53) official, officious
(54) oral, verbal
(55) practicable, practical
(56) pride, vanity
(57) raise, rear
(58) recollect, remember
(59) respectfully, respectively
(60) reverend, reverent
(61) sin, crime
(62) stationary, stationery
(63) synonym, antonym, homonym
(64) triumphal, triumphant
(65) veracious, voracious
(66) yield, submit

6. In a descriptive or narrative theme that you have already written, underline every adjective and adverb. In the margin give two synonyms for each. See whether a synonym or your original choice is the better.

7. Follow the plan explained above in connection with each of your verbs.

2. Connotation, or the suggestive Power of Words

There are two parts to a word just as there are two parts to a man; namely, body and soul. The body of the word is the core or kernel of it, its bare, literal, root meaning. This in rhetoric and logic is called *denotation.* The second part of a word, its soul, is composed of the emotional fringe or halo, all the associations and suggestions with which time and use have surrounded it. This is called *connotation.* It is from this second element, connotation or suggestiveness, that words get their richness and flavour. Denotation fixes the basic meaning; connotation adds power and appeal. It is from connotation, too, that each word derives its own individuality, its distinct personality, as it were, so that its place cannot be taken by any other word.

There is the classic example of *fist. Fist* means "the closed hand", or "the hand doubled up". Then, "The lady held a white lily in her delicate fist" ought to be a perfectly correct use of words. We smile, however, at the incongruous suggestion of *lady*, *lily*, *white*, and *delicate* on the one hand, and of *fist* on the other. The denotation of *fist* is correct, but its connotation makes it an impossible word for that sentence.

Boy, someone has said, means merely "boy", but *lad* means "a boy with a man's hand on his shoulder".

In fact all language, except the cold, clear, technical language of science, is tinged either faintly or decidedly with characteristic and often unexpected connotations and suggestions. Here are seven groups of familiar words which show interesting variations in connotation:

1. COMMONPLACE AND PROSAIC

fried fish, dust pan, coal scuttle, suspenders, biscuits, kitchen sink, toothbrush, pig pen

2. COARSE AND UNREFINED

nertz, gents, booze, nigger, sloppy, wench, victuals, swig, bloke, duds, bug-house

3. BOOKISH AND OVERLEARNED

meticulous, peruse, mendacity, expeditious, surreptitious, deleterious, adventitious, minutiæ

4. CHILDISH

naughty, fairy princess, once upon a time, moo cow, birdie, doggie, kitty, dolly

5. ARCHAIC

oft, ne'er, forspent, surcease, frore, dight, wot, methinks, forsooth, eke, eld, yore

6. ROMANTIC

the Spanish Main, buccaneer, bourgeon, manor, castle, the East, doubloons, gypsy, Arabian, galleon, lagoon

7. POETIC

dell, glade, vale, glen, isle, skylark, evening star, nightingale, blithe, steed, maiden

All writers, of course, avail themselves of the word magic latent in the connotation of words. Read aloud the two following passages and taste the difference. They form striking contrasts in connotation.

1. The Witches' Brew

(The three weird sisters in *Macbeth* mix their sinister brew on the blasted heath.)

Round about the cauldron go;
In the poison'd entrails throw.
Toad, that under cold stone
Days and nights has thirty-one
Swelt'red venom sleeping got,
Boil thou first i' the charmèd pot. . . .
Scale of dragon, tooth of wolf,
Witches' mummy, maw and gulf
Of the ravin'd salt-sea shark.
Root of hemlock digg'd i' the dark,
Liver of blaspheming Jew,
Gall of goat, and slips of yew
Sliver'd in the moon's eclipse,
Nose of Turk and Tartar's lips . . .
Make the gruel thick and slab . . .
Cool it with a baboon's blood,
Then the charm is firm and good.
—*Macbeth*, IV. i

2. The Lover's Feast

(Porphyro prepares the table for his sleeping sweetheart, Madeline.)

And still she slept an azure-lidded sleep,
In blanchèd linen, smooth and lavendered,
While he from forth the closet brought a heap
Of candied apple, quince, and plum, and gourd;
With jellies soother than the creamy curd,
And lucent syrops, tinct with cinnamon;
Manna and dates, in argosy transferred
From Fez; and spiced dainties, every one,
From silken Samarcand to cedared Lebanon.
—KEATS, "The Eve of St. Agnes"

THE ROUND TABLE

1. List what you consider the five most beautiful words in the language.

Try to decide what it is that appeals to you in them, whether (1) meaning, (2) suggestion (connotation), (3) sound—or all three.

2. From the individual lists make a class list of the ten most beautiful words, and if there are other sections of your same English class, ask the teacher to compare lists.

3. What two (or three) words do you dislike most? Can you tell why you dislike them?

4. A well-known columnist once composed a poem on the basis of the mere sound and suggestiveness of words. Here are four stanzas. Read them aloud for pleasure and, using words of your own choice, compose another stanza like them. Since the stanzas in the poem need not be connected, choose the six or eight best stanzas composed by the members of the class and put them together into a poem like this one.

THE BALLAD OF BEAUTIFUL WORDS

Amethyst, airy, drifting, dell,
Oriole, lark, alone,
Columbine, kestrel, temple, bell,
Madrigal, calm, condone.

Emerald, swallow, tawny, dawn,
Silvery, starling, lane,
Radiance, rosary, garland, fawn,
Pastoral, valley, vane.

Smouldering, sombre, tumbrel, tomb,
Indigo, ember, shorn,
Sonorous, sorrow, cloven, doom,
Pendulum, dirge, forlorn.

Charity, gloaming, garnering, grain,
Curfew, candle, loam,
Benison, mother, lassie, swain,
Children, evening, home.

—JOHN T. MCCUTCHEON in the *Chicago Tribune*

3. Words General and Specific

All of our contacts with the world around us come through the five doors that open inward on our consciousness—the eye, the ear, the tongue, the nose, and the touch. When we wish to tell anyone else about our experiences, whether we are relating an incident or are describing a scene, the only way we can do it successfully is to reproduce in words the particular sensation and the definite detail just as they came to us through the eye or the ear. Or, to express it differently, **to write vividly, we must feel vividly too, and use concrete, specific words.** In the last analysis, that is the secret of all good writing.

(1) GENERAL WORDS

All our experiences are definite and concrete. Man, however, is not only an animal that sees and feels, but also an animal that thinks. And when we think, we need not only specific concrete words, but general, abstract words as well. We thus have thousands of general words, which, instead of naming a particular, individual thing, name a group, or class, or species. For example, take *animal*, *vegetable*, *automobile*, *flower*, *house*, *book*, *bird*, *child*, *tool*, and *tree*. Each of these words names a class, not an individual or particular object. Hence general words cannot call up pictures or images in the mind. While riding along in an automobile, someone may exclaim, "Isn't that a beautiful tree?" What he really sees, and what you see when you look where he points, is not a tree in general, but one particular tree—a towering pine, a moss-covered oak, or a graceful elm. Your companion *says tree*, but your eye *sees the picture made by the pine, oak, or elm.* But when you are writing, and hence cannot point to the tree you mean, you cannot say *tree*, but must name a definite specific kind of tree, or your reader sees nothing. If the word *tool* is spoken, you cannot image in the mind a tool in general but you can and do image the definite sort of tool that you are most familiar with, probably a hammer, a saw, or a pair of pliers. What does the word *dog* suggest to you? If your father likes hunting, it will probably call up the image of a red Irish setter with soft brown eyes and a plumy tail, or maybe a white-and-liver pointer, while to the student next to you it may suggest a graceful collie, an alert fox terrier, or a powerful German police dog with a sharp muzzle and pointed ears. **We must translate a general word into a specific one before we can see a picture.**

(2) ABSTRACT WORDS

When we come to abstract words, still less than general words do they call up images or paint pictures. Abstract words name nothing that you can see, hear, smell, taste, or touch. **Abstract words name only the qualities, actions, and conditions that exist in the thoughts of man.** Read over the following list of abstract nouns. Not one of them suggests an image or paints a picture.

existence	beginning	influence
knowledge	repetition	falsehood
certainty	frequency	vigour
agreement	newness	obscurity
equality	weakness	happiness

All of these words are both familiar and important. We use them almost every day. The point here is, however, that in spite of their familiarity and usefulness they are abstract nouns, and hence pale and colourless. They are concerned with thought, not with feeling, and are useful in an essay of explanation but not in a story or a description. In stories and descriptions abstract words, like general words, must be avoided at all cost. It takes a concrete, specific word to bring the feeling to a focus, as it were, and to penetrate to the centre of feeling. General and abstract words are broad and blunt, and glance off without making any impression. Consider the difference in effectiveness between the most general and the most specific words in the diagrams on page 333.

Compare, too, the following examples, and notice how as the word becomes more and more specific the idea becomes correspondingly sharper and more vivid:

1. Bird, song-bird, canary
2. Bird, game bird, partridge
3. Utensil, kitchen utensil, frying pan

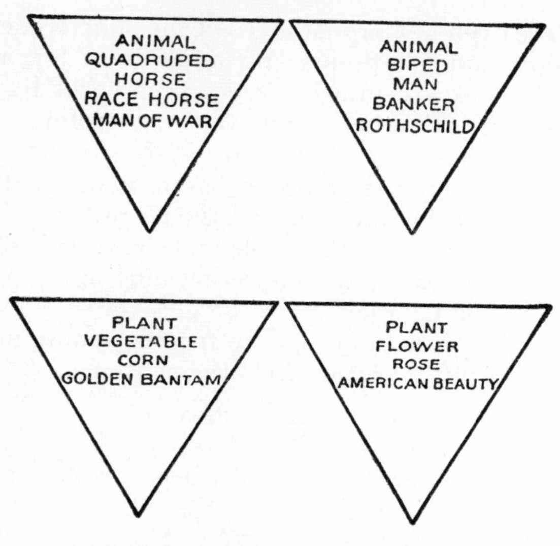

BRINGING IDEAS TO A SPECIFIC FOCUS

4. Colour, red, crimson
5. Knife, pocket knife, a two-bladed Barlow
6. Furniture, parlour furniture, gate-legged table

Take the ever-interesting topic of the weather. Two of the commonest remarks in the language are, "It's a warm day today", and the opposite, "It's a cold day today". In describing the weather in a story, however, it isn't enough to call it warm or cold. We must specify, and specify exactly and vividly, if we wish our readers to swelter or to shiver with us. There are more than a score of highly specific, hence highly descriptive words for each of the two sensations.

Hot: warm, mild, genial, tepid, lukewarm, ardent, aglow, sunny, torrid, tropical, close, sultry, stifling, stuffy, suffocating, oppressive, fiery, glowing, blazing, smoking.

Cold: cool, chill, chilly, frigid, fresh, keen, bleak, raw, inclement, bitter, biting, cutting, nipping, piercing, pinching, shivering, frosty, icy, glacial, freezing, wintry, arctic, polar.

Verbs are even better instances of the effectiveness of being specific than are nouns and adjectives, for, with the exception of a few useful but colourless verbs like *be* and *seem*, most verbs denote action. When, therefore, you take action and movement and make it highly specific, you flash a vivid picture on the minds of your readers. Take the sentence, "'No,' she said, and left the room." The idea that these words convey is both simple and clear. It is also absolutely colourless, for *say* and *leave* are among the most general verbs in the language.

Let us look at some of the more specific synonyms for *say* and *leave*, and put a picture into the sentence.

SPECIFIC WAYS OF "SAYING"

bawl
bellow
bleat
blubber
blurt
croak
cry out
drawl
falter
groan
growl
grumble
grunt
howl
jabber
jeer
lisp
moan
mumble
murmur
mutter
plead
rant
roar
scream
screech
shout
shriek
shrill
smile
snap
snarl
snort
sob
sputter
squall
squeal
stammer
stutter
tease
thunder
titter
twitter
whine
whisper
whoop
yell

SPECIFIC WAYS OF "LEAVING"

bolt
bounce
crawl
creep
dart
dash
flash
glide
hobble
hop
hurry
jerk
jump
leap
limp
lunge
lurch
march
mince
plod
plunge
poke
prance
race
recoil
reel
romp
run
rush
scamper
scoot
scramble
scuffle
shoot
shuffle
sidle
skip
slip
sneak
sprint
stagger
steal
stumble
tiptoe
toddle
totter
tramp
trip
trot
wabble
waddle
waltz
wander
whirl
wriggle

Think of how definite and vivid is the action described by these words, and contrast them in this respect with the entirely colourless word *leave* or with some of its pale synonyms like *advance, depart, go, journey, move, proceed, wend.* There is not a picture in a car-load of words like these.

Looking back over the two lists of specific synonyms, let us take the original sentence and add life, movement, and colour to it. In short, let us put a picture in it. Here are eight of the possibilities in the case.

1. "No," she groaned, and tottered from the room.
2. "No," she jeered, and marched from the room.
3. "No," she lisped, and sidled from the room.
4. "No," she moaned, and crept from the room.
5. "No," she shrieked, and dashed from the room.
6. "No," she sobbed, and stumbled from the room.
7. "No," she tittered, and minced from the room.
8. "No," she whispered, and tiptoed from the room.

Exercises in Choosing Effective Words

Choose the words which express the meaning most precisely.

A

A big 1.(frothy, foaming, white, lathery, creamy) sea came out of the mist; it 2.(approached, neared, moved towards, made for, came towards) the ship, roaring 3.(wildly, noisily, loudly, strongly, forcefully), and in its rush it looked as mischievous and discomposing as a madman with an axe. One or two, shouting, 4.(climbed, hurried, clambered, started, scrambled) up the rigging; most, with a 5.(sudden, quick, convulsive, jerky, irregular) catch of the breath, held on where they stood. Singleton 6.(braced, dug, pressed, forced, kept) his knees under the wheel-box, and carefully 7.(eased, moved, turned, revolved, adjusted) the helm to the 8.(sudden, abrupt, unexpected, spasmodic, headlong) pitch of the ship, but without taking his eye off the coming wave. It 9.(rose, became visible, appeared, towered, was seen) close-to and high, like a wall of green 10.(vegetation, trees, glass, brush, stucco) topped with snow. The ship 11.(rose, ascended, mounted, climbed, shot up) to it as though she had 12.(fluttered, soared, moved, been transported, floated) on wings, and for a moment rested 13.(motionless, quiet, inert, poised, quiescent) upon the foaming crest as if she had been a great sea-bird. Before we could 14.(breathe, take a breath, respire, exhale, draw breath) a heavy 15.(puff, gust, breeze, wind, draught) struck her, another roller took her unfairly under the weather bow, she gave a toppling 16.(stagger, lurch, roll. sway, movement) and filled her decks. Captain Allistoun 17.(leaped, jumped, hopped, stepped, rose) up and fell; Archie rolled over him, 18.(crying, shouting, saying, screaming, exclaiming): "She will rise!" She gave another lurch to leeward; the lower deadeyes dipped heavily; the men's feet 19.(went, slipped, flew, glided, slid) from under them, and they 20.(remained, lingered, were seen, were suspended, hung) kicking above the slanting poop. . . . Forward the forecastle doors 21.(flew, swung, came, fell, were forced) open, and the watch below were seen 22.(hurrying, leaping, running, moving, rushing) out one after another, throwing their arms up; and, falling on hands and knees 23.(hurried, ran, moved, scrambled, went) aft on all fours along the high side of the deck, sloping more than the roof of a house. From leeward the seas rose, 24.(following, going after, pursuing, moving upon, attending) them; they looked wretched in a hopeless struggle, like vermin 25.(fleeing, hurrying, escaping, running, running away) before a flood; they 26.(climbed, struggled, clambered, went, fought) up the weather ladder of the poop one after another, half naked and 27.(glancing, looking, watching, staring, gazing) wildly; and as soon as they got up they 28.(hurried, shot, were sent, went quickly, were forced) to leeward in 29.(groups, twos and threes, clusters, scattered groups, bunches), with closed eyes, till they 30.(bumped, came, brought up, were sent, were forced) heavily with their ribs against the iron stanchions of the rail; then, groaning, they 31.(revolved, rolled, rotated, turned, fell) in a confused 32.(group, assemblage, jumble, mass, pile). The immense volume of water thrown forward by the last 33.(rise, movement, motion, scend, lift) of the ship had 34.(burst, broken, forced open, opened, split) the lee door of the forecastle. They could see their chests, pillows, blankets, clothing come out floating upon the sea. While they 35.(moved with difficulty, turned, worked, climbed, struggled) back to windward they looked in 36.(surprise, dismay, alarm, astonishment, apprehension). The straw beds 37.(floated, remained, swam, were carried, drifted) high; the blankets, spread out, 38.(vibrated, undulated, surged, waved, rose and fell); while the chests, waterlogged and with a heavy list, 39.(pitched, tossed, swam, dipped, plunged) heavily like dismasted 40.(vessels, barges, ships, hulks, frigates) before they sank. . . . A black squall 41.(blew, swept, moaned, came, howled) low over the ship that lay on her side with the weather yard-arms pointing to the clouds. . . . At that moment the topsail sheet parted, the end of the heavy chain 42.(shot noisily, was jerked, clattered, racketed, flew) aloft, and sparks of red fire 43.(came, streamed, poured, fell, sparkled) down through the 44.(rushing, foaming, flying, dashing, swift) sprays.

—JOSEPH CONRAD, *The Nigger of the Narcissus*

B

There seemed no flies to 1.(annoy, bother, worry, vex) him, and he was languid with rest. But there came a time when the buck's ears lifted and 2.(stretched, tensed, stiffened, became rigid) with swift eagerness for sound. At the sound he snorted with a sudden start that 3.(sent, moved, carried, transported, jerked) him through the air from water to meadow. The green screen was 4.(burst, moved, separated, pushed) asunder, and a man peered out at the meadow and the pool and the sloping hill. From out of the screen of vines and creepers he 5.(cast, threw, flung, tossed) ahead of him a miner's pick and shovel and gold-pan. He 6.(poured, sprinkled, dribbled, spattered) a little water in over the depressed edge of the pan. With a quick flirt he sent the water 7.(sluicing, trickling, pouring, sliding, running) across the bottom, turning the grains of black sand over and over. Like a shepherd he 8.(collected, gathered, assembled, accumulated, herded) his flock of golden specks so that not one should be lost. He could not 9.(resist, check, forbear, hinder) another survey of the hill before filling the pan farther down the stream. Into the fire he 10.(put, thrust, placed, set, deposited) the gold-pan and burned it until it was blue-black. He turned and 11.(cast, gave, flung, sent, threw) a measuring glance at the sun poised above him in the azure of the cloudless sky. The green screen 12.(moved, stirred, bent, trembled, surged) back and forth in the throes of a struggle. A second horse 13.(came, walked, scrambled, moved) into view.

—JACK LONDON, "All-Gold Cañon"

C

The old brick building had 1.(vanished, gone, departed, withdrawn) before the wreckers in a cloud of broken brick and plaster. Already the muddy floor was 2.(covered, filled, crowded, dotted) with the toadstool tents of the excavators, and day and night unceasingly wagonloads of sticky clay and mud 3.(went, moved, dragged, were drawn) up the incline to the street. In ordered plan the crossbeams 4.(were put, were placed, were set, fell) into their places, and the great lattice of the substructure shaped itself. With incredible rapidity the gaunt frame 5.(was built, was lifted, piled, rose, was constructed) upward.

Against the pale sky the black ribs of the building 6.(rose, surged, went, were built) higher. As each new story was bolted down, the derricks 7.(were transported, were moved, were lifted, lifted themselves) heavily to the new level. Like beetles the steel workers 8.(walked, moved, stepped, clambered) sure-footed over the empty frame. Far out on the end of the narrow beams they 9.(rested, were placed, hung, could be seen) above the void. Like flies they caught the slim-spun threads of the derricks and 10.(moved, went, were carried, swung) up to some inaccessible height. On flimsy platforms the glow of their forges 11.(shone, could be seen, was seen, blinked red) in the twilight. Through the tangle of its skeleton frame the flaming red and yellow of an electric sign 12.(sent, spattered, threw, spilled) a trail of jewelled fire against the sky. Far down in the streets the glare of automobile lights 13.(lighted, contrasted with, illuminated, stroked) the gleaming blackness of the pavement.

—JOSEPH HUSBAND, *America at Work*
Reprinted by permission of, and by arrangement with Houghton Mifflin Company.

THE ROUND TABLE

1. Choosing among the specific words for *hot* and *cold* given above, describe a day (*a*) pleasantly warm; (*b*) disagreeably hot; (*c*) pleasantly cool; and (*d*) disagreeably cold. Have a definite day in mind each time and make the descriptive phrases as pointed and vivid as possible.

2. Using specific words in place of *say* and *leave*, make up five definitely picture-making sentences.

3. Choose one of your themes which received a low grade. Strike out every adjective and adverb. Draw a ring around every verb and underline every noun. Go back through the theme substituting as highly specific verbs and nouns as you can find for the ones you first used. Compare the two versions.

4. Give four specific synonyms for each of the following general, class nouns:

(1) School
(2) Student activity
(3) Food
(4) Dwelling place
(5) Exercise
(6) Waterfowl
(7) Writer
(8) Sport
(9) Vehicle
(10) Storm
(11) China
(12) Fuel
(13) Precious stone
(14) Insect
(15) Weapon
(16) Drink
(17) Moisture
(18) Clothing
(19) Profession
(20) Trade

5. Give three specific synonyms for each of the following general verbs:

(1) Injure
(2) Take
(3) Think
(4) Want
(5) See
(6) Ask
(7) Carry
(8) Go up
(9) Go down
(10) Help

6. Compose specific picturesque phrases for the following general, colourless phrases:

(1) An impressive tree
(2) An expensive automobile
(3) A dark night
(4) A bad storm
(5) A melodious sound
(6) A cheerful noise
(7) A melancholy noise
(8) An attractive odour
(9) A threatening sound
(10) A disagreeable odour

7. Bring to class, from either prose or poetry, the best illustration you have ever seen of the force and effectiveness of specific words in painting pictures.

4. Idioms

An Idiom is a word or turn of expression peculiar to a language. Usually there is something odd about either the meaning or the grammar of an idiom that marks it off from regular and expected usage and makes it practically untranslatable into any other language. An interesting example is the English idiom *a friend of mine*, or *a friend of John's*, in which the possessive instead of the objective follows the preposition. In translating *a friend of mine* into French we can only say *un de mes amis* (one of my friends); and so with all other languages as well. Another familiar idiom is "How do you do?" For this the French idiom is *Comment vous portez-vous*? (How do you carry yourself?) and the German idiom, *Wie befinden Sie sich*? (How do you find yourself?).

Idioms are among the most racy and distinctive forms of expression in the language. To borrow a phrase from John Galsworthy, they possess an unusual amount of sheer stingo. They make for a strong, homely, vivid style.

Idioms

at arm's length
bad blood
by and by
to make a clean breast of
to fall asleep
to fall flat
to gain ground
to get used to
to beat about the bush
to cap the climax
to carry on
to catch cold
to cast in one's teeth
child's play
a clean sweep
to come off
well-to-do
ill at ease
to make both ends meet
in the nick of time
odds and ends
once for all
to keep pace with
to play safe
to make a point of
to pull through
to put off
the rank and file
without rhyme or reason
to run riot
to run amok
to get wind of
to give out
to give in
had rather
from hand to mouth
on hand
to take heart
out of one's head
to hit upon
out of keeping
a labour of love
to make light of
not to mince matters
by all means
to show one's hand
on the sly
to take back
to take to heart
touch and go
through thick and thin
it stands to reason
tit for tat
to turn the tables

THE ROUND TABLE

1. Which of these idioms could be included in the list of trite phrases on pages 349-351? Which seem to you strongest and most original?

2. List two other interesting English idioms and be prepared to explain them if called on.

3. If you are studying a foreign language, can you mention and explain a few of the most peculiar idioms from that language?

4. Write sentences using effectively about ten of the idioms in the list above. Then rewrite the sentence without using the idiom.

CHAPTER XX

Figurative Language

God wove a web of loveliness,
  Of clouds and stars and birds,
But made not anything at all
  So beautiful as words.

—ANNA HEMPSTEAD BRANCH

FIGURES OF SPEECH

By using words in a figurative instead of a literal sense, we increase the number of uses to which they can be put three-fold or even four-fold. And we do more than that: we increase their force and suggestiveness ten-fold or even a hundred-fold. This increase in vividness through the imaginative use of words is the peculiar province of figures of speech.

The older rhetorics recognized more than twenty figures of speech and devoted much space to defining and illustrating them. Of these we need consider only the leading five: Simile, Metaphor, Personification, Metonymy, and Onomatopoeia.

1. Figures Based on Imaginative Resemblance

1. Simile 2. Metaphor 3. Personification

Simile and metaphor are the two basic figures. Both depend upon the fundamental principle of imaginative resemblance, or analogy—that is, the resemblance of qualities, relations, or functions.

(1) SIMILE

Simile is directly expressed comparison, the point of resemblance being stated by means of *like* or *as* or *as if*.

Thy soul was like a star, and dwelt apart.
The Assyrian came down like the wolf on the fold.
When she had passed, it seemed like the ceasing of exquisite music.

In "To a Skylark" the poet Shelley is seeking for beautiful things to which to compare the birds' singing. He asks:

What thou art we know not,
What is most like thee?

Then he answers the question in a succession of beautiful similes:

Like a poet hidden
In the light of thought—

Like a high-born maiden
In a palace tower—

Like a glow-worm golden
In a dell of dew—

Like a rose embowered
In its own green leaves.

Similes, however, are of course not limited to poetry. They are used constantly in prose, particularly in description. Many a vivid touch in a story owes its power to a striking simile. Recent writers, particularly, have vied with each other in coining apt, unexpected, whimsical similes. Here are a few of the best:

As futile as a swinging door.—J. W. EMMERSON

Her mind is like a sundial; it records only pleasantness.

As worn-out as a woodpecker in a petrified forest.
—RICHARD HOWELLS WATKINS

As anonymous as a pair of headlights.
—THELMA S. CROSNOE

Picture frames like doorways to other worlds.
—ALDOUS HUXLEY

(2) METAPHOR

Metaphor is implied comparison, or imaginative identification. There are no words of comparison such as *like* or *as*. The two things that are compared are fused into one by the energy of the imagination and the intensity of the emotion.

> Thine eyes are stars of morning,
> Thy lips are crimson flowers.

> One generation blows bubbles, and the next breaks them.

The pages of poetry are full of beautiful metaphors like these; so, too, are the pages of prose and our everyday conversation. As has been noted, slang itself usually consists of violent metaphor. Nor is metaphor always complimentary. We can refer to a girl not only as a peach but also as a lemon; and we can call a man not only a prince but a hog, or a fox or a snake in the grass. A popular magazine in lighter vein gathered the following descriptive metaphors taken from various stories:

His voice broke His heart sank His face fell His hair rose His eyes blazed His words burned His blood froze	and yet	he pulled himself together. he kept a stiff upper lip. he did not show a yellow streak. he put his best foot foremost. he did not show the white feather.

(3) PERSONIFICATION

Personification is a variety of metaphor, and, like metaphor, is based on imaginative resemblance or likeness. The word *personify* comes from two Latin words, *persona*, a person, and *facere*, do or make. Personification thus means the process of "making a person", and that is exactly what this figure of speech does. It makes a person out of abstract ideas and things without life, or out of the lower animals, and thus attributes to them the thoughts, feelings, and characteristics of human beings.

> Sport that wrinkled Care derides,
> And Laughter, holding both his sides . .
> And in thy right hand lead with thee
> The mountain nymph, sweet Liberty.
>
> —MILTON

> Blow, winds, and crack your cheeks.
>
> —SHAKESPEARE

Occasionally a poet will start with a personification, and build a whole poem around it. Sir Philip Sidney does this in his beautiful sonnet:

> With how sad steps, O Moon, thou climb'st the skies!
> How silently, and with how wan a face!

Other well-known poems built around personifications are Shelley's "To Night", "Ode to the West Wind", and "To a Skylark"; Dante Gabriel Rossetti's "A Superscription"; William Blake's "To the Evening Star"; Joyce Kilmer's "Trees"; Carl Sandburg's "Fog".

2. Figures Based on Association

(1) METONYMY AND SYNECDOCHE

Associates are persons, or things, that are so often found together that every time we see one we expect to see the other. To illustrate by using algebraic symbols, X and Y usually occur together. When, therefore, X is mentioned we think at once of Y; or when Y is mentioned we think at once of X. *Lily*, for example, suggests purity and grace; a rose calls to mind beauty and fragrance; an onion, its strong characteristic odour; a hog, greediness; a fox, shrewdness and trickery; an eagle, mastery of the air and kingship among the birds; a lion, strength, courage, and kingship among the beasts.

Among figures of speech, metonymy is based on this principle of the association of ideas. Formerly metonymy and synecdoche were treated as separate figures, the term synecdoche being reserved especially for those figures (as in

1 and 4 below) in which the part stands for the whole, or vice versa. The line dividing them, however, is shifting and shadowy at best, and now both are commonly considered together as one figure under the name "metonymy". **Metonymy, then, consists in mentioning one of two things or ideas that are so closely associated that the mention of the first immediately suggests the second.**

Some of the important varieties of association on which metonymy may be based are the following:

1. *A significant part for the whole*: He employs three hundred hands; A fleet of thirty sail; He was an old hand at the game.
2. *Cause for effect, or effect for cause*: Wrinkles and gray hairs (for old age); The bright death quivered at the victim's throat (for dagger).
3. *The container for the thing contained*: The kettle is boiling; He loves the bottle; A man in his cups; Fond of his pipe.
4. *The material for the object made of it*: She has beautiful household linen; She wears silks and satins.
5. *An author for his works*: Are you fond of Dickens? Do you ever read Sandburg?
6. *The instrument for the agent*: A troop of a thousand bayonets.
7. *The concrete for the abstract or the abstract for the concrete*: The pen is mightier than the sword.

3. A Figure Based on Suggestiveness of Sound

(1) ONOMATOPOEIA

Onomatopoeia is made up of two Greek words, *onoma*, meaning "name", and *poieo*, "do or make". That is, **onomatopoeia is an imitative figure involving the use of words whose sound suggests the sense.** Our vocabulary is full of onomatopoetic words. Examples are *click*, *clank*, *clack*, *cluck*, *cackle*, *hiss*, *pop*, *boom*, *whiz*, *siss*, *splash*, *murmur*, *tinkle*, *buzz*, *crash*, *roar*, *swish*, *plunk*, *zip*, *sizzle*. Even a foreigner who did not know a word of English could gather the meaning of most of these words if they were read aloud to him.

The poets have availed themselves fully of the principle of onomatopoeia in their verses, and by this means gain some of their most skilful results. Read the following passages aloud and consider their imitative effects:

1. And the silken, sad, uncertain rustling of each purple curtain.
—POE

2. Bang-whang-whang goes the drum, tootle-te-tootle the fife.
—BROWNING

3. Soft is the strain when zephyr gently blows,
And the smooth stream in smoother numbers flows:
But when loud surges lash the sounding shore,
The hoarse rough verse should like the torrent roar.
When Ajax strives some rock's vast weight to throw,
The line, too, labours, and the words move slow:
Not so when swift Camilla scours the plain,
Flies o'er the unbending corn, and skims along the main.
—POPE, *Essay on Criticism*

Sometimes the poet goes further than to use onomatopoeia in a line or in a short passage, and builds a whole poem out of it. Southey's "Cataract of Lodore" and Poe's "Bells" are probably the most familiar and obvious examples. Other good instances are Poe's "Ulalume", Tennyson's "Blow Bugles, Blow", Browning's "How They Brought the Good News from Ghent to Aix", and Masefield's "Cargoes".

THE ROUND TABLE

1. Can you think of any bird that is named after the sound it makes? Any animal?

2. Invent two imitation words and see if the class can guess th meaning from the sound.

3. Try to find two lines or short passages from either prose c poetry which get their effect through onomatopoeia, like the quotations given above.

EFFECTIVE FIGURES OF SPEECH

Read the following figures of speech for the pleasure afforded b their aptness, suggestiveness, and beauty. Then, as directed by th teacher, name the kind of figure and tell upon which principle each is based.

1. Haply I think on thee, and then my state,
Like to the lark at break of day arising
From sullen earth sings hymns at heaven's gate.

—SHAKESPEARE

2. Thick as autumnal leaves that strew the brooks
In Vallombrosa.

—MILTON

3. A good book is the precious life-blood of a master spirit, embalmed and treasured up on purpose to a life beyond life.

—MILTON

4. If a man be gracious and courteous to strangers, it shows he is a citizen of the world, and that his heart is no island cut off from other lands but a continent that joins them.

—FRANCIS BACON

5. But pleasures are like poppies spread,
You seize the flow'r, its bloom is shed,
Or like the snow falls in the river,
A moment white, then gone forever—
Or like the rainbow's lovely form
Evanishing amid the storm.

—ROBERT BURNS

6. Stern Daughter of the Voice of God!
O Duty!

—WORDSWORTH, "To Duty"

7. I clutched at the hem of sleep and sought to pull it over me again.

—MANNING LONG

8. Still as a slave before his lord,
The ocean hath no blast.

—COLERIDGE

9. My only books
Were woman's looks,
And folly's all they've taught me.

—THOMAS MOORE

10. Time writes no wrinkle on thine azure brow—
Such as creation's dawn beheld, thou rollest now.

—BYRON, "To the Ocean"

11. Then felt I like some watcher of the skies
When a new planet swims into his ken.
—KEATS

12. I warmed both hands before the fire of life,
It sinks, and I am ready to depart.
—LANDOR, "On His Seventy-Fifth Birthday"

13. Love took up the harp of Life, and smote on all the chords with might,
Smote the chord of Self, that, trembling, pass'd in music out of sight.

14. The life of every man is a diary in which he means to write one story and writes another.
—J. M. BARRIE

15. These laid the world away; poured out the red
Sweet wine of youth.
—RUPERT BROOKE, "The Dead"

16. As a white candle
In a holy place,
So is the beauty
Of an agèd face.
—JOSEPH CAMPBELL

17. By the margin, willow-veiled,
Slide the heavy barges trailed
By slow horses; and unhailed
The shallop flitteth silken-sailed
Skimming down to Camelot.
—TENNYSON

18. You are beautiful and faded,
Like an old opera tune
Played upon a harpsichord.
—AMY LOWELL, "A Lady"

19. A silver plane pinned on the lapel of a cloud.
—ARDYS ARONSON

20. Poplars at attention, willow trees at ease.
—CHARLES A. MYERS

21. A coiffure that looked like a sparrow taking a bath.
—MARGARET FISHBACK

22. The carter cracked a sudden whip.
—WILFRED WILSON GIBSON

23. In this soft, this somewhat languid air, the ship glowed like an immense and brilliant jewel. All of her lights were on: they burned row by row straight across her 900 feet of length, with the small, hard twinkle of cut gems: it was as if the vast black cliff of her hull, which strangely suggested the glittering night-time cliff of the fabulous city that was her destination, had been sown with diamonds.

—THOMAS WOLFE, *Of Time and the River*

24. The dim white gleaming days succeeded one another like pearls on a string. The sun hung a pale disk over a channel veiled in torn silver webs, and in the short, misty twilight Marlingate showed like a pewter town beside a pewter sea.

—SHEILA KAYE-SMITH

For additional examples see "Selections for Paraphrasing", pages 103-106 and "The Suggestive Power of the Single Detail", pages 445-446.

THE ROUND TABLE

1. What is alliteration? Find and bring to class two good examples.
2. Make up and bring to class one serious and one humorous simile.
3. What is your favourite quotation? Does it contain a figure of speech? If so, what figure?

4. The Avoidance of Trite, Hackneyed Language

As was pointed out on page 331 and following, two kinds of words that should be avoided at all costs are abstract and general words. To these must now be added a third class, namely, stale, common-place, worn-out words, phrases, and figures of speech. Words become stale with unbelievable quickness. This has been strikingly expressed in a modern free verse poem:

The Word

The first time the emperor Han heard a certain Word he said, "It is strange." The second time he said, "It is divine." The third time he said, "Let the speaker be put to death."[1]

[1]Allen Upward, "The Word", from *Scented Leaves from a Chinese Jar.*

The pity of it is that it is usually the cleverest expression and the catchiest phrase that wear out first. Their very popularity ruins them. This, among other reasons, is why slang is so short-lived.

In avoiding triteness we must be on the watch against two varieties in particular: (1) trite comparisons (usually similes), and (2) trite quotations and phrases.

(1) TRITE COMPARISONS

It is appallingly easy to fall into stale, commonplace comparisons either from hurry or from sheer laziness. Take a column of such common descriptive words as the following, and try to complete the comparison:

1. black as ____	6. light as ____
2. white as ____	7. cold as ____
3. quick as ____	8. clear as ____
4. busy as ____	9. green as ____
5. heavy as ____	10. hard as ____

When we read over this list, instantly into the minds of four out of five people come the following comparisons—all of them the essence of triteness:

1. ink or night	6. a feather
2. snow or milk	7. ice
3. a flash or lightning	8. crystal
4. a bee	9. grass
5. lead	10. a rock

The very fact that the second half of such comparisons slips so easily into the mind is a danger sign. It means that nearly everyone else would use the same simile. And this, in turn, is exactly what constitutes triteness.

By way of contrast, glance back over the original, vivid similes given on page 342 and the figures of speech quoted on pages 346-349. There we have true originality and suggestiveness.

(2) TRITE PHRASES

In the second place, make the acquaintance **of a number**

of rubber-stamp words and expressions like those given below, and cross them definitely out of your vocabulary. All of them went on the retired list before you entered school. So convenient are they, however, that one still meets them here and there in the sentences of unskilled or lazy writers. Such expressions bear the same relation to real writing that a rubber stamp does to a signature.

Rubber-Stamp Expressions

reach one's destination
tired but happy
no sooner said than done
wended our way
favour with a selection
reigned supreme
all nature seemed
goodly number
doomed to disappointment
delightful feature
beggars description
partake of refreshments
old Sol
with bated breath
fit as a fiddle
rank outsider
apple-pie order
view with alarm
tempest in a teapot
conspicuous by its absence
so near and yet so far
the irony of fate
the psychological moment
burn the midnight oil
institution of higher learning
sober as a judge
guardian of the law
broad daylight
beat a hasty retreat
the sleep of the just
twinkling stars
all too soon
last but not least
sigh of relief
a few well-chosen words
sadder but wiser
proud possessor
fond parent
fair sex
downy couch
wee, small hours
sands of time
sea of life
faultlessly attired
colourful spectacle
square meal
the inner man
point with pride
eagle eye
too funny for words
tiller of the soil
but it was not to be
human form divine
combine business with pleasure
generous to a fault
brown as a berry
ripe old age
clocklike precision
lead a dog's life
throw caution to the winds
twittering birds

THE ROUND TABLE

1. Which, if any, of the trite (*a*) comparisons or (*b*) expressions
you remember having ever used in your writing?

2. Choose five of the similes listed on page 350 and complete tl
comparison as originally and vividly as you can.

3. Can you add any examples to the rubber-stamp expressio
listed above?

4. O. Henry has an amusing story called "Calloway's Code",
which a war correspondent in Mexico got a forbidden dispatch throu
the censor by the clever expedient of using the first half of certa
well-known, hackneyed expressions. The editor of the paper w
shrewd enough to take the second half of the expressions and make
story of them which scooped all the other papers. Read the sto
and explain how Calloway worked it.

5. The Avoidance of "Fine" Writing

Many inexperienced writers have a curious tendency
use big words and indirect methods of expression whenev
they begin to write. They may talk simply and interestingl
but give them paper and pencil and they seem hypnotiz
out of their true selves. Naturalness and ease fly away, ar
in the effort to measure up to the situation they try to be to
dignified, and end by becoming stiff, stilted, and wooden.

Too often in high-school themes, for example, the writ
does not get ready to leave, but "spends much time in pr
paring to depart"; he does not "go on", but "wends h
way" or "proceeds on his journey"; he never gets to whe
he is going, but always "arrives at his destination"; he do
not eat, but "enjoys a delicious repast". And so it go
throughout most of the theme: inflated words and rubbe
stamp expressions where simple words and specific expre
sions are needed.

The tendency toward "fine writing" or "tall writing" h
always been the bane of all writers, both amateur and pr
fessional, who have the urge to make their little fishes ta
like whales. As long ago as the American Civil War Jam
Russell Lowell satirized it in comparing what he called tl

"old style" and the "new style" of writing. It does not take much thought to determine which style is better.

Old Style	*New Style*
A great crowd came to see	A vast concourse was assembled to witness
Was hanged	Was launched into eternity
Great fire	Disastrous conflagration
The fire spread	The conflagration extended its devastating career
House burned	Edifice was consumed
Man fell	Individual was precipitated
The frightened horse	The infuriated animal
Sent for the doctor	Called into requisition the services of the family physician
I shall say a few words	I shall, with your permission, beg leave to offer some brief observations
Began his answer	Commenced his rejoinder
Asked him to dine	Tendered him a banquet
She sang	She rendered a vocal selection
No	The answer is in the negative
I received your letter	I am in receipt of your esteemed favour
Was given	Was made the recipient of

As the final word on the whole matter of style, therefore, **let us always use the simplest words the subject will bear.**

THE ROUND TABLE

1. Look back over some of your themes to see whether you have a tendency toward "fine writing". Ask your teacher's opinion on this point.

2. Read aloud in class Æsop's fable about "The Frog Who Tried to Make Himself As Large As an Ox". The application here is obvious.

3. One of the best take-offs on fine writing is the following, which was suggested by a similar sentence of H. L. Mencken's:

> If you think a flea is as large as a Newfoundland dog, as beautiful as the Queen of Sheba, and as dignified as the Archbishop of Canterbury, then say "A conflagration destroyed the edifice"; otherwise say, "The house burned down".

4. Paraphrase two familiar proverbs into the most polysyllabic and magniloquent English you are capable of. Discuss results in class, and put the two or three most inflated specimens on the board.

PART FOUR

SPECIAL FORMS OF WRITING

CHAPTER XXI

Letters

The ninety-and-nine will write letters throughout life, and they will write nothing else.

—THOMAS C. BLAISDELL

The Importance of Letter Writing

Next only to conversation, letters are both the most universal and the most personal form of communication. In school and college we get useful practice in many varieties of writing—usually in the story and in both kinds of essay, the expository and the informal, as well as in verse and plays. After graduation, however, not more than one person out of a thousand develops sufficient talent to have his work accepted for publication, and thus embark upon the career of an author. There is, however, one kind of writing which we shall all have to do as long as we live—everyone at least once a month, many probably every week, and a few possibly every day. That kind of writing is, of course, letters.

The ability to write a good letter means far more than we are likely to realize. For example, it frequently makes the difference between an average and an exceptional businessman; and, what is more important, it often makes the difference between a commonplace acquaintance and a lifelong friend. On the dollar-and-cents side the business world has no time to waste on a firm that conducts its correspondence in a careless, slipshod way; and on the human side as we grow older we come to set increasing store by those among our friends and families who can—and do—write bright, attractive, sincere letters.

Universal and important as letter writing is, it is something more besides: it is the most personal and intimate form of writing. A letter from you is as much a part of you as your voice, your smile, your frown. It represents and reflects you with unforgiving faithfulness: it is you who have chosen the kind of ink and paper; it is you who have selected the person to whom the letter goes; what you say and how you say it depend upon you and you alone. Your letter proclaims as it is opened and read: "Mark me well. I come to you as the personal representative of my sender. From me you can tell much of the kind of person he is and what he thinks of you. I only hope that if I look hasty, careless, and inaccurate, you will not judge my sender by me alone, but will let your past and future face-to-face dealings with him remedy my own imperfections."

Too often when writing home we dash off a few scrappy details and close with a request for money or some article that we forgot to take with us—a request that forms the real motive for the letter. This style of letter was once humorously parodied by a father who had a son playing summer baseball in a town nearby and who was not hearing from him as often as he wished. He sent his son a batch of stamped, self-addressed envelopes with a dozen typewritten copies of the following:

Dear Dad,

We played today against .... and won (lost) by the score of .... to ..... I went to bat .... times and got .... hits (doubles ...., triples ...., home runs ....). I struck out .... times and walked .... times. I am feeling ..... Please send me cheque for $.....

Love,

.....

THE ROUND TABLE

1. As interesting evidence of the place letter writing fills in life, let each pupil ask the adult members of his family to answer the following questionnaire. Have you ever written (1) a play? (2) a poem? (3) a magazine article? (4) a news article? (5) a short story? (6) a salable joke? (7) a letter to a good friend? (8) an order for goods

out of a catalogue? (9) a letter of complaint? (10) a letter of adjustment? (11) a letter of application? (12) a letter of recommendation? (13) Do you type your letters or use a pen or a pencil?

Tabulate the answers and discuss them in class.

2. In order to make the exercises in letter writing as practical as possible, try the plan of collecting five cents from each member of the class and having a class committee, in consultation with the teacher, select and buy for the class a suitable supply of (*a*) business letter sheets 8½″ × 11″, (*b*) note paper, and (c) correspondence cards. Get as neat and attractive stationery as possible.

3. Ask that member of the class who has the largest collection of stamps and who knows most about them to bring his (her) collection to class and make a ten-minute talk on Interesting Things about Stamps.

4. If another section of the English class in your school is also studying letter writing, work out with the teacher a plan for exchanging and comparing letters.

5. While the chapter on letter writing is being studied prepare a class notebook to contain the best examples of business letters, formal invitations and replies, and friendly letters. If the notebook is good enough, keep it as a permanent school exhibit or put it into the library for the use of next year's class.

6. Be prepared to answer the following questions about our postal system:

(1) If you direct a letter wrongly, so that it cannot be delivered, what becomes of it?
(2) What happens to a letter if it has insufficient postage?
(3) Make a report on interesting facts concerning the Dead Letter Office.
(4) What is meant by first-class mail? Second-class mail? What is the difference in rates?
(5) In sending packages by parcel post what are the limitations of size and weight? What are the "zones" and how do the rates differ?
(6) Can you insure a package by parcel post? For how much?
(7) What are the cost and advantage of sending a letter or package by registered mail?
(8) What are the cost and the advantage of air mail? Of special delivery?
(9) How close to you does the nearest air-mail route come?
(10) How many rural routes run out from your town or from the nearest large town?

Kinds of Letters

In general there are three kinds of letters, the forms of which are to be carefully distinguished and mastered. They are as follows:

1. Business Letters
2. Formal Invitations and Their Replies
3. Friendly Letters

Since both (1) the business letter and (2) formal invitations have a fixed, definite form, they will be taken up first and explained briefly.

1. Business Letters

As the first requirement, **a business letter must present a pleasing impression while the envelope is being opened and the letter taken out.** Good taste should be evident in every detail: neatness; quality and colour of the paper; kind, colour, and arrangement of the type in which the firm's name is stamped on the letter sheet; the care with which the letter itself is centred on the page, with ample margins on each side and equal spacing at the top and the bottom. All such details, which go to make up what is called the letter picture, must be above reproach in dignity and refinement. A letter must please the eye before it pleases the mind.

Practically all business letters may be included in the following classes:

1. Letters making requests or inquiries
2. Letters replying to requests or inquiries
3. Letters ordering goods
4. Letters acknowledging orders
5. Letters of remittance
6. Letters acknowledging remittances
7. Letters requesting adjustment
8. Adjustment letters
9. Credit letters
10. Collection letters

11. Sales and advertising letters
12. Letters of introduction
13. Letters of application
14. Letters of recommendation

A business letter must strictly observe the general principles of all writing. It must be perfect in spelling and punctuation. Above all it must be paragraphed with careful strictness, each different item of information being carefully set off by itself in its own separate paragraph, so that the reader can instantly grasp and as easily answer each different point.

(1) THE FIVE *C*'S

In addition to such general requirements, to reach its highest effectiveness a business letter must have five qualities pre-eminently. **It must be (1) clear, (2) correct, (3) complete, (4) concise, and (5) courteous.** Each of these five adjectives obviously justifies itself, and does not need further elaboration. We might call them the Five *C*'s of Good Business Correspondence. They should unfailingly characterize every business communication.

All five are important, but the stress that the business world lays on courtesy and friendliness can be seen from the following significant directions on this point.[1]

When reading your dictated correspondence, just measure letters according to the following table:

I	II
Courteous	Discourteous
Sincere	Curt
Pleasant	Sarcastic
Friendly	Sharp
Cheerful	Impatient
Warm	Cold
Helpful	Peevish
	Overbearing
	Harsh

[1] W. H. Leffingwell's *Office Management*, quoted in Lucia B. Mirrieless. *Teaching Composition in High School*, Harcourt, Brace and Company, p. 279,

If to each of the words in the first column you can answer "Yes", then your letters are all right as far as tone is concerned. Should you have to answer "Guilty" to any of the points given in the other column, then revise the letter or letters before they leave your hands, even if it is necessary to hold them until the next day. An unfriendly letter is nothing more than the dropping of a wrench into the gears which drive the business machine. Whether the whole letter, or only a sentence, violates this principle makes no difference. A sentence, or even a word, can undo months and years of effort.

(2) SPECIAL FORM

The business letter is a strictly utilitarian document. It exists for business, not for pleasure, and its object is to convey information as clearly, correctly, completely, concisely, and courteously as possible. For this purpose the long experience of the business world has developed a fixed, definite form. This form consists of six distinct parts. There is a good reason for each part, and hence little cause to alter the arrangement and no excuse for making a mistake.

Its six parts are these:

(A) Heading
(B) Inside Address
(C) Salutation
(D) Body of the Letter
(E) Complimentary Close
(F) Signature

So far as the letter sheet is concerned, these six parts are distributed and grouped as shown on page 363.

1. The Two Arrangements of Lines and the Two Systems of Punctuation

With special reference to parts one and two, the heading and the inside address, and likewise the outside address on

LETTER FORM

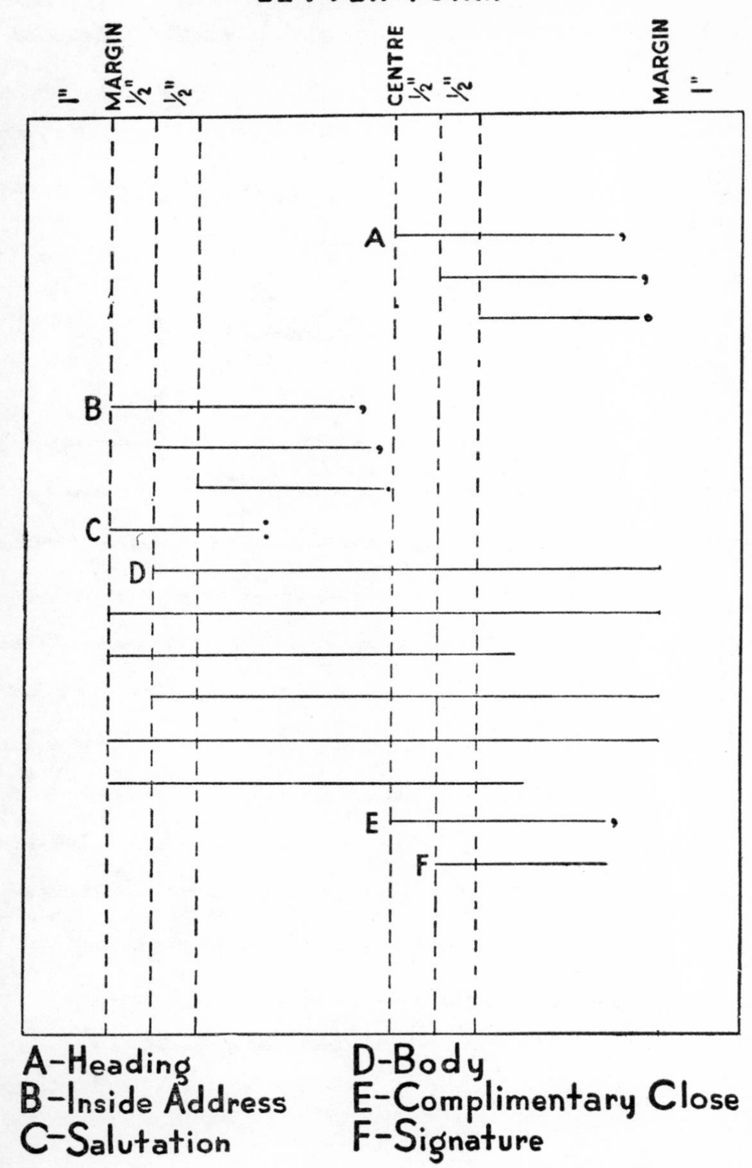

A-Heading
B-Inside Address
C-Salutation
D-Body
E-Complimentary Close
F-Signature

512 Leonard Street,
Calgary, Alta.,
September 7, 1946.

The Norton Company Limited,
211 Prairie Avenue,
Regina,
Saskatchewan.

Gentlemen:

Thank you for your promptness and courtesy in forwarding your interesting catalogue of sports equipment. The covering letter gave me the special information requested.

Football helmet No. 21 C appears to be what I require, but it is difficult to be sure. Will you please send me one of these on approval, as suggested in your communication.

Yours truly,
George C. Scott

the envelope, two arrangements of lines are permissible. The older method, which is still standard, (and indeed recommended by the Post Office Department), is **the indented or slanting order.** In this order, each successive line is set back or indented like the first line of a paragraph, in this fashion:

———————————————
        ———————————————
                ———————————————

The other method, which is newer, and is now growing in favour for typewritten business letters, is **the block system.** In this, the successive lines are not indented, but begin flush with the same margin, in this fashion:

———————————————
————————————
—————————

The indented arrangement is still usually followed by those who write a letter by hand. The block system is fairly common among those who use typewriters.

2. THE TWO SYSTEMS OF PUNCTUATION: CLOSED AND OPEN

There are two prevailing ways of punctuating the heading, the inside address, and the outside address on the envelope. **The older method is the closed, in which commas are used after each line except the last, and a period after the last line.** Closed punctuation can be used with either the indented or the block arrangement of lines. **In the open system no commas or final periods are used at the ends of the lines,** unless of course a line ends with an abbreviation; then the period is essential to the spelling of the abbreviation.

CLOSED PUNCTUATION

Indented Arrangement	*Block System*

Mr. Thomas Gray,
  405 Simcoe Street North,
    Oshawa, Ontario.
	Mr. Thomas Gray,
	405 Simcoe Street North,
	Oshawa, Ontario.

OPEN PUNCTUATION

Indented Arrangement	*Block System*

Mr. Thomas Gray
  405 Simcoe Street North
    Oshawa, Ontario
	Mr. Thomas Gray
	405 Simcoe Street North
	Oshawa, Ontario

Again, either the closed or the open system of punctuation is correct. The closed system is the older, and is usually followed by those who use the indented arrangement of lines and write their letters by hand. The open system is growing in favour with those who use the block system and typewrite their letters.

Note that the heading begins at the centre of the line and that the date is given in numerals only: October 1, 1946, not October 1st or October first.

Common salutations in business letters are the following:

Dear Mr. Jones:	Dear Mrs. Jones:
My dear Mr. Jones:	My dear Mrs. Jones:
Dear Sir:	Dear Madam:
My dear Sir:	My dear Madam:

Note that the use of "My" in the salutation increases the formality.

The plural forms are these:

Gentlemen: Mesdames:

"Dear Sirs", the older form of salutation, is becoming obsolete in Canadian business usage.

(3) THE BODY OF THE LETTER

The body of the letter is the main thing. All the other parts are merely incidental or preliminary to it. We should make sure that each letter that leaves our hands is characterized by the Five *C*'s mentioned above—that is, is clear, correct, complete, concise, and courteous. To these should be added the sixth golden essential of business efficiency—namely, promptness. If possible, all business houses try to answer every letter either the day or the day after it is received. "A clear desk at the end of the day" is a maxim in most offices.

As to form, a large majority of Canadian business concerns (*a*) indent each paragraph, (*b*) single space the lines throughout the entire letter, and (*c*) double space between paragraphs. In a very short typewritten letter of fifty words or less double spacing is used throughout. Some business houses, however, do not indent the paragraphs. Both styles are exemplified in the sample letters on the following pages.

The best usage today is away from the stereotyped short cuts, abbreviations, and rubber-stamp expressions of the past, such as the following:

> ult. (for ultimo), the last month
> inst. (for instant), the present month
> prox. (for proximo), the next month
> Yours of the 15th inst. received and contents duly noted. Will say in reply, etc.
> I beg to advise
> Your esteemed favour
> Your valued order

Likewise the somewhat complicated participial close, which used to be in favour, is losing its hold. Most correspondents avoid such expressions as

> Thanking you for past favours and hoping for a continuation of the same, I remain,
> Thanking you in advance for your kindness in attending to this matter, I am,
> Hoping to be favoured with an early order, I am

Notice that the complimentary close, like the heading, starts at the middle of the page.

The complimentary closes in common use are these:

Yours truly,	Truly yours,
Yours very truly,	Very truly yours,

In letters to superiors you may use *Yours respectfully* or *Respectfully yours.*

A letter indicating a friendly business relationship may close with *Yours sincerely* or *Sincerely yours, Yours cordially* or *Cordially yours.*

The position of the signature is determined by the use of the indented or the block arrangement.

A woman should make clear by her signature how she is to be addressed.

Unmarried woman	(Miss) Mary Webster
Married woman	Mary Williams
	(Mrs.) G. A. Williams
Widow	(Mrs.) Mary Williams

(4) THE ENVELOPE

The envelope should contain the two following items clearly and correctly given:

1. The name and address of the sender, in the upper left-hand corner of the envelope.
2. The name and address of the recipient neatly spaced across the main part of the envelope.

These two addresses (1) may be in either the indented or the block form, and (2) may use either the closed or the open system of punctuation. Post office authorities favour a double-spaced address with the name of the province or state on a separate line from that of the city or town.

The following pages contain examples of correct forms for business letters and envelopes. Since we are concerned here with form rather than with content, the same letter is used throughout in order to make comparison easier.

1618 Western Avenue,
Vancouver, B. C.,
October 1, 1946.

The Macmillan Company of Canada Limited,
70 Bond Street,
Toronto, Ontario.

Gentlemen:

Can I secure from you a set of Scott's novels in the same binding and at the same price per volume as the edition of Thackeray's works which I ordered from your firm last month? I find this set both useful and attractive and should like to duplicate it if possible.

What grade of paper, size of type, and colour of binding are used in your Standard Series of American and English Poets? If you have specimen pages or a more detailed description than that contained in your general catalogue, I should appreciate your letting me know.

Yours truly,

Thomas B. Graves

The spacing and signature changes indicated on page 370-371 are according to best modern practice.

1. **Typewritten; block system; closed punctuation:**

1618 Western Avenue,
Vancouver, B.C.,
October 1, 1946.

The Macmillan Company of Canada Limited,
70 Bond Street,
Toronto, Ontario.

Gentlemen:

Can I secure from you a set of Scott's novels in the same binding and at the same price per volume as the edition of Thackeray's works which I ordered from your firm last month? I find this set both useful and attractive, and should like to duplicate it if possible.

What grade of paper, size of type, and colour of binding are used in your Standard Series of American and English Poets? If you have specimen pages or a more detailed description than that contained in your general catalogue, I should appreciate your letting me know.

Very truly yours,

Thomas B. Graves

Envelope

Thomas B. Graves,
1618 Western Avenue,
Vancouver, B.C.

The Macmillan Company of Canada Limited,
70 Bond Street,
Toronto,
Ontario.

2. **Typewritten; block system; open punctuation:**

1618 Western Avenue
Vancouver, B.C.
October 1, 1946

The Macmillan Company of Canada Limited
70 Bond Street
Toronto, Ontario

Gentlemen:

Can I secure from you a set of Scott's novels in the same binding and at the same price per volume as the edition of Thackeray's works which I ordered from your firm last month? I find this set both useful and attractive, and should like to duplicate it if possible.

What grade of paper, size of type, and colour of binding are used in your Standard Series of American and English Poets? If you have specimen pages or a more detailed description than that contained in your general catalogue, I should appreciate your letting me know.

Very truly yours,

Thomas B. Graves

Envelope

Thomas B. Graves
1618 Western Avenue
Vancouver, B.C.

The Macmillan Company of Canada Limited
70 Bond Street
Toronto
Ontario

3. Handwritten; indented arrangement; closed punctuation:

Envelope

George C. Scott,
513 Leonard St.,
Calgary, Alta

The Norton Company Limited,
211 Prairie Avenue,
Regina,
Saskatchewan.

THE ROUND TABLE

1. "Zero for an Error." So clear and definite is the form of the business letter that, once it is learned, no errors should be permitted. After reading this section and writing two specimen business letters, are you willing to agree that no business letter will receive a passing grade that contains a single mistake in any of the six parts? This means an error in form, not in the body of the letter.

2. First getting permission, bring to class several business letterheads from local professional or business men. Prepare a neat display of them in scrapbook form.

3. If possible, bring to class any actual business letters that you can courteously and legitimately procure. Call attention to any unusual features.

4. Choose the business or profession you prefer and draw up your own letterhead. What colour of paper and kind of type will you select?

5. Among the six following assignments in the strictly business letter, use the indented style with closed punctuation. If the letters are typed, the block style and open punctuation might be used for one letter.

(1) Address two envelopes (or slips of paper cut to envelope size, usually $3\frac{5}{8}'' \times 6\frac{1}{2}''$) to advertisers in a national magazine.

(2) Write the inside address and salutation only to two of the following: the Governor-General; the Prime Minister; one of the members of Parliament; the Lieutenant-Governor. Consult your teacher for the proper form of salutation.

(3) Answer an advertisement in any Canadian magazine requesting a catalogue.

(4) Write a letter subscribing for your favourite magazine. Mention how you are sending the money.

(5) Write a business letter ordering several items from a store or factory advertising in a local paper.

(6) Write to a school principal or to a secretary of a board of education in your province applying for a position as teacher. Be definite as to what grade or subject you feel best fitted to deal with. State your qualifications fairly and fully.

6. Find in a daily paper an advertisement in the "Help Wanted" column which you think you could fill. Imagine that getting this place is very important to you just now. Apply for it.

7. Appoint a small class committee to represent the employer, and (*a*) let them judge the letters of application written in Exercise 5 (6) on looks only, on paper, handwriting, margins, neatness, etc.—rejecting all that fail to come up to a high standard; (*b*) then let the committee read over the accepted letters, and on the score of correctness and effectiveness appoint personal interviews for those who deserve them.

8. Write to the publishers of one of your textbooks ordering new books for the entire class.

9. Write to the registrar of the college you would most like to attend requesting a catalogue, information about entrance requirements, and an estimate of a year's average expenses.

10. Write as secretary, in the name of your class, inviting a prominent man or woman to deliver the commencement address. Remember that this is asking a good deal of a busy person. Give some details as to why you wish this particular person to speak for you, and state whether a fee or simply expenses will be paid, and where and how entertainment will be provided.

11. A friend whom you both know and like is applying for a position in the nearest large city. Having in mind an actual friend and a position he (she) is fitted to fill, write a letter of recommendation.

12. You are business manager of your school annual or paper. Write a letter soliciting an advertisement from some business firm. Try to write a logical, persuasive letter.

13. Write to the principal asking permission to make a canvass in

the school in behalf of the Society for Prevention of Cruelty to Animals. Go into some detail.

14. Write a sales letter boosting some product that is either manufactured or grown in your community. You will have to know the product thoroughly and believe in it before you can convince others. An effective sales letter is the hardest of all business letters to write well. Select the best two or three letters written by members of the class for this exercise and submit them to the manufacturer, merchant, or farmer whose product is described.

15. Write to the manager of the best high-school team (basketball, football, hockey, baseball) in the neighbourhood proposing a game with your team.

16. Decide what single improvement the school needs most and write a letter to the board of trustees through the chairman petitioning for this improvement. Select the two best letters and, if the teacher and the principal both approve, send them to the chairman of the board.

17. Order from a mail-order catalogue five dollars' worth of musical supplies, sporting goods, or automobile accessories.

18. Write to the principal petitioning for a holiday or for a desired school privilege. Have an actual situation in mind and try to write logically and convincingly.

19. You do not approve of a recent article or editorial which appeared in the school magazine. Write a formal letter to the editor stating your objections and the reasons for them.

20. You are attracted by a contest in which a prize is offered for the best advertisement of a certain make of shoes. Write for particulars.

21. The school band practises in a room on the east side of the building. Just across the street is a very ill woman, who is disturbed by the noise. You are the woman's nurse. Write to the leader of the band on the subject.

22. Using a pen name and an imaginary address, write a letter of complaint. Your letter should suit the character of the person who you imagine is writing it, and need not be written correctly. Exchange letters within your own class or with another class, and reply to the letter of complaint you have received. This time your letter should be correct both in form and in style. It should deal adequately with the complaint. Seal your letter in a properly addressed envelope and return it to the sender. Distribution and return of letters can be simplified by appointing two or three pupils to act as postmen.

2. Formal Invitations and Replies

A special form of social communication, as fixed in its form and conventions as the business letter itself, is the formal invitation and its reply. The **formal invitation** has neither heading, inside address, greeting, complimentary close, nor signature. All necessary information as to time, place, person, and purpose is given in one brief paragraph. It is written throughout in the third person. It is usually either written by hand or engraved. It is never typewritten or mimeographed and should not be printed if this can possibly be avoided. It is usually centred upon a correspondence card or upon very heavy white paper approximately 3½ by 5¼ inches, or slightly larger than regular notepaper folded. So far as possible all abbreviations are avoided and even figures are written out in full, for both abbreviations and figures suggest business and lack of leisure. Everything about a formal invitation savours of formality, dignity, good taste, and the avoidance of the cheap and the commonplace.

If the invitation is engraved, the company that does the engraving will have sample forms and styles to go by. The language is highly formal, but the lines may either be arranged in the block style or separated according to the different items of the invitation, each line being centred exactly on the page. If this latter style is followed, the name of the person or the organization occupies the first line, the invitation itself the second line, the purpose the third line, the date the fourth line, the hour the fifth line, and the place the sixth line. If an answer is expected, there are placed in the lower left-hand corner the letters R. S. V. P. or R. s. v. p., standing for the French phrase *Répondez, s'il vous plaît* (Reply, if you please).

If written out by hand, the invitation either may follow the group arrangement of lines described above or may be in block style, centred on the card, with no indentations.

REPLIES

Replies to formal invitations follow exactly the style of the invitation itself, rewording every item except the hour.

Examples

1. Invitation: engraved; group arrangement of lines:

The Forest Lake Country Club
requests the pleasure of your company
at its annual Ladies' Night Dance
on Friday evening, December the first
from eight till twelve o'clock
at the clubhouse

R. S. V. P.

1. Acceptance: handwritten; group arrangement of lines:

Mr. Donald G. Whitman
accepts with pleasure the invitation of
The Forest Lake Country Club
to its annual Ladies' Night Dance
on Friday evening, December the first
at the clubhouse

2. **Invitation: handwritten; group arrangement of lines:**

The Evening Music Club
requests the pleasure of Mr. Traymoor's presence
at its open meeting
on Tuesday evening, December the first
at eight-thirty o'clock
in the Crystal Room of the Colonia Hotel.

Please reply

3. **Refusal: handwritten; block arrangement of lines:**

Miss Alice Carpenter regrets that
a previous engagement prevents
her from accepting Mr. and Mrs.
Robert T. Gray's kind invitation
to dinner on Tuesday evening
August the nineteenth

1611 Avondale Street
Monday, August the twelfth

THE ROUND TABLE

1. Let as many students as can do so bring to class an engraved or handwritten formal invitation or announcement. Display these in class. Select the best and keep them for the class notebook.

2. Your parents are giving a formal dinner two weeks from today. (*a*) Write an invitation to your teacher; (*b*) write her acceptance or refusal.

3. Your class is giving a formal afternoon reception to the high-school staff. Write an invitation to your parents to attend.

4. Your grandparents will soon celebrate their golden wedding. Write the invitation for them.

5. The junior class is giving the senior class a dance on the night of the last school day before the Christmas holidays. Write an invitation to the principal and his wife.

6. Write your acceptance of an invitation from a school friend to a formal birthday party.

7. Write to the class next below yours inviting them to attend a play your class is giving soon. Be specific as to the play itself and the time and the place.

8. A club to which you belong will have at its next meeting an especially interesting programme. Write a formal invitation to a teacher who formerly sponsored this club.

3. Friendly Letters

A man that hath friends must shew himself friendly.
—PROVERBS XVIII. 24

(1) THE FORM OF FRIENDLY LETTERS

The **friendly letter** is different in both form and purpose from the business letter and the formal invitation. The only part of the friendly letter that is strict in form is the address on the envelope. Since this address guides the letter to its destination, it should of course be as accurate and as complete as the address on a business envelope. Friendly letters are usually written by hand, and the address can follow either the indented or the block system of arranging the lines, and either the closed or the open style of punctuation. It is well to put your own return address on the upper left-hand corner of the envelope as is regularly done in business correspondence. The Post Office Department advises this in all cases.

Notice that the greeting in friendly letters is punctuated with a comma instead of with a colon as in business letters.

The notepaper itself should be of first-class quality and in perfect taste. White, cream, or pale gray is preferable to the gaudier colours. **The ink should be black or blue-black,** not red, green, or violet. Strongly perfumed paper should be avoided. Everything about the letter should suggest refinement and good taste.

(2) THE LETTER ITSELF

So various in tone and purpose are our manifold friendly letters that no single prescription will cover them all. Perhaps the best is the beautiful sentiment from Proverbs quoted at the beginning of this section: "A man that hath friends must shew himself friendly." That is, friendship carries its own obligation; if we have friends, we must show ourselves worthy of them by carrying out the obligations of friendship and affection. Not the least of these is, in absence, to keep alive and cherish the friendly feeling by means of bright, attractive letters, as intimate and affectionate as the mutual relationship warrants. Whatever other qualities such letters should have, they should above all be natural, sympathetic, and as interesting as we can make them.

THE ROUND TABLE

1. Name all the different kinds of friendly letters (*a*) that you have had occasion to write during the past twelve months, and (*b*) that you think you may have occasion to write during the next twelve.

2. A former schoolmate who has gone away to college has recently won distinction in athletics, public speaking, debating, scholarship, or writing. Write him (her) a cordial note of greeting and congratulation telling him (her) how proud you are of him (her).

3. Write to a close personal friend of your family asking permission to use his name as reference in applying for a position you are seeking.

4. Write a note to the mother of a friend who has entertained you at their cottage in the mountains (or at the seashore) for a week-end.

5. Write a note acknowledging an unexpected Christmas gift of five dollars from an uncle who lives in a distant city and whom you see but seldom.

6. Write a note to an elderly woman friend of your family who sent you some flowers during your recent illness.

7. Write to a friend in a nearby town who entertained another friend of yours at dinner when he (she) was visiting in that town last week.

8. You are in a boys' (girls') camp for the summer. Write to the father of a close friend urging that he let your friend spend a month at the same camp. Describe the advantages of the camp, state the cost, and tell what equipment each camper must bring.

9. Write a cheerful letter to a friend (boy or girl) who has had a bad automobile accident and is laid up in bed with a broken leg.

10. The family of one of your classmates (boy or girl) is moving to a distant city. You have a first cousin there whom you wish your classmate to meet. Write your cousin an informal letter of introduction about your friend.

11. Your mother (or father) is away on a visit. Write an interesting detailed letter about some recent important or funny or unusual event in school or community life.

12. You are sending some flowers to a sick friend. Write a cheerful little note to accompany them.

13. An unexpected automobile trip out of town with friends has made you forget an engagement to be present at a friend's party. Write a note of explanation and apology.

14. If a member of the class is sick or laid up from an accident, write a cheerful note telling him (her) how much you miss him (her) and giving some interesting or funny school news. These letters might be sent.

15. Write a note of congratulation to a schoolmate who has won a contest or tournament in which you were a contestant.

16. Write a letter to an old friend of your family's telling him of the two professions you are debating entering, and asking his advice as to which to follow.

17. Write to a classmate who left school last year and went to work in a neighbouring town, telling him about your studies this year and giving him some interesting class news.

Effective Letters

1. Thomas Bailey Aldrich, the author of Marjorie Daw, writes a guest letter to William Dean Howells, the novelist:

Ponkapog, Mass.
December 13, 1875[1]

Dear Howells,

We had so charming a visit at your house that I have about made up my mind to reside with you permanently. I am tired of writing. I would like to settle down in just such a comfortable home as yours, with a man who can work regularly four or five hours a day, thereby relieving one of all painful apprehensions in respect to clothes and pocket-money. I am easy to get along with. I have few unreasonable wants and never complain when they are constantly supplied. I think I could depend on you.

Ever yours,

T. B. A.

P. S. I should want to bring my two mothers, my two boys (I seem to have everything in twos), my wife, and her sister.

2. Robert Louis Stevenson to his friend W. H. Low:

Chalet La Solitude, Hyères
October 23, 1883[2]

My dear Low,

I am now a person with an established ill-health—a wife—a dog possessed with an evil, a Gadarene spirit—a chalet on a hill, looking out over the Mediterranean—a certain reputation—and very obscure finances. Otherwise, very much the same, I guess; and were a bottle of Fleury a thing to be obtained, capable of developing theories along with a fit spirit even as of yore. Yet I now draw near to the Middle Ages; nearly three years ago, that fatal Thirty struck; and yet the great work is not yet done—not yet even conceived. But so, as one goes on, the wood seems to thicken, the footpath to narrow, and the House Beautiful on the hill's summit to draw further and further away. We learn, indeed, to use our means; but only to learn, along with it, the paralysing knowledge that these means are only applicable

[1]From *Letters of Thomas Bailey Aldrich*, Houghton Mifflin Co. By permission of the publishers.
[2]By permission of the publishers, Charles Scribner's Sons.

to two or three poor commonplace motives. Eight years ago, if I could have slung ink as I can now, I should have thought myself well on the road after Shakespeare; and now—I find I have only got a pair of walking-shoes and not yet begun to travel. And art is still away there on the mountain summit. But I need not continue; for, of course, this is your story just as much as it is mine; and, strange to think, it was Shakespeare's too, and Beethoven's, and Phidias's. It is a blessed thing that, in this forest of art, we can pursue our wood-lice and sparrows, *and not catch them*, with almost the same fervour of exhilaration as that with which Sophocles hunted and brought down the Mastodon.

Tell me something of your work, and your wife.—My dear fellow, I am yours ever,

R. L. STEVENSON

My wife begs to be remembered to both of you; I cannot say as much for my dog, who has never seen you, but he would like, on general principles, to bite you.

3. An unexcelled example of the hardest of all kinds of letters to write:

JAMES MEMORIAL UNIVERSITY
JAMESON, TENNESSEE

October 11, 19—[1]

Mrs. E. P. Waters
Richmond, Virginia

My dear Mrs. Waters:

Something happened here this morning that I want you to know.

About nine o'clock a young fellow swung on to the campus with a long-legged stride that would have been astonishing anywhere else. He had come a hundred miles from his home in the mountains of North Carolina.

I turned him over to Dean Stuart, but I listened to the conversation. He had brought with him the sum of just $10,—no more,—all he had on earth. The dean told him that it was hard to know what to do with him, and explained as kindly as he could that all our rooms were occupied.

I looked at the young man; he never flinched; he smiled, confidently faced us both, clear-eyed and steady, and this is what he said: "Dean, I didn't come here to get a room or to get a bed; I came to get an education. I can sleep on the floor."

[1]From Roy Davis and C. H. Lingham, *Business Letter-Writing*, Ginn and Co. By permission of the publishers.

There was no answer to that. At least, neither the dean nor I could think of one, and we simply made a place for him; we had to. We cannot refuse this sort, and we will not do it as long as there is a dollar in sight.

These boys are the salt of the earth—big, strong, upstanding fellows; old Revolutionary stock, most of them; mountain-born; fearless, quiet, loyal, high-principled, and clean. They must have help. They need it and they deserve it. The sum of $25,000 is required at once for the actual current expenses of the year. We must have that amount at hand or in prospect at an early day.

We are asking not only because the money is needed for the great work that we are doing but because it is right that you should have an opportunity to give if you can. Your gift may make the difference between a life of ignorance and a life of knowledge, to some mountain boy.

Sincerely yours,

SHERIDAN P. EDWARDS,
President

DCM

4. From *Letters from a Bald-Headed Dad to His Red-Headed Daughter,* by Robert Quillen:

September 19—[1]

My dear Louise,

This letter isn't prompted by the fact that you live in a small town. Human nature is changed very little by population statistics, and a large community is merely a collection of small ones.

In all communities of which I have knowledge, the people are divided into two classes—those who talk about things and those who talk about people. Of course the classes aren't wholly distinct. Those who talk about things—about politics, books, current events, music, law—these may at times discuss their friends and their servants; but the other class, composed of those who talk about people, is incapable of talking or listening unless the topic of conversation is a neighbour.

You are now forming the social habits that will stay with you through life. The next five years will determine which class is yours. Environment will decide the matter for you if you make no effort to do anything for yourself. You will develop the habit of making conversation as your daily companions do.

[1]By permission of the author and of Publishers Syndicate, 30 N. La Salle St., Chicago, Ill.

Don't fool yourself by assuming that you can spend your youth in discussion of your neighbours and then blossom out overnight and become a charming conversationalist capable of discussing anything under the sun. Habit isn't formed that way. Your future way of life won't be decided upon next year or the next. You are cutting the pattern now.

Do you wish to be a common scold? That is the ultimate fate of every woman who talks about nothing but people. You can't make conversation about your neighbours' virtues and triumphs. Ordinary things aren't interesting. If you make it a practice to talk about people, you will talk about their faults and their sins, their mistakes and their failures. And after a few years of that your mind will travel in a rut and you won't be able to open your mouth without saying something uncomplimentary about somebody.

You can't change after the habit jells. Once you become a confirmed neighbour discusser, you will be happy only among others of your kind. When chance places you in a group that talks of other things, you will be as dumb as an oyster.

Talk of many things, Honey. Otherwise you'll be tongue-tied when you meet a stranger who doesn't know the Joneses.

Love,
DAD

CHAPTER XXII

Incident

1. The Love of Stories

The world has always kept the warmest spot in its heart for its story-tellers. We cheer our orators; we admire our essayists and our scientific writers; we applaud our dramatists; we honour our poets; but we love our novelists and story writers. The names that stand highest in our affection are such names as Dickens, Scott, Stevenson, Dumas, Mark Twain, Louisa Alcott, Bret Harte, Kipling, and O. Henry. How could we help being warmly drawn to those who gave us *A Tale of Two Cities*, *Treasure Island*, *The Three Guardsmen*, *Huckleberry Finn*, and *Little Women*? If you want the key to the world's heart and to the world's treasure chest, tell the world absorbing stories, and make it laugh and weep and thrill over your characters.

2. Kinds of Narrative

There are many different kinds of stories, or rather types of literature which have a narrative backbone. Merely to name these over is interesting, and makes a significant display. We may divide the entire field into (*a*) fact and (*b*) fiction, and list the various types as follows:

Fact	*Fiction*
Personal Anecdote	Epic (poetry)
News Stories	Ballad (poetry)
History	Drama
Letters	Tale
Diary	Fable
Memoirs	Short Story
Biography	Novel
Autobiography	
Travelogues	

These various kinds of narrative writing are not hard-and-fast divisions, for some of them shade very gradually into one another, and sometimes it would be puzzling to say whether a given incident should be classed as a personal anecdote, a news story, a tale, or a short story. In general, however, the types are clearly recognizable. Together they offer impressive testimony to the far-flung scope of narration and the tremendous place it occupies in the literature of the world.

Important as these various narrative types are, only three of them concern us this year in the composition course. These are (1) letters, (2) simple incident, and (3) the story. The narrative element in friendly letters was dealt with in the last chapter. The present chapter, as its title implies, is devoted to the incident and the next chapter to the story.

3. Simple Incident

Most of your narrative writing this year will be concerned with what is usually called **simple incident.** Simple incident, might also be accurately termed "single incident". It consists of a single interesting or significant event that has chanced to happen to you or that has fallen under your observation. It is complete in itself, and in the form in which you tell it is cut away both from what went before it and from what came after it. It just happens, as it were, out of a clear sky. You may have walked by a certain corner for years without seeing anything worth telling about, but one day something exciting takes place as you pass—a runaway, an automobile wreck, a fight, a fire, a mad-dog scare, any of the dozen things that find their way into the newspaper and that you talk about for several days afterwards to your family and friends.

Things like these happen now and then to all of us—and then we have material for an incident. The incident may be thrilling, but it does not have to be. It can be funny, sad, typical, or even commonplace, if only we observe it with seeing eyes and relate it accurately and minutely. Among the incidents, for example, written by high-school students and quoted in this chapter are experiences no more exciting in themselves than returning a lost dog to its home and visiting an exhibition of white mice.

Of course the incident does not have to be actually and literally true. You may have invented it in whole or in part. Often it is a combination of fact and fancy. Something that we have seen or heard or read gives us a hint, and our imagination pieces it out, adds to it here, takes away from it there, heightens the interest and trims it to the desired length. All that is demanded of us is that the incident seem true as we tell it.

Here are two simple incidents as told by high-school students.

A Modern Traveller

He seemed to be only a poor, lost dog, aimlessly wandering about the streets wondering what all the noise was about, and vainly seeking to find his master. His tail drooped disconsolately and he moved along slowly, indifferent to the cars which raced around him.

There were shrieks of fear and a grinding of brakes as a car, narrowly missing the forlorn-looking creature, slid to a stop near the curb.

"Whew," breathed an occupant of the car. "That surely was a narrow escape for that dog!"

"Look! He seems to be a thoroughbred," cried another. "He has a collar. Let's find out where he belongs. It would be a pity to let him get killed."

So saying the girls opened the door and called the dog. He immediately hopped in and placed himself upon the back seat as if he were accustomed to riding there. His eyes brightened and he showed his appreciation by placing his cold muzzle upon the driver's shoulder.

A name plate was on the collar and the girls discovered that his master lived only a short distance away; so they drove to the address given.

When they let the dog out, he bounded joyfully up the steps and sat down before the door wagging his tail. One of the girls rang the doorbell and told the butler how they had found the dog wandering on the street. The butler grinned and replied,

"Yes, miss. He sure am a smart dog. He go off lak dat all de time, and when he gits tuckered out, he jest wander out in de road and look lak he lost, and someone always bring him home. Yes, miss, he shore am a smart dog."

Page the Pied Piper

"Oh, aren't they adorable?"

"Adorable nothing! They're horrible!"

"Eeee! Let's get away from 'em! They scare me to death!"

What on earth could be in that big tin box to bring forth such a variety of opinions, the reporter wondered. Investigation revealed—mice: fifty or more real live white mice in the Mickey Mouse carnival at a local theatre last Saturday.

Such a time they were having!

Some of them were whirling dizzily in a diminutive ferris wheel, some sliding down the sliding board; and, believe it or not, one versatile little fellow was performing breath-taking feats on an acting bar at the dizzy height of four inches from the ground.

Was the dainty little creature looking up at the performer his girl friend? It must have been, for its two bright eyes gazed in worshipful admiration at Tailspin Tommy. And surely the scornful little fellow to the left with the "Aw, that's nothing" look in his eyes was Tommy's rival for the fair white paw of little Susy Bright Eyes.

But the best laid plans of mice and men often go astray, and poor Tailspin Tommy tried to show off once too often, and down he fell—thump! Much chagrined, he scampered away, a sadder and wiser mouse. Was it merely fancy, or did the reporter really hear a tiny "ha! ha!" from Tommy's rival?

After watching these fascinating little creatures for fully thirty minutes, the reporter turned her steps homeward, wishing that she could buy for her pet cat a ticket of admission to this carnival.

4. Details

Three-fourths of being interesting consists in giving definite details. The other fourth doesn't matter.

The art of telling a story is the art of going into details. There are two requirements: first, we must give enough details; and secondly, the given details must be definite, so that the reader can get the picture and visualize the action; or, to state it more accurately, so that the reader can from the given details create the action for himself and visualize the scene. Without details the reader is helpless. The writer may be quivering with excitement—or shaking with indignation—or bursting with laughter—or choking back the tears—but unless he gives us the actual, specific details which so moved him, he leaves us cold. It is as if he took us into a closed room to show us a wonderful picture and then failed to turn on the light.

This principle is fundamental. Every writer must realize it and train himself to write in accordance with it before any solid progress can be made. It is Swift's skilful handling of details that makes *Gulliver's Travels*, impossible as much of it is, a convincing story as well as one of the world's great books. It is Defoe's realistic use of details that for more than two hundred years has made *Robinson Crusoe* one of the most widely read books in English and that has caused it to be translated into nearly all languages. Similarly it is the wealth of details that makes Pepys's *Diary* and Boswell's *Life of Johnson* the two greatest books in their respective fields. Again, it is by details that the famous French story writer de Maupassant has created his masterpieces of succinct narration, particularly "A Piece of String" and "The Necklace", which are as popular in the English-speaking world as they are in France. The way of details is the way of all successful writers.

Here is a good example of the power of details to make a scene come alive before our eyes. The two following passages were written by the same person and deal with a minor crisis in the lives of a newly married couple.[1] The only difference between the versions is that the first does not go into detail and the second does, but this makes all the difference between poor writing and good.

First Version

Bob and Audrey were sitting at the dinner table when one of Bob's friends called up to see if he could play golf in the morning. Audrey had been dreading this, for she hated the idea of being a golf widow.

[1]Ruth Herrick Myers, "Improve by Re-Writing", *Writer's Digest*, November 1934, p. 18.

Second Version

The telephone pealed. . . . Simultaneously they knew that the fatal moment had come.

Bob took the telephone. "Oh, hello, Tom. How are you?"

Audrey, sitting on one foot, a childish trick she had never outgrown, traced the outline of her shoe round and round through her skirt.

"Oh, it is? Chuck and I were saying yesterday that it ought to be open pretty soon. Why—wait a minute. Audrey?"

Audrey looked up smiling. "Yes?"

"Care if I play golf tomorrow?"

Here is another striking illustration of the power of the concrete detail to arouse interest and to create an impression of reality. In it the details are neither grouped nor selected, but just set down one after the other as they happened. It is part of a letter from an English clergyman to an old friend written about a hundred and fifty years ago.[1] It gives the commonplace, routine experiences in a most uneventful day, but it gives them so concretely and definitely that we cannot help being interested in spite of ourselves:

Went to the ploughs—set the foot a little higher; went to the other plough—picked up some wool and tied over the traces—mended a horse-tree, tied a thong to the plough-hammer—went to see which lands want ploughing first—sat down under a bush—wondered how any man could be so silly as to call me *reverend*—read two verses and thought of His loving kindness in the midst of His temple—gave out "Come, all harmonious tongues" and set Mount Ephraim tune—rose up—whistled—the dogs wagged their tails, and on we went—got home—dinner ready—filled the pipe—drank some milk, and fell asleep—woke by the carpenter for some slats, which the sawyer must cut. The Reverend Messrs. A........ in a coat, B........ in a gown of black, and C........ in one of purple, came to drink tea, and to settle whether Gomer was the father of the Celts and Gauls and Britons, or only the uncle—proof sheet from Mr. Archdeacon—corrected it—washed—dressed—went to meeting and preached from, "*The end of all things is at hand; be ye sober and watch unto prayer*"—found a dear brother *reverence* there, who went home with me, and edified us all out of Solomon's Song with a dish of tripe out of Leviticus and a golden candlestick out of Exodus.

[1]Robert Robinson to an "Old Friend", Chesterton, May 26, 1784. (E. V. Lucas, *The Gentlest Art*, p. 277.)

Not an exciting day, you'll agree. But suppose Mr. Robinson had written it this way:

Nothing interesting has happened lately. Yesterday I went out to the farm and attended to several matters. Three brother clergymen, the Reverend Messrs. A........, B........, and C........, dropped in for a cup of tea, and we discussed the Celtic question. After church another clergyman came home with me and expressed himself at length on certain parts of the Old Testament.

This is a summary or synopsis of what took place, not the things themselves. A few general statements are given us, but not enough details for us to enter imaginatively into the writer's experiences and share them with him. **The summary or synopsis style is sure death to all interest and effectiveness.** It is the bane of story writing, and must be avoided at all costs. Our aim should be, "Always the details, never the general statement, never the synopsis or summary."

THE ROUND TABLE

As an exercise in observing and recording details, work out the four following assignments. Remember that your purpose is to get as many tiny, accurate, definite details as possible. Proceed somewhat along the lines of the Reverend Mr. Robinson's letter on page 390.

1. Watch someone unobtrusively but closely, for five minutes. Notice and record anything he (or she) does within that length of time—every movement, every expression, every gesture, every act—even if it is as simple and homely a one as coughing or scratching his nose.

2. Listen closely to a conversation in a public place such as a street corner, a bus, a store, a grandstand, etc. Try to reproduce exactly what was said, and also to describe how it was said—whether fast or slowly, with or without a pause, in what tone of voice, accompanied by what gesture, movement, or facial expression, etc.

3. Run through the accumulation of details gained in Exercises 1 and 2 and see if you can work each of them into a readable account. Leave out both the altogether trivial and the conflicting details. Touch up and heighten the others, trying to unify them into a character sketch or the impression of a mood. In other words, turn yourself from an observer of facts into a writer of fiction.

4. Try the following "five-minute projects":
   (a) Stand at the classroom window and record faithfully in vivid detail exactly what you see.
   (b) Maintain absolute silence in the classroom and record with vivid verbs each sound you hear.

5. Vivid Verbs

Any discussion of details brings up at once the necessity likewise for specific, concrete words. Details cannot be pictured in general terms. Review again the sections on specific, concrete words, pages 330-335. Remember, as was pointed out there that we cannot see *a tree, a tool, a dog*; what we see is *a big oak, an old pair of pliers, a graceful collie.* Remember, too, that no picture was ever suggested by a sentence like " 'No,' she said, and left the room." To give the picture we must use specific action words like those listed on page 334. **A definite detail can be suggested only in definite words.**

This principle holds true of four parts of speech in particular: adjectives, adverbs, nouns, and verbs. Adjectives and adverbs are, by definition, the parts of speech that exist for the purpose of describing.

Along with adjectives and adverbs, however, concrete, specific nouns also have the power to describe and to suggest pictures. Few adjectives are able to call up images more vividly than such highly specific nouns as the following synonyms for *light*: *flare, flash, flicker, glare, gleam, glimmer, glitter, glow, shimmer, sparkle.*

Few readers would be interested in a statement by an Englishman who lived during the time of Charles II that on April 4, 1663, he "enjoyed an unusually big dinner with many different kinds of meat and fish." With astonishment and growing admiration, however, we read the following entry from Pepys's *Diary* for that date: "Very merry at, before, and after dinner, and the more for that my dinner was great, and most neatly dressed by our owne only maid.

We had a fricassee of rabbits and chickens, a leg of mutton boiled, three carps in a dish, a great dish of a side of a lamb, a dish of roasted pigeons, a dish of four lobsters, three tarts, a lamprey pie (a most rare pie), a dish of anchovies, good wine of several sorts, and all things mighty noble and to my great content."

Great is the power of details and specific words.

The most vivid of all words, however, are not adjectives, adverbs, or nouns, but verbs. The verb is truly the king of words in suggestive power. Adjectives, adverbs, and nouns are in general quiet and stationary. The verb denotes action, and depicts life in motion. It combines action and description, the action vivifying the description and the description vivifying the action. Many concrete verbs really carry their own adverbs on their back, both naming and describing the action at the same time. *To leap* means to jump quickly, and is a much better way of expressing the same idea. Likewise *to drawl* means to say slowly; *to whisper*, to say softly; *to gleam*, to shine brightly; *to crawl*, to move very slowly; *to dart* or *to dash*, to move very fast; *to adore*, to love devotedly; *to dawdle*, to waste time idly; *to hound*, to pursue unrelentingly; *to collapse*, to break down utterly; *to swarm*, to throng together in crowds. Consider the picture in such words as *dodged*, *glared*, *limped*, *shoved*, *winked*, *squatted*, and *lounged*.

Nearly all effective narration and much effective description depend alike upon vivid, picture-making verbs. Here is a sentence that endeavours to suggest the idea of a fast train as it rushes along the track: "The needle of the speed indicator moved quickly to and fro, the cinders fell upon the roof, and a whirl of dust followed the whirling wheels." But somehow the idea of speed is not vividly suggested. Change the colourless verbs *moved*, *fell*, and *followed* back to the verbs that the author originally used, and the train picks up speed before our very eyes: "The needle of the speed indicator flicked and wagged to and fro, the cinders rattled on the roof, and a whirl of dust sucked after the whirling wheels."

Read the following paragraph from Kipling's *Captains Courageous* describing how the little schooner, *We're Here*, was almost run down by an ocean liner in a fog. Read it first for the picture as a whole.

> A jaunty little feather of water curled in front of it, and as it lifted it showed a long ladder of Roman numerals—XV, XVI, XVII, XVIII, and so forth—on a salmon-coloured gleaming side. It tilted forward and downward with a heart-stilling "Sssooo"; the ladder disappeared; a line of brass-rimmed portholes flashed past; a jet of steam puffed in Harvey's helplessly uplifted hands; a spout of hot water roared along the rail of the *We're Here*, and the little schooner staggered and shook in a rush of screw-torn water as a liner's stern vanished in the fog.

Now reread it analytically with special reference to the verbs and participles. The passage contains twelve descriptive adjectives, four adverbs, twenty-eight nouns, and eleven verbs. Its effectiveness, however, depends mainly upon its specific, picture-making verbs—*curled*, *tilted*, *flashed*, *roared*, *staggered*, *shook*. The four participial adjectives *gleaming*, *heart-stilling*, *uplifted*, and *screw-torn* also effectively denote action.

Adjectives, adverbs, nouns, and verbs—in telling a story or describing a scene we must watch them all, but chiefly we must watch the verbs. Like Atlas, they bear the burden on their shoulders.

6. Three Don'ts

In writing narratives there are **three constructions to be avoided:** (1) Beginning a sentence with "There is" or "There are"; (2) using the passive voice; and (3) ending a sentence with a participial phrase. Each of these constructions weakens the narrative vigour and slows up the movement. The first two are useful in explaining, but not in telling a story.

(1) BEGINNING A SENTENCE WITH "THERE IS" OR "THERE ARE"

Weak: 1. There is no reason for us to fear a storm at this time of the year.

Better: 1. We have no reason to fear a storm at this time of the year.

(2) THE PASSIVE VOICE

Weak: 1. As the car approached the hairpin curve at a high rate of speed, it was seen by the horrified crowd to leave the track and crash into the fence.

Better: 1. As the car approached the hairpin curve, the horrified crowd saw it leave the track and crash into the fence.

(3) PARTICIPIAL CLOSE

Weak: 1. He played on the scrub team faithfully for three years, making his letter his last season.

Better: 1. He played on the scrub team faithfully for three years and made his letter his last season.

Still Better: 1. After three years of faithful playing on the scrub team, he made his letter his last season.

THE ROUND TABLE

1. In your own work try again an experiment already advised. After you have written the first draft of a simple incident, run through it and draw a ring around every verb and underline every adverb. Try to substitute the most specific and vivid verb possible in each instance. After doing this, see if all the adverbs are still needed, omitting any that may now seem useless.

2. If this second draft still seems dull and lifeless, run through it again, underlining all nouns and adjectives. For these try to substitute more specific and striking synonyms. Then compare the versions.

7. Dialogue

Dialogue is of great service in narrative. It quickens and livens it up, and makes it easier to read. Good dialogue serves two distinct purposes: (1) it advances the action and tells the reader in an interesting way what is going on, and (2) it reveals character and thus makes the people in the story more real and vivid. A story with a good deal of conversation in it is apt to be an interesting story.

Skilful dialogue often serves both to strike the right tone at the beginning and to put the reader into instant touch with the characters. O. Henry, a master of dialogue, in his story "The Day Resurgent", introduces one of his characters in this way:

"'Tis Easter Day," said Mrs. McCree.
"Scramble mine," said Danny.

These two remarks introduce Danny to us better than a page of explanation could do. We know his mood from that moment.

The student incident on page 388, "Page the Pied Piper", is very short and opens briskly:

"Oh, aren't they adorable?"
"Adorable nothing! They're horrible!"
"Eeeee! Let's get away from 'em. They scare me to death!"

In Joel Chandler Harris's pathetic Negro dialect story, "Free Joe and the Rest of the World,"[1] the following bit of dialogue between Free Joe and Spite Calderwood, who owns Free Joe's wife, Lucinda, does two things and does them supremely well; it advances the action by telling us that Joe will no longer be allowed to visit Lucinda, and it reveals Calderwood's brutal nature as if by a lightning flash. We know about him all that we need to know, and hate him from that moment.

One Sunday he was sitting in front of Lucinda's cabin, when Calderwood happened to pass that way.

"Howdy, marster?" said Free Joe, taking off his hat.

"Who are you?" exclaimed Calderwood abruptly, halting and staring at the Negro.

"I'm name' Joe, marster. I'm Lucindy's ole man."

"Who do you belong to?"

"Marse John Evans is my gyardeen, marster."

"Big name—gyardeen. Show your pass."

[1]By permission of the publishers, Charles Scribner's Sons.

Free Joe produced that document, and Calderwood read it aloud slowly, as if he found it difficult to get at the meaning: "To whom it may concern: This is to certify that the boy Joe Frampton has my permission to visit his wife Lucinda."

This was dated at Hillsborough and signed "John W. Evans."

Calderwood read it twice, and then looked at Free Joe, elevating his eyebrows, and showing his discoloured teeth.

"Some mighty big words in that there. Evans owns this place, I reckon. When's he comin' down to take hold?"

Free Joe fumbled with his hat. He was badly frightened.

"Lucindy say she speck you wouldn't min' my comin', long ez I behave, marster."

Calderwood tore the pass in pieces and flung it away.

"Don't want no free niggers 'round here," he exclaimed. "There's the big road. It'll carry you to town. Don't let me catch you here no more. Now, mind what I tell you."

(1) THE DIFFICULTY OF DIALOGUE

Bright, natural dialogue is very hard to write, and always gives inexperienced writers a great deal of trouble. Try as we may, our characters at first will always insist upon talking in a stilted, artificial, unnatural way. Someone once remarked concerning the many uninteresting people he came into contact with in real life: "I am really amazed at the way people can talk and talk without ever showing that they have lived, consciously, in this world. I want to stick a pin in them, to get one genuine reaction." After writing a story, that is the way we are apt to feel toward our characters: they just don't talk like real human beings.

To remedy this situation we must **avoid long speeches and too many complete, dignified sentences.** Conversation is not a series of speeches which the characters address to each in turn. It is more like a verbal game of tennis, with short, quick returns and unexpected volleys and rallies. Real speech is brief, broken, incomplete, pieced out and made intelligible by gestures, tones of voice, and facial expressions.

In writing dialogue we must try to give this impression of quickness, incompleteness, and life-likeness. Without going to an extreme, feel free to use colloquial and abbreviated expressions, exclamations, and slang whenever and wherever they are needed. An excellent way to write dialogue (as well as to revise it) is to repeat it aloud in emphatic and animated tones. Often the sound of your voice itself will call forth exactly the right word or turn of expression; and, what is equally important, tell you when it is time for one character to stop talking and another to answer him. Only first-class dialogue can stand the test of being read aloud.

Notice, too, how the successful writers manage dialogue. Take any of your favourite chapters from Dickens or Thackeray, or stories by Kipling, Stevenson, or O. Henry, or passages from more recent writers like John Galsworthy or Sinclair Lewis, and see how their characters talk. Watch for such things as the length of the speeches, exclamations, interruptions, questions, echoes, and so forth. Intelligent analysis of this kind will prove very helpful in your own writing.

Incidentally dialect is much harder than straight dialogue. When well done it is exceedingly effective. Do not, however, attempt it in any extended way unless (1) you know intimately the dialect you are using and (2) are willing to revise and rewrite carefully and often.

(2) "STAGE DIRECTIONS" IN DIALOGUE

It is not enough to give *what* was said; we must also give *how* it was said. The reader must know not only which person is speaking, but also in what manner and in what mood: whether his voice is soft, loud, bored, angry, affectionate, anxious, timid, pleased, doubtful, or what. We must hear the very tones themselves. Likewise, what look, action, or gesture accompanies each remark? What is he doing while he is speaking? And, of equal importance, what is the person he is speaking to doing, and how is he reacting to the speech? Finally, at what rate of speed is the conversation taking place? Real conversation goes by fits and starts, now fast, now slow. Where do the breaks and pauses come as the characters talk to each other? All of these accompaniments of conversation are called "stage directions". They are of paramount importance in lending an air of reality and vividness to dialogue. Careful attention must be given them both in writing and in revising.

The following examples will illustrate their value.

WITHOUT STAGE DIRECTIONS

"No, no, silly," she said. "That's not the way to do it. Let me show you."

WITH STAGE DIRECTIONS (1)

"No, no, silly. That's not the way to do it," and in her voice was all the affectionate impatience of big-sister-aged-ten for little-brother-aged-five. "Let me show you," and she took the crayon from his chubby fingers and drew the head of a black cat with big, staring eyes.

WITH STAGE DIRECTIONS (2)

"No, no, silly. That's not the way to do it," and turning from the stove she smiled affectionately at her tall brother home from college for the holidays. "Let me show you," and she took the big wooden spoon from his strong but inexperienced fingers and began expertly to beat up the eggs for the omelet.

(3) SYNONYMS FOR *SAY*

In order to get away from the monotonous repetition of "he said" and "she said", various specific synonyms should be used as needed. By actual count there are between two hundred and three hundred of them. Some of the more usual and useful ones are these:

acquiesced	faltered	put in
agreed	grinned	remarked
assented	hesitated	retorted
besought	implored	roared
breathed	laughed	shouted
burst out	maintained	sighed
coaxed	mimicked	smiled
continued	murmured	sobbed
denied	nodded	stammered
echoed	pleaded	warned
exclaimed	promised	whispered

(4) THE PUNCTUATION OF DIALOGUE

Both while writing and while revising dialogue there **are four definite items of punctuation to watch for.**

1. Make a new paragraph every time the speaker changes.
2. Begin each speech with a capital letter.
3. Enclose each speech in quotation marks. Note particularly that each part of a divided speech is enclosed in its own set of quotation marks.
4. Use a comma to separate *say* or its equivalent from the speech, whether *say* comes first or last.

All of these uses are explained and illustrated in the chapter on punctuation. Unless you are thoroughly familiar with them, review them briefly at this time.

Examine the opening dialogue of Katharine Brush's story, "Night Club", for stage directions, substitutes for *say*, paragraphing, and use of quotation marks.

The foyer was a blackness, an airless velvet blackness like the inside of a jeweller's box. Four drum-shaped lamps of golden silk suspended from the ceiling gave it light (a very little) and formed the jewels: gold signets, those, or cuff-links for a giant. At the far end of the foyer there were black stairs, faintly dusty, rippling upward toward an amber radiance. Mrs. Brady approached and ponderously mounted the stairs, clinging with one fist to the mangy velvet rope that railed their edge.

From the top, Miss Lena Levin observed the ascent. Miss Levin was the checkroom girl. She had dark-at-the-roots blonde hair and slender hips upon which, in moments of leisure, she wore her hands, like buckles of ivory loosely attached.

This was a moment of leisure. Miss Levin waited behind her counter. Row upon row of hooks, empty as yet, and seeming to beckon—wee curved fingers of iron—waited behind her.

"Late," said Miss Levin, "again."

"Go wan!" said Mrs. Brady. "It's only ten to ten. *Whew*! Them *stairs*!"

She leaned heavily, sideways, against Miss Levin's counter, and applying one palm to the region of her heart, appeared at once to listen and to count. "Feel!" she cried then in a pleased voice.

Miss Levin obediently felt.

"Them stairs," continued Mrs. Brady darkly, "with my bad heart, will be the death of me. Whew! Well, dearie? What's the news?"

"You got a paper," Miss Levin languidly reminded her.

"Yeah!" agreed Mrs. Brady with sudden vehemence. "I got a paper!" She slapped it upon the counter. "An' a lot of time I'll get to *read* my paper, won't I now? On a Saturday night!" she moaned. "Other nights is bad enough, dear knows—but *Saturday* nights! How I dread 'em! Every Saturday night I say to my daughter, I say, 'Geraldine, I can't,' I say, 'I can't go through it again, an' that's all there is to it,' I say. 'I'll *quit*!' I say. An' I *will*, too!" added Mrs. Brady firmly, if indefinitely.

Miss Levin, in defence of Saturday nights, mumbled some vague something about tips.

"Tips!" Mrs. Brady hissed it. She almost spat it. Plainly, money was nothing, nothing at all, to this lady. "I just wish," said Mrs. Brady, and glared at Miss Levin, "I just wish *you* had to spend one Saturday night, just one, in that dressing-room! Bein' pushed an' stepped on and near knocked down by that gang of hussies, an' them orderin' an' bossin' you round like you was *black*, an' usin' your things an' then sayin' they're sorry, they got no change, they'll be back. Yeah! They *never* come back!"

"There's Mr. Costello," whispered Miss Levin through lips that, like a ventriloquist's, scarcely stirred.

"An' as I was sayin'," Mrs. Brady said at once brightly, "I got to leave you. Ten to ten, time I was on the job."[1]

THE ROUND TABLE

1. Who is your favourite writer of fiction? Glance through one of his (her) books and examine the use of dialogue.

2. Bring to class any particularly bright and interesting bit of dialogue you have come across recently.

3. Select any two interesting or strongly contrasted people, imagine a situation, and write a page or so of the resulting dialogue. Here are a few suggestions. Ask the teacher to read aloud to the class several of the best dialogues.

   (1) A tramp knocks at the door of a suspicious housewife.
   (2) A school (or college) athletic idol meets a gushing girl admirer.
   (3) A boy explains to his father why his grades are so much lower this time than last (or a girl explains to her mother).
   (4) A boy takes a girl to her first football game.

[1]From "Night Club" by Katharine Brush published by Garden City Publishing Co. By permission of the Author.

(5) A book agent tries to sell a book to a busy housewife.
(6) A farmer shows the farm to a girl who has never been in the country before.
(7) A small boy goes on his first train trip with his father or older brother.
(8) A green clerk and a quick-tempered shopper.

4. If you have written an unusually interesting narrative incident try turning it into dramatic form by using only dialogue with added stage directions. Place the names of speakers before their respective speeches.

5. Invent a dialogue between two famous characters in literature or history such as Samson and Hercules, Helen of Troy and Cleopatra, Alexander and Cæsar, Enoch Arden and Sidney Carton, D'Artagnan and Cyrano de Bergerac, Robin Hood and Davy Crockett, Queen Elizabeth and Queen Victoria, Benjamin Franklin and Thomas A. Edison.

6. A polite little girl tries to entertain a caller while mamma is dressing.

7. A daughter who has just completed a business course argues with her father about taking a position in an office or a store.

8. If you are familiar with any dialect or peculiar manner of speech, try to reproduce it in a page or less of dialogue.

9. As directed by the teacher, let the whole class take the following skeleton plot and write it out in full, furnishing characters, setting, description, dialogue, details, and so forth, in three steps or stages:

(1) Told as an incident, with only the necessary amount of dialogue.
(2) Told entirely in dialogue.
(3) Turned into a one-scene play.

The Plot

A man (boy, girl, woman, tramp, Negro, Irishman, Jew, Swede, Italian, sailor, autoist) went into a store, and asked for a dime's worth of bananas. The storekeeper gave them to him, whereupon he asked if he could exchange them for a dime's worth of apples instead. The storekeeper agreed and gave him the apples. The man took them and started out of the store. The storekeeper asked him for the money.

"The money for what?" he asked.

"The money for the apples," said the storekeeper.

"But I gave you the bananas for the apples," answered the man.

"Well, then, the money for the bananas."

"But you've still got the bananas."

Whereupon the man walked out, leaving the storekeeper to figure it out as best he could.

10. Record a conversation between a dog and a cat revealing their mutual distrust and dislike (either realistic or humorous.)

8. Paragraphing a Story

In telling an incident the paragraph is managed differently from the way it is managed in explaining. In exposition each paragraph is devoted to explaining a single topic idea, and a new paragraph indicates a new idea. This idea is usually stated in the topic sentence. Successive paragraphs are linked with each other by means of transition words and phrases. The development of the thought is orderly and logical, and we pass from one topic to the next as we go from one room to another in a house, or climb a ladder rung by rung. This type of paragraph is explained at length in the chapter on Chain Paragraphs and Jointed Subjects.

In narration, however, no such logical or clear-cut use of the paragraph is possible. **The narrative paragraph is a much looser, and generally a shorter subdivision than the expository paragraph.** In dialogue, for example, which plays an important part in narratives, a new paragraph is made every time the speaker changes. This is done if only one sentence or a phrase or even a single word is spoken. This device helps the reader follow the conversation intelligently, and is a great aid to clearness.

In the story itself, when the characters are not talking, a new paragraph is used to introduce any new stage of the incident, or a bit of description inserted in the narrative, or a piece of explanation or characterization, or a comment or reflection, or any decided break or change in the continuity of the story. These reasons for paragraphing obviously differ from one another, so that in the last analysis much depends upon the exact impression the writer is trying to convey. If given the same story to paragraph, several trained writers would, within certain limits, paragraph it differently, and none would be clearly wrong, though one arrangement would certainly be superior to the others.

In your own work, on the one hand, avoid paragraphing each sentence by itself; and, on the other, examine any long stretch of over half a page to see whether it should not be divided.

THE ROUND TABLE

1. Relate (or invent) a concrete illustration of the truth of some familiar proverb.

2. Relate (or invent) an incident, with dialogue, illustrating some single trait of character or motive such as unselfishness, greed, stinginess, ignorance, courage, good nature, true friendship, loyalty, etc.

3. Choose one of Æsop's fables and transfer the scene to modern times, giving ample details, dialogue, characterization, etc.

4. Relate an incident in your life that had an important influence on your character, ambitions, or future.

5. Give an instance of everybody's natural desire to be someone else.

6. Relate an incident or a situation that made you very angry.

7. Relate an unsuccessful mouse hunt from the point of view of (*a*) the cat; (*b*) the mouse.

8. A false report has gotten out that a distant relative has died and left you $1,000. What do your friends do and say?

9. Situations Suggesting Incidents[1]

(1) A child; a swift mill-race; a large dog.
(2) Two young girls alone in a farmhouse at night; footsteps; a knock at the door.
(3) Girl; pile of unwashed dishes; telephone.
(4) Handsomely dressed woman; powder puff; monkey.
(5) Girl; umbrella; windstorm.
(6) Pretty girl; snake; man.
(7) Child; toothache; dentist.
(8) Ragged little girl; window of toys; well-dressed man.
(9) A small child on the porch roof; a slip; a scream; a man runs up and catches her like a ball.

10. Titles for Incidents

(1) How I Came to Admire —— (some friend)
(2) An Experience with Hypnotism (actual or observed)
(3) Absent-Mindedness Was To Blame

[1]Thomas C. Blaisdell, *Ways to Teach English*, Doubleday, Doran and Co. pp. 521-524.

(4) Believe It or Not ——
(5) A Mad-Dog Scare
(6) The Most Exciting Thing I Ever Saw (Heard)
(7) An Interesting Legend of My Locality
(8) How I Broke Myself of —— (any bad habit)
(9) Hiving a Swarm of Bees
(10) How I Caught and Tamed —— (a curious pet)
(11) Locked Out
(12) The Cleverest Trick I Ever Saw Played
(13) My First Experience with Cows
(14) Why I Almost Believe in Ghosts
(15) Was My Face Red?
(16) The Worst Break I Ever Made
(17) I Would Have Been a Hero if —
(18) My Most Exciting Plunge
(19) On the Stage—and No Memory
(20) I Argue with My Family about —(anything, such as a larger allowance, more free nights, not taking a certain school subject, the way to dress, etc.)
(21) The Bravest Act (Narrowest Escape) I Ever Saw
(22) The Autobiography of a Counterfeit Dime
(23) He Laughs Best Who Laughs Last
(24) How We Solved the Mystery
(25) Much Ado About Nothing
(26) Stranded
(27) Catching the Thief
(28) A Family Hero
(29) I Take a Dare
(30) An Unexpected Visitor
(31) How I Balanced the Budget

INCIDENTS (By Students)

My First Jump[1]

After a restless night of disturbing dreams, I awoke early that morning to a realization that this was the day for which I had been hardened and trained. Today I was to make my first parachute jump. I looked out of the window. The wind-sock on the tower hung limply. Good weather for jumping, I thought.

At seven-thirty, our class of thirty men picked up our "number one", adjusted parachutes, signed for our reserve parachutes, bid the girls who packed them a fond farewell, listened to a quick briefing by the jump-master, answered the roll-call, and then lined up on parade

[1]By permission of the author and the *Magnet*.

in "sticks" or sections of ten men each. We jump in sticks and today there were three.

Carrying the forty-pound chute like a baby, I climbed with the other men into the camp bus, which was impatiently waiting, and soon we arrived at Brandon R.C.A.F. Flying Station. There we formed up in our respective stick order, and, placing our chutes on the ground, stood at attention.

"Break off!" came the command.

We relaxed and awaited further developments in the recreation room nearby.

At nine-thirty, the aeroplanes arrived over the field, circled and landed. The pilots seemed in cheerful spirits. We clambered outside and lined up before our packs.

"Into your chutes," came the order.

We swung our main packs over our shoulders. The pilots manned their planes. The engines of the Lodestars burst into a mighty roar, eased down gradually, and commenced to purr. The tenth man of each stick waddled awkwardly to the doorless opening and clambered aboard. The others followed in order. Being the first man of the third stick, I was the last person to step into the passage-way of the third plane.

Then the jump-master gave us a pep talk to help our morale. In a few minutes the other two planes cleared the field. Then our plane taxied into position.

Again we waited.

"Up, first five."

Four men and I stood up and walked to the front of the plane, so that properly balanced, it could take off more easily. Without warning the engines boomed. The plane rolled slowly along and then picked up speed. As the noise became deafening, we mounted into the air. At an altitude of three hundred feet, we sought our original positions on the bench. I heaved a sigh of relief as I glanced at Rusty, my pal, who wanly smiled at me. I wondered if I looked as I felt.

Resting my chute on the bench, I sat back as comfortably as possible with my static line tucked behind my reserve pack for convenience and looked about me. I noticed the strong steel cable running close to the ceiling the full length of the plane. The wide bench ran from the front of the plane near the cockpit along the right side to where I sat across from the opening. Cylindrical cardboard containers, set in racks, were arranged along the other side. My stomach was seized with a sudden emptiness. I didn't feel well. With every bank of the plane I could see the ground far below, whizzing by. I checked my position—left foot, one step ahead of the right—and gripped the bench beneath me. The boys started to sing to get rid of the butterflies in their stomachs.

Within thirty minutes the planes circled about our camp. I noticed how small the two-hundred and fifty-six foot practice tower appeared far below and I wondered why I had been afraid to jump from there.

As the flight crossed over the flying field into the wind, I watched the centre plane for I knew "Oscar" would be hurled from it. Oscar is the three hundred-pound dummy used to drop-test the parachutes and to indicate the drift of the wind.

There he goes!

The dummy twisted and tumbled through the air and suddenly disappeared from view as his chute burst open. The jump-master gave the wind speed—ten miles per hour.

Then, as we approached the jumping area, the jump-master barked his commands.

"Hook up!"

"Check your equipment!"

"Sound off for equipment check!"

The tenth man shouted, "Ten o-kay." The ninth shouted, "Nine o-kay," and so forth along the stick until I heard Rusty shout in my ear, "Two o-kay!" I yelled "One o-kay!"

Another command. "Close up and stand in the door!"

I pivoted on my left heel and right toe to the door and threw my static line to the end of the cable, where the assistant master held it.

I waited—for hours, it seemed—in the open doorway, my arms outstretched on either side, my body straight, my knees bent, my head up, and my face thrust into the prop-blast.

Then a sudden slap on my leg and a mighty Ho! gave me my initial start.

I leaped out.

One thousand—two thousand—it didn't take long. A sharp shock suddenly jolted my whole body, flinging my arms and legs apart, and snapping my eyes wide open. With a sigh of relief, I reached up to grasp the risers.

My parachute had blossomed out above me. Glancing at the white silk, I checked for any malfunctions; there were none. My chute had blossomed out fully. Carefully I searched for the other chaps; if one is not alert, collisions and often death result. The other fellows were to the right and above me.

Far below, the ground passed slowly by. Far below stood the ambulance and the sound truck. Far below a voice crackled indistinct instructions.

I floated down to Mother Earth without a care in the world. This feeling of floating down is difficult to describe. It is as if one were suspended in the sky and slowly being lowered. By experience alone can this feeling be fully secured.

Then it happened!

Another chute floated directly underneath me and remained there. As my chute was no longer catching air, I dropped to the chute beneath me, sinking to my knees in silk. Suddenly my risers grew slack in my hands.

With my heart in my mouth, I took three quick steps across the silk and pulling my front risers down hard, leaped off the edge of that chute. The cross-wind whipped me away from disaster.

I breathed deeply as my chute fully opened again. I seemed to be gaining speed, and at one hundred feet I broke into the wind and prepared to land.

My head on my chest, my knees slightly bent and my feet together, I relaxed. The ground came up fast. A last oscillation of the parachute, and automatically I turned my feet off, and came in for an abrupt front roll.

"Abrupt front roll" is scarcely the phrase for my landing. I landed with a tremendous thud and the swift forward motion caused me to bounce a few times before coming to rest.

Hardly had I stopped when my chute, gathering wind, dragged me across the prairie. After nearly a hundred yards of this merciless treatment I was able to collapse my chute, and I lay back on the silk. My body felt intact, but bruised in certain places.

Then rolling up my chute, I happily realized that I had completed my first parachute jump successfully.

HENRY HENSHALL

GUILTY!

The rain beat down with a rhythmic sound. I stood before the judge awaiting my sentence. At last the jury filed solemnly in.

Strange as it may seem, each member of the jury gave his verdict separately. Juror number one arose.

"I find the defendant guilty of making incomplete statements when answering in class, and of referring to everything pleasant as being nice," he stated in rhythm with the rain. It reminded me of music lessons with a metronome. Then juror number two stood up.

"I find the defendant guilty of not punctuating her letters correctly, and of not recognizing an intermediate expression in a sentence." I writhed in my chair and waited for juror number three.

"The defendant is guilty of neglecting her study of salesmanship." He resumed his seat with a very pleased expression on his face.

The verdicts that followed were similar to the preceding ones. I was guilty of every crime imaginable. It seemed I had done nothing right in all my life. When at last each of the jurors had delivered his verdict, the judge solemnly told me to stand up. Quaking, I arose and waited with a sinking heart. In deep, booming tones he pronounced my sentence.

"When you hear a bell ring, your head will be cut off!"

"She's guilty and we'll kill her!" cried the jurors in unison.

With each nerve throbbing, both knees knocking, and my spine turning from hot to cold, I stood there waiting. In an awful moment the bell rang.

I groped for something with which to defend myself. There was nothing at hand. Then I felt myself sinking down, down, down, still groping. Suddenly my hand found something. I grasped it, and with every bit of energy I had, I threw the weapon up at the judge and jurors who were, by this time, far above me.

Then I heard a crash. My weapon had fallen. With surprise and shock I leaped to my feet. The rain was still pouring down. The fire had gone out, and my room was cold. Rubbing my eyes, I looked at the clock, but it wasn't there. I looked around and saw it lying in a mangled heap at the other end of the room. With relief I remembered that it had all been a dream, and began to dress myself.

—GRACE YOUNGER

CHAPTER XXIII

The Story

1. Story versus Incident

The story differs from the simple incident in several ways. For one thing, it is apt to be much longer. An incident may run anywhere from a page or two up to five or six pages. A story is apt to run anywhere from five or six pages up to ten, twelve, fifteen, or even twenty. Along with this increased length goes more emphasis on both the characters and the plot. The characters are presented more in detail, and thus there is more opportunity for dialogue. The plot is more complicated, and is usually managed so as to lead up to an intense or surprising final scene, called the climax. The climax brings events to a focus and thus leads to the conclusion. The story should end after the climax has been reached.

2. The Three Elements of a Story

Every story has three elements: (1) plot or action, (2) characters, and (3) setting. They may be simply defined as follows:

1. Plot or Action = the events that happen
2. Characters = the persons to whom the events happen
3. Setting = (*a*) the place where and
   (*b*) the time when the events happen

All narratives, whether short stories, novels, or dramas, have these three elements, though one of the three is apt to be more important than the other two in any given short story. Indeed stories usually suggest themselves to writers primarily either as a story of action, as a story of characterization, or as a story of setting. As Robert Louis Stevenson expressed it: "There are, so far as I know, three ways, and three ways only, of writing a story. You may take a plot and fit characters to it, or you may take a character and choose incidents and situations to develop it, or lastly . . . you may take a certain atmosphere and get action and persons to express and realize it."[1]

(1) THE PLOT OR ACTION

The plot or action of a story consists of events, happenings, incidents. It is a plot that makes a story move. Most readers prefer stories with swiftly moving plots to stories which are concerned mainly with portraying character or depicting setting. As we grow older we become more interested in quieter stories, but in youth we crave action. Call to mind the three or four stories you like best and the odds are that they will be plot stories. Practically all adventure, mystery, and detective stories, which together form such a large part of current fiction, are chiefly stories of plot.

Keep in mind that it is easier to handle successfully a short, simple plot than a crowded, unusual one. Many stories by students fail because they are overloaded by a long, complicated plot which would require fifty pages instead of ten or twenty to develop properly. Choose the simple plot and go into many and minute details. Remember that the section on details, pages 388-391, applies as forcibly to the story as to the incident. Not even Kipling or Stevenson could take a lengthy, complicated plot and treat it successfully in ten or fifteen pages of your handwriting. They would probably either make a novelette of it, as Stevenson does in *The Strange Case of Dr. Jekyll and Mr. Hyde,* which runs to about seventy-five printed pages; or they would throw away three-fourths of the plot, select a single episode or situation, and unfold it in detail. One of

[1]Graham Balfour, *Life of Robert Louis Stevenson,* II, 168, 169.

the most unprofitable exercises in the entire narrative field is to try to put into short-story form the plot of an interesting moving picture we happened to see. All that can be done within our limits of time and length is to give an unconvincing summary or synopsis of the action. If you wish to use something from a moving picture or an action-crammed plot from some other source, single out one scene or situation and concentrate on that.

1. Divide the Plot into Parts or Stages

Very few plots are suited to being told straight through from beginning to end in one narrative rush or surge, as it were. Most plots profit greatly by being planned as a series of scenes or stages, usually three, four, or five in number. Then each scene or stage is worked on as an individual unit or step in the story, and developed in sufficient detail to be interesting and convincing. All the stages lead up to the final stage or climax, and thus when put together form a continuous narrative road, with steadily increasing interest, up to the climax and conclusion.

Take the following skeleton plot as an example. It is not original, but is a good illustration of the principle under discussion.

FOR THE HONOUR OF THE NAME

A young man, whose forefathers had a long and an unbroken record for gallantry in war, enlists at the first declaration of war. His friends and family expect great things of him. He goes to the front and at the first call volunteers for spy duty inside the enemy's lines. He is captured and condemned to be shot. Faced with the certainty of death he loses his nerve and breaks down utterly. His mother, who has managed to get permission to visit him the night before his execution, sees with horror his tears and cowardice. He will disgrace the name on the morrow. Knowing that there is absolutely no hope of reprieve, she tells him that she has overheard the commanding officer say that an exchange of prisoners has been arranged and hence order all the cartridges to be loaded with blanks. The boy takes heart, and goes to his death next morning at sunrise with a smile on his face.

The scenes or stages into which this plot may be conveniently divided for ease of handling are these:

1. The family tradition
2. War and enlistment
3. Spy duty and capture
4. Condemnation and breakdown
5. The mother's visit in prison: the good (!) news
6. Bravery (!) and execution

Other divisions than this might be proposed according as a writer might wish to vary the proportions or the emphasis of the plot. The six stages suggested above, however, are the obvious ones. Numbers one and three could be very much condensed or even combined respectively with numbers two and four.

The thing to be determined at the outset is whether it is the boy's story or the mother's. It could be told from either his or her viewpoint. If it is the mother's story, number five is the climax and number six should be condensed into a few striking sentences, closing with a tribute from the officer in charge of the firing squad. If it is the boy's story, number six is the climax and should be related in greater detail. In either case, however, the most dramatic situation is the prison scene. Most students agree that it is the mother's story.

THE ROUND TABLE

1. In your opinion, is "For the Honour of the Name" the boy's story or the mother's story? Discuss this point in class.
2. In the plot of "For the Honour of the Name", several students once proposed substituting the wife for the mother. Discuss this suggestion.
3. One of the trouble spots in "For the Honour of the Name" is to make possible the interview between mother and son during war conditions. If you were writing the story, how would you set about making this seem natural?

2. Do Not Begin at the Beginning

The way to pick up a story is the way to pick up a puppy—a little in front of the middle.

—C. N. GREENOUGH AND F. W. C. HERSEY

As has just been stated in the previous section, one fault of inexperienced writers is trying to crowd too much plot into one story. The other chief weakness is beginning the story at the beginning instead of in the middle or just before the end. One of the best directions ever given amateur story writers is that quoted above: **the way to pick up a story is the way to pick up a puppy—a little in front of the middle.**

Time, space, and human nature being what they are, if we rush into writing too soon and begin at the beginning of the story, what happens only too often is this: we start writing the story with considerable enthusiasm, and do fairly well for the first few pages. Then we get tired and begin to slow up. The minutes slip by, and the story seems to stretch out longer and longer, with the end not much closer than it was at the outset. Finally, having covered the required number of pages with writing, tired out from the extended effort to do our best, we bring the story to a hurried and inadequate close.

A story written in this way exactly reverses the correct procedure, and almost always results in a weak climax and a lame ending. Instead of the story's getting better as it goes along, it gets steadily worse until it just runs out of breath, gasps a few times, and curls up and quits.

The remedy for this situation is fairly simple and easy. It is to plan the story as a series of scenes or stages and think it through from beginning to end in the mind, but **actually to start writing only on the last scene or the next to the last.** Into this scene put all the time, energy, dialogue, and detailed vividness that you have at your command.

For example, in writing the spy story outlined in the preceding section, leave the first four stages untouched for the moment and begin with the mother's visit to her son in prison. Do all in your power to enter fully into that situation; try to put yourself into her place and into his place. How did each feel? How did each look? How did each act? What did each say? Extend yourself to the limit of your possibilities for dramatic feeling. Make your readers see and feel all that went on in the hearts of the grief-stricken mother and her unfortunate son. Relate the execution briefly but as suggestively as you can. Then stop.

The next day, or the next night, read over what you have written, and tighten and improve it in all the ways suggested in the sections on revising. Then run back in your mind through the first four stages of the story and write them out in only enough detail to make your climax and conclusion clear and probable. It is surprising, if the story is written in this way, how little time and space have to be given to the first half of the plot. Its complications and difficulties seem to vanish into thin air, the path to the climax is short and easy, and the climax itself stands out vividly in all its details and impressiveness.

THE ROUND TABLE

1. Taking a plot of your own or one assigned by the teacher, divide it into scenes or stages; and, following the plan suggested in this section, indicate where you would begin the story. Write out the opening sentence.

2. Read how Poe says he wrote "The Raven" in his suggestive essay, "The Philosophy of Composition". He tells us that he first put pen to paper at the third stanza from the end. The whole essay is a masterly description of writing "from the end to the beginning". It will repay class discussion.

3. In planning your plot try to visualize definitely what will be the final word, gesture, and look of the characters in the last scene.

(2) CHARACTERS

The second important element in a story is the characters, the people to whom the events happen.

To depict character is harder than to narrate events. Even in a plot story, however, the characters should be made as real and life-like as possible. If we can *see* and *hear* the actors in the plot, the action itself will of course be more interesting and vivid.

1. Imagining a Character

Most professional writers take their characters from real life, or rather take hints and suggestions for their characters from real people they have come into contact with. They will meet a person with some outstanding or unusual trait, perhaps mental alertness, or good nature, or extreme slowness of thought and speech, or irritability, or quickness in repartee, or courage, or marked charm, or the habit of exaggeration, or fondness for gossip, or boastfulness—any of the thousand and one physical, mental, and moral characteristics that make people interesting. Then with this trait as a starting-point, the writer will mould and change the rest of the character in accordance with it, adding here and taking away there until the character fits the plot and the part in it he is supposed to play. This was the way both Scott and Dickens conceived their characters. And Stevenson tells us that Long John Silver in *Treasure Island* was modelled in part after his friend, the English poet William Ernest Henley, though Stevenson altered the portraiture so greatly to fit the needs of the story that no one except himself could have identified the source. Eden Phillpotts, the novelist, said: "My characters are composite and I never transfer a living person to a story, though I seldom meet a living person who does not offer me something to be recorded. Thus my puppets are built on live men and women."[1]

THE ROUND TABLE

1. Choose an incident or a single stage in the plot of a short story, and by means of what the character does (and how) and what the character says (and how) reveal him (or her) directly to us. Use little or no description and no explanation at all. For instance, try one of the following situations:

(1) A conceited athlete meets an admiring girl.
(2) An angry motorist comes home after a minor collision.
(3) A timid child is sent upstairs in the dark to get mother's glasses or father's slippers.

[1]Quoted in *Writing Well*, p. 285.

(4) A tired mother and a fractious child in a railroad station waiting room are waiting for a train that is a half hour late.
(5) A deaf old lady by mistake underpays a taxi driver.
(6) A cat and a dog meet each other in a narrow alley.
(7) A messenger boy tries to deliver a telegram in a yard guarded by a large dog.
(8) A confident book-agent encounters a timid housewife.
(9) A boy (or girl) who knows more than his (her) parents argues with them at the table.
(10) The census taker tries to get information from a suspicious (ignorant) householder.

2. Imagine a character (man, woman, or child) who exemplifies one of the following traits and invent an incident, with dialogue, to depict him: hate, love, greed, timidity, boldness, fear, anxiety, ill temper, good nature, lonesomeness, loyalty, suspicion.

Use no explanation. Read aloud the incident and let the class name the trait it illustrates.

3. Revising

It goes without saying that a story needs revising before it is submitted either to an editor or to the teacher. Glance through the chapter on Revising, slowly turning the pages and noting again the section headings and the examples.

In revising your own narrative writing, train yourself to ask the following questions:

1. **Does your story begin and end effectively?** If you had not written it and did not have to read it, would the first few lines make you want to go on with it, or would you feel inclined to toss it into the wastebasket?

2. **Is the ending definite, pointed, and clear-cut, and does it bring the incident to a focus and a climax?**

3. **Are you making general statements and giving a summary of events** instead of furnishing your reader with details, details, details?

4. **Are your adjectives, adverbs, and nouns specific enough,** or are you letting yourself use general words?

5. **Is there enough dialogue,** or could you heighten the interest by making your characters talk more? Is the dia-

logue that you have included paragraphed and punctuated correctly?

6. **Are your verbs the strongest, most specific verbs possible?** In this connection avoid "There is", the passive voice, and the participial close.

7. **How are the paragraphs running?** Too long or too short? Divide or combine them as seems advisable.

8. **Is your story plausible?**

9. **Are your characters individual, colourful, interesting?**

10. **Are the names of your characters suitable** and suggestive without being too obvious?

11. **Have you made use of contrast?**

12. **Always remember that the title is an integral part of the story.** Is your title suggestive? Is it brief? Would it attract a reader to your story? Does it reveal too much?

WRITING A STORY IN HIGH SCHOOL

Writing a story is a formidable matter, and calls for extended effort. It is the longest and hardest piece of writing which this book deals with. In fact, it offers material for the unit method of work, rather than for a single daily assignment or two in the regular class routine. A week is not too long to put on a single story.

Some such plan as the following will be found helpful. The teacher will of course adapt it to the needs of each class.

1. Choose a plot from those either given in this chapter, or assigned by the teacher, or suggested and discussed in class. Feel free to change or adapt this plot to your particular purpose.

2. As the first assignment (a) divide the plot into scenes or stages, according to the plan suggested on pages 412-413, and (*b*) settle on where you are actually going to begin writing. (*c*) In two or three sentences each, describe the appearance and disposition of the one, two, or three leading persons in the story. (*d*) In a half-dozen sentences describe the setting. Submit (*a*), (*b*), (*c*), and (*d*) to the teacher for criticism and suggestions.

3. As the second assignment, run through in your mind your plot, characters, and setting to see whether any changes or improvements occur to you, and begin the actual writing of the story at or near the middle.

4. As the third assignment, read over and touch up what was previously written, and continue writing the story.

5. The fourth assignment continues the third, and is devoted to revising what has already been written, and completing the writing of the story.

6. The final assignment is to revise the whole story, and to copy it neatly by hand or in type for handing in the next day.

4. In Conclusion

If in spite of your best efforts your plot seems to lag and drag, and your characters insist on talking like wooden dolls, do not feel permanently discouraged. There is no way to improve except by the try-try-again method. Ray Long, who for twenty years was a successful and influential magazine editor, once said that the recipe for success in writing stories is simple: "Think better and work harder than your competitors."

His "Think better" is especially significant.

THE ROUND TABLE

1. Which of the following are good titles: "The Word", "Mr. Looney Passes Out", "An Unusual Experience", "A Terribly Strange Bed", "I'm in a Hurry", "The Purloined Letter", "The Word That Screamed", "The Horseman in the Sky", "Leave It to a Woman", "Caught with a S-Cent", "They", "Was He Afraid?", "Ice Water, Pl——!", "Revenge", "Oooh!", "In Borrowed Plumes", "The Key", "The Untangled Tangle", "The One That Got Away", "B'ars Will be B'ars", "A Municipal Report", "Mr. Onion"? Give reasons for your selection.

2. What kind of person does each of the following names suggest: Carter Druse, Gussie Bloom, Willie Winkie, Horace Tidway, Ezekiel Snipe, Rufe Apley, Percival Launcelot Muggins, Jasper MacGregor, Fancy Day, J. Altrus Browne, Timothy Summers, Henrietta Pratt,

Augustus H. Price, Wilbert Squibb, Abner Dawson, Victoria Wagonseller, Daphne Eustasia Smythe, Angus Munro? Why do the names suggest certain characteristics?

3. In two stories that you like read again carefully the opening and the closing pages, and see whether you think the end is implied in the beginning.

4. Have you noticed an incident or a person this week that might contain the material for a story? Be on the look-out for such a suggestion for the next twenty-four hours and jot down in synopsis form any ideas that occur to you.

5. Is there a historical or folk legend of your neighbourhood that would make an interesting narrative?

6. Do you know an exciting situation or happening that you have heard the older members of your family tell which might be turned into a story?

7. Try giving each story that you write three titles, and then select the best.

8. In choosing a plot and characters, think carefully before deciding on a love story. Love stories are pitfalls for the unwary writer, and are apt to be either over-sentimental or unintentionally humorous.

9. Let each member of the class submit in tabloid form the best plot he can think of. From these plots the teacher will select several to be read to the class and discussed for further possibilities.

10. Invent one plot for a mystery or horror story. Discuss the plots in class and agree on the best, whether or not the story is written out.

11. Invent one dream story, full of fanciful or impossible incidents, with a surprise ending.

Suggestions for Stories

12. Try to find in the day's news a suggestion for an unusual or human interest story. Here are some actual headlines that offer possibilities:

(1) Pond ninety feet deep where back yard was.
(2) Moving clock around upsets whole town.
(3) Using shirt for sail, boy embarks on busy bay.
(4) Two fiancées claim train-wreck victim.
(5) School-house wrecked by besieged intruder.
(6) Skeleton dug up in wooden cage.
(7) Bruin returns to life in auto.
(8) Eulogized by boss when thought dead, man returns to be amused by kind words.
(9) "Crusading Carrie" lands in cell after parking-sign smashing campaign.
(10) Artful art critic hoaxes judges.
(11) Ban on snoring enforced in court.

13. PLOTS FOR STORIES

(1) Of two men seeking the favour of a lady, one tries to win an advantage over the other by telling the lady of his rival's stinginess. It develops later that the rival is saving every penny for a praiseworthy purpose—to pay off his father's debts, or to make possible a surgical operation for a mother or sister, or start a cripple in business.

(2) A boaster has built up a tissue of exaggerations about the things he has seen and the people he has met in another city. Travelling with friends, he is unexpectedly compelled to stay for some hours in that city. One by one his falsehoods find him out, and he has to put up the price of a dinner for the party.[1]

(3) A very bright attractive girl had become egotistical and dictatorial. Her opinions had always been accepted by her parents and younger sisters as conclusive. Her family moved to a larger town where she attended the central high school. Dorothy continued her habit of giving advice. Some of her schoolmates, becoming weary of her dictation, decided to cure her. Within the space of two or three days every one of them asked her opinion about dress or entertainment or school activities. Not until more than a dozen, both boys and girls, had humbly consulted her did she begin to suspect a plot. When her friends confessed, she was at first furiously angry but ultimately accepted the device as a very just criticism and changed her ways.[2]

SHORT-STORY READING LIST

Aldrich, Thomas Bailey . . . . *Marjorie Daw*
The Arabian Nights . . . . . . *Ali Baba and the Forty Thieves*
Barrie, J. M. . . . . *Two of Them*
Bierce, Ambrose . . . . *The Horseman in the Sky*
Brown, John . . . . *Rab and His Friends*
Cable, George Washington . . . *"Posson Jone"*
Jean-ah Poquelin
Chesterton, G. K. . . . . *The Blast of the Book*
Connell, Richard . . . . *The Most Dangerous Game*
Conrad, Joseph . . . . *Youth*
The Heart of Darkness
Daudet, Alphonse . . . . *The Death of the Dauphin*
De la Mare, Walter . . . . . . *Seaton's Aunt*
de Maupassant, Guy . . . . . . *The Necklace*
The Piece of String
Dickens, Charles . . . . *A Christmas Carol*

[1]Plots (1) and (2) from J. K. Slater, *Freshman Rhetoric,* D. C. Heath and Co.

[2]From Virginia J. Craig, *The Teaching of High School English*, Longmans, Green and Co., p. 172. By permission of the publishers.

Edwards, Harry Stillwell	*Eneas Africanus*
	The Woodhaven Goat
Freeman, Mary E. Wilkins . . .	*The Revolt of Mother*
	A New England Nun
Galsworthy, John	*Quality* (in *Inn of Tranquillity*)
Garland, Hamlin	*Up the Coolly*
	Under the Lion's Paw
Hardy, Thomas	*The Three Strangers*
Harris, Joel Chandler	*Six Uncle Remus Stories*
	Free Joe and the Rest of the World
Harte, Bret	*The Luck of Roaring Camp*
	Tennessee's Partner
	The Outcasts of Poker Flat
Hawthorne, Nathaniel	*Dr. Heidigger's Experiment*
	The Great Stone Face
	The Ambitious Guest
	David Swan
Henry, O	*A Retrieved Reformation*
	The Gift of the Magi
	The Last Leaf
	A Municipal Report
	The Ransom of Red Chief
Irving, Washington	*Rip Van Winkle*
	The Legend of Sleepy Hollow
	The Stout Gentleman
Jewett, Sarah Orne	*Marsh Rosemary*
	A White Heron
Kipling, Rudyard	*The Man Who Would be King*
	Rikki-Tikki-Tavi
	The Man Who Was
	On Greenhow Hill
	An Habitation Enforced
London, Jack	*All-Gold Cañon*
	To Build a Fire (in *Lost Face*)
Marshall, Edison	*The Heart of Little Shikara*
Moffett, Cleveland	*The Mysterious Card* (in Carolyn Wells's *American Mystery Stories*)
O'Brien, Fitz James	*What Was It? A Mystery*
Page, Thomas Nelson	*Marse Chan*
Poe, Edgar Allan	*The Gold Bug*
	The Murders in the Rue Morgue
	The Purloined Letter
	The Masque of the Red Death
	The Fall of the House of Usher
	The Cask of Amontillado

CHAPTER XXIV

Description

My senses five are five great Cups
  Wherefrom I drink delight!
For them to God a grace I sing
  At morning and at night,
For five fair loving cups are they
  That feed me with delight.

—RACHEL ANNAND TAYLOR,
"A Child of Joy"

1. What Description Is

Description is that form of writing whose purpose is to suggest a picture. It seeks in the main to portray the outside world as it is revealed to us by means of our five senses—sight, smell, hearing, taste, and touch. During every waking moment we are receiving impressions through the eye, the nose, the ear, the tongue, and the skin; and whenever we try to tell anyone else how something looks, smells, sounds, tastes, or feels, we are describing. Description deals with places, things, scenes, persons, and animals. We can also try to depict an interesting or curious character we have come in contact with, or to portray our own moods and feelings. What we say or write under these circumstances is description too.

Description rarely extends to the length of a book or even to that of a chapter. Description is at its best when it comes in little spurts and sparkles and flashes, to lend reality and vividness to stories and to plays.

THE ROUND TABLE

Exercises in *Expository Description*

1. Write an advertisement for a lost dog or cat. Have a definite animal in mind.
2. Write a letter to the chief of police or the sheriff describing a young friend who has disappeared, or a horse or a cow, or a valuable household article that has been stolen.
3. Write a description of a kitchen utensil, an automobile tool, a farm implement, an article of furniture.
4. Without naming it, describe briefly an important building in town (or a person), or a bird or an animal, so that the class can recognize it from your description.

2. Two Aids to Clearness

(1) The Point of View (2) The Basic Comparison, or the Fundamental Image

(1) THE POINT OF VIEW

When a photographer takes a picture of a building or of the crowds at a football game, what he does first is to pick out the best place to set up his camera. Likewise, in describing, the writer (*a*) selects the most suitable spot from which to view the scene, (*b*) lets the reader know what this spot is, and (*c*) does not change this point of view without telling the reader.

The same scene looks entirely different according to the place from which it is observed. A mountain viewed from the foot up is unlike the same mountain viewed from the top down. A near view of a building or of a monument does not give the same impression as a distant view. What is seen from an aeroplane flying over a city is different from what is seen from an automobile following the same route through the streets. What you see depends in large measure upon where you stand.

In writing description be sure to settle in your own mind your exact point of view, and stick to it as you write. Make it clear to the reader if you change places—if, for instance, you walk around a building or a pond to the other side, or go from room to room or from floor to floor in a building, or from a vantage point shift your gaze from left to right or from front to rear. Sometimes a description is written from a moving point of view, as a hike or an automobile trip. Be careful to let your reader know what progress you are making, and to keep him informed as the scene changes.

(2) THE BASIC COMPARISON OR FUNDAMENTAL IMAGE

It is usually best to begin a description by giving the size, shape, colour, and general appearance of the thing described. The reader needs a preliminary idea of the object as a whole into which he can fit the details as they are given later, one by one. This general plan or outline of the scene or object is known as the fundamental image, or, as it might be called, **the basic picture.** It is of the greatest service to the reader, for it gives him a mental outline or ground plan, and helps him keep the proportions and the relations of the different parts accurately and clearly in mind.

We are using a fundamental image when we speak of a carpenter's T-square; or describe a building as L-Shaped, or built like an E with the middle bar left out; or refer to a curve as an S or horseshoe or hairpin curve; or mention Half Moon Pond or Crescent Lake; or name a mountain Sugar Loaf, Caesar's Head, Chimney Rock, Table Rock, or Hawk's Beak; or call a baseball field a diamond and a football field a gridiron.

A basic comparison is very helpful in describing a comprehensive view or a large landscape such as a river valley, a state, or a country. Italy may thus be likened to a boot, with the island of Sicily playing the part of a football, Naples high up on the instep, and Rome much farther up toward the knee. Stevenson compared the Bay of Monterey, California, to a bent fishhook. Thoreau compared Cape Cod to a bent arm and fist, with Provincetown at the end of the fist.

Familiar images such as these help the reader to form an idea of the general outline or contour of a scene, and to locate smaller divisions or definite places in relation to the outline. The size of the landscape is also important, and should be given along with the shape at the outset. In describing Crescent Lake, for instance, it makes a big difference whether the lake is half a mile long from tip to tip and a quarter of a mile wide at its widest part, or ten miles from tip to tip and five miles wide. Likewise, if no reference is made to size, confusion is almost certain to result. It is possible to describe the jerboa, or jumping rat, in terms that will instantly call to mind a kangaroo, though the jerboa is five inches long without its tail and the kangaroo is five feet tall. Similarly, if neither the name nor the measurement is given, the description of a black cat will suggest a black panther, and the other way around.

By a well-chosen basic comparison, give your reader at the start a clear idea of the shape, size, and colour of what you are describing. He needs a frame to fit the details of the picture into.

THE ROUND TABLE

1. Look up in an atlas the basic comparisons mentioned above, and add any others you have heard of or can find for yourself.
2. On a large-scale map of your neighbourhood see if you can find any familiar image for any county, lake, section, or natural formation.
3. Using a large dictionary and a small encyclopedia, write a brief description of a jerboa so as to suggest a kangaroo, and try it on some member of the family.

3. The First Requisite: Close Observation

Talent is long patience.—GUSTAVE FLAUBERT

To repeat an important point made several times before, you can't build a brick wall without bricks or erect a stone house without stones. No more can you write an incident or a description without details. With details it is easy; without details it is impossible.

The gathering of details depends solely upon close observation, the noticing and the noting of the separate items in the unending stream of consciousness that flows in upon us every waking moment and, through our dreams, even in our sleep. Five avenues of entrance we have for receiving outside impressions: sight, hearing, touch, taste, and smell. Through each of these channels a host of stimuli come crowding in upon us day after day, week after week, and month after month, as long as we live. Upon the number and vividness of these sense impressions depend **both our intenseness in living and our success in writing.**

(1) LACK OF OBSERVATION

One reason why it is hard for us to give enough details in writing is that we do not observe closely enough in life. We have not trained ourselves to look carefully and steadily at things around us. Eyes we have, but they see not. For instance, there is the familiar question as to which way the figure six on the dial of a watch is turned, up or down? Or take any well-known public building that you pass frequently. How many stories, columns, and outside steps has it? If there is a monument on the town square, how accurately can you sketch it, giving its dimensions, material, design, and inscription? Has it ever fallen within your experience to take a walk in the country with a forestry expert, a botanist, a biologist, an experienced hunter, or an old woodsman? If so, you can faintly realize the thousand and one details of earth, sky, and water that most of us miss entirely as we pass from place to place and go from year to year. We should endeavour to form the habit not only of looking at things, but of really seeing what we look at. Without that ability, we can never narrate or describe successfully. With it, we can not only improve our writing but also enlarge our experience and increase our zest for living.

Listen to what Helen Keller has to say about intense observation. With two of her chief avenues closed from childhood—sight and hearing—she trained and intensified the sense of touch till it became miraculously delicate and responsive. She says to us:

I who am blind can give one hint to those who see—one admonition to those who would make full use of the gift of sight: Use your eyes as if tomorrow you would be stricken blind. And the same method can be applied to the other senses. Hear the music of voices, the song of a bird, the mighty strains of an orchestra, as if you would be stricken deaf tomorrow. Touch each object you want to touch as if tomorrow your tactile sense would fail. Smell the perfume of flowers, taste with relish each morsel, as if tomorrow you could never smell and taste again. Make the most of every sense; glory in all the facets of pleasure and beauty which the world reveals to you through the several means of contact which Nature provides. But of all the senses, I am sure that sight must be the most delightful.[1]

THE ROUND TABLE

1. From memory make a list of descriptive details of a familiar building, monument, or your own front or back yard. Then compare the list with the actual scene itself.

2. From memory make a list of what can be seen from your bedroom window. Then look out of the window to see how complete and accurate the list is.

3. Off-hand try to tell how your pet dog or pet cat or horse differs from all other dogs, cats, or horses. Then study the animal to see what additional differences you can discover.

4. With a friend walk slowly by a crowded store window and observe its contents. Make lists and compare them (*a*) with each other and (*b*) with the window itself.

5. Devote a recitation period, a class party, or an English Club meeting to an Observation Game of the Five Senses. Try several or all of them.

(1) Sight

Prepare a table with a number of miscellaneous objects laid out upon it, such as several kinds of knives, pieces of different coloured chalk, several different fountain pens, a bunch of keys, a small note-book, a large note-book, several small dolls, several china figurines, a top, marbles, fishing line, several kinds of fruits and flowers, doll dishes, pocket-books, a bottle of ink, and so forth.

Let the class in sections walk slowly around the table once, and

[1] "Three Days to See", from *Atlantic Monthly*, Jan., 1933. By permission of Famous Features Syndicate.

then list from memory what was on it. Compare the lists with each other and with the official list.

(2) Smell

Arrange containers all alike, such as small glasses or butter plates. Upon them put a number of familiar objects with a distinctive odour. One set might be these: a slice of banana; kitchen soap; a slice of lemon; a geranium leaf; a spoonful of lard; clover (or grass); leather; a flower; turpentine; rubbing alcohol; tobacco; tea; coffee; a moth-ball.

Blindfold the class, and let two others, one carrying the containers and the other a scoring pad, go down the line recording the answers after each person has taken a smell.

(3) Touch, (4) Taste, and (5) Hearing

These tests are made after the same fashion as that of smell.

Getting up the "exhibits" will entail some trouble, but if a different committee is appointed from the class to prepare and administer each test, the work will be divided up fairly, each committee will be interested in making a good showing, and no little interest and entertainment will result.

6. It is a matter of common knowledge that honest eyewitnesses will give utterly unlike accounts of the same accident or incident. As an instance, try this experiment. Let the teacher select someone outside the class to pay it an unexpected visit. Let him be dressed in some unusual or outlandish costume and wear a false face. Let him carry certain objects such as a clock and a walking stick, or a sofa cushion and an umbrella, or a small baseball bat and a bunch of flowers. Let him walk around the room and speak two unrelated sentences such as "Caesar conquered Gaul, but time and tide wait for no man", or "The weather has been unusually rainy thus far this year; however, the British navy is still sailing the seven seas." Let him do certain definite things with the objects he is carrying, when he gets to the table or desk in the front of the room. If desired, the teacher can remonstrate with him, and seem to try to persuade him to leave the room. (Of course, if this experiment is tried, it need not follow exactly these directions.)

Then, either toward the end of the period, or the next day, ask the class to write out a full and accurate account of exactly what happened, including a full description of the visitor.

Compare versions in class, and have the visitor describe his costume and tell what he did and said.

4. Details in Description

Recall the constant emphasis that has been put upon details throughout this book. Let us paraphrase one of the opening statements of this book, which by this time should be entirely familiar, and make it read, "Three-fourths of describing consists in giving definite details. The other fourth doesn't matter."

When you have a descriptive paragraph to write, or a descriptive passage in a story, try some such plan as this in order to gather the material—that is, the necessary details. **Settle, first, on the exact moment or circumstances under which you are viewing the scene or object you are describing.** This may concern the time of day, as early morning, noon, twilight, or night; it may be the season of the year, as winter, summer, spring, or autumn; or it may be a particular moment in an important incident or accident. Whatever it is, fix it definitely in your mind. **Determine, secondly, the prevailing mood or impression you wish to arouse,** whether of confusion, peacefulness, alarm, beauty, ugliness, decay, pleasure, danger, heat, cold, or what. **Thirdly, list all the details you can think of,** using as many of the five senses as possible, with particular reference to movement and action.

1. Variety of Sense Appeal

To ensure thoroughness at first and to gain practice, use some such diagram as the following, which can be conveniently drawn on regular theme paper by turning the sheet lengthwise and writing along the red margin line.

1. *Subject:* —— 2. *Time:* —— 3. *Mood or Impression:* ——

Sight	Hearing	Smell	Taste	Touch	Movement

As illustrations of the relation between the separate details and the description itself, take the following analysis of two descriptive paragraphs.

I

A. The Material (Details) of the Picture

1. Subject: Westminster Abbey 2. Time: Twilight
3. Mood or Impression: Increasing darkness and gloom

Sight	*Sound*
Last beams of sun streaming through high, coloured windows.	Distant footfall of a verger has a dreary sound.
Lower parts of Abbey in obscurity.	The door jars shut and fills the building with echoes.
Chapels and aisles getting darker.	
Statues of kings and figures on the monuments fading uncertainly.	
Evening breeze cold as from a grave.	

B. The Picture

TWILIGHT IN WESTMINSTER ABBEY

BY WASHINGTON IRVING

The last beams of day were now faintly streaming through the painted windows in the high vaults above me; the lower parts of the Abbey were already wrapped in the obscurity of twilight. The chapels and aisles grew darker and darker. The effigies of the kings faded into shadows; the marble figures of the monuments assumed strange shapes in the uncertain light; the evening breeze crept through the aisles like the cold breath of the grave; and even the distant footfall of a verger, traversing the Poets' Corner, had something strange and dreary in its sound. I slowly retraced my morning's walk, and as I passed out at the portal of the cloisters, the door, closing with a jarring noise behind me, filled the whole building with echoes.

II

A. The Material (Details) of the Picture

1. Subject: A compound yard in India 2. Time: Afternoon
3. Mood or Impression: Silence, seclusion, and tranquillity

Sight	*Sound* (here, absence of sound)
Inn cow poking about.	Country seclusion emphasized.
Dog asleep stretched out in the sun.	Place tranquil and restful.
Servants coming and going in white.	Crows not there.
Elephant rocking in shade of a large tree, begging with trunk and playing with brown children.	Servants barefooted and made no sound.
Camels here and there.	Camels went on padded feet and fitted in with the silence and serenity.

B. The Picture

The Compound Yard in Jeypore, Rajputana, India[1]

BY MARK TWAIN

The inn cow poked about the compound and emphasized the secluded and country air of the place, and there was a dog of no particular breed, who was always present in the compound, and always asleep, always stretched out baking in the sun and adding to the deep tranquillity and reposefulness of the place, when the crows were away on business. White-draperied servants were coming and going all the time, but they seemed only spirits, for their feet were bare and made no sound. Down the lane a piece lived an elephant in the shade of a noble tree, and rocked and rocked, and reached about with his trunk, begging of his brown mistress or fumbling the children playing at his feet. And there were camels about but they go on velvet feet, and were proper to the silence and serenity of the surroundings.

Turning to our own writing, suppose we have to write a description of a city cafeteria at lunch time. Using the suggested form of analysis, we might get some such results as the following:

(1) DETAILS FOR DESCRIPTION

1. Subject: A city cafeteria 2. Time: The noon rush hour
3. Mood or Impression: Hurry, bustle, confusion

Sight	*Sound*	*Smell*	*Movement*
A number of white-topped tables, some seating two, others seating four.	Noise of chairs being pushed back on floor.	The heavy moist odour of food and crowded humanity as one first enters the door.	Assistants hurrying to and fro among the tables balancing heavy trays on their hands.
Most of the seats occupied by busy men, women and children, eating, facing various ways.	Rattle of china and of knives and forks on the hard-topped tables.	Then specialized smells of cabbage, string beans, boiled beets, vegetable soup, fried beefsteak, cigarette smoke, coffee, as one passes down the line near the tables and past the food counter.	Other assistants clearing off dishes and wiping tables for waiting customers.
Walls coloured a light green with an interlaced border of darker green outlined in pink.	An occasional louder crash as an assistant stacks dishes hurriedly in large piles in clearing the table.	A whiff of whiskey on one man's breath.	Those who have finished leisurely gathering their hats and wraps and strolling toward the door.
The male assistants clothed in white.	The buzz and murmur of conversation from all over the room.	An odour of cheap violet cologne on a heavily rouged girl.	A long row of waiting diners standing in line.
The serving girls clothed in green trimmed with pink.	The whir of the cash register and the sharp ting of the bell as the cashier rings up a sale and makes change.		Another line, slowly pushing their trays along the white metal rails, pausing at the counters to get soup. meat, bread, salad, a drink, and a dessert.
Steam rising from the meat counter and the huge polished coffee urn.	The click of the ice-water cooler as the glasses are filled.		

[1]By permission of the publishers, Harper and Brothers.

Sigh.	*Sound*	*Smell*	*Movement*
The evident embarrassment of a big sister aged fourteen over little brother's loud talking and acrobatic stunts on the heavy steel rail along the serving counter.	A child's shrill voice protesting at being made to leave the sugar dish alone and finish his spinach.		Fumbling for change in purse or pocket to pay the cashier.
The smiles and side glances of the serving girls at the good-looking young men in line.	The crash of a feeble old man's half-filled tray as he pushes it uncertainly along the rails and tilts it over the edge.		Then following the assistants with the trays, looking anxiously all over the room for a vacant table.
These glances returned with interest by the fat middle-aged men who want extra large helpings or choice portions.	The consequent titter of some of the diners.		A small boy running back and forth to refill water glasses for his table.
The disapproval of the obviously efficient business woman whose usual twenty-five-cent luncheon creates no interest on the part of the cashier.	The loud objection of the small boy whose sister made him stop playing on the steel rail.		A little girl with an air of great importance exchanging a special order slip for a dish of chocolate ice cream.
Fussy old woman who can't decide what she wants — chooses fish — rejects it in favour of chicken pie — serving girl looks very bored as the old lady finally decides she'll have soup instead of meat.			

Here then, in list form, is the material (details) for a description of a cafeteria during the rush hour. In writing out the description it will not be necessary to use all the details, but only the most suggestive ones, particularly those that contribute to the special mood, impression, or purpose of the writer. If, for example, you do not object to cafeterias, but rather like their democratic air, choosing your own dishes, and the absence of tipping, your choice and grouping of details would be entirely different from that of a person who frankly dislikes cafeterias and prefers a quiet café or tea shop. And whether you are describing the cafeteria in a complimentary or an uncomplimentary mood, the details will not be separated according to the different senses, as in the analysis, but will be given in the order in which they most naturally came to us. We do not first see and then hear and then smell, but frequently do all three at the same time. Which of the three impressions we shall present first—whether of eye or ear or nose—will depend upon which impression seemed strongest at the time and which we want our reader to realize first. The chief value of this exercise is that it insures an abundant supply of eye-ear-nose-touch-and-motion details, which can be selected and grouped as needed.

Closer to the actual process of writing is the way the following details of a storm in the country are listed—that is, not according to the different senses but according to the time order in which they were perceived.

(2) MORE DETAILS FOR DESCRIPTION

A Storm in the Country

1. Simpson's farm. Hot afternoon; corn droops. (Make it very hot.)
2. Old mule asleep. He stands with his weight on three legs; a straw sticks from his mouth; his lower lip wiggles as if he had something to say, but couldn't remember what it was.
3. Thunderheads on horizon; then darker, nearer.
4. Storm about to break. Wind in trees, windmill clanks wildly; horses race along pasture fence; air cool; farmer's wife rushes to drive a brood of little chicks under shelter; shutters drawn; thunder and lightning.
5. Rain pours. Big drops first, then sheets. Old mule still asleep.
6. Attitudes of animals. Chickens under corn-crib, rooster on one leg. On porch, cat curled up in a ball, disgusted; dog licking his paws.
7. Cow in barnyard, pleasantly chewing cud, eyes half closed; water runs off her in little rivers.
8. Pigs in pen. Ducks active.
9. Frogs start a chorus; sound of rain on shingles. Old mule all this while asleep.
10. Comedy: Little girls rush up—have been on picnic—soaked.
11. Chattering crowd of children on porch. Scrape off mud. What's the use?
12. Tragedy: Little girls take out wet lunch; try to eat it.
13. Charity: Farmer's wife helps out.
14. Merry sound of talk and laughter louder than beat of rain.
15. Appearance of flooded road and field.
16. Heroism: Farmer, with boots and rubber coat, goes out to rescue a drowning hen.

17. Storm slackens; birds in eaves begin to tune up.
18. Little girls depart with thanks and more chattering.
19. One little girl stuck in mud. Rest all shriek and laugh.
20. Sunshine. Old mule suddenly wakes up, shakes one ear, and looks surprised.

Specimens of Description

Read the passages below critically, paying close heed to (1) the number and grouping of the details, (2) the sense or senses appealed to, and (3) the writer's prevailing mood or the impression the description is intended to make on the reader.

(3) DETAILS OF SMELL

Remembered Odors[1]

BY THOMAS WOLFE

Yes, and the smell of hot daisy-fields in the morning; of melted puddling-iron in a foundry; the winter smell of horse-warm stables; of old oak and walnut; and the butcher's smell of meat, of strong slaughtered lamb and of brown sugar melted with slivered bitter chocolate; and of crushed mint leaves, and of a wet lilac bush; of magnolia beneath the heavy moon, of dogwood and laurel; of an old caked pipe and Bourbon rye, aged in kegs of charred oak; the sharp smell of tobacco; of carbolic and nitric acids; the coarse true smell of a dog; of old-imprisoned books, and the cool fern-smell near springs; of vanilla in cake-dough; and of cloven ponderous cheeses.

(4) DETAILS OF SIGHT, SOUND, SMELL, TASTE, FEEL

Childhood Memories[2]

I can call back the solemn twilight and mystery of the deep woods, the earthy smells, the faint odors of the wild flowers, the sheen of rain-washed foliage, the rattling clatter of drops when the wind shook the trees, the far-off hammering of woodpeckers and the muffled drumming of wood pheasants in the remoteness of the forest, the snapshot glimpses of disturbed wild creatures scurrying through the grass—

[1] *Look Homeward, Angel*, Charles Scribner's Sons. By permission of the publishers.

[2] From Mark Twain's *Autobiography*, Harper and Brothers. By permission of the publishers.

I can call it all back and make it as real as it ever was and as blessed. I can call back the prairie, and its loneliness and peace, and a vast hawk hanging motionless in the sky, with his wings spread wide and the blue of the vault showing through the fringe of their end feathers. I can see the woods in their autumn dress, the oaks purple, the hickories washed with gold, the maples and the sumachs luminous with crimson fires, and I can hear the rustle made by the fallen leaves as we plowed through them. I can see the blue clusters of wild grapes hanging among the foliage of the saplings, and I remember the taste of them and the smell. I know how the wild blackberries looked, and how they tasted, and . . . the pawpaws, the hazelnuts, and the persimmons; and I can feel the thumping rain, upon my head, of hickory nuts and walnuts when we were out in the frosty dawn to scramble for them with the pigs.

Nocturne

BY CHARLES HOMER NEWTON[1]

I lay quite still on the ground looking down on the stars. One of them floated near a lily pad in the centre of the pond, and quivered on the water as it did in the air. The water stretched away like a pit; it seemed to appear only in dark splotches, where it buoyed up some shimmering star or photographed a pine sleeping on the shore. The pines rocked in vapid columns, and whenever a breeze floated upon them they only nodded in unison. I saw some black blades of grass spike up before me. When I looked to the right, I smiled at two dark clovers growing on top of the grass—they seemed so alone as they drooped in gentle arcs, bending forward to be impaled on the stiffened stumps beneath them. I wondered why the clovers should look so graceful beside the grass—I couldn't see any difference in their daily shades of green. A leaf fell from somewhere above me and drifted slowly down. I thought it would fall beside me; but I saw a breeze snatch at it, and it whirled out over the pond, only to drop once more. It landed in the water on top of a star, and all I could see was the silhouette of the leaf's stem and a fringe of silver tracing up one side. I saw the wind glide over the lake in ripples and

Felt its coolness strike the warmth of my body. One wisp loosed a lock of hair which fell down over my forehead, and another stole in through my open collar and laid its hands on my neck and chest. I pressed closer to the earth; I felt its dryness against me and the bristles of grass bend under me. A breeze rushed the night's dampness into my face, and I shivered. I felt something crawl over my hand, and

[1]The Choate School, Connecticut. From Prize-Winning Essays, Atlantic Essay Contest for High School Students, 1931-1932. By permission of Atlantic Monthly Company.

Heard it chirp in the grass beside me: it was a cricket. I heard a frog burble somewhere on the shore of the pond; then he and the cricket were still, and I could hear the silence a long way off. But the ripples on the pond began to lap its shores; and the frog must have been frightened, for he burbled twice again and then splashed into the pond. It was so silent that I heard a leaf drop in the grass beside me; I jumped, then the wind swished through the pines, and

I smelled their fragrance. It was ever so fresh, and I thought of the sea. Then I smelled the grass, but it smelled of earth. A faint aroma, dripping from the clovers in the grass, drifted into my face. I breathed in something else—I lifted my elbow and found a crushed patch of violets underneath it. I sniffed at the dampness like a whimpering puppy, but I liked its coolness and its smell of heaviness. I liked the night, too, for it smelled so empty—like myself lying there in the grass.

THE ROUND TABLE

1. Using the details of the cafeteria scene given above, and adding or substituting others of your own if you wish, write a descriptive paragraph either in class or at home as the teacher directs. Read aloud several of the best paragraphs to show what different results can be obtained from the same material.

2. Suggest in class other subjects rich in sense impressions, and from them or from the subjects given below (*a*) choose one and analyse it according to the diagram on page 431, giving as many definite details under each sense as you can; (*b*) take another subject in class and, with the teacher at the board, work together, suggesting all possible details.

Suggested Subjects

An Early Morning Walk in the Woods (City)
A Noon Walk in the Woods (City)
A Late Afternoon Walk in the Woods (City)
The Railroad Station Just before the Train Comes In
The Railroad Station Just after the Train Has Left
A City (or Town) Street on Saturday Afternoon
A City (or Town) Street on Sunday Afternoon
Running from an Unexpected Shower
The Big Parade Passes
A Fashionable Church Wedding
The Grandstand Just before the Kick-off
The Grandstand between Halves
A Schoolroom Just before the Bell Rings
A Schoolroom Just after the Bell Rings

3. After the model of Mark Twain's "Childhood Memories", recount your most vivid childhood impressions and recollections. Go into minute detail, and appeal to as many senses as possible.

5. Mood or Impression in Description

There are two factors that fix the character of any piece of description. The first is the kind of person or scene described, and the second is the mood of the writer and the impression he wishes to make on the reader. As to the scene itself, there is almost as much personality in places as there

Courtesy of Collier's Weekly and Charles Dana Gibson

HIS FORTUNE

"You are going on a long, long journey."

is in people. A scene is prevailingly beautiful, ugly, quiet, noisy, squalid, heated, cool, confusing, restful, attractive, or unattractive. This definiteness of impression that a scene makes is sometimes called "dominant tone". It is what Stevenson had in mind when he said: "There is a fitness in events and places. . . . Some places speak distinctly. Certain dank gardens cry aloud for a murder; certain old houses demand to be haunted; certain coasts are set apart for shipwreck." Consider, for example, the difference between the block of handsomest residences in your town and the row of tumbledown shacks in a back alley or lining the railroad tracks. Or compare the prettiest woodland pool you know of with an old pond in a deserted brickyard or a mud puddle in an automobile graveyard.

The nature of the scene itself, therefore, is obviously one of the determining factors in description. More important than this, however, is the mood of the person viewing it.

Courtesy of Collier's Weekly and Charles Dana Gibson

TWO STRIKES AND THE BASES FULL

Our feelings are like bits of coloured glass through which everything we see is transformed. Look through a piece of red glass, and everything appears rosy. Change the glass to blue or green or yellow or black, and the landscape changes with it. When we feel well and happy, every person and thing we see seems pleasant and likeable. But if we are tired or disappointed or grieving or angry, we look out upon a different world. A touch of flu or malaria will make any future look dark, and an attack of ptomaine poisoning will for several days cause any life to seem a failure.

Much of the description in a story is thus coloured by the moods and the emotions of the characters. The practical point in this connection is the need of giving not all the possible details of the scene but only those which match the mood and will hence produce a similar impression on the reader.

If you will glance again at the descriptions of "Twilight in

Courtesy of Collier's Weekly and Charles Dana Gibson

FANNED OUT

Westminster Abbey", and "The Compound Yard in India", you will find that both are alike in this particular: they do not try to give a complete, general description of the respective scenes, but a special kind of description resulting from a particular mood in the writer and designed to produce a particular impression on the reader. In the first, Washington Irving is not so much concerned with Westminster Abbey as with the increasing gloom, both physical and mental, of the twilight moment; in the second, Mark Twain is interested mainly in producing an impression of sleepy silence and restfulness. In each case the writer selects only those details that will suggest the desired mood and make the desired impression, and omits all others. In the picture of Westminster Abbey, for instance, the setting sun is spoken of as throwing its beams through the coloured windows. There was probably reflected, therefore, somewhere in the interior a bright cheerful spot of yellow or blue or red light. Irving does not mention it because it does not accord with the prevailing mood of his description.

This is the method of all descriptions that proceed by mood and impression. The writer is highly selective; he gives only those details that chime in with his mood and that minister to his impression, and he rejects all others. It is conceivable, for instance, that a description of a town by a person who likes and admires it would not have a single detail in common with a description by someone who dislikes and scorns it. Similarly, an enemy and a friend would describe the same person in entirely different terms.

Read the following descriptions with special regard to their mood. Notice that the details match one another perfectly and are so grouped as to produce one definite impression.

1. The East[1]

And this is how I see the East. I have seen its secret places and have looked into its very soul; but now I see it always from a small boat, a high outline of mountains, blue and afar in the morning; like faint mist at noon; a jagged wall of purple at sunset. I have the feel of the oar in my hand, the vision of the scorching blue sea in my eyes. And I see a bay, a wide bay, smooth as glass and polished like ice, shimmering in the dark. A red light burns far off upon the gloom of the land, and the night is soft and warm. We drag at the oars with aching arms, and suddenly a puff of wind, a puff faint and tepid and laden with strange odours of blossoms, of aromatic wood, comes out of the still night—the first sigh of the East on my face. That I can never forget. It was impalpable and enslaving, like a charm, like a whispered promise of mysterious delight.

—JOSEPH CONRAD

[1]By permission of Doubleday, Doran and Company.

2. The Miracle of Purun Bhagat

Immediately below him the hillside fell away, clean and cleared for fifteen hundred feet, where a little village of stone-walled houses, with roofs of beaten earth, clung to the steep tilt. All round it the tiny terraced fields lay out like aprons of patchwork on the knees of the mountain, and cows no bigger than beetles grazed between the smooth stone circles of the threshing-floors. Looking across the valley, the eye was deceived by the size of things, and could not at first realize that what seemed to be low scrub, on the opposite mountain-flank, was in truth a forest of hundred-foot pines. Purun Bhagat saw an eagle swoop across the gigantic hollow, but the great bird dwindled to a dot ere it was half-way over. A few bands of scattered clouds strung up and down the valley, catching on a shoulder of the hills, or rising up and dying out when they were level with the head of the pass. And "Here shall I find peace," said Purun Bhagat.

—RUDYARD KIPLING

3. A Young Mountaineer in Prison[1]

There was no question about his strength. As he stood in the glare of the overhead light I could trace the muscles through his rough homespun—for he was a mountaineer, pure and simple, and not a city-bred thief in ready-made clothes. I saw that the bulging muscles of his calves had driven the wrinkles of his butternut trousers close up under the knee joint, and that those of his thighs had rounded out the coarse cloth from the knee to the hip. The spread of his shoulders had performed a like service for his shirt, which was stretched out of shape over the chest and back. This was crossed by but one suspender, and was open at the throat—a tree-trunk of a throat, with all the cords supporting the head firmly planted in the shoulders. The arms were long and had the curved movement of the tentacles of a devilfish. The hands were big and bony, the fingers knotted together with knuckles of iron. He wore no collar nor any coat; nor did he bring one with him, so the Warden said.

—F. HOPKINSON SMITH, "Bud Tilden, Mail Thief"

4. Stop! Go![2]

Red light. Bell.

A block deep, four ranks of cars wait at the grade crossing, fenders in tail-lights, mudguards scraping mudguards, motors purring hot,

[1]From *The Under Dog*, Charles Scribner's Sons. By permission of the publishers.

[2]Harcourt, Brace and Company. By permission of the author and the publishers.

exhausts reeking, cars from Babylon and Jamaica, cars from Montauk, Port Jefferson, Patchogue, limousines from Long Beach, Far Rockaway, roadsters from Great Neck . . . cars full of asters and wet bathing suits, sun-singed necks, mouths sticky from sodas and hot-dawgs . . . cars dusted with pollen of ragweed and goldenrod.

Green light. Motors race, gears screech into first. The cars space out, flow in a long ribbon along the ghostly cement road, between black-windowed blocks of concrete factories, between bright slabbed colors of signboards towards the glow over the city that stands up incredibly into the night sky like the glow of a great lit tent, like the yellow tall bulk of a tent show.

—JOHN DOS PASSOS, *Manhattan Transfer*

THE ROUND TABLE

1. Look carefully at the three Gibson drawings just given. They are striking studies in contrasts. Choose either the two baseball pictures or "You Are Going on a Long Journey" and describe the contrast as vividly as you can.

2. Is there any house, street, or scene in your neighbourhood that seems to have a marked personality or "dominant tone"? If so, name it and describe its effect in a single sentence.

3. Can you give an example from your own experience when your own mood coloured or influenced strongly your feeling toward a particular place or person?

4. In a few sentences describe the following:

(1) A baby as seen by (*a*) its mother, (*b*) a bachelor friend of the family, and (*c*) a nervous old man who lives in the flat above.

(2) An automobile as it seems to (*a*) the man who owns it, (*b*) a man who drives a much finer car, and (*c*) a man too poor to afford a car.

(3) A football game as seen by (*a*) a brother of one of the players and (*b*) a trustee opposed to football.

(4) A dinner table as seen by (*a*) a hungry boy and (*b*) a dyspeptic old man.

(5) A student theme as seen by
(*a*) the student who wrote it,
(*b*) his teacher,
(*c*) the class, and
(*d*) the writer's mother.

5. Describe some acquaintance as if you (*a*) liked him very much and (*b*) disliked him extremely.

6. Describe some person in two of the following moods, letting him (her) reveal himself (herself) by what he (she) does or says:

(1) Blue
(2) Merry
(3) Quarrelsome
(4) Stubborn
(5) Exhausted
(6) Vexed
(7) Disgusted

7. Describe a scene trying to convey an impression of heat, cold, restfulness. confusion, fear, horror, nervousness, untidiness, desolation, or haste. Open with a topic sentence something like one of these:

It was a terrifically hot day.
It was the coldest day of winter.
The scene was extremely restful.

Then read the paragraph aloud, omitting the topic sentence, and see whether your choice and grouping of details convey the desired impression to the class.

8. Write a descriptive paragraph on one of the following:

(1) Rain! Rain! Rain!
(2) I Hate the Place
(3) Description of My Room for My Mother
(4) Description of My Room for My Chum
(5) A Haunted House
(6) An Abandoned Water Mill
(7) A Sickroom
(8) The Most and Least Attractive Parts of Town
(9) Before and After Dinner
(10) Piano Lessons As Viewed by Father, Mother, and Young Son
(11) A View on a Clear and a Rainy Day

6. The Suggestive Power of the Single Detail

Long descriptions are hard to write and tiresome to read. The way recent writers manage description differs from the way of the older writers. A present-day story may contain as much description as one written fifty years ago; but the description, instead of being given solidly all at once at the beginning of the story, is distributed bit by bit throughout the narrative. In this way the reader gets as definite an impression of the scenes and the characters as formerly, but he gets it gradually, and is rarely confronted with more than two or three descriptive sentences at one time. Instead, therefore, of writing your description in one solid block, break it up into bits and distribute it throughout the story.

Often, too, the writer tries to make his impression not by giving a number of details, but by selecting only one or two and expressing them as suggestively and vividly as possible. If this plan is followed, naturally the detail must be chosen carefully and phrased strikingly. Here are some good examples:

The velvet hum of bees.—H. G. WELLS
Puddles puckered with raindrops.—BEVERLEY NICHOLS
Her voice stamped its foot just a little.—*Cosmopolitan Magazine*
He received the news with his eyebrows.—JOHN GALSWORTHY
Breezes honed on icebergs.—*Reader's Digest*
Angry waves charging in with their coats off.—LEO MURTAGH
On the face of the bluff a brave tree with toes dug in leaned against the wind.—BETTY MACDONALD
Upon a dozen tracks great engines, passive and alert as cats, purred and panted softly.—THOMAS WOLFE
Father was a patient boulder in the stream of Mother's chatter. —BESS STREETER ALDRICH
The type of woman whose eyes not only sweep the room, but dust it.—RUTH HICKMAN
Small rain that left a mist of seed pearls on our clothes. —TOM HANLOW
Cheeks nutmegged with freckles.—W. O. MITCHELL
A sentry marching his shadow back and forth.—TED BENTZ
She was all sugar and spice with a dill pickle for a tongue. —JOYCE FAULKNER
A cat wove itself in and out of the railings.—ELIZABETH BOWEN
A few belated drifts of snow stretched like fingers of winter, keeping a last grip on the soil.—WALTER PRITCHARD EATON
He came into the house voice first.—Capt. ARNOLD WERLOW
She never enters a room; she raids it.—PETE MARTIN
The day was fine, but not convincingly fine. A long line of woolly yet possibly wicked little clouds were putting their heads together.—H. G. WELLS
The cat was stropping its backbone against the watering trough. —P. G. WODEHOUSE
The tails of little birds trying to roost were blown inside out like umbrellas.—THOMAS HARDY

THE ROUND TABLE

1. Try to give an unusually vivid detail of some scene or action like those quoted above. Ask the teacher to read aloud several of the best in class.

7. Revising Description

In revising description, look carefully to the following five points:

1. Maintain the physical point of view accurately, and keep the reader informed whether it is stationary or changing. See "The Point of View", pages 425-426.

2. Adhere strictly to the mood or impression and follow and reinforce it throughout. See "Mood or Impression in Description", pages 439-442.

3. Be sure to give enough definite details to enable the reader to realize the object described and your feeling toward it. See "Details in Description", page 431.

4. Appeal to as many of the five senses as possible—sight, smell, sound, taste, feel, and motion. See "Variety of Sense Appeal", page 431.

5. Try to sharpen and focus each detail so that it will be as vivid and suggestive as you can make it. See "The Suggestive Power of the Single Detail", pages 445-446.

SPECIMENS OF DESCRIPTION

1. THE STORM[1]

The door of the cavern was big enough to roll a hogshead in, and on one side of the door the floor stuck out a little bit and was flat and a good place to build a fire on. So we built it there and cooked dinner.

We spread the blankets inside for a carpet, and eat our dinner in there. We put all the other things handy at the back of the cavern. Pretty soon it darkened up and begun to thunder and lighten; so the birds was right about it. Directly it begun to rain, and it rained like all fury, too, and I never see the wind blow so. It was one of these regular summer storms. It would get so dark that it looked all blue-black outside, and lovely; and the rain would thrash along by so thick

[1]From *The Adventures of Huckleberry Finn*, Harper and Brothers. By permission of the publishers.

that the trees off a little ways looked dim and spider-webby; and here would come a blast of wind that would bend the trees down and turn up the pale underside of the leaves; and then a perfect ripper of a gust would follow along and set the branches to tossing their arms as if they was just wild; and next, when it was just about the bluest and blackest—fst! it was as bright as glory and you'd have a little glimpse of tree-tops a-plunging about, away off yonder in the storm, hundreds of yards further than you could see before; dark as sin again in a second, and now you'd hear the thunder let go with an awful crash and then go rumbling, grumbling, tumbling down the sky towards the under side of the world, like rolling empty barrels down stairs, where it's long stairs and they bounce a good deal, you know.

"Jim, this is nice," I says. "I wouldn't want to be nowhere else but here. Pass me along another hunk of fish and some hot corn-bread."—MARK TWAIN

2. Autumn Twilight in a Small, Medieval French Town[1]

It was September, 1429; the weather had fallen sharp; a flighty piping wind, laden with showers, beat about the township; and the dead leaves ran riot along the streets. Here and there a window was already lighted up; and the noise of men-at-arms making merry over supper within, came forth in fits and was swallowed up and carried away by the wind. The night fell swiftly; the flag of England, fluttering on the spire-top, grew ever fainter and fainter against the flying clouds—a black speck like a swallow in the tumultuous, leaded chaos of the sky. As the night fell the wind rose, and began to hoot under archways and roar amid the tree-tops in the valley below the town.

—ROBERT LOUIS STEVENSON

3. The Race

To a horse-lover, a great deal of the attraction and enjoyment of a race is to be found, not only on the track, but "behind the scenes" as well. Never go to a race and sit in the stands waiting for the starting-gun—go back to the stables, watch all the feverish last minute activity there, and it will be strange indeed if you do not become infected with some of that excitement which all track-addicts know.

This afternoon, as I arrive at the Woodbine track, few people are in the gaily-coloured stands, as the race is scheduled for half-past two, and it is not quite two o'clock now. Quite content, I wander back to

[1]From "The Sire de Maletroit's Door," Charles Scribner's Sons. By permission of the publishers.

the stables, enjoying the balmy spring afternoon and the smell of fresh hay. About a dozen horses are in the stalls along the muddy dirt road, and it is good to see such a fine collection of racers. Every eye bright and alert, polished coats glistening, proud heads tossing, it is impossible to say which will be the victor in an hour's time. Many people move around—the little negro groom, resplendent and beaming in his best livery, patting possessively his charge's gleaming neck, grinning proudly at whoever passes the stall; the trainer, inspecting the horse's feet, making a last-minute check-up; the owner, nervously pacing about, peering at his watch, and seeking reassurance from his trainer and the jockey; the jockey himself, who will have the responsibility of guiding his precious charge to victory; the buyer, sharp-eyed, looking for a good purchase, appraising every animal, and talking craftily with owners. All these play their part before the horses even leave the stalls.

And now, to return to the track. The stands have filled up, and only ten minutes remain till starting-time. There is a steady din throughout the stands. Candy vendors, in bright smocks, sell their candy, peanuts, and pop, to hundreds, bookies receive bets, and anxious betters watch the odds feverishly. Cameramen set up their tripods at the starting-gate and at the finishing-line, and the loud-speaker emits strange noises as it is being tuned. Then the announcer drones out the names of the entries. But wait! The horses are coming out. A hush falls over the crowd, as they line up at the starting-gate—a flag falls—a gun roars—and they're off!

There are few things more exhilaratingly beautiful than a horse-race on a cloudless afternoon. The sun picks out the gay flags of the stands, the brilliant satins of the jockeys, the gleaming flanks of the galloping studs, glints on the silver in the bridles, and turns to bright emerald the grass in the centre of the track.

From the very beginning, it is evident that this is a contest between two horses. They are running neck-and-neck—a chestnut ridden by a red-coated jockey, and a black urged on by a jockey in bright green. The odds are high on the chestnut, but the black is a newcomer, and his odds are low.

They are on their second lap, the chestnut in the lead, and the crowd shouts madly. Desperately the other jockey urges on the black and he comes up inch by inch. Only one more lap to go! The noise is deafening, but over it sounds the pounding of hoofs as the horses round the bend once more. The black is even closer, but the chestnut has a steady pace which has won for him many times. Now they're coming around for the last time, and it looks as if the chestnut has won. But no! With a last desperate effort, the jockey stands up in his stirrups, shouts and urges the black to a mighty effort. The crowd goes mad. And the black crosses the line half a length before the chestnut!

I return home, absurdly elated over winning fifty cents on my two-dollar bet, and resolved to return to this fascinating sport of kings as soon as possible.

VIVIEN HUDDART
(H. S. Student)

4. Northern Lights[1]

At midnight we noticed a strange, chill glare spreading from the northern horizon. In contrast with the warm velvet of the night sky, it was a weird radiance. We were witnessing the northern lights at their best. The spectral reflections radiated and extended to the east and west, shifting back and forth like curtains. Rods of frigid light—green, saffron, and purple—shot into the summit of the sky, faded away, and then reappeared seconds later more intense and breath-taking than before. We thought we overheard a faint crackle like the breaking of thin ice or the echo of electric sparks.

In brilliance and variety of colour the marvellous phenomenon resembled a nocturnal rainbow.

5. The Atomic Bombing of Nagasaki[2]

Even though we were turning away in the opposite direction, and despite the fact that it was broad daylight in our cabin, all of us became aware of a giant flash that broke through the dark barrier of our arc welder's lenses and flooded our cabin with intense light.

We removed our glasses after the first flash, but the light still lingered on, a bluish-green light that illuminated the entire sky. A tremendous blast wave struck our ship and made it tremble from nose to tail. This was followed by four more blasts in rapid succession, each resounding like the boom of cannon-fire hitting our plane from all directions.

Observers in the tail of our ship saw a giant ball of fire rise as though from the bowels of the earth, belching forth enormous white smoke rings. Next they saw a giant pillar of purple fire, 10,000 feet high, shooting upward with enormous speed.

By the time our ship had made another turn in the direction of the atomic explosion, the pillar of purple fire had reached the level of our altitude. Only about forty-five seconds had passed. Awe-struck, we watched it shoot upward like a meteor coming from the earth instead of from outer space, becoming ever more alive as it climbed skyward through the white clouds. It was no longer smoke, or dust, or even a cloud of fire. It was a living thing, a new species of being, born right before our incredulous eyes.

[1]From "Night Watch" by Bill Firstbrook, University of Toronto Schools, printed in *The Twig*, 1945. By permission of *The Twig*.
[2]By permission of the author and the *New York Times*.

At one stage of its evolution, covering millions of years in terms of seconds, the entity assumed the form of a giant square totem pole, with its base about three miles long, tapering off to about a mile at the top. Its bottom was brown, its centre was amber, its top white. But it was a living totem pole, carved with many grotesque masks grimacing at the earth.

Then, just when it appeared as though the thing had settled down into a state of permanence, there came shooting out of the top a giant mushroom that increased the height of the pillar to a total of 45,000 feet. The mushroom top was even more alive than the pillar, seething and boiling in a white fury of creamy foam, sizzling upwards, and then descending earthward, a thousand Old Faithful geysers rolled into one. In a few seconds it had freed itself from its gigantic stem and floated upward with tremendous speed, its momentum carrying it into the stratosphere to a height of about 60,000 feet.

But no sooner did this happen than another mushroom, smaller in size than the first one, began emerging from the pillar. As the first mushroom floated off into the blue, it changed its shape into a flower-like form, its giant petal curving downward, creamy-white outside, rose-coloured inside. It still retained that shape when we last gazed at it from a distance of 200 miles.

—WILLIAM L. LAURENCE

THE ROUND TABLE

1. Describe, in one sentence each, any five of the following (five sentences in all): an animal, a bird, a boy, a girl, a man, a voice, a flower, a pair of eyes, someone's hair, a laugh.

2. Bring to class and be prepared to read aloud one of the following:

    (1) The best description of a storm you ever read
    (2) The best description of a scene you ever read
    (3) The best description of a person you ever read
    (4) The best description of dogs you ever read
    (5) The best description of horses you ever read

3. Describe your most vivid childhood memory.

4. In what words would you suggest the sound of a typewriter, a sewing machine, a vacuum cleaner, a lawnmower, an aeroplane, sawing wood, frying, boiling, thunder, surf, a rifle, a shotgun?

5. Try to describe in a sentence any two of the following: the feel of silk, worsted, velvet, sandpaper, a just-caught fish, a cat's fur, a dog's nose, diving, riding rapidly with the windshield open, caught in a sudden shower of rain.

6. Try to describe in a sentence any two of the following: a bed

of sweet peas, hay, an old attic, a cellar, burning leaves, burning paper, cigar smoke, wood smoke, coal smoke.

7. Try to describe in a sentence any two of the following tastes: bacon, bananas, oranges, apples, orange marmalade, cheese, green apples, honey, coffee, vinegar.

8. Describe two of the following birds that are most familiar to you: an English sparrow (cock or hen), a redbird (cardinal), a robin, a wren, a crow, a bluejay, a woodpecker or sapsucker, a pigeon, a lark.

9. List the tastes in food and drink that you (*a*) like and (*b*) dislike. Try to describe one of each in a single sentence (two sentences in all).

10. Describe the scene when a long-winded visitor comes just as the family have packed a picnic lunch and are ready to get into the automobile for a day's outing. Introduce the mother, the father, a grown daughter, and a younger son. Use plenty of dialogue.

Subjects for Description

1. A Street in the Rain
2. The Spoiled Child
3. A Nervous Mother
4. The Deserted Farm
5. A Snowy Morning
6. The Old Oak
7. Class Dismissed
8. A Crowd Waiting for a Parade
9. While Waiting for Her to Come Downstairs
10. Pleasing Noises of a Large City (the Country)
11. Disagreeable Noises of a Large City (the Country)
12. Five Members of the Family Discussing What Kind of Dog They Shall Buy
13. Having a Group Picture Taken
14. Washing the Dog (Cat)
15. Stage Fright
16. When Father Is Ill
17. My Little Brother on Christmas Morning
18. The Barnyard on a Rainy Day
19. The Street I Live On
20. A Student's Room
21. After Church
22. Voices I Could Identify
23. When I Thought I Heard a Burglar
24. A Cat Stalking a Sparrow
25. An Old Landmark

26. Feeling Your Way in a Dark Room in Search of the Electric Light Switch
27. Night Sounds in the Woods
28. On the Bus
29. A Hen Protecting Her Chickens
30. A Cat Protecting Her Kittens
31. At a Bargain Counter
32. A Pawnshop Window
33. A Cat Washing Its Face
34. The "Limited" Goes Past
35. A Calm Night
36. A Cold Winter Morning
37. The Top Pantry Shelf
38. A Small Boy (Girl) Taking Medicine
39. After Company Has Gone
40. A Town Character
41. My Favourite Walk
42. Five Minutes to Six in a Five-and-Ten-Cent Store
43. Housecleaning Sounds
44. When Father Shaves
45. A Traffic Jam
46. A Display of Fireworks
47. Our Choir
48. The Auctioneer
49. The "Panhandler"
50. Waiting for the Train
51. The Attic on a Rainy Day
52. A Busy Machine
53. Blossom Time
54. A Skier (Figure Skater) in Action

CHAPTER XXV

Argument

Perhaps the principal objection to a quarrel is that it interrupts an argument.

—G. K. CHESTERTON

In the earlier chapters on the paragraph and on chain paragraphs we have studied how to express our thoughts clearly and effectively. (See pages 73-89 and 165-188.) Many of the themes we have written may have been themes of exposition. In exposition we try to make clear the basic facts about something such as how to make a cake, or the interesting features of a book. Sometimes in exposition we set forth our opinions and the bases upon which those opinions are founded. In all this the power to write clearly will stand us in good stead. In no field of writing will it prove more valuable than in the writing of argument.

Argument might be defined as "exposition with a bias". In argument we do more than set forth our opinions and the bases upon which they are founded; we try, in addition, to persuade the reader or the listener that our opinions, or our interpretations of facts, are better than his. The purpose of argument, then, is to persuade someone that upon some point where difference of opinion exists, our opinion is the right one. If our opinion is based upon facts which can be clearly demonstrated, and the opposing opinion is based upon ignorance of those facts, we should be able to convince an opponent merely by bringing the facts to his knowledge. To that extent argument is founded upon exposition, and ultimately the most successful argument will be that in which the writer or speaker most effectively marshals the facts to make the truth most clear.

But it is not always so easy to persuade others that we are right. For one thing, our opinions are not always based upon clearly demonstrable facts. We often, as we say, "put two and two together", and guess at conclusions; we draw inferences, probable conclusions to which known facts point but which they do not absolutely establish. In drawing inferences we display the complexity of our personalities. The emphasis which we give to one fact or deny to another, our prejudices, our emotions will often lead each of us to quite different inferences from the same facts. Here, then, argument comes into play. It will be necessary to convince our opponents that their interpretations of the facts are wrong.

Of course, people do not like to be proved wrong. In argument, therefore, we must somehow win a willing concession from our opponents. We must not only demonstrate by clear reasoning that our conclusions are logical, and that they follow naturally from the facts, but we must also argue so persuasively that our opponents will change their way of thinking upon the facts. The failure to win this concession very often turns an argument into a quarrel, for the quarrel is merely the resort to anger and perhaps force where persuasion has proved unsuccessful. We can be most persuasive if we observe the following rules:

(1) arrange ideas logically
(2) guard against being misled by emotion or prejudice
(3) show patience and understanding when dealing with the ignorance, prejudice, or emotional thinking of others.

It is as important to observe these rules in written argument as in spoken. We should develop our powers to observe them by constant practice in classroom discussions, in debate in student councils, and in articles or letters in the school paper.

THE ROUND TABLE

1. Write a letter to a friend urging the attractiveness of a seaside holiday.

   Write the friend's reply urging you to spend the summer in camp.

2. Put down the most persuasive arguments for having a recreation centre in your town.

   Put beside them the arguments which might be produced by those who oppose the recreation centre.

3. Prove to the satisfaction of your teacher that the new car you most like is really the best buy.

4. Write a letter to a newspaper urging immediate action in clearing a slum area.

1. Handling the Argument

As we take our practice steps in argument, we must learn not to develop bad habits. We must avoid behaving badly; we must also avoid "emotional thinking" by which we allow our feelings to control our reason and so deceive ourselves about the strength of our argument. We shall deal with them in turn.

(1) OUR BEHAVIOUR IN ARGUMENT

First of all, we must avoid becoming impatient with our opponent. If we become irritated by his refusal, or seeming refusal to accept our opinion or interpretation, we shall perhaps try being dogmatic. The dogmatic person, because he is too impatient to reason with his opponent, argues that his conclusion is right merely because he says so. He often becomes belligerent, trying to conquer by sheer volume of words or loudness of speech. Remember that over-emphasis is frequently an indication of weakness and uncertainty. Therefore, be patient and courteous. In the formal debate, quiet courtesy is encouraged by the rules of debating; one must always address the audience rather than the opposing debaters, and one must always refer to one's opponents in the third person as "the last speaker" or "the first speaker for the motion" or "my honourable opponents".

(2) EMOTIONAL THINKING

Sometimes the appeal to the emotions is a very strong appeal in argument, and it is a valid appeal so long as the emotion has some relation to the argument. But we deceive ourselves when we allow our reason to be swayed by appeals to emotions which have little or no relation to the point in question. We are all guided in our actions and our thinking by such emotions as love, fear, patriotism, self-esteem, the desire to belong to the group. Cunning rabble-rousers, cheap politicians, advertising quacks—all endeavour to substitute emotional thinking for reasoning in their audiences. By arousing prejudices and irrelevant emotions they may the better conceal the weakness of their logic. The manufacturers of soap stress the danger we run of being excluded from our group if we do not use their soap; the glamour advertisements, appealing to our self-esteem, suggest, sometimes quite wrongly, that we too can be beautiful like our favourite movie star; those who object to "foreigners" and wish to restrict immigration often carry their sentiment for the "Motherland" to ridiculous extremes. Their emotional thinking leads them to consider everything bad that is not British. Be wary of appeals to irrelevant emotion. Practise by looking carefully at the assertions of advertisements and by reading accurately the argument they present. When you argue, keep your own emotions under control.

2. The Materials of Argument

We shall discuss the materials of argument under three headings, The Proposition, The Issues, and The Proof.

(1) THE PROPOSITION

All argument must be upon some proposition or assertion which is debatable. Until this proposition is clearly, simply, and completely stated we can discuss indefinitely without forwarding our argument at all. For example, it is quite impossible to "argue" about the library. There are a thousand things we might say about it, but until we come to grips with some specific debatable statement regarding it, we would be like two blind-folded boxers in a twenty-foot ring. The assertions that "The library is very inefficiently run" or that "The library grant should be increased by one hundred dollars" are propositions about which there might be differences of opinion, and upon which we could have a reasonable argument. In setting forth our proposition we should observe the three following rules:

1. **Express in the proposition only one debatable idea.** Only confusion will result from argument upon such a proposition as this: "The world needs an international police force, and the British Empire should proceed to organize one".

2. **Define precisely the meaning of words used in the proposition.** If we fail to do so, we shall find ourselves arguing at cross-purposes, with no prospect of reaching a conclusion. If, for example, our proposition is "It is better to go to a small university than a large one" we shall have to define what we mean by "large" and "small" and perhaps what we mean by "better".

3. **Limit the proposition in scope sufficiently so that a conclusion may be reached.** In other words, the argument should be confined to a few debatable points. An argument upon the proposition "A scientific education is more valuable than an education in the humanities" is too broad to admit of any conclusion. People do have to make up their minds on such questions, but they do so on very broad bases, not upon points that are easily debatable.

(2) THE ISSUES

The debatable points referred to in the last paragraph are the **issues** in the argument. They are the points upon which difference of opinion is likely to be most marked. In the preparation of your argument, it is wise to clear away any issues upon which both sides will be in agreement. Concentrate upon the debatable issues. You can best do this by writing a series of questions which might arise in either your mind or the mind of your opponents as you think about the proposition. Try to discover the answers to those questions as each side might present them in turn. If, for example, our proposition were "The state should afford free university training for qualified matriculants" some of the debatable issues might arise out of questions like the following:

How would such a policy affect university attendance?
Could our present universities handle such a programme?
What would be the financial problem in such an undertaking?
Should we revise our standards of university entrance?
What services would be provided—free board, lodging, books?
Would there be regimentation of students into particular courses?

THE ROUND TABLE

1. Which of the following would you accept as satisfactory debatable propositions? Give reasons for rejecting the others.

(1) The failure of the rugby team this season.
(2) The editor of the school paper should be elected by the students, and he should represent the school at all official functions.
(3) The school board should provide all pupils' supplies free of charge.
(4) Basketball has more interest for the spectator than football.
(5) Honesty is the best policy.
(6) The evils of being too self-satisfied.
(7) Every high-school student should receive instruction in swimming.
(8) The value of good books.
(9) The librarian should be given an annual grant for the purchase of new books.
(10) Examinations are unfair estimates of ability, and promotions in school should be based either on objective tests or on term work.

2. Consider the proposition "The school-leaving age should be 18". Write a list of about fifteen to twenty questions to which your argument might give the answers. Then try to group your questions under

two or three main "issues" such as "The drawbacks of the present leaving age", "The benefit to the student of the higher leaving age", and so on.

3. What would be the main issues in a discussion upon the proposition that there should be no speed limit on highways outside the city?

4. After deciding the main issues, list the arguments both for and against the proposition "The milk industry should be operated by the municipality".

3. Proof

We are familiar with the word "proof" in our work in geometry, though our use of mathematical symbols, which are merely short cuts for words, sometimes obscures the fact that we are arguing and often reduces geometric proof to mere memorization. We use the word "proof" also in our reports of scientific experiments in which we try to establish the truth of a scientific law, or a conclusion that we have drawn. We say, for instance, that "The volume of a gas varies inversely with the pressure". To state the proposition and to insist upon it is not sufficient to prove it. We must bring forth our **evidence.** For any debatable proposition, those of an opposing opinion will bring forth evidence to contradict ours. In formal argument we call this contrary evidence **refutation** or **rebuttal.** Frequently rebuttal is only negative evidence—evidence that what has been asserted is not true. This is not sufficient to establish that a given alternative is necessarily true, for the evidence that *A is not true* does not establish that *B is true.* You cannot argue that a tree must be a maple because it is not a pine. For any positive conclusion we must produce positive evidence.

Evidence falls into two main categories: first, **evidence of fact**; and second, **evidence of inference.** If so-called facts were unquestionably true, and our inferences were always justified, arguments would be quickly settled. Because of human fallibility, however, it is necessary to subject all evidence to the closest examination to test its validity.

(1) EVIDENCE OF FACT

Let us consider first evidence of fact. There are two kinds of factual evidence: (1) **evidence of observation** and (2) **evidence of authority.**

Evidence of observation is the statement of that which we ourselves have observed and know to be true. It is true that Mr. Mackenzie King was the leader of the Liberal party in Canada; it is also true that he held office as Prime Minister longer than any other man. These are facts. That Mr. King was a popular Prime Minister is only an inference from these facts and cannot be established by observation alone.

Evidence of authority is the presentation of facts which are vouched for by the observation of those upon whose accuracy we rely. We must rely upon the meteorological office for records of variations in temperature and humidity; we must accept reports and statistics prepared by trained economists since we have not access to the sources of their information nor the time to repeat their studies. We may quote these authorities as evidence. But we must remember that evidence of authority will be strong only so long as the authority is recognized as dependable and up-to-date. There is no value in quoting authorities who are not known, or not recognized as worthy of our trust. It is important to question any "authority" who is likely to be unreliable or who has some personal interest which is affected by the evidence he gives.

(2) EVIDENCE OF INFERENCE

Under evidence of inference we must mention **evidence of circumstances,** or **circumstantial evidence** which consists of observed facts from which some conclusion may be drawn even when no absolutely conclusive observed evidence may be present. It may be true that no one saw Binks drawing pictures in a fellow-student's notebook. It may be possible, however, to conclude that he did so if

(a) the notebook was defaced during a classroom period
(b) the drawings were done in green pencil
(c) the stub of a green pencil is in Binks's pocket.

Note that the evidence would lose most of its value if another green pencil stub were found in the waste basket.

Again, there is evidence of analogy which rightly or wrongly is based upon the assumption, that what happens in one situation will happen in another situation which resembles the first in many respects but which is not absolutely identical. By way of illustration we may say that as sons show respect for their mothers and are quick to defend them in danger, so, by analogy, we can account for the loyalty with which the Dominions rallied to the defence of Great Britain, the Motherland, in two World Wars. In such analogies, the similarity of the situations is assumed and may, of course, be entirely false. Suffice it to say that argument by analogy, and argument upon circumstantial evidence are very uncertain, and taken by themselves are not conclusive proof.

Let us resolve, therefore, to test all evidence by submitting it to such questioning as this:

(1) Have we observed sufficiently closely or examined a sufficient amount of evidence to justify drawing a conclusion? (For some statements it might be necessary to examine ten thousand cases.)
(2) In our anxiety to find a conclusion are we
  (a) allowing our observation to be prejudiced?
  (b) deliberately concealing evidence which might prove the contrary?
(3) Are the authorities we quote
  (a) unbiased observers?
  (b) familiar with the most up-to-date information?
  (c) qualified to speak on this particular issue?
  (Most newspapers have a definite political bias.)
(4) Does the evidence exclude any other conclusion?
(5) Are the inferences we have drawn justified by the facts?
(6) Is any analogy we have used reasonable and valid?

THE ROUND TABLE

1. Suppose that by actual count of 10,000 persons it was discovered that 20% of them suffered from pyorrhea. Could you safely argue that one-fifth of your class suffers from pyorrhea?

2. When food goes bad we throw it out. When a boy breaks a school rule, he should be expelled. Is this a good analogy?

3. On what conditions would you accept the opinions of the following persons on the subjects indicated:
   (a) a famous airman on the political situation in Germany
   (b) a clergyman upon Russia
   (c) a millionaire mining prospector on the selection of a university president
   (d) your best friend on your chances of getting a job
   (e) a boy suddenly wakened from a sound sleep about an accident seen from his bedroom
   (f) your English teacher on your skill in writing.

4. Two Types of Reasoning

(1) INDUCTIVE REASONING

When we argue, we move from that which is accepted to that which we wish to establish and have accepted. Sometimes we bring together many items of evidence all of which seem to point towards a broad general conclusion. From these items of evidence we can frame a generalization which will cover or include all the known evidence. Our generalization then becomes an accepted fact and we govern our behaviour by it. When in argument we move thus from the particular instance to the general conclusion, we are said to argue **inductively** or to use **inductive reasoning.** Many experiences have been brought forth to establish such generalizations as these: "It is dangerous to drive with badly-worn tires", "It is best to stay with a tipped canoe", "Dirt harbours disease". These generalizations are based on good evidence and are therefore valid. If we should discover evidence which seems not to support our generalization, we must either correct our generalization, or account for the inconsistent evidence. This is another way of saying that we must not generalize too hastily from insufficient evidence. We could not say that skating is a dangerous sport because occasionally a person falls and breaks an arm.

(2) DEDUCTIVE REASONING

Sometimes we start our argument from a generalization which is accepted by everyone. We then go on to show that this generalization is applicable to a particular instance. Everyone will admit that smoking is very dangerous where paints and varnishes are stored. If a particular room in a factory houses paint, we shall recognize that the generalization applies and shall forbid smoking. When we thus proceed from the general rule to the particular instance, we argue **deductively,** or use **deductive reasoning.** In its simplest form, deductive reasoning can be presented in the **syllogism.** The syllogism consists of three main parts: the generalization which is known as the major premise; the application of the generalization to the particular situation, known as the minor premise; and the conclusion which follows naturally from the two premises taken together.

You may find that it will help you to think clearly if you try putting your argument into the form of syllogisms. You may detect weaknesses which might otherwise be concealed in the flow of many words. Keep in mind that your major premise must be true and admit of no exceptions, that your minor premise must deal with an example covered by the major premise. The use of simple diagrams like those below will often help to keep the argument clear. If we take the generalization "All downtown intersections are places that need signal lights" and the statement "King and James is a downtown intersection", then the conclusion must follow that "King and James should have a signal light". The largest circle represents "places that need signal lights"; the smaller circle represents all downtown intersections and falls entirely within the larger; and the smallest represents King and James and it in turn falls within the smaller circle.

In diagram B the intersection at 45th and Main falls within the circle of those that require signal lights, but not within the circle of downtown intersections. It is not covered by the same premises as the argument for establishing lights at King and James. It is presumably a busy intersection though not downtown. What premises would you use to justify putting lights at 45th and Main?

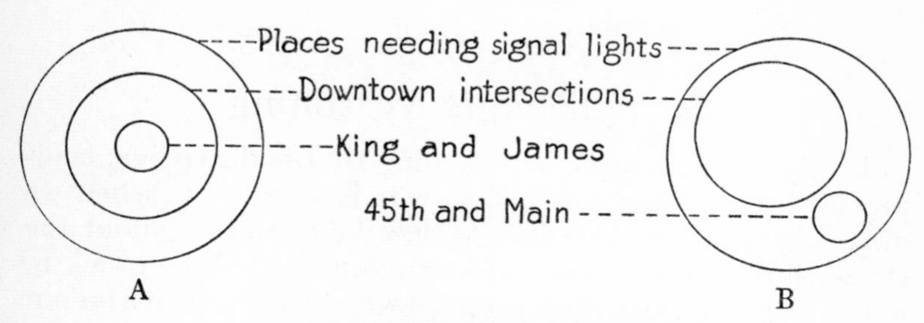

THE ROUND TABLE

1. For each of the following draw a large circle to represent those who study Latin, and then draw the arrangement of smaller circles to represent the class and the individual. Sometimes there is more than one possible arrangement.

(a) All members of 2A study Latin and Halliday is in 2A
(b) None of 2C studies Latin and Miss Harkins is in 2C
(c) Some members of 2C study Latin and Brewer is one who does
(d) Some members of 2C study Latin and Miss Marsh is one who does not
(e) Not all members of 2C study Latin and Jackson is in 2C
(f) No member of 2C studies Latin and Arthur is in 2A.

2. If you have done the first exercise carefully you will have realized the confusion that may arise when we are talking of "some" and not "all" the members of a group. Now you can go on to point out the major and minor premises upon which the following arguments are based. Are they sound arguments?

(a) He ought to give up all games so that his work will improve.
(b) Bill is a snob. He never comes to the school dances.
(c) She stays home every night and does her homework. No wonder she is unpopular.
(d) Certainly the strike was started by communists. Don't they always start strikes?

(e) We ought to pay miners high wages. Their work is very dangerous.
(f) Street car fares should be reduced now that the company is showing a profit.
(g) The house is a fire hazard. The wiring was not done properly.
(h) This paint brush is not my father's. He would never leave a brush in that condition.
(i) I guess Camp Wigwam is on a canoe trip. Here is another dirty campsite.

5. Fallacious Reasoning

Fallacious reasoning is reasoning that is deceptive, leading to unjustifiable conclusions. It is very easy, when we are eager to prove a point, to deceive ourselves about the strength of our argument. Our opponents will be quick to notice our fallacious reasoning; so we must be always on our guard to avoid it. We shall deal with only a few forms of fallacious reasoning, and we shall consider them under three headings:

1. Faulty observation of evidence
2. Faulty judgment upon evidence
3. Faulty expression.

(1) FAULTY OBSERVATION OF EVIDENCE

Our observation is at fault when we do not note all the facts that are relevant to the discussion, or when we fail to distinguish the facts which are relevant from those which have no bearing on the discussion. Prejudice easily leads us to faulty observation. Those who are prejudiced against such minority groups in our communities as the French, the Japanese, the Negroes, the pacifists, will quickly note the faults of these groups. Any isolated happening will be seized upon to prove that they are ignorant, unco-operative, unpatriotic, or disloyal. The prejudiced observer will completely overlook the rich contribution which any one of these groups has made to our culture or our thinking. The prejudiced observer does not see all the facts. The relevance of facts is also important. You would be foolish to assume that you passed the algebra examination because you carried a rabbit's foot, or that cotton wool was cold because it looked white like snow. The rabbit's foot and the whiteness of cotton wool are not relevant to these conclusions.

(2) FAULTY JUDGMENT UPON EVIDENCE

Our judgment upon evidence can be at fault when we assume that what happens after a given event is necessarily caused by that event. This kind of reasoning is at the root of all popular superstitions such as the belief that thirteen at a table is bound to have unhappy consequences. Again, we must not, from a group of possible causes for an event, select the wrong one and base an argument upon it. Often our prejudices will lead us to leap to conclusions when other conclusions are actually more reasonable. It is easy, for example, to convince ourselves that poor marks in an examination are due to the harshness of the examiner, or to the fact that the examination time-table was bad.

These might be the reasons, but the chances are that our poor marks are due to inadequate preparation. Our judgment may be wrong, too, if we assume that what happens two or three times is bound to happen always. We may need the evidence of a thousand cases to establish such a general rule.

Finally, we should not assume that a change in one relationship necessarily involves a correspondingly equal change in some other relationship. We would be wrong if we thought that two pounds of lead would fall twice as fast as one pound, or that we could run twelve miles in an hour because we can run one mile in five minutes.

(3) FAULTY EXPRESSION

Under faulty expression we shall group several forms of fallacious reasoning that are due to the careless use of words.

The first is **ambiguity.** Ambiguity occurs when we use the same expression in two different senses. We may assume, by way of illustration, that rigid discipline is necessary in learning composition. We know that rigid discipline can be maintained by the use of corporal punishment. Would we be right in saying that corporal punishment is necessary in teaching composition? Surely not. In this argument "rigid discipline" is used in two differing senses, first as self-discipline and secondly as enforced discipline. Ambiguity may also occur if we confuse the word "all" meaning "all together" with "all" meaning "each one". It would not be fair to say that each member of a rival school was a poor sport because the spectators from that school booed the referee at a rugby match. It is true that the Italians are a musical people, but the Italian organ grinder is not necessarily a musical genius. The converse of the previous form of ambiguity is the hasty assumption that what is true of individuals taken separately is necessarily true of the same individuals taken as a group. A group of all-star hockey players may on occasions be defeated by a well-coordinated team of less brilliant players.

Other forms of faulty expression will be illustrated briefly.

Begging the question. This is false reasoning which hopes to convince by cunningly assuming that the point at issue is already proved. This is done by prefacing the issue by a phrase like "It is only too clear that", or "No one but a fool would argue that ——". Sometimes, as in the following example, the trick is to assume as acceptable a general thought which includes the point at issue: "You should not have a student council because any form of student council is bound to be a poor form of government."

Arguing in a circle. As the name implies, this uses a premise to prove a conclusion which in turn supports the premise. It can best be represented thus:

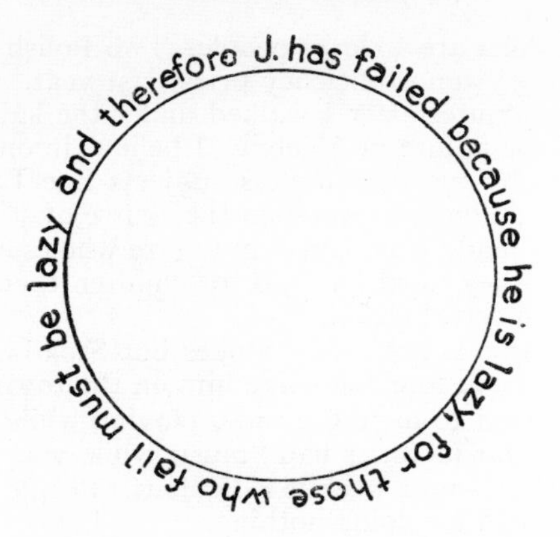
J. has failed because he is lazy, for those who fail must be lazy and therefore J. has failed

Irrelevance. One form of this is the attack on the person rather than on the issue. We hope to win by calling our opponent unpleasant names such as "Red" or "scab".

Reductio ad absurdum. This is the attempt to make an opposing argument seem ridiculous by carrying it to an extreme. Here is an example. "You say that you want the students to have some voice in school administration. Why, pretty soon you will have them hiring the teachers!" You can counter this form of faulty reasoning by pointing out that one need not maintain either of two extreme positions. While it is true that black is the opposite of white, there are nevertheless many shades of grey between the two extremes.

THE ROUND TABLE

Point out all the examples of unsound reasoning in the following arguments. In each case name the fallacy and show why the reasoning is faulty. Three of the arguments are logical.

(1) We certainly need a swimming pool in the recreation centre because a pool brings the crowd. We shall need all the patronage we can get if we are going to spend so much on the building.

(2) Our cottage is a two-hour drive from here along a road very treacherous in the dark. Since darkness falls at eight, we should leave before six to be safe.

(3) The Poles are a clever people. Two Polish students at our school won proficiency prizes last year.
(4) Five minutes after I walked under the ladder, I got news of my failure in Algebra. I believe in omens.
(5) It is obvious that useless subjects like Latin and Greek should be dropped from the course of study.
(6) Foods made from cereal grain are wholesome for children. Whiskey must be good for children then, for it is made from cereal grain.
(7) His name is not really Stokes but Stokowski. We should not have foreigners like him on the town council.
(8) It is good to have the radio playing while you study. All the war factories had "music while you work".
(9) The forty-hour week is ridiculous. People simply want to be paid for doing nothing.
(10) We should promote Stephenson for he has clearly demonstrated his ability to handle the work.
(11) This radio is priced at $50. I think we ought to have the other at $100 because it will be twice as good.
(12) Miss Blank is a poor teacher. I failed in her subject last year.
(13) For ten years the Newtown High School has maintained an average of 92% successful candidates in departmental examinations. The teaching must be effective.
(14) Democracy is a failure. Anyone can see how much more efficient a dictatorship is.
(15) It will rain on the twenty-fourth of May. It always rains on a holiday.

6. The Brief

One step in the preparation of effective argument remains to be discussed, the writing of the argument **brief.** The brief is the well-ordered setting out in tabular form of the issues and evidence upon which proof of the proposition is based. In the brief we demonstrate the power to marshal the forces of our argument in the most effective fashion. If we pay strict attention to the form of our brief, we shall have our argument under perfect control. We shall be able not only to test the strength of each step in our argument, but to establish the relative value of each step, and so our argument will move with clarity and convincing power to its goal.

The form of the brief is very important. The brief begins by firmly stating the proposition to be proved. It then progresses from the proposition to each main supporting argument in turn, each again expressed in a sentence. Within each supporting argument, it moves through each subordinate supporting argument until it reaches the point of evidence which is least in importance. Each in turn is expressed in a complete sentence and is joined to the preceding statement by a conjunction like *for* or *because.* Thus the most minor step in the development of the argument supports a larger step and it in turn a still larger step until the proposition provides the coping-stone to the whole structure.

The preparation of the brief will reveal any weakness in each step. We must then correct even the smallest weakness if the whole argument is not to suffer. Be sure, therefore, that your brief consists of a series of complete statements, each properly connected to its supporting statement. Lay out your brief in such a way that by lettering and indentation those steps which are equal and those steps which are subordinate in importance will be easily seen, so that the whole process of your reasoning will be clear at a glance. The following pattern will make the technique clear.

The Main Issue Stated
- I First main supporting argument
    - A Evidence supporting I
        1. Evidence supporting IA
        2. Evidence supporting IA
            - (a) Evidence supporting IA2
            - (b) Evidence supporting IA2
- II Second main supporting argument
    - A Evidence supporting II
    - B Evidence supporting II
    - C Evidence supporting II
        1. Evidence supporting IIC and so on.

You will, of course, use only as many headings, sub-headings, and sub-sub-headings as your argument requires, but the important thing is that you use a uniform scheme of headings which will keep your relative values clear. The accomplished writer of argument may do much of this automatically and unconsciously, but the student writer will be well advised, whether in debate or in formal written argument, to write out the brief in complete form.

In his essay on Education in *Proper Studies* Mr. Aldous Huxley writes enthusiastically about the Dalton Plan of instruction. This is a scheme whereby students are guided in their studies rather than formally taught, and under which individual assignments of study are completed by students at their own speeds of work. Under the Dalton Plan rigid time-tables and formal classes cease to be of importance. Mr. Huxley, after defining the scheme and illustrating its methods, proceeds to argue as follows. The completed argument can be found in his *Proper Studies*.

Brief on the Dalton Plan

The Dalton Plan is superior to any other educational method because

I. Older systems were harmful in their effects because,
  A. They were too rigid because
    1. They did not consider individual differences
    2. They forced individuals into conventional patterns.

II. The Dalton system is beneficial in its effects because
  A. It allows freedom to the individual because
    1. It allows for variation in ability because
      (a) Children can work at speeds normal to them
    2. The individual can develop his own personality because
      (a) The bright student can advance beyond his years
      (b) The slow child becomes a more effective student because
        (i) He is not unnaturally hurried
        (ii) He is not handicapped by thinking himself stupid
    3. Students of outstanding ability can develop their fullest powers
    4. Students with obvious weaknesses are given opportunity to correct these weaknesses.

III. The Dalton learning process is more effective as a means of learning because
   A. Children are not taught mechanically
   B. Work is done more consistently because
      1. Children work as individuals
      2. Even the lazy students must work harder to complete assignments
   C. Students remember better what they have learned because
      1. They are not passively accepting ready-made knowledge
      2. They have learned the art of teaching themselves.

IV. The Dalton Plan achieves good discipline because
   A. The students are not mischievous because
      1. They are busy at their work
      2. They are interested in their studies
      3. They have no desire to create difficulty
   B. A class from the London slums under the Dalton Plan were models of behaviour for,
      1. They were courteous and independent
      2. Their manners were good but easy
      3. They worked industriously because
         (a) They did not fear their teachers
         (b) They regarded their teachers as friends
         (c) They moved about freely and easily
      4. Their behavior was a marked contrast to that of the average class because
         (a) They did not observe an unnatural strained silence in the classroom
         (b) They did not break out into uproar at recess
         (c) They behaved like rational responsible beings.

In the actual writing of the theme each of these headings will naturally be expressed more fully and will be enriched by comment and illustration. The above brief, since it is merely an extract from an essay, lacks an introduction and a conclusion which would define the issue and terms, and sum up the argument, respectively. It will serve, however, as a model on which you can construct your own argument briefs. Keep always in mind the fundamental rules for effective argument:

(1) Define your issue clearly
(2) Think clearly and rationally
(3) Argue calmly and logically
(4) Write with emphasis and conviction.

THE ROUND TABLE

1. Proposition. *The speed limit on the highway should be abolished.* Select the three or four main issues in the following list and group the others with them in a brief.

(1) An arbitrary speed limit has no real value
(2) More accidents occur in the city than on the highway
(3) To abolish the speed limit would be beneficial
(4) Slow drivers hold up long queues of cars
(5) Drivers vary greatly in their ability to drive
(6) A truck may be out of control at 30 miles per hour
(7) Inexperienced drivers are more numerous in cities
(8) Police officers could more profitably be used elsewhere than in checking speeders
(9) Some nervous drivers are dangerous even at slow speeds
(10) There are fewer driving hazards on the highway
(11) The worst offenders on highways are the very slow drivers
(12) Motorists would be more conscious of safety precautions if there were no limit
(13) Drivers in queues become impatient
(14) A new car may be perfectly safe at 70 miles per hour
(15) Safety depends on many factors other than speed
(16) The number of accidents due to speed is relatively small.

2. Prepare a proposition and a supporting brief upon issues arising from the following questions:

(1) Is our country less wealthy in forest products than it was fifty years ago?
(2) To what causes is the present condition attributed?
(3) What provision is being made to counteract this situation?
(4) How can these methods be made more effective?

3. Select three or four main issues upon which to base your argument upon any of the following propositions. Prepare your brief and write the argument.

(1) Operating a paper route is good training for business
(2) The best time to study is before breakfast in the morning
(3) Every adolescent should have a hobby
(4) Games should be compulsory for all those in school who are physically fit
(5) All secondary schools should be co-educational
(6) Every student in Canadian High Schools should speak French
(7) It is better to buy than to rent a house

4. Choose any subject for argument listed on pages 487-497, and after clearly defining your proposition write your argument.

5. Debate in class one of the following propositions:
   (1) Organized sport should be permitted on Sundays
   (2) Midnight shows should be forbidden by law
   (3) Our country should require one year's military training of every citizen who is physically fit
   (4) The present schemes of educational broadcasting are unsatisfactory.

CHAPTER XXVI

The Personal Essay

It is myself I pourtraye.—MONTAIGNE, 1580

A personal essay may be about anything in the heavens above, the earth beneath, or the waters under the earth. Nothing in life is too large or too small, too sad or too funny, too weighty or too trivial, to sparkle for a moment in the white light of the essayist's reason or to glow in the rainbow tints of his imagination. In the table of contents of a recent collection of essays[1] are to be found the following diverse titles: "On *And*", "A Little Debit in Your Tonneau", "The Truth about Women", "He Tries a Cafeteria", "In Praise of a Lawnmower", "Holding a Baby", "Concerning Revolving Doors", "On Wearing a Hat", and "Talkability".

In form, too, the personal essay is varied and elastic. It has no set form, no outward pattern by which it can be recognized. A personal essay is indefinite because its sole purpose is to reflect its writer's mood or to voice his feeling. About all we can say of it is that if it isn't interesting, it is negligible.

Thus the virtue of a personal essay comes not from its subject but from its writer. In the words of a modern English novelist: "An essayist, indeed, is a kind of autobiographer, one who begins anywhere and is always beginning over again. Our indifference to his subject is the mark of a real essayist. We do not care a fig what Lamb writes about, just as we do not care what an old friend talks about; so long as Lamb writes, the old friend talks, that is good

[1]Raymond Woodbury Pence, *Essays by Present-Day Writers*, Macmillan Company.

enough for us."[1] It is the writer's personality that attracts us, revealing itself in unexpected turns of thought, in new and original ways of looking at things, in flashes of fun and sadness, in cordial sympathy and in simple kindness of judgment.

One person may travel through Europe, and return only to bore us, but another cannot take a bus ride or go to the corner drug store without making us sorry when he stops talking about it. It is that kind of person who writes good personal essays.

1. Writing the Personal Essay

Because the personal essay is both highly personal and exceedingly varied, no definite pattern or prescription can be given for writing it. The best plan is to read thoughtfully the personal essays in some good collection. A number of these collections will be in your school library. Your teacher will suggest the titles of half-a-dozen or more essays in them for your reading.

(1) SEVEN SUGGESTIONS

In choosing a subject, in settling on your mood and the approach to it, and in writing out the essay, consider the seven following suggestions.

1. **The subject does not matter much.** It is your attitude toward it, your mood, that makes or breaks the essay. Among possible fields for subjects are the manners, morals, and customs of today, either considered by themselves or in contrast to those of former times; interesting animals, persons, or places; authors, books, plays, stories, or poems; your own personal experiences, recollections, opinions, and confessions; the world of nature in any of its varied manifestations—bird, beast, tree, flower, river, lake, or season; a character sketch; your own fads, foibles, hobbies, prejudices,

[1]J. B. Priestley, "Test of a Good Novel", *English Journal*, Vol. 18, 1929, p. 330.

whims, impressions, moods, desires, feelings, fancies gay and fancies grave; in short, anything at all that concerns you personally and that you have strong feelings or decided opinions about. From one of the fields named above you can select a subject that fits you individually as your glove your hand.

2. **Your approach to your subject should be frank and intimate.** Remember that the appeal of your essay to others will come not from the subject but from your attitude toward it, from your own thoughts and feelings concerning it—in short from the way you reveal yourself as you talk about it. Avoid stiffness, formality, dignity. As was said in connection with the friendly letter, "Be yourself". "Be yourself", it might be added, at your best, at your highest pitch of wit, individuality, observation, and sympathy. Try to write as you would talk to a close friend sitting in the woods on the bank of a stream as twilight comes down or as you would do before a leaping log fire in the winter time, with the light turned low and the wind tugging at the windows. Let us see your real self.

3. Because it is personal and frank, **the light personal essay has a casual, informal tone which no other form of writing except the friendly letter has.** It does not begin with a sentence of enumeration naming over the topics to be discussed and telling us in advance what is coming. It begins suddenly and unexpectedly, with the air of an old friend suddenly joining us in a walk and starting in to tell us an interesting experience or a funny story. Consider how informal—and how attractive—are the opening sentences of the following essays:

SUMMER

If, like me, you are more interested in seeing things happen than in seeing them when they have happened, you will not be such an advocate of Summer as of other, any other, seasons.

—MAURICE HEWLETT

The Master

The master of a ship I remember first as a slim lad, with a shy smile, and large hands that were lonely beyond his outgrown, reefer jacket.—H. M. TOMLINSON

Family Group

One of the things which make children so expensive—and it is an item which nobody seems to budget for in advance—is that at least once a year it becomes necessary to have them photographed.

—JAN STRUTHER

Americans Are Queer

Americans are queer people: they can't rest.—STEPHEN LEACOCK

On Lying in Bed

Lying in bed would be an altogether perfect and supreme experience if only one had a coloured pencil long enough to draw on the ceiling.—GILBERT K. CHESTERTON

The light essay not only begins casually and informally, but proceeds on its way informally and easily. Colloquial language, slang, and exclamations all find a place if needed. The paragraphing is loose and seems done in a happy-go-lucky manner. Even the sentence structure is relaxed, and in order to build up a desired effect words and phrases and clauses are allowed to do the work of sentences. Formal transitions like *first*, *secondly*, *in the next place*, are conspicuously absent. As we read, we almost feel that most of the laws of composition are temporarily repealed, and that the writer is taking a vacation from serious work. We are also apt to feel that it is no trouble to write a light essay, and that we could toss one off in half the time it takes to write a serious theme.

4. Be not deceived. **Informality is not carelessness, and some of the most attractive strokes and happiest effects result from long, thoughtful effort and frequent revisions.** A bright, careless air of ease and naturalness is much harder to achieve than a more serious, explanatory style. It is much easier, for example, to write a perfect sentence of enumera-

tion like those described on pages 175-176 than it is to start an essay off on exactly the right note through such happy openings as those quoted on the two preceding pages. As the story-essayist William Saroyan expressed it: "A beginning is always difficult, for it is no simple matter to choose from language the one bright word which shall live forever." The more we study sentences like these the more we realize their artistry. Remember that the highest art is to conceal art, and the reason that such work seems easy and spontaneous is that the author toiled long and arduously over it. In your own work, too, do not forget what was said about the value of revision. You will probably have to go over your essay not once but several times, in different moods, to make it what you want it.

5. As a matter of fact **what holds the light essay together and keeps it from flying off in fragments into space is the writer's mood.** This mood may be anything—mock indignation, mock despair, gentle satire, gaiety, whimsical nonsense, sadness, wistfulness, yearning, or sheer nonsense. Whatever it is, however, it is the essay's reason for being, and holds the essay in itself as a soap bubble holds its colours and its own shimmer. The mood gives unity to the whole, and however random and unrelated the different parts may seem, they all cohere in the central feeling. The essay may be narrative in tone, or it may be largely descriptive; but it is not told for the sake of its story or its description. It is told for the sake of the author's mood; and whether narrative or descriptive, what chiefly matters is not what the writer saw or what happened to him, but how he feels about it. The mood, the feeling, is the thing.

6. Whatever other qualities we may try to write into our light essays, we should do all that lies within our power to **be whimsical, humorous, and unusual.** This is not easy on paper. We laugh and joke and make ourselves very entertaining when among friends, but we too often put on a long face and pull a stiff wooden overcoat over our feelings when we take pen in hand. It may be hard to be whimsical or

funny; it is impossible unless we were born that way. The point here is to encourage any, even the least, spark of fun we may have to shine forth in our writing. If we can't be funny we can at any rate try to say witty, unusual, or unexpected things. Say anything except the expected thing; take any attitude except the usual one. Recall here again one of the sayings that follow the title page of this book: Learning to write is a serious business, but it need not be a solemn one.

7. In the last place, **get as bright and attractive a title as you can.** The title is your invitation to the reader. It is bone-of-the-bone and flesh-of-the-flesh of what you are writing. Usually you can get a better title after you have written the essay than before. Don't think you have to write your title across the page first and then begin your opening paragraph. You must of course have definitely in mind your *subject*—that is, what you are going to write about; but your *title*, or what name you give it, can very well wait till last. Many professional writers write their essays or stories first and then cast about on all sides, sometimes for days and weeks, for a good title.

In conclusion, not everyone is fitted by nature to write light essays. It may be that you are made of sterner stuff, and do not share your feelings easily with others. In this case your field is the expository essay, and you should put redoubled effort on that. If, however, you can write informally, whimsically, and humorously, you will become an increasing source of pleasure both to yourself and to others.

Suggested Titles for Light Essays

1. Fashions
2. Fat Men
3. On Spanking Children
4. More About Grapefruit
5. Reminiscences on Seeing My Shoes in a Row
6. The Fun of Being Poor
7. The Disadvantages of Having Ears
8. The Cruelty of Children to Parents

9. The Bad Result of Good Intentions
10. Noses
11. On Being Teased
12. Women Should Propose
13. How Colours Affect Me
14. Brighter Clothes for Men
15. The Beauty of Weeds
16. In Defence of Laziness
17. What Animal I Should Like to Be for a Day
18. On Getting Up in the Morning
19. On Being Cheerful before Breakfast
20. On Being an Only Child
21. Rich Uncles
22. Maiden Aunts
23. Hitchhiking—by a Hitchhiker
24. Hitchhiking—by a Car Driver
25. Garden Pests
26. On the Word "Don't"
27. In Defence of Rainy Days
28. Handshakes
29. Inventions I Should Like to See
30. Ghosts I Should Like to Meet
31. What's in a Name?
32. Getting Away From It All
33. On Being Small (Tall)
34. Hair Cuts
35. The Absurdities of English Spelling
36. Balancing That Budget
37. Sleeping Outdoors
38. On Sunburn
39. Old Clothes
40. My Pet Aversion
41. Those Hats!
42. Pests I Have Known
43. "They Say"
44. On Being Owned by a Summer Place
45. The Art of Doing without Things
46. Telephone Manners
47. Those Good Old Days
48. Some Reflections on Bridge
49. Modern Chivalry

THE ROUND TABLE

1. Looking back upon your English course this year, about how many explanatory themes have you written as compared with verse, incident, description, or informal essays?

2. If you have not read them, look up Lamb's "Dream Children" and "Dissertation on Roast Pig". They are famous personal essays.

3. Taking suggestions from Addison's *Sir Roger de Coverley Papers*, satirize gently some modern fad, foible, custom, or type of person that has fallen under your observation recently.

4. Which, if any, of the personal essays you read previously to starting this chapter could you recommend to the class as interesting?

5. Speaking of humour, what is the funniest (*a*) poem, (*b*) story, (*c*) essay or sketch you ever read? Give the class the benefit of it.

Essays By Students

I

Reminiscences on Seeing My Shoes in a Row

Shoes are interesting things. I have a passion for them myself; but, unlike most people, I do not think of them merely as a very important item in my wardrobe. With a slight stretch of the imagination, I am able to see in them friendly little story-tellers, each with its own particular chapter of my life's story to relate. From silver dancing slippers to well-worn brogues, my collection of shoes stands ready to remind me of days gone by.

The ridiculous network of thin leather straps, which claims the title of "dancing slippers", always manages to attract my attention first. "You don't wear us very often," they timidly say, "but just think of the fine occasions when you do! We always go to weddings and formal parties and dances. Remember the first party you took us to? You said that it made you feel just like a Cinderella, except, perhaps, that your mother's last-minute reminder to be home sharp at twelve was a little less romantic than the fairy godmother's warning! It was a wonderful party, though! You took us to Cousin Stella's wedding too. Remember how furious you were when we tripped you half-way up the aisle? Ha! Ha! We have never laughed so much in all our lives!"

Then, while the tiny voice chuckles merrily, another pipes up. "Remember us? Maybe our adventures haven't been so lovely as those, but they've been just ten times as exciting! We are just old, brown hiking-shoes, but we have fun, too. On Good Friday you took us miles along sunny country roads, through budding, green woods, beside rocky-bedded streams, and even through the streams! We knew you couldn't climb that slippery rock, but what could we do? All our lives we've been terribly abused, and we can never say a word!" But mingled with the complaints and grumbling, one can notice with little difficulty a note of pride and secret pleasure in such glorious adventures.

"Now, look here!" cries one more voice. "You can't ignore us this way. Why, who takes you to work in the morning? Who takes you shopping? We do, of course! We're crowded into elevators, jammed into streetcars, and trampled on at bargain counters. It's no wonder our toes are scuffed and worn! But we see more than do the others. We see the old friends you meet on the street; we see the frightened, lost child uptown; we see the big stores, the office, and your home; we see your everyday life, the little things that mean so much to you. Oh, yes! We are quite as important as the other shoes!"

And on and on they ramble, each and every pair—interesting, friendly companions. "Just imagination!" you say. Maybe that's true too, but, if it is, I still do not know what I would ever do without either my imagination or—my shoes!

—HELEN WALTON

II

What's in a Name?

Psychologists inform us that 73.5% of the inmates of most of the C.A.F.C.P.W.D.T.T.C.B.O.P.C.T.T.A. (Canadian asylum for crazy people who don't think they're crazy but other people convince them they are) are in there for reasons which can be traced indirectly to their names. Isn't that appalling? You must remember that at one time all these people were just as normal as you or I. They lived a normal life. They did the normal things. Every morning they would rush off to work although they would rather have stayed in bed. At night they would go visiting and be bored to death, but they would tell their host they'd had a lovely time. They would go to bridge parties and trump their partner's king. Oh yes, at one time these people lived a normal life, but now, because of a name . . . alas!

Dr. I. Semore tells us that many of these unfortunate people suffer from "nomen commonosis". This is a disease which affects people with common names such as Smith, Jones, Doe, Brown, Green, and the rest of the colours. No matter where these people go, they see their name up before the public. When they go to vote, they see their name on the sample ballot. Every time a victory loan is launched, their name is on the specimen copy. But this maltreatment is not confined to the adults alone. Oh no! If their children attend school, they learn that John Doe has a draft due on July 22, that Mr. Brown owes Mr. Smith twenty dollars which he is to pay in eight monthly payments, that Mr. Jones is bankrupt and is selling his business to Mr. Green for 20% of the cost of all the lemons in the store which are three for ten cents. Finally, when they can stand it no longer, these tortured slaves of society develop an acute case of "nomen commonosis". They usually end their days in a small, quiet room trying to stick small pieces of paper together.

Those of the 73.5% who do not suffer from the disease mentioned in the last paragraph are suffering from a mental disorder known as "nomen associatosis", the association of names. This disease usually affects the weaker minded members of a society. Whenever they hear or see their name they think of someone who has the same name but whom they despise. Every day they are introduced to someone who, on hearing their name, says "Oh, you're Mr. So 'n So, the one that . . ."

"Oh no!" they break in hurriedly. "He just has the same name as I do."

This goes on day after day, week after week. All the time they must be on their guard, watching, listening, explaining. At last, they can defend themselves no longer. They submissively surrender to this constant bombarding and decide that they are someone else. The common trend is Napoleon; they seem to favour the militarist. However, there are a few original ones, perhaps with more artistic natures, who imagine they are a vase or a statue. These poor creatures usually end by living as "he" would have lived and dying as "he" would have died.

What is the solution of this problem? Must we go on living this way? Is it necessary that we must always have those 73.5%? No!! After careful study, a solution has been found! We shall live in a world in which no one has a name. Already there is a small group in our community who are endeavouring to bring this plan about. Often, you will hear them address one another like this: "Hey, You", or simply "Hey!" However, there is another school of thought. Its followers choose a few common names and address each other so: "Hey, Mac", or "Hello, Jo". But this plan might bring about a mass attack of "nomen associatosis".

—ROY JONES

III

Castles in The Air

The interior of a dilapidated mill is not generally considered the ideal place to idle away the hours in blissful reverie. I mean that here there is no scope for imagination such as may be found on the shaded bank of a clear brook, with a tableau of pastoral beauty stretching out as far as the eye can see. There is, however, nothing like the sweet, musty smell of grain and the dark, sombre atmosphere which may be found only in old mills, to banish the present and allow the imagination to run wild. Mine is doing exactly that now, as I wait for my father to come back from the fields.

The rusty, antique implements and the rotting, low-hanging rafters, as well as the sun-kissed meadow which I can see through the doorless doorway, all gradually slip out of my conscious sight, and I begin to glide softly, ever so softly, into the phantom world of my dreams. First comes the strange moment of transition which lies just beyond the frontier of reality, yet not quite over the rim in fantasy. All I need now is a slight push—there! Over the brink I go, drifting among my castles in the air. This is my Utopia—my ideal world.

Here I am no longer the awkward, gangly Tom Tickson of reality. Now I am Don Carlson (what a smart and dashing name!), tall, but not too thin, carefree and confident. Twenty-five is the ideal age, I think—so much more interesting than fourteen. I live in a large, bustling city, miles away from farms. I have no bothersome parents to be continually bossing me, but I live in a big apartment where I may come and go as I please. Since I have a responsible position in a prominent business firm, I have an abundance of money with which to make life easy and enjoyable. The ladies worship me because I am handsome, charming, and rich.

There is one in particular who seeks a permanent place as the object of my attentions. Strangely enough, she bears a striking resemblance to a certain Miss Nancy Cole, but she is a little taller and has fewer freckles. She has the same laughing eyes, though, and the bright red hair. I can see her now, smiling at me with adoration. I am making a witty remark which causes her to throw back her head with silvery ripples of laughter. Now I am driving her to a party in my bright new limousine, and she is being very gracious and lovely, for she secretly hopes that I will ask her to marry me.

Besides Nancy and me, there are other characters in my dream-world. My older brother Arthur lives with me, and he is just as understanding and kind as he is in real life. There is only one change in him—instead of being lame, his legs are straight and strong, so that he is just as able to have enjoyable times as I. He can swim, play baseball, and walk briskly, as he has always wanted to do. He is racing me up the stairs of our apartment, laughing his deep laugh which no longer has its sad, hollow tinge.

We are all very happy, my dream-people and I. We live in a land where love and joy flourish, where hate and discord do not exist. Our worries and infirmities drop from us like October leaves the moment we cross the border into fantasy.

Suddenly I hear a sharp voice calling my name. "Tom! Hey, Tom! Stop your confounded daydreaming and help me with these cows."

—MARGARET WEST

Theme Topics

Here are hundreds of suggestions as to what to write about. In order to make topics a little easier to find, the list has been divided, the titles being grouped under headings that represent different phases of life—observations, preferences, reading, thoughts on better citizenship, and so forth.

I. Watching the World

(Your aim in writing on these topics is to report to others concerning certain things you have seen or found out. Your accounts will be vivid but often impersonal.)

1. Birds I Have Studied
2. Setting a Hen
3. A Dyspeptic in a Restaurant
4. How I Classify People
5. A Freak I Knew Once
6. My Experiences with Goldfish
7. The Most Stupid Kind of Animal I Know
8. The Greeting of a Dog to His Master
9. Birds I Know
10. Trees That Keep Their Leaves Longest
11. The Best Hour's Walk from Here
12. The Study of Insects As a Source of Pleasure
13. Which Trees Put on Leaves First
14. Seeds
15. Intelligence of Horses
16. Tricks of Horses
17. The Flight of Birds
18. Where Salt Comes From
19. The Age of Trees
20. Mimicry in Nature
21. The Firefly's Light
22. Life of Bees
23. The Carrier Pigeon
24. Hibernation
25. How a Bee Makes Honey
26. How a Spider Weaves
27. What Is Ore?
28. Where Iron Comes From
29. Where Silk Comes From
30. Tree Surgery

31. Baby Swallows a Piece of Ice
32. Having a Toothache
33. The First Cold Snap
34. Our Family at the Breakfast Table
35. A Man in the Rain
36. Before the Curtain Rises
37. Before the Examination
38. A Cafeteria
39. Bargain Day
40. The Man Who Never Smiles
41. The Doctor's Office
42. An Old-Fashioned Kitchen
43. The Country Store
44. The Mosquito
45. Temperamental Susie (Give contrasting moods with her change in appearance.)
46. The Boy in the Back Row
47. The Back-Seat Driver
48. The Two Gigglers
49. Intelligence in Animals (Describe evidences you have seen.)
50. The Questions She Asked at the Game
51. Overheard in a Pullman
52. Overheard in a Day Coach
53. A Squirrel and a Dog on the Campus
54. My Church
55. The Back-Yard Cat
56. The Country Store As a Social Centre
57. The Boy Scout
58. A Barber Shop for Women
59. Little Willie Shows Off before Company
60. The Lucky Piece
61. My Favourite Class (Describe it.)
62. Our Best Bird Friend
63. A Dialogue between a Farmer and His Hired Man
64. When Mother and Father Disagreed
65. A Rough Road
66. Some Local Superstitions
67. Talking to a Deaf Person
68. Souvenirs I Have Collected
69. The Billboard
70. The Camp Fire Girl
71. What I Have Learned from .... (Tell what you have learned from watching some animal.)
72. A Display in a Store Window (Describe it.)

73. Coming from Church (Describe people coming from church, particularly two or three.)
74. A Description of Some Unfamiliar Animal (Let the class guess it.)
75. Animal Tracks
76. My Young Brother
77. What Roots Do
78. What Leaves Do
79. The Wisdom of Cats (Describe evidences you have seen.)
80. Overheard in a Street Car
81. School Noises
82. A Distant Relative
83. A Parade

II. Money Value

84. How I Could Earn a Living if I Left School Now
85. My Father's Business
86. On Working during Vacation
87. Getting Nothing for Something
88. What Is a Bank?
89. Where Do Taxes Go?
90. How to Get a Patent
91. Wiles of a Book Agent
92. The Use of Advertising Slogans

III. The World Is My Oyster

(What I Can Do in the Future)

93. A Man Famous in My Chosen Profession
94. My Future As I See It
95. Why I Am (Am Not) Going to College
96. Chances for Success in My Profession
97. What I Expect College Life to Be
98. What Constitutes Real Success?
99. The Greatest Influence in My Life
100. My Career (A humorous account of all the careers you have selected and why.)
101. What I Should Like to Do for My Life Work

IV. Notions and Preferences

(Notions of my own about many things—and some notions of other people)

102. On Wearing a Hat
103. Queer Names

104. Luck
105. Things I Like to Do on a Rainy Day
106. Things I Should Like to Forget
107. Stamp Collecting
108. Collecting Postcards
109. Putting Away Childish Things
110. The Dictionary for Entertainment
111. Things I Can Do Without
112. Trials of an Only Daughter (Son)
113. Why I Want to Grow Up
114. The Greatest Fear of My Childhood Days
115. Does My Cat Think?
116. The Fascination of the Forbidden
117. The Quickest Way to Make Me Furious
118. Radio Announcers
119. People Who Bore Me
120. On Keeping a Secret
121. Hair Cuts
122. Lending Books
123. Borrowing Books
124. Second-hand Books
125. My Nicest Compliment
126. How It Feels to Be Red-Headed
127. How it Feels to Be Left-Handed
128. How It Feels to Be Fat (Thin)
129. My Pet Extravagance
130. My Pet Economy
131. A Dog's Love of Motoring
132. The Thoughts of a Dog on a Running Board
133. Proof That the Earth Is Flat
134. "Where's My Compact?"
135. Gossip
136. On Deceiving Children
137. The Blues
138. The Nerve of Some People
139. The Most Enjoyable Party I Ever Attended
140. My Greatest Fear
141. What My Dog Has Taught Me
142. The Importance of Having Someone to Whom to Explode
143. On Lending Money to Fellow Students
144. Have I Enough Curiosity?
145. The Value of a Real Sense of Humour
146. What Pictures Impress Me
147. Effects of Weather on My Thoughts

148. Do Animals Know When Sunday Comes?
149. Pictures I Should Like to Paint
150. Pies
151. Pride
152. Fairies
153. Secrets
154. Impressions While Sick (Sounds, Tastes, etc.)
155. How Music Affects My Imagination
156. Day-Dreaming—Examples
157. On Hearing the Alarm Clock Go Off
158. On First Discovering That the World Is a Big Place
159. On Getting a New Pet
160. On Making a Little Garden
161. When You Take Up a Newspaper, What Do You Read First? (Give the answers of several people who are talking this over.)
162. What Names Do You Like Best for Boys and for Girls? (Let several people give their preferences in talking.)
163. Who Is the Most Interesting Person You Have Ever Met, and Why? (Report a conversation in which several people take part.)
164. A Very Interesting Dream (Let several persons tell their dreams.)
165. Which Is the Most Beautiful Season of the Year? Which Is the Most Enjoyable? (Give a conversation in which two or three persons exchange opinions.)
166. What Are Some Clever Pieces of Advertising You Have Noticed Lately? (Give the comments of several people in conversation.)
167. White Shoes
168. Household Chores I Most Dislike
169. Sounds That Keep Me Awake at Night
170. How Persons I Dislike Help Me
171. Things I Have Lost
172. The Inconvenience of Owning a Bicycle
173. The Disadvantages of Having Too Many Friends
174. My Favourite Musical Instrument
175. My Bugbears Among Words
176. Nicknames I Have Survived
177. Fears of Childhood

V. Fair Field and No Favour—Both Sides of Some Questions and More than One View of Some Topics

178. My Opinion of Co-education
179. Should Examinations Be Abolished?

180. The Value of Examinations
181. A Best Seller *vs.* a Classic
182. Should Grades Be Posted?
183. Why Pay Taxes?
184. What Is the Most Important Change That Should Be Made in Our School?
185. Talking *vs.* Silent Pictures
186. Is a Lie Ever Justified?
187. Should Capital Punishment Be Abolished?
188. Are Moving-Picture Shows Harmful to Children?
189. Speaking *vs.* Writing
190. Biology Is More Useful than .... (any other school subject)
191. Is Science a Menace to the Peace of the World?
192. Should the School Leaving Age Be Raised?
193. Does the Amateur Provide a Better Game than the Professional?
194. Should Homework Be Abolished?
195. What Should Be Done with Students Who Cheat?
196. Should a Student Sell His Textbooks?
197. Is the Party System of Government Better than a Coalition Government?
198. Does Education Increase Happiness?
199. Have the "Comics" a Harmful Influence on Children?
200. Should Conversation Be Permitted in Classrooms?
201. Should Students Be Ranked on Reports?
202. Practice in Balancing Differences between
    - Setter and Pointer
    - Airedale and Irish Terrier
    - Snow and Hail
    - Rain and Dew
    - Elm and Oak
    - Wool and Cotton
    - Walking and Running As Exercise
    - Jersey Cow and Holstein (or Guernsey)
    - High School and College
    - Intelligence of Cats and Dogs

VI. Sports

203. The Service in Tennis
204. Heroes of the Sports Page
205. A Ping-Pong Game
206. The Popularity of Softball
207. What Is the Best Outdoor Sport?
208. Professional Hockey
209. On Riding a Horse

VII. My Nose in a Book

210. Words from Mythology
211. Unfamiliar Words
212. My Seven Wonders of the World
213. Three Books I Want to Own, and Why
214. How Literature Misrepresents Life
215. Folk Lore
216. Fabulous Animals
217. What Do You Consider the Best Moving Pictures You Have Ever Seen, and Why?
218. What You Like to Read Outside of School
219. A Character from a Play by Shakespeare (any character)
220. My Hero (My Heroine) in History or Fiction
221. The Best Short Story—an Appreciation
222. Four Books Recommended—for a Classmate Who Has Never Been Fond of Reading
223. My Favourite Actor (Actress)
224. Prometheus and Fire
225. Pandora
226. Hyacinthus
227. Niobe
228. Midas and the Golden Touch
229. Actæon
230. Cupid and Psyche
231. Atalanta's Race
232. Hero and Leander
233. Orpheus and Eurydice
234. Exploits of Hercules
235. Jason and the Golden Fleece
236. Ulysses and Polyphemus
237. Ulysses and Circe
238. A Bible Story (Choose any well-known story.)
239. The Most Interesting Animal Story I Ever Read
240. A Scene I Remember from a Motion Picture or a Book
241. My Favourite Comic Strip

VIII. Thoughts on Making the World Better and More Pleasant—Morals and Manners, Speeches and Customs, Comforts and Conveniences

242. What Is an Educated Man? A Gentleman?
243. On What Virtues Is Self-Respect Based?
244. The Most Useful Man or Woman in Our Community
245. The Essentials of Good Breeding

246. The Smoke Nuisance
247. Drives to Obtain Funds
248. Slang
    Yesterday's Slang
    Childish Misconceptions of Words
    Why is Slang Undesirable?
249. Decline in Church Attendance
250. Judging Character by Personal Appearance
251. The Decline of Courtesy toward Women
252. How I Broke Myself of a Bad Habit
253. Modern Inventions Have Revolutionized Home Life
254. Protection of Birds (Forests, Wild Life)
255. Modern Conveniences on a Farm
256. Forms of Stinginess
257. The Essentials of a Comfortable Living-Room
258. How to Improve the Appearance of This Street (This School)
259. Blunt Speech As a Good (Bad) Trait
260. When Not to Laugh
261. Harmful Recent Inventions
262. When I See Dumb Animals Abused
263. What I Consider the Greatest Invention
264. Tact
265. By Their Words You Shall Know Them
266. The School Bully
267. The Chaperon

IX. Glorious Adventure—and Some Not So Glorious

268. A Night with the Mosquitoes
269. My Greatest Surprise
270. My Proudest Moment
271. The Most Reckless Thing I Ever Did
272. A Card Trick
273. A Test of Courage
274. Stuck in the Mud
275. The Spelling Match
276. Amateur Doctoring
277. Making a Dime Go a Long Way
278. Sleeping Class
279. Stuck in an Elevator
280. The Most Important Bridge I Ever Burned
281. We Ran Out of Gas
282. It Hurt
283. When My World Tottered
284. Getting Acquainted with the Neighbour's Dog

285. Investigating a Bumblebee's Nest
286. Thrown from a Pony
287. My First Fight
288. A Curious Dream
289. My First Trousers
290. Moving into a Strange House
291. The Early Worm Gets Caught by the Bird
292. Talking with Two People Who Are Not on Good Terms with One Another
293. Interviewing the Town's Worst Grouch
294. Talking to Some Person You Know but Cannot Place
295. Meeting a Speaker at the Train and Taking Him to a Hotel
296. Visiting a Friend Confined in a Hospital
297. Being Introduced to an Important Personage
298. Carrying on a Conversation with a Silent Dinner Partner
299. An Accident (Give the points of view of the driver of the car, the vendor whose pushcart has been hit, and a passer-by.)
300. My First Hero Worship
301. When My Intuition Played Me False
302. Guaranteed Hole-Proof
303. My First Dance
304. Sunday-Night Suppers at Home
305. Every Dog Has His Day
306. A Bird in the Hand
307. It Never Rains but It Pours
308. A Miss Is As Good As a Mile
309. Catching Up with Father
310. Why I Was Late
311. The Teacher Fails to Appear
312. My Narrowest Escape
313. The Story I See in a Picture

X. Things Every Student Knows—or Might Know

314. New Fashions in Slang
315. How to Develop a Vocabulary
316. How I Improved My Memory
317. Defects in My High-School Training
318. How to Distinguish Four Kinds of Birds (Trees)
319. Explanation of the Equinox
320. The Leading Extra-Curricular Activities in My School
321. School Politics
322. School Tradition
323. Staying Out of School a Year
324. What Is School Spirit?

325. Teaching a Boy to Swim
326. Colds and How to Avoid Them
327. Library Etiquette
328. Learning to Swim
329. How to Keep an Automobile (or a Bicycle) in Good Condition
330. How to Pack a Trunk
331. How to Generate Hydrogen
332. Some Things I Learned from Being a Boy Scout (a Girl Guide)
333. Some Fine Points of Automobile Driving
334. How to Sew on a Button
335. Something I Learned in
    Botany
    Chemistry
    Physics
336. The Cause of the Seasons
337. First Aid in Fainting
338. Living by Schedule
339. How the Summer Camp Benefited Me
340. First Aid for Burns
341. The Best Fuel for Your Neighbourhood (wood, coal, coke, oil, gas, etc.)
342. Why Days Are Short in Winter
343. What Should Be the Length of Vacations?
344. How to Measure the Height of a Skyscraper or a Tall Tree
345. How to Study
346. How to Teach a Dog Tricks
347. Keeping a Diary
348. Patching Tires
349. Ways to Amuse a Baby Sister or Brother
350. Why the Leaves Fall
351. How to Learn to Remember Names
352. How to Measure the Area of a Pond
353. How to Feed and Care for a Bird
354. What's a Volcano?
355. Names of the Months
356. Hallowe'en Customs
357. Variations of the Boiling Point
358. The Causes of Dew
359. Why Do We Have Leap Years?
360. In the Next Twenty Years We'll See Many Interesting Inventions
361. The Man I Marry Must (or Must Not) Be a Dreamer
362. What I Want to See in France

363. What I Would Do with a Thousand Dollars
364. What City, Domestic or Foreign, Should You Like Best to Visit?
365. In the Days of .... (If you could live one day in any period of history, which period would you choose?)
366. If I Were
    A Missionary Opening a Barrel Sent by the Ladies' Aid
    A Fat Girl
    A Fat Boy
    A Poet at a Football Game
    An Old College Athlete Soliloquizing
367. The Site of the High School a Thousand Years Ago—If I Could See It
368. Three (Four) Reasons Why I Like Dogs

INDEX

David Gill

English

Suggested

Comp. 40%

Sentence Correction 8 16%

Run. Exe 10%

Precis 14%

Clause An 10%

Homoymns 10%

Lit.

Poetry - 3 contexts 10% 3x3

Poetry Appreciation 10%

Asked to write on 2 novels ~~15%~~ 30%

Prose 2 essays 30%

The Blood is Strong 1 essay 2